AIR TRAFFIC CONTROL ASSOCIATION

AIR TRAFFIC CONTROL

HOW TO BECOME AN
FAA AIR TRAFFIC CONTROLLER

WALTER S. LUFFSEY

RANDOM HOUSE

NEW YORK

AIR TRAFFIC CONTROL ASSOCIATION

AIR TRAFFIC CONTROL

HOW TO BECOME AN FAA AIR TRAFFIC CONTROLLER

WALTER S. LUFFSEY

RANDOM HOUSE

NEW YORK

Library of Congress Cataloging-in-Publication Data

Luffsey, Walter S.
    Air traffic control: how to become an FAA air traffic controller
    /Walter S. Luffsey.
      p.   cm.
    At head of title: Air Traffic Control Association.
    ISBN 0-679-73050-8
    1. Air traffic control—United States—Vocational guidance.
I. Air Traffic Control Association. II. Title.
TL725.3.T7L83 1990
629.136'6'024—dc20   90-40726
                                             CIP

Manufactured in the United States of America

1 2 3 4 5 6 7 8 9

First Edition

*To my wife Louise and to all those who love aviation,
and to those who have been and will be air traffic controllers.*

ABOUT THE AIR TRAFFIC CONTROL ASSOCIATION

——*Dedicated to progress in the science of air traffic control.*——

The Air Traffic Control Association (ATCA) is an independent, nonprofit, professional membership organization dedicated to advancements in the science of air traffic control. Its members are individuals and corporations concerned with the continuing safety, reliability, and efficiency of the United States Air Traffic Control System and developments in air traffic control worldwide. They include air traffic controllers, flight service specialists, pilots, electronics engineers, electronics technicians, and representatives from related aviation industries. ATCA members play a significant role in improving the present ATC system and in planning for its future.

The major goal of ATCA is to contribute new knowledge to the National Aviation System by making known to the aviation world any significant work, improvements, or research accomplished in air traffic control disciplines. To this end, ATCA publishes the world-renowned periodical, the *Journal of Air Traffic Control*, the monthly *ATCA Bulletin* newsletter, and the *Fall Conference Proceedings*, an annual source book of ATC technical information. The association testifies before Congress and works within the aviation community on behalf of the ATC system. It also provides a channel of communications between military and civilian segments of the system.

Each fall, ATCA conducts an annual meeting, including an international technical program and exhibits. The meeting provides a forum of the foremost aviation experts and the largest display of exhibits anywhere in the world devoted exclusively to air traffic control products and services. A highlight of the annual meeting is ATCA's awards program, recognizing persons and organizations for extraordinary achievement and outstanding contributions to, or within, the National Air Traffic Control System.

Throughout the year ATCA conducts symposia and other educational events designed to keep air traffic control professionals abreast of the latest in aviation technologies and public policy issues.

ATCA makes a substantial contribution to aviation education each year by awarding scholarships to deserving students pursuing an aviation-related course of study at recognized institutions of higher learning. These scholarships are awarded both to full-time students seeking an advanced degree, and to full-time aviation career employees taking courses part-time to enhance their job skills.

Additional information about the Air Traffic Control Association and its programs may be obtained from:

Air Traffic Control Association, Inc.
2020 North 14th St., Suite 410
Arlington, VA 22201
Phone: (703) 522-5717

ACKNOWLEDGMENTS

The author and producers are grateful for the willing assistance of many individuals, government agencies, and companies.

The Federal Aviation Administration's Office of Public Affairs responded with advice and information, and assistance with photos and diagrams. We are grateful to Phillip S. Woodruff, Director of Aviation Education, and his colleagues MaryJo Byberg, Fraser Jones, and Pat Tomasetti. Superintendent of the FAA Academy Robert S. Bartanowicz, and Claudia Jackson and Gwen Sawyer helped with understanding the curriculum and training of air traffic control specialists.

Terry Dobson, the FAA Air Traffic Manager at Sioux City, Iowa, and Col. Denny Swanstrom, commander of the Iowa Air National Guard's 185th Tactical Fighter Wing, provided details and understanding of the United Airlines 232 accident. Their assistance was invaluable. Edmund Pinto helped with education information.

Many others helped with photos and information. These deserve particular mention: Gulfstream Aerospace, IBM, Westinghouse, E-Systems, Raytheon, Unisys, Hughes Aircraft, and the Aviation/Space Writers Association.

AUTHOR'S PERSONAL ACKNOWLEDGMENTS:

Probably everyone in aviation with whom I had contact influenced this book. Among them were the unsung heroes of the system whose names may have passed into oblivion for many, but not for me. Also, the public heroes who have been enshrined in history had an influence by virtue of their visible impact and public acclaim.

The "big" and "little" people of aviation, all of equal stature and status to me, touched my life and I am grateful for that. All the FAA Administrators from Jim Pyle (of the CAA) to the current Administrator, Jim Busey, shaped my views. Individuals who played a special role in shaping my career include Nicholas Proferes, Joe Blatt, Ray Yeager, Jack Ludlam, Sam Sorkowitz, Bob Martin, Paul Bradbury, Don Brinkley, and Mel Sivils.

A person who shaped all of air traffic control from its infancy and into maturity was my very good friend Glen Gilbert, for whom an ATCA award is named.

Many others influenced my career and the practice of air traffic control. This book is a tribute to all of them. It is intended to pass on to those who follow in the air traffic control system a feeling of belonging, just as those who preceded and tracked along with me did for me. There is no greater gift by anyone's definition than to be made a part of "Air Traffic Control."

To those who assisted directly in this book a special thanks and a public expression of my debt of gratitude. To Jim Loos: many thanks, pal, I couldn't have done it without you. To ATCA, Gabe Hartl, Suzette Matthews, Bill LaLiberte, and all of the ATC Committee: you made me do what I often thought was impossible. To Clif Berry and staff: very special recognition of your patience, diligence, tolerance, and perseverance. To all those FAA folks in Washington Headquarters and at "Oke" City: you supplied the right stuff at the right time, as you always do! Of course, I acknowledge the assistance of all the aforementioned with full recognition I may have missed someone. If so, my apologies and thanks. To all of you I say: this book has been a labor of love. I hope it does justice to you and the system. I did my best.

Walter S. Luffsey

CONTENTS

PART III. KNOWING THE SYSTEM

APPENDIXES

PREFACE

SCOPE OF THE BOOK

This book shows how individuals become air traffic controllers with the Federal Aviation Administration (FAA). It also describes how they operate within the national air traffic control system.

The Air Traffic Control Association (ATCA) cooperated in the book's preparation. ATCA is dedicated to progress in the sscience of air traffic control and to spreading knowledge about the air traffic control profession.

Part I explains the qualifications a person needs in order to apply for a position as an FAA air traffic control specialist. It also covers the entire hiring process and the training given to men and women who are selected. Part II shows how controllers at key places within the system do their jobs. In Part III, details of the air traffic control system are explained. The Appendixes provide useful reference information.

IMPORTANCE OF AIR TRAFFIC CONTROLLERS

The job of air traffic control specialist is one of the most demanding, yet satisfying, careers possible. Without the skill and dedication of air traffic controllers, our skies would be turned into chaos.

Consider a few numbers that show the size of the task. Each year 57 million passengers arrive and depart from Chicago's O'Hare International Airport alone, the country's busiest airport. Nearly 48 million fly into and out of Atlanta's Hartsfield International Airport. New York's three major airports handle more than 55 million travelers annually. Nationwide, each year nearly one-half billion passengers fly safely and efficiently through crowded skies. In addition, millions of other persons fly safely on aircraft operated by the military, by businesses, and by private fliers of the general aviation community.

Those millions of flights operate safely because the United States has an efficient system of air traffic control. The system includes a lot of high-technology equipment, of course. Powerful radar sets identify aircraft and pinpoint their location, altitude, and speed. Other equipment such as radios tie the system together into a national control network.

But all of the high-technology equipment in the world would be useless without the people who are the true brains of the air traffic control system. Called air traffic control specialists, they are the trained and dedicated men and women whose skills ensure safe and efficient operation of the air traffic control system.

Air traffic control specialists make the system work properly. In simplest terms they keep aircraft separated from each other. However, to achieve that simple goal controllers' tasks are much more complex. They might be seated in a darkened room in front of a radar scope, controlling dozens of aircraft in a chunk of airspace hundreds of miles across. Or they might be standing in a control tower high above a busy airport giving instructions over the radio to airplanes landing and taking off. Other air traffic control specialists may be talking with pilots in a flight service station. They could be discussing the flights being planned and providing information essential to those pilots' decisions.

DEMANDS ON CONTROLLERS

No matter where they are working air traffic control specialists are vital ingredients in this country's safe air transportation system. They carry unique responsibilities. They must work well under pressure, make decisions quickly, work with a minimum of supervision, adjust rapidly to changing circumstances, and operate as team players.

Controlling aircraft requires an ability to create a complex mental picture. Aircraft move in three dimensions and at different speeds. They climb, descend, and turn. When a series of aircraft take off from a runway, each in its turn, they do so upon the instructions of air traffic controllers. As each airplane sets off on its voyage through the skies its path diverges from the flight paths of other aircraft going to different places. At a busy airport when many aircraft are arriving they must converge again to land on an arrival runway, again upon instructions from air traffic controllers.

Aircraft fly at different speeds and their performance varies. Pilots in command of the aircraft possess standard skills but at different levels of competence and experience. Aircraft are fitted out with different communications and navigation equipment. Whatever the differences among pilots, aircraft, and equipment, one thing is certain. Aircraft must not arrive at the same spot on the same runway at the same time or, for that matter, occupy the same point in the airspace at the same time. That is where controllers come in.

Controllers employ an assortment of high-technology tools to accomplish this challenging task. More advanced tools are always being developed to improve the air traffic control system. Whatever the technological advances, the men and women who are the nation's air traffic controllers remain indispensable.

Air traffic control specialists work hard. They know the importance of their skills and of the thousands of people relying on their ability to make the right decisions in instants. In recognition of their demanding profession controllers are among the highest paid of federal government workers. They earn their pay, every day.

PART I

BECOMING A CONTROLLER

CHAPTER ONE

ON THE FRONT LINE

THE CONTROLLER WORK FORCE

LaCharliere Hydrogen Balloon, 1783. First flight with a barometer to measure altitude; rocks for ballast, gas valve to stop ascent. J.A.C. Charles and M. Robert.

Men and women who have qualified as Air Traffic Control Specialists are very special individuals. They are responsible for the safe operation of the nation's complex air traffic control system. Air traffic controllers ensure that the millions of persons flying through our skies do so in safety and confidence. They are truly on the front line of air traffic control.

More than 20,000 air traffic control specialists are employed by Federal Aviation Administration (FAA), which is a part of the Department of Transportation.

Each year, thousands of individuals apply to the FAA to become air traffic controllers. They are given a screening test and background and health examinations. About 3,000 persons pass those hurdles and become controller candidates. Hired as trainees by the FAA, they attend the rigorous air traffic controller course at the FAA Academy in Oklahoma City, Oklahoma. Of those 3,000 trainees, about 60 percent complete the 11-week controller course. Once through the course, they are called "developmental controllers," because they are beginning the process of career development.

Developmental controllers who are new graduates from the FAA Academy are sent out to FAA air traffic control facilities to begin work. ("Facilities" is a word the FAA gives to the places where its air traffic controllers work. The different types of facilities are explained later in the chapter.) The developmental controllers are ready to learn the profession. They replace older controllers who will be retiring, moving into staff and managerial positions, or leaving the FAA.

The FAA is still building up the total number of qualified and experienced controllers from the low point experienced after the controllers' strike of 1981. Therefore, it must annually produce more graduates from the FAA Academy than the number of controllers who are leaving the front lines. The controller workforce is increased by about 500 to 600 men and women each year.

Developmental controllers begin building their careers upon arriving at their first assignment. Their object is to continue improving their skills and experience until they reach the status of full-performance level controllers, or FPLs. The process takes about three years. Not everyone makes the grade. About 30 percent of developmental controllers do not succeed in reaching FPL status. They leave the FAA or are transferred to non-controller jobs at less active facilities.

Control tower at Washington Dulles International Airport. It is in Northern Virginia about 25 miles west of Washington, D.C. The tower and Dulles's distinctive terminal were designed by Eero Saarinen. (FAA photo)

MORE CONTROLLERS NEEDED

The need for recruiting new controllers has been pressing for some time. In August 1981, the Professional Air Traffic Controllers Organization (PATCO) organized an illegal strike against the FAA and the U.S. Government. More than 11,000 controllers were fired. Only 4,000 qualified controllers were left. The FAA had to begin the monumental task of rebuilding the workforce around those few remaining controllers. Many controllers were recalled to the front line from staff and manager positions.

Today, the controller workforce (those in towers and centers) is more than

17,000 and approaching 18,000 persons, a number higher than the pre-1981 number. However, the experience level of the controller workforce is lower than before the strike. Out of necessity, the FAA has not transferred as many former controllers into staff and managerial positions. Older and experienced controllers are needed on the front lines.

Also, there is a relatively large age gap in the controller work force between staff and managerial personnel. Many top managers are at or near retirement age. On the other hand, controllers hired after the 1981 strike are relatively young. Consequently, the demand for young people to enter the field over the next few years will remain strong. The FAA must keep feeding qualified younger controllers into the force as experienced controllers are shifted into management positions.

STEPS UP THE CAREER LADDER

Before getting into the details of becoming an air traffic controller, it will be helpful to understand the career ladder that controllers can expect to experience.

Tower crew at Washington Dulles. James Stephenson (foreground) is the area supervisor and is working Local Control. He is observing an aircraft on final approach to runway 1R. Background, left, is Andy Papageorge. He is a developmental controller working on Ground Control, checking the position of an aircraft requesting permission to taxi. David Arnold (in background) is training Papageorge. He is also discussing gate hold and release time for a departing aircraft with Sharon Compher, a developmental controller working on flight data and clearance delivery. (FAA photo by Bruce Beuzard)

Air traffic control personnel may be divided into several categories. Their roles are explained using certain specialized FAA terms. These terms, or descriptive labels, begin with describing entry-level personnel and progress through training and experience to the most qualified controllers.

Trainees—students at the FAA Academy. They have passed all the screening tests, have been hired by the FAA, and are taking the basic air traffic control course at the FAA Academy, the Mike Monroney Aeronautical Center in Oklahoma City.

Seal of the Federal Aviation Administration, responsible for the safe and efficient operations of the National Airspace System. (FAA)

Developmental Controllers—persons who have completed the basic course at the FAA Academy. They have been transferred from Oklahoma City to their first job in the system. That means they are in training at an ATC facility. A "facility" could be one of several types. For instance, it might be an airport control tower. Or the facility might be an Air Route Traffic Control Center, keeping track of aircraft passing through their assigned space. Or it could be a Flight Service Station, working with pilots to prepare their flight plans.

Operational Controllers—developmental controllers who have become certified for two or more positions at the ATC facility where they are assigned. They work part of the time without supervision on the positions for which they have been certified. At other times, they train to become qualified on additional positions. For example, at an airport control tower, an operational controller might be qualified on two positions: (1) processing pilot requests for flight routes and granting clearances for approved routes, and (2) providing ground control to aircraft moving about on the airport. That same individual may also be training to control aircraft ready for takeoff or approaching to land. Controllers are trained to become qualified on all of the positions at a given facility, and to be ready for the next step up the career ladder.

Full-Performance Level Controllers (FPLs)—operational controllers who have become certified on all required positions at the facility they are assigned to. The number of FPL required positions varies among facilities and so do the description of the various positions. The control tower at JFK International Airport, for example, handles a heavy volume of traffic day and night. It also requires close coordina-

At one of the busiest U.S. airports, airliners form a queue for takeoff. Deregulation and more air travel have increased demands on the air traffic control system. (FAA photo)

tion with nearby high-volume airports such as La Guardia and Newark. Thus, the JFK tower "facility" has more FPL positions than the control tower at Martinsburg, West Virginia, where the traffic is lighter. All FPL controllers at JFK, therefore, have to be qualified in the same number of positions to be considered FPL controllers at JFK. Likewise, at Martinsburg, all FPL controllers have to be qualified in the same number of positions, but there are fewer positions.

Traffic Management Unit Controllers (TMU)—FPL controllers who are assigned duties involving the orderly flow of traffic into and out of a facility's airspace. They regulate air traffic so that the system does not develop bottlenecks.

First-level Supervisors—FPL controllers assigned to supervisory jobs directly involving air traffic control. They supervise and train the controllers for whom they are responsible.

JOB SPECIALIZATION

The FAA offers three broad areas of job specialization to controller candidates leaving the FAA Academy and going to their first assignment—terminal, center, and flight service station. They are explained below, along with descriptions of the positions one finds in each type.

ATC candidates may express a preference for the specialization area they prefer. However, the FAA assigns people where the needs are greatest and where individual aptitude suggests the person will perform most successfully.

Follow the numbers for the sequence of a flight: pilot files flight plan and receives approved routing; controllers in the airport tower cab clear the aircraft to taxi and takeoff; en route controllers at Air Route Traffic Control Centers (ARTCC) monitor progress against flight plan, provide separation; as the aircraft nears destination approach controller guides aircraft to final approach to the airport; terminal controllers clear aircraft to land, then provide guidance for it to taxi to assigned gate. (Unisys)

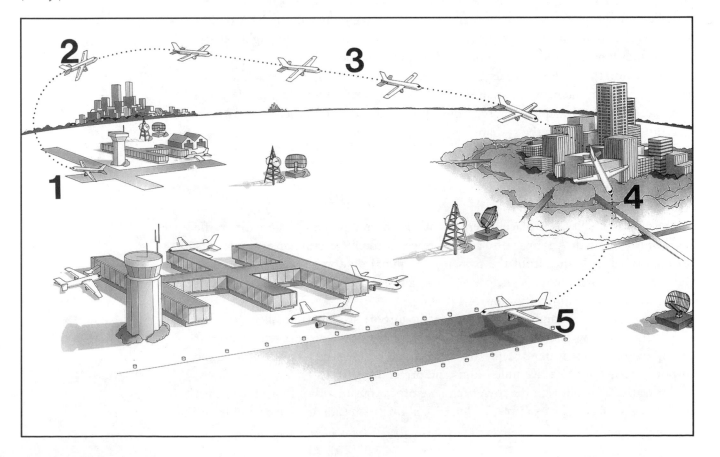

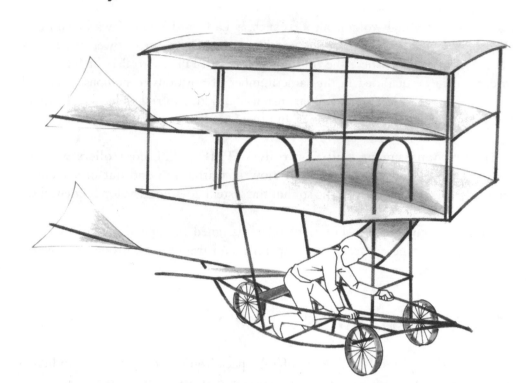

"Boy Lifter," 1849. World's first manned, heavier-than-air flight. Unnamed boy glided 30 ft. off a hillside in Sir George Cayley's design.

After developmental controllers reach full-performance level, they have the option of "bidding" on vacant positions at other facilities. In practice, however, bidding is limited by the staffing at the bidder's present facility. That is, if the bidder's present facility is understaffed, it might be a year or more before a release may be granted for transfer to another facility. Also, the money in the FAA budget for moving people has not kept pace with the costs of moving. This tight budget may further limit the number of transfers that can be made.

The section that follows discusses the three major areas of specialization and the positions within each of them. Refer to the diagram "Flying in the National Airspace System." It depicts the relationship between the air traffic control activities and aircraft flying in the system.

TERMINAL

A "terminal" facility is a place where flights begin and end, and where air traffic control is exercised. An air traffic control tower is the most familiar example of a terminal facility. Rising from the passenger terminal or dominating some remote part of the airport, the glass enclosed tower cab is easily recognizable. To many, it is the symbol of the air traffic control system.

The tower is high, and it is situated on the airport so that controllers have an unobstructed view. They need to be able to see areas of the airport where aircraft are operating on the ground. They also must be able to see the airspace around the airport, at least out to a five-mile radius and preferably further.

Air traffic controllers in the tower regulate operations of aircraft into the airport and on its surface. For example, to "taxi" an aircraft means to move it under its own power on the surface of an airport. A pilot wishing to taxi an aircraft must ask the controllers for "permission to taxi" before moving the airplane.

Tower controllers also supervise activities of vehicles and people at places on the airport where they might affect aircraft movements. Examples include aircraft parking ramps, gates where passengers board or leave aircraft, aircraft taxiways, and runways.

Controller at a terminal radar console observes bright data blocks on the display screen. Each block represents an aircraft in flight, either approaching to land or departing from the airport, whose location is depicted at the center of the screen. (Unisys)

WORK POSITIONS IN CONTROL TOWERS

Terminal positions vary slightly with local requirements. In most control towers, one or more persons are assigned to the following positions:

Flight Data—In this liaison position, the controller dispatches essential information about flights to tower people who require it.

Clearance Delivery—The controller at this position receives requests from pilots for the routes they wish to fly. The request is passed into the system. It goes to the Air Route Traffic Control Center, or ARTCC. Soon, the ARTCC issues a "clearance." It is an authorization for the aircraft to fly a specified route, very precisely defined and spelled out. The clearance delivery controller passes the clearance to the pilot over the radio. To make sure the pilot understood the clearance accurately, he reads it back to the clearance delivery controller.

Ground Control—The ground controller issues taxi directions to aircraft. The directions guide departing aircraft from the parking ramp or passenger gate to the active runway. Arriving aircraft, once they are clear of the active runway, are directed to a ramp or gate by the ground controller.

Local Control—This controller keeps track of arriving aircraft on their final airborne approach and issues permission for them to land (clears them to land) on the active runway. The local controller also issues permission for departing aircraft to taxi onto the active runway and take off from it. (Cleared for takeoff.) This controller also makes sure that safe distances are maintained between aircraft. That is, the controller separates arriving aircraft ("arrivals") from each other, and depart-

Air traffic control specialist S. Michael McKean works at a console in the Houston Terminal Radar Control (TRACON) facility during a busy time. (FAA photo by S. Michael McKean.)

ing aircraft ("departures") from each other. He also separates arrivals from departures by ensuring that the pilots in the aircraft maintain the appropriate separation distance from each other. Minimum separation distances, both horizontally and vertically, are prescribed by the Federal Aviation Administration.

Control towers that are busy might have two local controllers and two ground controllers working at the same time. They might also employ one or more coordinators. Coordinators are trained to spot potential conflicts among traffic being worked by one of the other controllers. Less busy towers might have only two controllers on duty at the same time. They would be performing the functions of all of the operating positions described above.

The number of people in the towers in the various positions is called the level of staffing. Staffing levels in control towers, and in other FAA facilities as well, are determined by two major factors. The first factor is the workload, the number of aircraft takeoffs and landings. The second, and lesser factor is the complexity of the airspace for which the particular facility is responsible.

Tower controllers collect information from a variety of sources that are valuable for pilots. For example, the Air Route Traffic Control Center (ARTCC) generates en route clearances. Flight clearances specify flight routes and key points along the way, along with essential information about the route. (Air Route Traffic Control Centers are explained later in this chapter.)

The tower controller passes the en route flight clearances on to pilots, along with special instructions required for local operations. The National Weather Service provides local and flight route weather information to controllers and pilots. Controllers use instruments in the tower cab to measure wind speed and direction. They read barometric pressure from other instruments and give pilots the appropriate setting for their airplane altimeters. With a transmissometer, they measure runway visual range (RVR)—the distance in hundreds of feet that one can see clearly down a specific runway. They also keep track of the status of navigational aids at the airport and in its vicinity.

RADAR ROOMS AND TRACONS

Radar rooms and TRACONS are also terminal activities where controllers operate. (TRACON is the acronym for Terminal Radar Control.)

Radar (Radio Detection And Ranging) is a fundamental tool of air traffic control. Radar was developed before and during World War II. Its first use in combat was by British forces during the Battle of Britain in the summer of 1940. Used first for air defense, radar was soon applied to aerial navigation and air traffic control. Radar truly revolutionized the air traffic control system. Radar transmissions can pierce through clouds and darkness for hundreds of miles.

Information collected by radar signals is interpreted and then converted into displays on video screens available to controllers. Thanks to radar and display technologies, terminal controllers can identify aircraft approaching their airport from many miles away. Then they are able to line up the aircraft in sequence for an approach to one of several runways at the airport. This can be done long before the approaching pilots have the airport in view.

In less busy towers, the radar display is probably in the tower cab itself. At busier terminals, however, the radar display is in a separate room, either below the tower cab or in another building.

In particularly congested localities, one radar room will provide service for more than one terminal. This is the case where several airports and control towers are in the same general vicinity, as in New York City. The New York Terminal Radar Control (TRACON) facility is a single radar room, with many displays and controllers working at them. The New York TRACON provides service for air traffic at three airports: Newark, La Guardia, and John F. Kennedy. A similar TRACON facility in Oakland, California serves the airports in both San Francisco and Oakland.

New York TRACON uses the new Magnavox full digital display, installed as part of an upgrade being performed by Unisys Corp. (Unisys)

POSITIONS IN RADAR ROOMS AND TRACONS

The number of controllers working in terminal radar rooms and TRACONs varies from place to place, again depending upon the workload. The basic functional positions include:

Flight Data—a liaison position, in which the controller dispatches essential information about flights to others who require it.

Departure Controller—a controller who accepts control responsibility for departing aircraft from the controller in the tower, who cleared them for takeoff. As the aircraft leaves the runway on takeoff, the tower controller directs the pilot to contact the departure controller on the radio. The departure controller "takes" the departure aircraft from the tower controller. He is responsible for control from then until the aircraft reaches a position where control responsibility is handed off to the Air Route Traffic Control Center (ARTCC). The ARTCC exercises control during the en route phase of flight.

Approach Controller—the controller who takes control of arriving aircraft from the ARTCC, and brings it to a point several miles from the airport. From there, control over the aircraft is turned over to the local controller in the airport tower.

Lateral boundaries of the Air Route Traffic Control Centers (ARTCC) in the mainland United States. Center locations are designated by the stars. (FAA.)

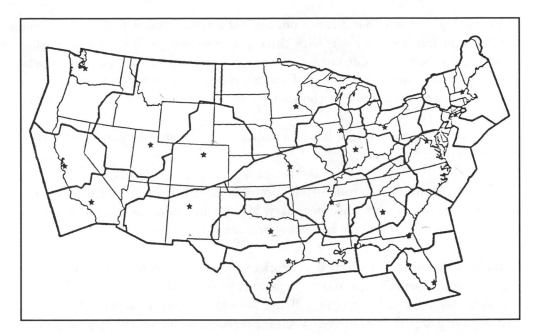

Handoff Controller—the controller who identifies arriving aircraft for the approach controller or, at another position, points out a departing aircraft to the ARTCC. The handoff controller makes sure that transfer of control responsibility is "handed off" promptly and properly.

Busy airports might have as many as three approach and two departure controllers, as well as a coordinator, working at the same time. A large TRACON like New York will field a team of three to five controllers of each type for each major airport and perhaps employ one or two more for the smaller airports in the area.

The number of aircraft arrivals and departures at a terminal facility is used by the FAA to place it on a five-level scale of activity. The levels are used as a basis for the pay grades of controllers working there. They range from Level I (least busy) to Level V (busiest). At Level I facilities, full-performance level (FPL) controllers have a pay grade of GS-10 on the General Schedule. The General Schedule pay chart is on page 16. At the busiest terminal facilities, those at Level V, the FPL grade is higher, set at GS-14.

EN ROUTE CENTERS

Air Route Traffic Control Centers (ARTCC), or simply "centers," control huge blocks of airspace, thousands of cubic miles in size, ranging across several states. Center controllers handle the en route segment of a flight. Remember that the departure controller transfers control responsibility for aircraft leaving his terminal to a center. Likewise, control responsibility for an aircraft nearing the end of its flight will be transferred. In that case, control is handed off from a center controller to an approach controller at the terminal facility that is the aircraft's destination.

The airspace of a center is divided into areas, and the areas are further subdivided into sectors. It helps to consider the sector the basic building block of a center's airspace. Sectors are defined in terms of lateral limits described on a map and vertical limits bounded by altitudes, such as from the ground to 17,000 feet or some other altitude.

Centers vary in size, but it is not unusual for a typical center to have five areas divided into five sectors each, with three persons on duty in each sector. That means 75 controllers on duty at the center at any given time. Total number of people working in centers, including staff and managerial positions, often exceeds 500.

The control personnel on duty controlling a sector typically occupy these positions:

Flight Data Specialist—the liaison position, transferring essential data to controllers who need it.

Handoff/Monitor Controller—the controller who performs the handoff function (transfer of control) when necessary. He also monitors the radar controller's radio frequency to detect any developing problems.

Radar Controller—this controller works with a large video display that shows locations and essential data about aircraft in the sector. The radar controller uses radios to communicate with pilots flying through the sector, working with them and assigning separation between aircraft according to minimum distances established by the FAA.

At the Washington, DC Flight Service Station, Temetri Suk, a specialist on en route flight advisory service, observes a weather radar display and provides information to pilots over the radio. Looks like heavy weather in the Washington area. (FAA photo by Robert Laughlin)

As in the terminal, when traffic warrants, a coordinator might also be on duty to ensure a smooth flow of air traffic from sector to sector and from sector to terminal. A note about the types of air traffic controlled by centers and control towers is in order. Control towers serve aircraft operating under both visual and instrument flight rules (VFR and IFR). However, centers mainly serve IFR aircraft. They separate fast and slow aircraft, spread them out as they leave terminal areas and start bringing them back together as they approach destination airports. Aircraft flying under VFR rules may receive assistance and information from centers, but mainly the center controllers concentrate on IFR aircraft.

As the tower controllers provide essential information to pilots, so do center controllers. They can use their computer to call up hourly weather observations provided by the National Weather Service (NWS). Also, a meteorologist is on duty in the center to tell controllers about significant weather in the area.

Centers may be categorized under three levels, with the level determined by the volume of air traffic through their airspace. But in reality all centers but one are classified as Level III. Full-performance level controllers at all of those centers are at the GS-14 pay grade. The sole exception to the Level III classification is the center at Anchorage, Alaska. It is at Level II, with a GS-13 FPL grade authorized.

FLIGHT SERVICE STATIONS

Recall that centers primarily serve IFR aircraft. Flight Service Stations (FSS) mainly serve general aviation aircraft operating under visual flight rules (VFR). General aviation aircraft, as well as some military flights, use these stations to get information pertinent to operating along intended routes, as well as within 200 miles of the station.

The pilot in command of an aircraft is responsible for obtaining all pertinent information affecting the flight before taking off. The FSS is a primary source of the necessary information which includes: factual data (terrain or weather peculiarities); preflight and inflight weather information; suggested routes; altitudes; pilot reports (PIREPS) radioed by airmen in flight reporting significant information such as turbulence or potential icing; and any other information important to flight safety.

The FSS is a direct descendant of the original communication stations established in the 1920s. They also serve as terminals for one of the FAA's teletype communications networks. This network carries several types of messages, including notices to airmen (NOTAMS). NOTAMS advise pilots of navigational aids that are out of operation, any unusual airport conditions, and other necessary safety information.

Pilots also use the FSS as the place to file their flight plans. The flight plan is just what the name implies; the pilot's plan for a particular flight. "Filing" a flight plan means entering its information into the computers of the air traffic control system. Although pilots flying under visual flight rules are not legally required to file flight plans, prudent pilots do so. By filing a flight plan, the pilot knows that the flight is entered into the air traffic control system.

A flight plan is like a free insurance policy. If something goes wrong during the flight, or the flight does not arrive at the planned destination within a reasonable time after the pilot planned to get there, the air traffic control system will be alerted. In an emergency, the information in the flight plan will be used for search and rescue operations.

The specialist on duty at the Flight Service Station is a trained preflight briefer, who provides pilots with pertinent facts necessary for a particular flight. A specialist cannot prevent a VFR pilot from taking off. However, if weather conditions dictate, a pilot will be advised that VFR flight is not recommended. A prudent pilot will heed this advice.

In the past, FSSs were found at airports. However, because of improvements in technology, this is no longer always true or necessary. The FSS system is being modernized. Existing FSSs are being replaced with fully automated flight service stations (AFSSs). The automated flight service stations are equipped with the most modern data processing and communication equipment. With that equipment, pilots must place a greater reliance on long-distance telephones and other devices such as computers, to get the information available from the AFSS network. Stations of the future can be expected to serve large areas, and at the same time require fewer control specialists. The project to automate flight service stations is expected to be completed in this decade.

Specialists at the most active flight service stations are authorized an FPL grade of GS-12. However, FPLs at the newer automated flight service stations are at the GS-13 pay grade.

Federal General Schedule Pay Scale.

	Step 1	Step 2	Step 3	Step 4	Step 5	Step 6	Step 7	Step 8	Step 9	Step 10
GS-1	$10,581	$10,935	$11,286	$11,637	$11,990	$12,197	$12,544	$12,893	$12,910	$13,232
GS-2	11,897	12,180	12,574	12,910	13,053	13,437	13,821	14,205	14,589	14,973
GS-3	12,982	13,415	13,848	14,281	14,714	15,147	15,580	16,013	16,446	16,879
GS-4	14,573	15,059	15,545	16,031	16,517	17,003	17,489	17,975	18,461	18,947
GS-5	16,305	16,849	17,393	17,937	18,481	19,025	19,569	20,113	20,657	21,201
GS-6	18,174	18,780	19,386	19,992	20,598	21,204	21,810	22,416	23,022	23,628
GS-7	20,195	20,868	21,541	22,214	22,887	23,560	24,233	24,906	25,579	26,252
GS-8	22,367	23,113	23,859	24,605	25,351	26,097	26,843	27,589	28,335	29,081
GS-9	24,705	25,529	26,353	27,177	28,001	28,825	29,649	30,473	31,297	32,121
GS-10	27,206	28,113	29,020	29,927	30,834	31,741	32,648	33,555	34,462	35,369
GS-11	29,891	30,887	31,883	32,879	33,875	34,871	35,867	36,863	37,859	38,855
GS-12	35,825	37,019	38,213	39,407	40,601	41,795	42,989	44,183	45,377	46,571
GS-13	42,601	44,021	45,441	46,861	48,281	49,701	51,121	52,541	53,961	55,381
GS-14	50,342	52,020	53,698	55,376	57,054	58,732	60,410	62,088	63,766	65,444
GS-15	59,216	61,190	63,164	65,138	67,112	69,086	71,060	73,034	75,008	76,982
GS-16	69,451	71,766	74,081	76,396	78,190	79,438*	81,708*	83,978*	85,470*	
GS-17	79,762*	82,420*	85,078*	85,470*	85,500*					
GS-18	86,682*									

*The rate of basic pay payable to employees at these rates is limited to the rate for level V of the Executive Schedule, which would be $78,200. SOURCE: The White House

CONTROLLER DISTRIBUTION AND SALARIES

Today 22 centers and 447 air traffic control towers, including more than 200 with radar systems, are operational. The number of controllers in the terminal facility specialty is nearly 9,500. At centers, nearly 8,000 controllers are employed. In the third specialty, flight service stations, nearly 3,000 specialists are employed.

Controllers are paid according to the Federal pay table, the General Schedule. For example, a full-performance level (FPL) controller at a Level V control tower is classified at the GS-14 pay grade. Look in the table for GS-14 on the left-hand side. Each of the GS pay grades is divided into steps. Suppose this controller is GS-14, Step 3. The steps are shown across the top of the table. Start at GS-14 on the left-hand side and move across that row until you are under Step 3. You can determine that the annual base pay is $53,698.

In addition to base pay, controllers can receive premium pay as follows:

Holiday Pay—controllers get an extra full day's pay for every Federal holiday they work. And if controllers work the day before or the day after a holiday that falls on their regular day off, they also receive an extra day's pay. For example, if a controller works on July 3 and is supposed to be off on July 4 (Independence Day) and July 5, then double time is paid for the day worked on July 3.

Sunday Pay—Controllers get 25 percent extra pay for time worked on Sunday.

Night Pay—Controllers get 10 percent extra pay for hours worked between 6:00 p.m. and 6:00 a.m.

Overtime—Controllers are paid time-and-one-half for working more than eight hours a day, or more than 40 hours in an administrative work week. Controllers are not allowed to work more than 10 consecutive hours and must have at least one calendar day off a week.

Revitalization pay—Center and tower controllers receive an incentive pay premium of five percent for working in such a facility. They also are paid 25 percent extra for time worked as an on-the-job training (OJT) instructor. Lastly, if staffing and traffic demands prevent their getting a 30-minute lunch or dinner break during an eight-hour shift, they are paid 30 minutes of overtime.

Demonstration Project Pay—In June 1989, the FAA began a five-year pay demonstration project to attract more people to the staff at selected facilities in New York, Chicago, Oakland, and Los Angeles. These controllers receive an extra 20 percent pay differential.

With premiums, a full-performance level controller's pay can amount to $75,000 or more. Most government employee earnings are limited to an amount set by Congress (presently $78,200). This is called a "pay cap." The pay of air traffic controllers is not capped.

RETIREMENT BENEFITS

New employees are covered by the Federal Employees Retirement System (FERS). In addition to Social Security, the FERS provides a guaranteed basic annuity coverage that allows employees to participate in a Thrift Savings Plan. The Thrift Savings Plan is a savings plan similar to an Individual Retirement Account. Taxes on the plan are deferred until after the employee retires and begins withdrawing from it, usually at a lower tax rate than while on active service.

In addition, air traffic controllers are eligible to retire earlier than other Federal employees. They may retire at age 50 after 20 years of controlling airplanes, and at any age after 25 years of controlling airplanes. The normal government retirement age is 55, with at least 30 years of government service.

WORKING CONDITIONS

Controlling air traffic is a seven-day-a-week, 24-hour-a-day job. Controllers work shifts. Thus, their days off often fall in the middle of the calendar week. They work Sundays and holidays and from midnight to eight o'clock in the morning. They work Christmas and New Year's Eve and often on their birthdays. On the other hand, controllers can go to the beach or the mountains during the week, and sleep late two weeks out of three. Some even get used to the unconventional schedule.

CONCLUSION

If the pay and benefits in the air traffic control field seem attractive, consider that there is a reason for these benefits. The job is tough. Not everyone can measure up to the demands. However, if you are looking for a challenging way of life and believe you have the potential to succeed in a most demanding career, then read on.

CHAPTER TWO

GETTING STARTED AS A CONTROLLER

QUALIFICATIONS AND APPLYING

Giffard's Dirigible, 1852. First manned, sustained, and powered flight, Sep. 24. Steam engine drove a pusher prop. Henri Giffard.

In Chapter One, we learned about the steps in a controller's career. In pursuing that career, a controller will progress upward in steps. After employment, the controller's career begins as trainee at the FAA Academy. Then the controller progresses through status as a developmental controller and eventually to full-performance level (FPL) controller a few years later.

Prospective controllers must go through lengthy job application and selection procedures. Our objective is to explain each stage of the process. The steps are taken in sequence.

If you are interested in becoming an air traffic controller, you should first determine if you meet the qualifications. If you do, then the next step is to apply for the Federal Aviation Administration's (FAA) written test. If you pass the test with high enough scores, the FAA will put you on a list of potential job candidates. Then, if the FAA decides to hire you, you will be notified to go through "preemployment processing." This requires filling out additional forms, having a medical examination, an interview, and a suitability investigation.

That process includes a lot of "ifs" and several steps. The entire procedure may take from four to six months, depending on the FAA's needs.

QUALIFICATIONS TO ENTER THE JOB

Let's begin with qualifications. Individuals who determine that they meet the qualifications can move on to the next stage, applying for the FAA written test. Check yourself against the qualifications first; if you meet them, then you are ready to make the written application.

You can determine for yourself whether you qualify to make the first application to the FAA to take the written test. This first determination is yours to make. It is based on your own record and experience. If you pass the test with high enough scores and are selected for employment, then your qualifications will be screened further. For example, you will be required to pass a physical examination. You also will be given a personal interview to evaluate your suitability. In addition, a check of your background will be made, with the FBI and local police agencies.

Many of the users of the National Airspace System are shown in this drawing. All of them operate safely and efficiently through the services of air traffic control specialists of the Federal Aviation Administration (FAA).

Radar scope display at a busy en route center shows bright data blocks for aircraft flying through the sector. The straight lines are airways; the large oval in upper right defines special use airspace. (Unisys)

EXPERIENCE REQUIREMENTS

The FAA selects as candidates for employment those men and women who have scored well on the written test and who also have the required experience. Two types of experience are specified: general and specialized. "General experience" is defined in three ways:

1) three years of progressively responsible experience in administrative, technical, or other work that demonstrates potential for learning and performing air traffic control work;

2) or four years of college;

3) or any combination of education and experience equaling three years.

Here's how to determine if your own combination of education and experience equals three years. The FAA considers one year (30 semester hours or 45 quarter hours) of undergraduate study as matching nine months of general experience. A person who has earned 60 semester hours (or 90 quarter hours) of college would have two years of college for purposes of this calculation. Since each year of college equates to nine months of general experience, those college credits translate to 18 months of general experience. To meet the three-year general experience requirement, the candidate would need 18 additional months of work experience that qualifies under the definition above.

Suppose you are still in college, and believe you will qualify with the credits you will earn by the end of the school year. You can still apply now. That is, if you will complete the amount of education required to qualify within nine months of the test date. You may apply and be selected, but must complete college studies before beginning work.

Part-time work also counts toward the general experience requirement. It is credited on the basis of a 40-hour week. Working 20 hours a week for two months would give you credit for one month of experience. If you went to college and worked also, you may get credit for both the education and work experience. If you worked two different jobs during the same time period, you may receive credit for both.

Tip: don't overlook any experience or college study.

Lillienthal's Gliders, 1891-1896. Otto Lillienthal made thousands of flights in heavier-than-air gliders, advancing knowledge of flight.

SPECIALIZED EXPERIENCE

The first kind of specialized experience defined by the FAA is gained from previous air traffic control work that "demonstrates possession of the knowledge, skills, and abilities required to perform the level of work" for which the person is applying.

The FAA also considers the following kinds of specialized experience as meeting its requirements. A candidate must pass the written test and have these kinds of specialized experience, and hold or have held the certificates that are appropriate:

1) **an appropriate facility rating and have actively controlled air traffic in civilian or military air traffic control terminals or centers;**

2) **an FAA certificate as a dispatcher for an air carrier;**

3) **an instrument pilot certificate;**

4) **an FAA certificate as a navigator, or have been fully qualified as a navigator/bombardier in the armed forces;**

5) **a pilot with 350 hours of flight time;**

6) **a rated intercept director with the Aerospace Defense Command.**

Three controllers at work in the control tower at Albany County (New York) airport. Area supervisor Norman Lizzul is in center. On the left is ground controller John Kerr, and local controller George Cerillo is on the right. (FAA)

COMBINATIONS OF EXPERIENCE AND SCORES

To be considered for employment, a person must achieve a high score on the FAA written test and have the appropriate experience. Persons scoring 90 or higher on the test have the best chances of being selected.

However, in theory a candidate for Air Traffic Control Specialist can be selected for employment if he or she has the right combination of test score and experience. That is, so long as the person's test score was at least 70. Persons scoring less than 70 are not considered for employment.

Thus, a candidate with a score between 70 and 75 on the written test might still qualify, if he also has a bachelor's degree and a year of graduate study, or a bachelor's degree and high academic standing. The FAA will require proof of academic standing before appointment.

Applicants who have scored 70 or higher on the written test, and who possess the required specialized experience may also be considered for employment

At first glance, figuring out the qualifications criteria might be considered a test in itself. However, it is really fairly simple. If candidates score higher than 75 on the written test and have three years of almost any kind of work experience they will qualify. If they score lower than 75, their names will probably never be reached on the selection list. Actually, persons with scores of 90 or higher have the best chance of being selected. That is because the standards are high and quite a few qualified men and women are applying.

AGE LIMITATION

Extensive studies and experience conducted by the FAA have determined that the unique skills and abilities necessary to control air traffic begin to decline at a relatively early age. This conclusion is also the basis for the early retirement benefits given to controllers.

Therefore, in May 1972, the 92nd Congress passed Public Law 92-297. The law recognized the unusually high standards required of FAA air traffic controllers. The law gave the Secretary of Transportation the ability to set a maximum entry age into the air traffic control career field. Consequently, a candidate can be no older than age 30 when entering service as an air traffic control specialist in the tower or center option. This age limitation does not apply to the flight service station option.

CITIZENSHIP

Applicants must be U. S. citizens at the time they apply for Air Traffic Controller Specialist positions.

APPLYING FOR THE TEST

If a person meets all of the qualifications, then the next step is the written test. All applicants are required to take the FAA's written aptitude test. It measures their ability to learn and perform air traffic control work. Persons who wish to apply to take the written test can do so in three ways. In each case, state that you want the application form to take the FAA's written test for air traffic controller.

Way 1. Contact the FAA's Aviation Careers Examining Division in Oklahoma City, Oklahoma by mail or by phone. The address is:

> Federal Aviation Administration
> Mike Monroney Aeronautical Center
> Attention: Aviation Careers Examining Division, Building BM144
> Oklahoma City, OK 73125
> The telephone number is 405/680-4657

Way 2. Contact the nearest federal government job information and testing center. These offices are operated by the Office of Personnel Management (OPM). Local OPM job information and testing offices are listed in most major metropolitan phone directories under "Federal Government." For convenience and ready reference, the addresses and telephone numbers are listed in Appendix I.

Way 3. Contact the closest FAA personnel office. These offices are located in Washington, D.C., New York, Boston, Atlanta, Kansas City, Chicago, Fort Worth, Los Angeles, Seattle, and Anchorage. Their addresses and telephone numbers are also listed in Appendix I.

Applicants are sent a copy of the current announcement for Air Traffic Control Specialist. The announcement describes the various options and contains other useful information. It also includes an essential form to complete. That is the OPM Form 5000. It is the actual application for the written test. The Form 5000 appears on the next page.

Applicants complete the Form 5000 and mail it to the OPM office nearest the city where they wish to be tested. When the OPM office receives the card, it puts the applicants' names on a schedule for testing. Well before the test is scheduled, the OPM office notifies the candidates by mail when and where to report for testing.

In some areas, the test is being given on a walk-in basis. You can contact either the FAA or OPM for information regarding location and time. The test is given on a first-come, first-serve basis. There is no need to take any supplies or forms along.

The written test takes approximately four hours to complete and consists of three subtests. They are covered in detail in the next chapter. Briefly, Test I and Test II measure aptitude to learn and perform air traffic controller work successfully. Test III is for extra credit. It measures knowledge of air traffic controller procedures gained through specialized experience.

It is possible to achieve a score of 100 solely on Tests I and II. Applicants can earn up to 15 extra points by scoring well on Test III.

When applicants take the written tests, they will be asked to complete Form B, "Occupational Supplement for Air Traffic Control Positions — 2152." On Form B, applicants give their name, mailing address, telephone number, and geographic

If the form below is missing, or if additional application forms are needed, contact a Federal Job Information Center or a larger post office for an OPM Form 5000 AB card to be used as a substitute.

You should bring with you to the examination room the following items:
—the form below when it is returned to you;
—a pen, three medium No. 2 black lead pencils, and an eraser;
—the completed SF-171 and OPM Form 1203-M (see pages 7 and 8 of this announcement).

IDENTIFICATION MAY BE REQUIRED FOR THE WRITTEN EXAMINATION. Impersonation in the examination room can result in being barred from competing in Federal civil service examinations or from accepting employment in the competitive service for 3 years.

Privacy Act Statement

This information is requested under the authority of sections 1302, 3301, and 3304 of title 5 of the U.S. Code. These sections require the Office of Personnel Management to conduct examinations for competitive positions in the Federal service. The information sought will be used to schedule you for a written examination, serve as an admission card to that exam, and to ascertain whether you may be affected by laws determining who may be tested or employed. Other possible uses of the data include disclosure to a source (e.g., former employer or school) who is requested to furnish information about you that will assist in determining whether to hire you; to a Federal, State, or local agency for checking on law violation; or to the courts where the Government is a party to a suit. Your Social Security Number (SSN) is requested under authority of Executive Order 9397, which requires agencies to use the SSN as the means of identifying individuals in Government information systems. The furnishing of your SSN and the other information is voluntary. Failure to provide your SSN will result in your not being scheduled for an exam. Failure to provide the other data may have the same result.

To apply for the test:

1. Please PRINT all the information CLEARLY in INK.
2. Mail your application to the OPM office which is closest to the city where you wish to be tested. OPM addresses are on the next 2 pages of this announcement.
3. Be sure to mail your application in a stamped envelope.

MAIL TODAY

OPM addresses next 2 pages. ▶

—————————— Cut Along Dotted Line ——————————

Cut Along Dotted Line

(Initial)

(First Name)

1. (Last Name)

2. YOUR ADDRESS (Street & Number, or R.D., City, State & Zip Code)

3. DATE OF BIRTH (Mo., Day, Year)

4. DATE OF THIS APPLICATION (Mo., Day, Year)

5. WHERE DO YOU WISH TO TAKE THE WRITTEN TEST? (City) (State)

1. **AIR TRAFFIC CONTROL SPECIALIST**   2. Announcement No. FAA/ATC 008

3. TELEPHONE NO. [____] _____   4. Social Security No. [| | | | | | | | |]

5. Where do you wish to take the written test?

City _____ State _____

6. If you observe the sabbath or religious holiday on a day other than Sunday or if you have a disability requiring special arrangements, specify the day of your sabbath or the nature and degree of your disability and the special arrangements you will need.

_____

7. If you performed active duty in the armed forces in the United States and were separated under honorable conditions, indicate periods of service: from month____ day____ year____   to month____ day____ year____
Do you claim veterans preference? ☐ yes ☐ no

8. Are you a United States citizen?   ☐ Yes ☐ No

PRINT OR TYPE YOUR NAME AND ADDRESS	FIRST, MIDDLE, AND LAST NAME
	NUMBER AND STREET, OR R.D., OR POST OFFICE BOX NO.
	CITY, STATE, AND ZIP CODE (Zip Code Must Be Included)

APPLICATION FOR WRITTEN TEST

DO NOT WRITE IN THIS SPACE

When this form is returned to you, bring it with you when you report for the test.

Office of Personnel Management Form 5000, shown here, is the application for the FAA written test for Air Traffic Control Specialist. (FAA)

preference for assignment. Applicants name the FAA region that is their first choice of geographic preference and may name up to two other regions as additional preferences.

PROCESSING AFTER THE TEST

After the test is completed, the answer sheets are optically scanned and scored by machine. Passing or failing the test is determined by the results of the first two parts, Tests I and II. Persons scoring less than 70 have failed. The third part, Test III, gives the applicant additional points. But the additional points are used only if the applicant makes a passing score on the first two parts.

A computer record is established for each person who takes the test. All records are referred to the Special Examining Unit (SEU) at the FAA's Mike Monroney Center.

All applicants receive a notice of results. This can either be a numerical passing score, or a code that says the person is ineligible. A written explanation is sent with the notice. It gives the applicant information about the rating.

Passing scores range from 70 to 100. Veterans who qualify for preference may add up to 10 points. Passing scores are valid for 18 months. Applicants who have passed the test but are not hired during this period must be retested in order to receive further consideration.

HOW APPLICANTS ARE HIRED

The FAA has nine regional offices across the country. They hire all of the controllers for the air traffic control facilities within their geographic responsibility. When vacancies occur or are forecast, the FAA regional personnel office takes action. It contacts the Special Examining Unit (SEU) in Oklahoma City to request a list of applicants, called a Certificate of Eligibles.

The SEU sends to the regional personnel office the records of applicants with the highest scores for that region. Usually three applications for each opening are sent. As a practical matter, the SEU usually does not have to dip below scores of 90 to fill the openings. From the list of eligibles, the FAA tries to honor first choices of geographic region. If there are not enough highly qualified eligibles available for a particular region, then the regional office will consider those applicants who selected that region as a second or third choice.

PREEMPLOYMENT ACTIONS

At this point the regional personnel office contacts the eligible applicants who have been referred from the SEU. They are asked to complete a preemployment package. Also, the regional office gives them information on scheduling the personal interview and the medical examination.

FAA REGIONAL BOUNDARIES

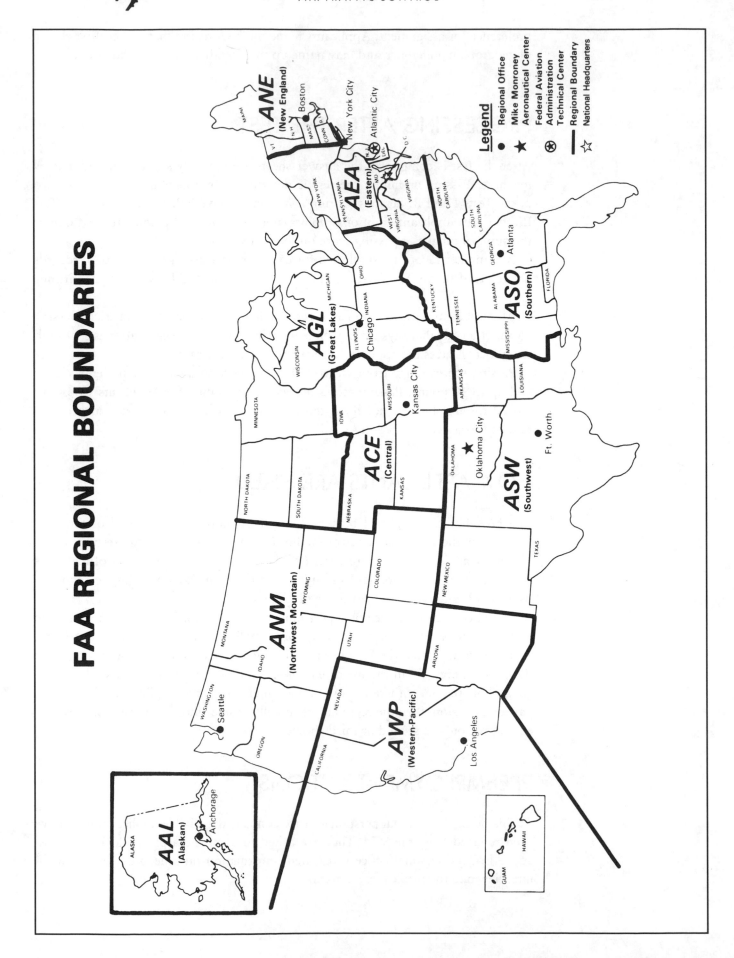

Preemployment processing normally takes from four to six months to complete. Once the processing is completed, each applicant will be considered with other candidates for ATCS positions. The FAA regional personnel office contacts individuals to tell them whether or not they have been selected for a position.

FORM SF-171, APPLICATION FOR FEDERAL EMPLOYMENT

This is the essential form that is completed by all persons hired by the Federal Government. It may appear long and cumbersome. But the information you furnish on the SF-171 is necessary to make an official determination of your basic experience and qualifications. The Office of Personnel Management suggests that you make copies of the forms for your own records. Throughout your career, you will be asked to complete other forms. Having the copies at hand will help you fill them out accurately and quickly.

Here are suggestions for completing the SF-171 properly. The complete form and its instructions appear on the next six pages.

You should list and describe all your work experience in detail. There is no need to attach extra paper for more space, but be specific. For example, although you could describe your experience as "worked in a service station," there is a far better way. That is to enter on the form: "service station attendant—dispensed gasoline, operated cash register, performed minor repairs, assisted travelers."

Answer all questions truthfully, and be sure to give the details requested. Usually a yes answer on page 4 of the SF-171 will not disqualify you from consideration. That is the section asking for background information. Examples include being fired from a job within the past 10 years, felony convictions, and such. Your answers will be reviewed by a specialist to determine if a serious problem exists requiring further investigation.

Be sure to sign Form 171 in ink.

All persons seeking jobs with the Federal government, including air traffic control specialists, must complete Standard Form 171. It is called "Application for Federal Employment." The complete form appears on the next six pages. Instructions for completing the form appear on the first page. Then come the four pages of the SF-171 itself, and a continuation sheet for use if necessary. It is important to answer all of the questions fully and correctly.

Standard Form 171
Application for Federal Employment

Read The Following Instructions Carefully Before You Complete This Application

- **DO NOT SUBMIT A RESUME INSTEAD OF THIS APPLICATION.**

- **TYPE OR PRINT CLEARLY IN DARK INK.**

- IF YOU NEED MORE SPACE for an answer, use a sheet of paper the same size as this page. On **each** sheet write your name, Social Security Number, the announcement number or job title, and the item number. Attach all additional forms and sheets to this application at the top of page 3.

- If you do not answer **all** questions fully and correctly, you may delay the review of your application and lose job opportunities.

- Unless you are asked for additional material in the announcement or qualification information, **do not attach** any materials, such as: official position descriptions, performance evaluations, letters of recommendation, certificates of training, publications, etc. Any materials you attach which were not asked for may be removed from your application and will **not** be returned to you.

- We suggest that you **keep a copy** of this application for your use. if you plan to make copies of your application, we suggest you leave items **1**, **48** and **49** blank. Complete these blank items each time you apply. **YOU MUST SIGN AND DATE, IN INK, EACH COPY YOU SUBMIT.**

- **To apply for a specific Federal civil service examination** (whether or not a written test is required) **or a specific vacancy in a Federal agency:**

 -- Read the announcement and other materials provided.

 -- Make sure that your work experience and/or education meet the qualification requirements described.

 -- Make sure the announcement is open for the job and location you are interested in. Announcements may be closed to receipt of applications for some types of jobs, grades, or geographic locations.

 -- Make sure that you are allowed to apply. Some jobs are limited to veterans, or to people who work for the Federal Government or have worked for the Federal Government in the past.

 -- Follow any directions on "How to Apply". If a written test is required, bring any material you are instructed to bring to the test session. For example, you may be instructed to "Bring a completed SF 171 to the test." If a written test is not required, mail this application and all other forms required by the announcement to the address specified in the announcement.

Work Experience *(Item 24)*

- Carefully complete each experience block you need to describe your work experience. Unless you qualify based on education alone, **your rating will depend on your description of previous jobs. Do not leave out any jobs you held during the last ten years.**

- Under **Description of Work**, write a **clear** and **brief**, but **complete** description of your **major** duties and responsibilities for each job. Include any supervisory duties, special assignments, and your accomplishments in the job. We may verify your description with your former employers.

- If you had a major change of duties or responsibilities while you worked for the same employer, describe each major change as a separate job.

Veteran Preference in Hiring *(Item 22)*

- **DO NOT LEAVE Item 22 BLANK.** If you do **not** claim veteran preference place an **"X"** in the box next to **"NO PREFERENCE"**.

- You **cannot** receive veteran preference if you are retired or plan to retire at or above the rank of major or lieutenant commander, **unless** you are disabled or retired from the active military Reserve.

- To receive veteran preference your separation from active duty must have been under honorable conditions. This includes honorable and general discharges. A clemency discharge does not meet the requirements of the Veteran Preference Act.

- Active duty for training in the military Reserve and National Guard programs is not considered active duty for purposes of veteran preference.

- To qualify for preference you must meet **ONE** of the following conditions:

 1. Served on active duty anytime between December 7, 1941, and July 1, 1955; (If you were a Reservist called to active duty between February 1, 1955 and July 1, 1955, you must meet condition 2, below.)
 or
 2. Served on active duty any part of which was between July 2, 1955 and October 14, 1976 or a Reservist called to active duty between February 1, 1955 and October 14, 1976 **and** who served for more than 180 days;
 or
 3. Entered on active duty between October 15, 1976 and September 7, 1980 or a Reservist who entered on active duty between October 15, 1976 and October 13, 1982 **and** received a Campaign Badge or Expeditionary Medal **or** are a disabled veteran;
 or
 4. Enlisted in the Armed Forces after September 7, 1980 or entered active duty other than by enlistment on or after October 14, 1982 **and:**

 a. completed 24 months of continuous active duty or the full period called or ordered to active duty, or were discharged under 10 U.S.C. 1171 or for hardship under 10 U.S.C. 1173 **and** received or were entitled to receive a Campaign Badge or Expeditionary Medal; **or**

 b. are a disabled veteran.

- If you meet one of the four conditions above, you qualify for 5-point preference. If you want to claim 5-point preference **and** do not meet the requirements for 10-point preference, discussed below, place an **"X"** in the box next to **"5-POINT PREFERENCE"**.

- If you think you qualify for 10-Point Preference, review the requirements described in the Standard Form (SF) 15, Application for 10-Point Veteran Preference. The SF 15 is available from any Federal Job Information Center. The 10-point preference groups are:

 -- Non-Compensably Disabled or Purple Heart Recipient.

 -- Compensably Disabled (less than 30%).

 -- Compensably Disabled (30% or more).

 -- Spouse, Widow(er) or Mother of a deceased or disabled veteran.

If you claim 10-point preference, place an **"X"** in the box next to the group that applies to you. **To receive 10-point preference you must attach a completed SF 15 to this application together with the proof requested in the SF 15.**

Privacy Act Statement

The Office of Personnel Management is authorized to rate applicants for Federal jobs under sections 1302, 3301, and 3304 of title 5 of the U.S. Code. Section 1104 of title 5 allows the Office of Personnel Management to authorize other Federal agencies to rate applicants for Federal jobs. We need the information you put on this form and associated application forms to see how well your education and work skills qualify you for a Federal job. We also need information on matters such as citizenship and military service to see whether you are affected by laws we must follow in deciding who may be employed by the Federal Government.

We must have your Social Security Number (SSN) to keep your records straight because other people may have the same name and birth date. The SSN has been used to keep records since 1943, when Executive Order 9397 asked agencies to do so. The Office of Personnel Management may also use your SSN to make requests for information about you from employers, schools, banks, and others who know you, but only as allowed by law or Presidential directive. The information we collect by using your SSN will be used for employment purposes and also may be used for studies, statistics, and computer matching to benefit and payment files.

Information we have about you may also be given to Federal, State and local agencies for checking on law violations or for other lawful purposes. We may send your name and address to State and local Government agencies, Congressional and other public offices, and public international organizations, if they request names of people to consider for employment. We may also notify your school placement office if you are selected for a Federal job.

Giving us your SSN or any of the other information is voluntary. However, we cannot process your application, which is the first step toward getting a job, if you do not give us the information we request. Incomplete addresses and ZIP Codes will also slow processing.

DETACH THIS PAGE – NOTE SF 171-A ON BACK

Application for Federal Employment—SF 171

Read the instructions before you complete this application. *Type or print clearly in dark ink.*

Form Approved:
OMB No. 3206-0012

GENERAL INFORMATION

1 What kind of job are you applying for? *Give title and announcement no. (if any)*

2 Social Security Number

3 Sex
☐ Male ☐ Female

4 Birth date *(Month, Day, Year)*

5 Birthplace *(City and State or Country)*

6 Name *(Last, First, Middle)*

Mailing address *(include apartment number, if any)*

City   State   ZIP Code

7 Other names ever used *(e.g., maiden name, nickname, etc.)*

8 Home Phone
Area Code | Number

9 Work Phone
Area Code | Number | Extension

10 Were you ever employed as a civilian by the Federal Government? If **"NO"**, go to Item 11. If **"YES"**, mark each type of job you held with an **"X"**.

☐ Temporary ☐ Career-Conditional ☐ Career ☐ Excepted
What is your **highest** grade, classification series and job title?

Dates at **highest** grade: FROM   TO

AVAILABILITY

11 When can you start work? *(Month and Year)*

12 What is the **lowest** pay you will accept? *(You will not be considered for jobs which pay less than you indicate.)*
Pay $ _____ per _____ OR Grade _____

13 In what geographic area(s) are you willing to work?

14 Are you willing to work:

	YES	NO
A. 40 hours per week *(full-time)?*		
B. 25-32 hours per week *(part-time)?*		
C. 17-24 hours per week *(part-time)?*		
D. 16 or fewer hours per week *(part-time)?*		
E. An intermittent job *(on-call/seasonal)?*		
F. Weekends, shifts, or rotating shifts?		

15 Are you willing to take a temporary job lasting:

	YES	NO
A. 5 to 12 months *(sometimes longer)?*		
B. 1 to 4 months?		
C. Less than 1 month?		

16 Are you willing to travel away from home for:

	YES	NO
A. 1 to 5 nights each month?		
B. 6 to 10 nights each month?		
C. 11 or more nights each month?		

MILITARY SERVICE AND VETERAN PREFERENCE

17 Have you served in the United States Military Service? *If your only active duty was training in the Reserves or National Guard, answer "NO". If "NO", go to item 22.*

YES	NO

18 Did you or will you retire at or above the rank of major or lieutenant commander?

YES	NO

DO NOT WRITE IN THIS AREA

FOR USE OF EXAMINING OFFICE ONLY

Date entered register

Form reviewed:
Form approved:

Option	Grade	Earned Rating	Veteran Preference	Augmented Rating

Veteran Preference:
☐ No Preference Claimed
☐ 5 Points *(Tentative)*
☐ 10 Pts. *(30% Or More Comp. Dis.)*
☐ 10 Pts. *(Less Than 30% Comp. Dis.)*
☐ Other 10 Points

Initials and Date

☐ Disallowed ☐ Being Investigated

FOR USE OF APPOINTING OFFICE ONLY

Preference has been verified through proof that the separation was under honorable conditions, and other proof as required.

☐ 5-Point
☐ 10-Point--30% or More Compensable Disability
☐ 10-Point--Less Than 30% Compensable Disability
☐ 10-Point--Other

Signature and Title

Agency   Date

MILITARY SERVICE AND VETERAN PREFERENCE *(Cont.)*

19 Were you discharged from the military service under honorable conditions? *(If your discharge was changed to "honorable" or "general" by a Discharge Review Board, answer "YES". If you received a clemency discharge, answer "NO".)* If **"NO"**, provide below the date and type of discharge you received.

YES	NO

Discharge Date *(Month, Day, Year)*	Type of Discharge

20 List the dates *(Month, Day, Year)*, and branch for all **active duty** military service.

From	To	Branch of Service

21 If all your active military duty was after October 14, 1976, list the full names and dates of all campaign badges or expeditionary medals you received or were entitled to receive.

22 **Read the instructions that came with this form before completing this item.** When you have determined your eligibility for veteran preference from the instructions, place an **"X"** in the box next to your veteran preference claim.

☐ NO PREFERENCE
☐ 5-POINT PREFERENCE -- You must show proof when you are hired.

10-POINT PREFERENCE -- If you claim 10-point preference, place an **"X"** in the box below next to the basis for your claim. **To receive 10-point preference you must also complete a Standard Form 15, Application for 10-Point Veteran Preference, which is available from any Federal Job Information Center. ATTACH THE COMPLETED SF 15 AND REQUESTED PROOF TO THIS APPLICATION.**

☐ Non-compensably disabled or Purple Heart recipient.
☐ Compensably disabled, less than 30 percent.
☐ Spouse, widow(er), or mother of a deceased or disabled veteran.
☐ Compensably disabled, 30 percent or more.

THE FEDERAL GOVERNMENT IS AN EQUAL OPPORTUNITY EMPLOYER

PREVIOUS EDITION USABLE UNTIL 12-31-90

NSN 7540-00-935-7150   171-109

Standard Form 171 (Rev. 6-88)
U.S. Office of Personnel Management
FPM Chapter 295

WORK EXPERIENCE *If you have no work experience, write "NONE" in A below and go to 25 on page 3.*

23 May we ask your present employer about your character, qualifications, and work record? *A "NO" will not affect our review of your qualifications. If you answer "NO" and we need to contact your present employer before we can offer you a job, we will contact you first. . . . .*

YES	NO

24 READ **WORK EXPERIENCE** IN THE INSTRUCTIONS BEFORE YOU BEGIN.

- Describe your current or most recent job in Block **A** and work backwards, describing each job you held **during the past 10 years.** If you were **unemployed** for longer than **3 months** within the past 10 years, list the dates and your address(es) in an experience block.

- You may sum up in one block work that you did **more than 10 years ago.** But if that work **is related** to the type of job you are applying for, describe each related job in a separate block.

- INCLUDE VOLUNTEER WORK *(non-paid work)--***If the work** *(or a part of the work)* **is like the job you are applying for,** complete **all** parts of the experience block just as you would for a paying job. You may receive credit for work experience with religious, community, welfare, service, and other organizations.

- INCLUDE MILITARY SERVICE--You should complete **all** parts of the experience block just as you would for a non-military job, including all supervisory experience. Describe each major change of duties or responsibilities in a separate experience block.

- IF YOU NEED MORE SPACE TO DESCRIBE A JOB--Use sheets of paper the same size as this page (be sure to include **all** information we ask for in **A** and **B** below). On **each** sheet show your name, Social Security Number, and the announcement number or job title.

- IF YOU NEED MORE EXPERIENCE BLOCKS, use the SF 171-A or a sheet of paper.

- IF YOU NEED TO UPDATE (ADD MORE RECENT JOBS), use the SF 172 or a sheet of paper as described above.

A

Name and address of employer's organization *(include ZIP Code, if known)*	Dates employed *(give month, day and year)*		Average number if hours per week	Number of employees you supervise
	From:	To:		
	Salary or earnings		Your reason for wanting to leave	
	Starting $ per			
	Ending $ per			

Your immediate supervisor			Exact title of your job	If Federal employment *(civilian or military)* list series, grade or rank, and, if promoted in this job, the date of your last promotion
Name	Area Code	Telephone No.		

Description of work: Describe your specific duties, responsibilities and accomplishments in this job, **including** the job title(s) of any employees you supervise. *If you describe more than one type of work (for example, carpentry and painting, or personnel and budget), write the approximate percentage of time you spent doing each.*

For Agency Use (skill codes, etc.)

B

Name and address of employer's organization *(include ZIP Code, if known)*	Dates employed *(give month, day and year)*		Average number of hours per week	Number of employees you supervised
	From:	To:		
	Salary or earnings		Your reason for leaving	
	Starting $ per			
	Ending $ per			

Your immediate supervisor			Exact title of your job	If Federal employment *(civilian or military)* list series, grade or rank, and, if promoted in this job, the date of your last promotion
Name	Area Code	Telephone No.		

Description of work: Describe your specific duties, responsibilities and accomplishments in this job, **including** the job title(s) of any employees you supervised. *If you describe more than one type of work (for example, carpentry and painting, or personnel and budget), write the approximate percentage of time you spent doing each.*

For Agency Use (skill codes, etc.)

IF YOU NEED MORE EXPERIENCE BLOCKS, USE SF 171-A *(SEE BACK OF INSTRUCTION PAGE).*

← ATTACH ANY ADDITIONAL FORMS AND SHEETS HERE

EDUCATION

25 Did you graduate from high school? *If you have a GED high school equivalency or will graduate within the next nine months, answer "YES".*

26 Write the name and location *(city and state)* of the last high school you attended or where you obtained your GED high school equivalency.

| YES | If "YES", give month and year graduated or received GED equivalency: . . . . |
| NO | If **NO**, give the highest grade you completed: . |

27 Have you ever attended college or graduate school? YES / NO ▸ If "YES", continue with **28**. If NO", go to **31**.

28 NAME AND LOCATION *(city, state and ZIP Code)* OF COLLEGE OR UNIVERSITY.. If you expect to graduate within nine months, give the **month** and **year** you expect to receive your degree:

	Name	City	State	ZIP Code	MONTH AND YEAR ATTENDED From	To	NUMBER OF CREDIT HOURS COMPLETED Semester	Quarter	TYPE OF DEGREE *(e.g. B.A., M.A.)*	MONTH AND YEAR OF DEGREE
1)										
2)										
3)										

29 CHIEF UNDERGRADUATE SUBJECTS *Show major on the first line*

		NUMBER OF CREDIT HOURS COMPLETED Semester	Quarter
1)			
2)			
3)			

30 CHIEF GRADUATE SUBJECTS *Show major on the first line*

		NUMBER OF CREDIT HOURS COMPLETED Semester	Quarter
1)			
2)			
3)			

31 If you have completed any **other courses or training related to the kind of jobs you are applying for** *(trade, vocational, Armed Forces, business)* give information below.

NAME AND LOCATION *(city, state and ZIP Code)* OF SCHOOL	MONTH AND YEAR ATTENDED From	To	CLASS-ROOM HOURS	SUBJECT(S)	TRAINING COMPLETED YES	NO
School Name 1)						
City State ZIP Code						
School Name 2)						
City State ZIP Code						

SPECIAL SKILLS, ACCOMPLISHMENTS AND AWARDS

32 Give the title and year of any honors, awards or fellowships you have received. List your special qualifications, skills or accomplishments that may help you get a job. *Some examples are: skills with computers or other machines; most important publications (do not submit copies); public speaking and writing experience; membership in professional or scientific societies; patents or inventions; etc.*

33 How many words per minute can you:

TYPE? TAKE DICTATION?

Agencies may test your skills before hiring you.

34 List **job-related** licenses or certificates that you have, such as: *registered nurse; lawyer; radio operator; driver's; pilot's; etc.*

	LICENSE OR CERTIFICATE	DATE OF LATEST LICENSE OR CERTIFICATE	STATE OR OTHER LICENSING AGENCY
1)			
2)			

35 Do you speak or read a language other than English *(include sign language)? Applicants for jobs that require a language other than English may be given an interview conducted solely in that language.* YES / NO ▸ If "YES", list each language and place an "X" in each column that applies to you. If "NO", go to **36**.

LANGUAGE(S)	CAN PREPARE AND GIVE LECTURES Fluently	With Difficulty	CAN SPEAK AND UNDERSTAND Fluently	Passably	CAN TRANSLATE ARTICLES Into English	From English	CAN READ ARTICLES FOR OWN USE Easily	With Difficulty
1)								
2)								

REFERENCES

36 List three people who are not related to you and are not supervisors you listed under **24** who know your qualifications and fitness for the kind of job for which you are applying. At least **one** should know you well on a personal basis.

FULL NAME OF REFERENCE	TELEPHONE NUMBER(S) *(Include Area Code)*	PRESENT BUSINESS OR HOME ADDRESS *(Number, street and city)*	STATE	ZIP CODE
1)				
2)				
3)				

BACKGROUND INFORMATION-- *You must answer each question in this section before we can process your application.*

37 Are you a citizen of the United States? *(In most cases you must be a U.S. citizen to be hired. You will be required to submit proof of identity and citizenship at the time you are hired.)* If **"NO"**, give the country or countries you are a citizen of: _____ | YES | NO |

NOTE: It is important that you give complete and truthful answers to questions 38 through 44. If you answer **"YES"** to any of them, provide your explanation(s) in **Item 45. Include** convictions resulting from a plea of nolo contendere *(no contest)*. **Omit:** 1) traffic fines of $100.00 or less; 2) any violation of law committed before your 16th birthday; 3) any violation of law committed before your 18th birthday, if finally decided in juvenile court or under a Youth Offender law; 4) any conviction set aside under the Federal Youth Corrections Act or similar State law; 5) any conviction whose record was expunged under Federal or State law. We will consider the date, facts, and circumstances of each event you list. In most cases you can still be considered for Federal jobs. However, **if you fail to tell the truth or fail to list all relevant** events or circumstances, this may be grounds for not hiring you, for firing you after you begin work, or for criminal prosecution (18 USC 1001).

38 During the last **10 years**, were you **fired from any job** for any reason, did you **quit after being told that you would be fired**, or did you leave by mutual agreement because of specific problems?. . . . . | YES | NO |

39 Have you **ever** been convicted of, or forfeited collateral for **any felony violation?** *(Generally, a felony is defined as any violation of law punishable by imprisonment of longer than one year, except for violations called misdemeanors under State law which are punishable by imprisonment of two years or less.)* . . . .

40 Have you **ever** been convicted of, or forfeited collateral for **any firearms or explosives violation?**. . . . .

41 Are you **now** under charges for **any** violation of law?. . . . .

42 During the **last 10 years** have you forfeited collateral, been convicted, been imprisoned, been on probation, or been on parole? Do **not** include violations reported in 39, 40, or 41, above. . . . .

43 Have you **ever** been convicted by a military **court-martial?** If no military service, answer **"NO"**. . . . .

44 Are you **delinquent** on any Federal debt? *(Include delinquencies arising from Federal taxes, loans, overpayment of benefits, and other debts to the U.S. Government plus defaults on Federally guaranteed or insured loans such as student and home mortgage loans.)* . . . .

45 If **"YES" In: 38** - Explain for each job the problem(s) and your reason(s) for leaving. Give the employer's name and address.
  39 through 43 - Explain each violation. Give place of occurrence and name/address of police or court involved.
  44 - Explain the type, length and amount of the delinquency or default, and steps you are taking to correct errors or repay the debt. Give any identification number associated with the debt and the address of the Federal agency involved.
  NOTE: If you need more space, use a sheet of paper, and include the item number.

Item No.	Date (Mo./Yr.)	Explanation	Mailing Address
			Name of Employer, Police, Court, or Federal Agency
			City State ZIP Code
			Name of Employer, Police, Court, or Federal Agency
			City State ZIP Code

46 Do you receive, or have you ever applied for retirement pay, pension, or other pay based on military, Federal civilian, or District of Columbia Government service?. . . . . | YES | NO |

47 Do any of your relatives work for the United States Government or the United States Armed Forces? Include: *father; mother; husband; wife; son; daughter; brother; sister; uncle; aunt; first cousin; nephew; niece; father-in-law; mother-in-law; son-in-law; daughter-in-law; brother-in-law; sister-in-law; stepfather; stepmother; stepson; stepdaughter; stepbrother; stepsister; half brother; and half sister.* . . . .
If **"YES"**, provide details below. If you need more space, use a sheet of paper.

Name	Relationship	Department, Agency or Branch of Armed Forces

SIGNATURE, CERTIFICATION, AND RELEASE OF INFORMATION

YOU MUST SIGN THIS APPLICATION.   Read the following carefully before you sign.

- A false statement on any part of your application may be grounds for not hiring you, or for firing you after you begin work. Also, you may be punished by fine or imprisonment (U.S. Code, title 18, section 1001).
- If you are a male born after December 31, 1959 you must be registered with the Selective Service System or have a valid exemption in order to be eligible for Federal employment. You will be required to certify as to your status at the time of appointment.
- I **understand** that any information I give may be investigated as allowed by law or Presidential order.
- I **consent** to the release of information about my ability and fitness for Federal employment *by employers, schools, law enforcement agencies and other individuals and organizations, to investigators, personnel staffing specialists, and other authorized employees of the Federal Government.*
- I **certify** that, to the best of my knowledge and belief, **all** of my statements are true, correct, complete, and made in good faith.

48 SIGNATURE *(Sign each application in dark ink)* | **49** DATE SIGNED *(Month, day, year)*

Standard Form 171-A— *Continuation Sheet for SF 171*

• Attach all SF 171-A's to your application at the top of page 3.

Form Approved:
OMB No. 3206-0012

1. Name *(Last, First, Middle Initial)*	2. Social Security Number
3. Job Title or Announcement Number You Are Applying For	4. Date Completed

ADDITIONAL WORK EXPERIENCE BLOCKS

☐ Name and address of employer's organization *(include ZIP Code, if known)*	Dates employed *(give month, day and year)*	Average number of hours per week	Number of employees you supervised
	From: To:		
	Salary or earnings	Your reason for leaving	
	Starting $ per		
	Ending $ per		

Your immediate supervisor			Exact title of your job	If Federal employment *(civilian or military)* list series, grade or rank, and, if promoted in this job, the date of your last promotion
Name	Area Code	Telephone No.		

Description of work: Describe your specific duties, responsibilities and accomplishments in this job, **including** the job title(s) of any employees you supervised. *If you describe more than one type of work (for example, carpentry and painting, or personnel and budget), write the approximate percentage of time you spent doing each.*

_____

For Agency Use (skill codes, etc.)

☐ Name and address of employer's organization *(include ZIP Code, if known)*	Dates employed *(give month, day and year)*	Average number of hours per week	Number of employees you supervised
	From: To:		
	Salary or earnings	Your reason for leaving	
	Starting $ per		
	Ending $ per		

Your immediate supervisor			Exact title of your job	If Federal employment *(civilian or military)* list series, grade or rank, and, if promoted in this job, the date of your last promotion
Name	Area Code	Telephone No.		

Description of work: Describe your specific duties, responsibilities and accomplishments in this job, **including** the job title(s) of any employees you supervised. *If you describe more than one type of work (for example, carpentry and painting, or personnel and budget), write the approximate percentage of time you spent doing each.*

_____

For Agency Use (skill codes, etc.)

THE FEDERAL GOVERNMENT IS AN EQUAL OPPORTUNITY EMPLOYER
PREVIOUS EDITION USABLE

Standard Form 171-A (Rev. 6-88)
U.S. Office of Personnel Management
FPM Chapter 295

THE PERSONAL INTERVIEW

A personal interview will be scheduled at a local air traffic control facility near the applicant's home. At the interview, an applicant's personal characteristics are assessed to see if they match the characteristics required of controllers. For example, applicants should possess common sense, job dedication, and a clear speaking voice. They are also evaluated on alertness, decisiveness, and poise.

THE MEDICAL EXAMINATION

Once the interview is completed, a candidate is scheduled for a medical examination. Part of this exam includes the testing of a urine sample for the presence of drugs. Controllers are required to pass an annual physical examination and are subject to random drug testing throughout their professional careers.

Following are medical requirements candidates must meet:

Vision standards for terminal and center specialist positions are strictest. Distant and near vision in each eye must test at 20/20 or better. In case an applicant wears glasses or contact lenses are worn, candidates may not meet FAA standards if the refractive error in each eye exceeds plus or minus 5.50 diopters or 3.00 diopter of cylinder.

For flight service station specialist positions, the vision standards are not as stringent. At least one eye must have distant and near vision of 20/20 or better. If a flight service specialist applicant wears glasses or contact lenses, a consultation with an ophthalmologist will be required if the refractive error exceeds plus or minus 8.00 diopters of spherical equivalent.

Applicants cannot be color blind. Their color vision should be normal without using x-chrome lenses.

Disqualifying medical history or clinical diagnosis include any of the following, according to the FAA:

1) **Psychosis; neurosis**

2) **Substance dependence. "Substance" includes alcohol, narcotics, and non-narcotic drugs**

3) **Any other mental or personality disorder that the Federal Air Surgeon determined a hazard to safety in the air traffic control system**

4) **Diabetes mellitus**

5) **Other organic, functional, or structural disease, defect, or limitation found by the Federal Air Surgeon to constitute a hazard to safety in the air traffic control system.**

The FAA regional flight surgeon will review the results of the examination and any military health records, if applicable. The purpose of the flight surgeon review is to determine if a candidate meets the medical requirements for Air Traffic Control Specialist. Those who do not meet these requirements will be told the reason(s) for disqualification.

Costs of the medical examinations are paid by the FAA. However, the applicant pays the travel costs necessary for reporting for the examination. If a problem arises which requires further evaluation to determine eligibility, the individual pays all associated costs. Once employed, costs of the annual medical examination required of all controllers are paid by the FAA.

SECURITY (SUITABILITY) INVESTIGATION

The final stage in the application process is a security investigation which includes inquiries to both former employers and/or schools. It also includes a review of pertinent FBI, military, and police files.

Candidates can be disqualified if the investigation reveals any questionable information concerning personal conduct, reliability, character, trustworthiness, or loyalty to the U. S. Government.

All questions must be answered truthfully. Do not enter false information on the SF-171. It may eliminate a person from further consideration for a job. If any falsified information is eventually discovered after appointment, the person may be dismissed.

CONCLUSION

Generally, it takes from 45 to 180 days to process an air traffic control candidate's medical examination and security clearance. Applicants should remain in their current jobs and not be discouraged if they do not hear immediately from the regional management.

When the region decides to hire a person, he or she is notified and given a date to report to the FAA Academy in Oklahoma city for training. Training at the FAA Academy is covered in Chapter Four.

Chapter Three comes next. It explains the FAA written test and provides sample questions and answers for its first two parts.

INSIDE THE WRITTEN EXAM

PREPARING FOR THE WRITTEN TEST

I n Chapter Two the FAA written test for air traffic controller applicants was outlined. Its place in the application and selection process was shown. This chapter provides a further explanation of the test, and includes sample questions and answers for illustrative purposes.

The written test consists of three subtests. Remember that Test I evaluates a person's air traffic controller aptitudes. Test II assesses an individual's ability to comprehend spatial relationships. The third test evaluates knowledge about air traffic control work.

A word about scoring. It is possible to achieve a score of 100 solely on Tests I and II. If a person achieves a passing score of at least 70 on Tests I and II, additional points achieved on Test III may be added to raise the score, but not to more than 100.

All supplies necessary to take the test are provided at the test site. However, you should bring certain essential items with you. The first three items are forms mentioned in Chapter Two, and which you have already completed. Bring these items:

> 1) **Form 5000, application for the written test, when it is returned to you;**

> 2) **Form B, occupational supplement (OPM Form 1203-M), completed;**

> 3) **SF-171, completed.**

You should also bring a pen, three medium No 2 black lead pencils, and an eraser.

Finally, be certain to bring identification that proves you are really you. You may be asked to show identification. This is to prevent someone's impersonating another, and taking the examination in his place.

Once in the examination room, persons taking the test are briefed on the procedures and any administrative details necessary. Then before each subtest, preliminary instructions are given. They help you read the information provided before you actually start taking the test.

The whole test takes approximately four hours to complete. Advice from the FAA to prospective test-takers: get a good night's sleep before reporting to the test site. Allow plenty of time to get there, so you are not rushed at the last moment.

TEST I, THE RADAR SCOPE

The first test consists of questions based on schematic drawings similar to information shown on radar scopes. They depict patterns of air traffic that are typical of what controllers see on real scope displays. Each problem in the test uses a sketch simulating a radar scope. It shows flight paths and symbols for aircraft flying along them. A table printed under the scope drawing contains information about each aircraft. It tells the altitude, speed, and route that each one is following.

The questions ask you to analyze the information on the scope to respond to specific questions about the aircraft depicted on it. For example, the questions require you to identify:

1) **potential midair collisions,**

2) **differences in aircraft routes,**

3) **distances between aircraft,**

4) **compass headings of different aircraft; that is, the directions they are flying, and**

5) **changes in routes based on the flight information provided.**

Before the test begins, applicants receive preliminary instructions that explain the information provided in the problems.

In Sample Question 1, the drawing of the radar scope shows flight paths of five aircraft. The aircraft can change their flight paths only at the intersection between two routes (this is a test parameter, not a real world restriction). Each "x" depicted on the routes represents an aircraft traveling in a particular direction, indicated by the trailing dots. The dots are a sort of trail, indicating where the aircraft has been. The number next to each "x" on the drawing corresponds to an aircraft listed in the table.

Simulated radar scope, showing characteristic patterns of air traffic.
Aircraft are designated by letters. Essential information about each aircraft is given in the table below the simulated scope. (FAA)

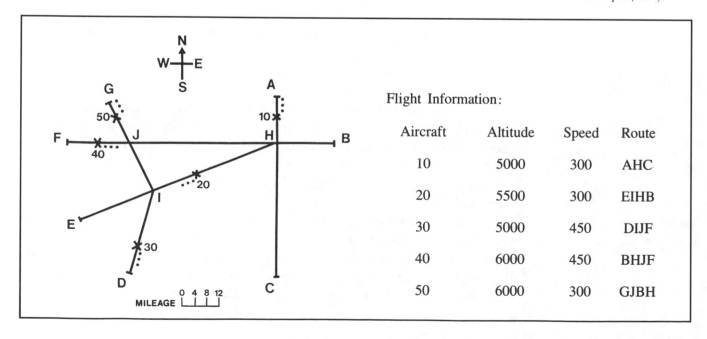

Flight Information:

Aircraft	Altitude	Speed	Route
10	5000	300	AHC
20	5500	300	EIHB
30	5000	450	DIJF
40	6000	450	BHJF
50	6000	300	GJBH

The flight information in the table tells about each aircraft depicted on the scope. Information includes the altitude, speed (in miles per hour), and the route that each of the five aircraft is flying.

When answering the questions, keep in mind that north is always at the top of the page. Also, be aware that separation between aircraft can be achieved either vertically or horizontally. Several variations of minimum vertical separation are possible, but for this example assume that the minimum distance is 1,000 feet. That is, aircraft must remain separated vertically by at least 1,000 feet.

Minimum horizontal separation also varies with the situation. Assume for this situation that the distance is five miles. That is, in the horizontal dimension aircraft must be separated by at least five miles of airspace. Again, the trail of dots indicates where the aircraft has been.

SAMPLE QUESTIONS FOR TEST I

Here are five questions that could be asked based on this example radar scope and situation. You can enter your answers on the sample answer sheet by darkening the bar that corresponds to the answer you have chosen.

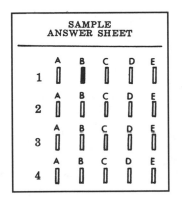

SAMPLE ANSWER SHEET

Sample answer sheet for written examination.

1. **Which aircraft travels a route that does not change direction?**
   (A) 50   (B) 30   (C) 10   (D) 20

2. **Will aircraft 20 and aircraft 10 conflict?**
   (A) Yes   (B) No

3. **How many miles does aircraft 50 travel on its route?**
   (A) 20   (B) 35   (C) 105   (D) 76   (E) 57

4. **Aircraft 20 travels:**
   (A) East then northeast
   (B) Northeast then east
   (C) South then southeast

5. **Will aircraft 30 and aircraft 50 conflict?**
   (A) Yes   (B) No

ANSWERS TO TEST I SAMPLE QUESTIONS

Solving the problems depends on a person's aptitude for understanding the diagram and the instructions. It does not require applicants to have any background in air traffic control or general aviation. The solutions are straightforward. Here are the answers and explanations for each.

1. **Identifying Changes in Direction**—Aircraft 50 changes direction at J, aircraft 30 changes at I and J, and aircraft 20 changes at H. Aircraft 40 does not change direction, but it was not among the possible choices. Aircraft 10 flies in a straight line. Therefore, C is the correct answer.

2. **Spotting a Potential Conflict**—Aircraft 20 is at 5,500 feet and aircraft 10 is at 5,000 feet. Vertical separation of 1,000 feet is required. Since the required vertical separation does not exist, the horizontal separation between the two aircraft must be calculated. Recall that a minimum of five miles horizontal separation is required in this situation. The aircraft are flying at the same airspeed, so they will cover the same distance in a given amount of time. Aircraft 20 is about 28 miles from point H, aircraft 10 is about 10 miles from point H. By the time aircraft 20 reaches point H, aircraft 10 should be about 18 miles south of the point. Therefore, aircraft 10 and 20 will not conflict. Answer B is correct.

3. **Calculating Miles Traveled**—Using the scale at the bottom of the diagram, you can measure the distance on the scope within plus or minus four miles. The correct answer is 76 miles. Answer D is correct.

4. **Observing Direction**—Using the compass points given, where north is straight up, south is straight down, east is to the right (at a 90-degree angle) and west is to the left. Aircraft 20 is traveling northeast and then turns east at point H. Again, note that the aircraft is traveling away from the dots, which form its trail. Answer B is the right one.

5. **Gauging a Potential Conflict**—Aircraft 30 is at 5,000 feet and aircraft 50 is at 6,000 feet. The minimum 1,000-foot vertical separation requirement applies, precluding any need to consider the route or speed of the aircraft. The two aircraft will not conflict. Thus, Answer B is the right one in this situation.

When doing exercises similar to this one, it helps to write the information from the table next to the "x" so you don't have to keep looking at the table. In fact, this practice simulates the data blocks that are displayed on the real-world scopes that controllers work with in today's system. The experience is likely to prove useful in the long term.

TEST II, SPATIAL RELATIONSHIPS

The second test contains questions dealing with relationships among sets of symbols and sets of letters. The following samples provided by the FAA illustrate the types of questions you can expect to encounter. Indicate your answers on the sample answer sheet provided by darkening the appropriate bar.

Each of the first four questions has two boxes at the left. The symbols in the second box are different from the symbols in the first box. There is a relationship among the symbols within the first box and a relationship among the symbols within the second box.

The relationship in the second box is similar but not identical to the relationship in the first box. Using these similarities and differences, choose from the five lettered alternatives (A, B, C, D, or E) the symbol that can best be substituted for the question mark in the second box. The correct answer is never based upon the series or progression of the symbols.

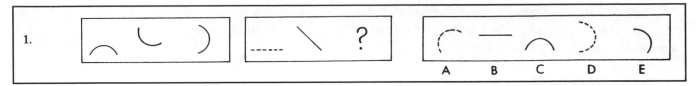

1.

Symbols for Test II, Question 1
Symbols in the second box are different from the symbols in the first box. There is a relationship among the symbols within the first box and a relationship among the symbols within the second box. (FAA)

In question 1 all the symbols in the first box are curved while the symbols in the second box are straight. Of the lettered symbols in the third box, only B is straight, so B has been marked on the sample answer sheet. (Note that although one symbol in the second box is made of dashes, the other is not, and so a dashed type of line is not the difference between the two boxes.) Now that you know how the relationships are defined, you are ready to try questions by yourself. Do questions 2 through 4 now.

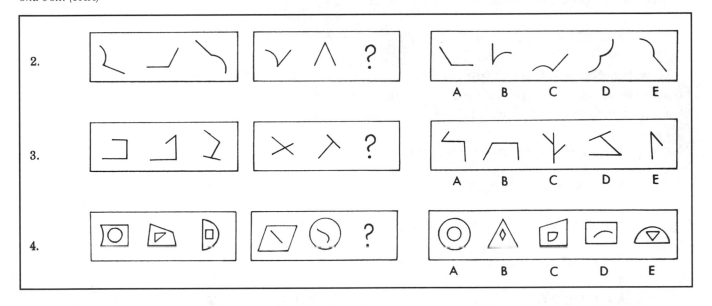

Symbols for Test II, Questions 2-4.

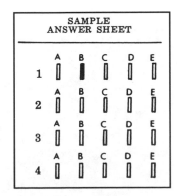

Sample answer sheet for written examination.

ANSWERS TO FIRST PART, TEST II

Recall that these questions test your ability to comprehend spatial relationships. The answers to questions 2-4 are:

2. **(B) is right.** The symbols in the left box contain two lines which form an angle of 90 degrees or more (an obtuse angle). The second box contains symbols with two lines forming an angle of less than 90 degrees (acute angles). Alternative (B) is the only symbol with two lines forming an angle of less than 90 degrees. Whether the lines are curved or straight is not a factor in deciding the correct choice.

3. **In this case, (E) is correct.** The first box has symbols with three connected lines. The second box has symbols with two connected lines. Alternative (E) is the only symbol with two connected lines.

4. **If you selected (D), you got it right.** The first box has a circle, a triangle, and a square inside the larger figure. The second box has a single line inside the larger figure. Only alternative (D) has a single line inside the larger figure.

Sometimes the mind tries to make the problem more difficult than it is, and we try to discern the pattern in the first two boxes before looking at the alternatives. Remember, it might be simpler than you think.

RELATIONSHIPS IN LETTER SERIES

In each of the next five questions (numbers 5-9) there are at the left a series of seven capital letters. The series of letters follow some definite order. At the right are five sets of two capital letters each.

Look at the letters in the left-hand series and determine what the order is. Then, from the suggested answers at the right, select the set that gives the next two letters in the series. Next to the question number on the sample answer sheet darken the bar that has the same letter as the set you have chosen.

5. X C X D X E X ...... A) F X   B) F G   C) X F   D) E F   E) X G

Answer to Number 5: the A space has been darkened for question 5. That is because the series consists of X's alternating with letters in alphabetical order: C, D, and E. Since F is the next letter in the alphabet, choice A is correct.

Now do sample questions 6 through 9 on your own.

6. A V A W A X A ...... A) Z A   B) Y Z   C) Y A   D) A Z   E) A Y

7. A T T B S S C ...... A) R R   B) R D   C) C R   D) D D   E) C C

8. A B D E G H J ...... A) K L   B) L N   C) J M   D) L M   E) K M

9. A R C S E T G ...... A) H I   B) H U   C) U J   D) U I   E) I V

ANSWERS TO QUESTIONS 6 THROUGH 9

With the explanation given for Question 5, you probably found that detecting the patterns in 6 through 9 was easier than you first expected. Here are the answers and explanations.

6. **(C) is the correct answer here.** Every other letter is an A, so you know the second letter in the answer should be an A. The alternate letters are V, W, and X. The next letter should therefore be Y and the answer is Y A.

7. **We can reason that (A) is correct for this situation.** The letter pattern indicates that the answer should be a double letter, so the A-B-C pattern is irrelevant. The double letters are T T and S S, which reverses the alphabet. The answer therefore is R R.

8. **Here, (E) is the right answer.** This is a continuous letter pattern. Every third letter of the alphabet is missing. There is no C or F or I. There should be a K, skip L, and retain M. The answer is K M.

9. **This time, (D) is correct.** Every other letter skips one letter in the alphabet. So you have A (B) C (D) E (F) G which leads to (H) I. The alternate letters follow the alphabet. You have R, S, T which leads to U. The answer is U I

A word about the questions and taking the written test. These questions are standard types found in all sorts of tests. They are not particularly related to air traffic control. However, they all test your ability to detect a pattern and project it out to the next logical step. The FAA has found these sorts of exercises to be good indicators of how a man or woman will perform as a controller.

In addition to working the questions, you will also be working against the clock. That may add to the stress of taking the test. But controllers work against the clock and under pressure every day. If you can handle the pressure during the written test, that is a good indication you can handle the job.

Persons who have passed all the hurdles of testing and examination enter the FAA Academy. Here, tower controller trainees learn airport operations, using aircraft models and a simulated airport. (FAA)

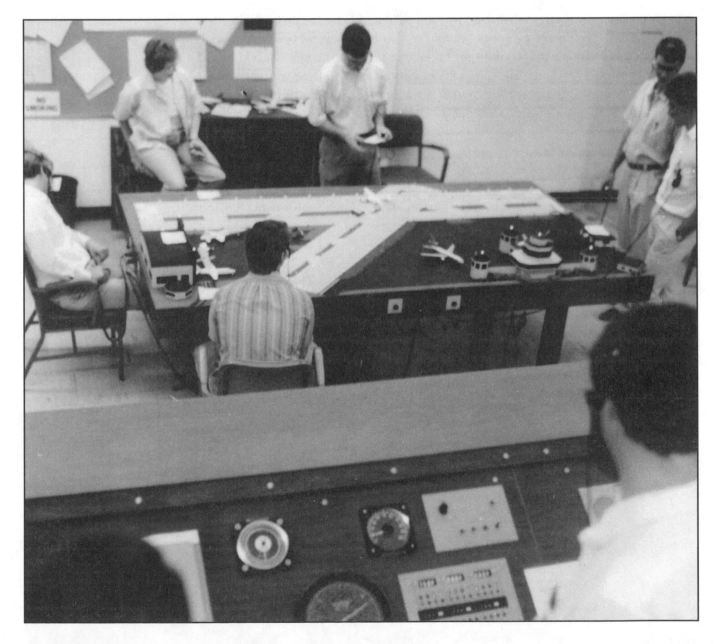

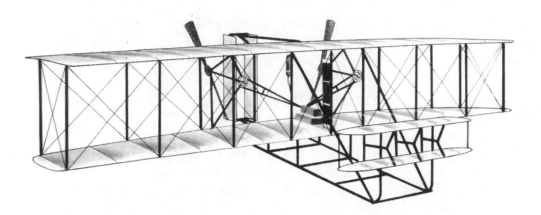

Wright Airplane, 1903. Orville Wright flew the first piloted, powered, sustained, and controlled heavier-than-air flight, Dec. 17. Orville and Wilbur Wright.

TEST III

Test III consists of questions which cover knowledge related to air traffic control work. The test demonstrates understanding of this knowledge. However, specialized knowledge is not a prerequisite for taking the test or for being selected by the FAA for controller training. The questions in this test deal with air traffic rules, air traffic procedures, inflight traffic control procedures, communications operating procedures, flight assistance procedures, air navigation and aids to navigation, and aviation weather.

Although the test is not shown here, when you have finished reading this book you will have gained knowledge that will prove useful in taking Test III.

Remember, the FAA written test is an aptitude test. The results should be understood as indicating your aptitude for a particular job. Your performance on this test has nothing to do with your overall intelligence, or with your aptitude for other jobs.

Suppose you have passed the written test with a score of 90 or better. You have gone through all of the preemployment screening successfully. The interview went well, your physical examination was fine, and the suitability checks were all fine. You have been hired by an FAA region, and have been given a reporting date for a class at the FAA Academy.

Oklahoma City, here you come.

While attending the Academy course, you will be paid at the GS-7 salary grade, $20,195 as of this writing. You will receive a paycheck every two weeks. In addition to the basic salary, you also receive a per diem allowance to cover living expenses while in school.

The next chapter covers training at the FAA Academy. Being selected for the training is a measure of your determination and your ability. It is also the beginning of a rewarding and very challenging career.

CHAPTER FOUR

ACADEMY TRAINING: MAKING CONTROLLERS

AT THE FAA ACADEMY

The FAA's Mike Monroney Aeronautical Center is in Oklahoma City, Oklahoma. Mike Monroney was a longtime United States Senator from Oklahoma with a lifelong interest in aviation. The center named for Senator Monroney is the home of the largest and perhaps finest government-run aviation school in the world—the FAA Academy. This is the place where most FAA controllers start their air traffic controller careers. It is also the place where 40 percent of controller trainees end their FAA careers.

The Mike Monroney Center is a sprawling complex of buildings located on the west side of Will Rogers World Airport, six miles southwest of Oklahoma City. In addition to the FAA Academy it is home to several other FAA facilities, including the Civil Aeromedical Institute (CAMI) and the FAA logistics center—both industry marvels.

CAMI oversees projects related to medical requirements for the aviation industry and conducts crash survival tests. The Institute also does extensive work in studying human factors and developing aptitude tests to identify promising air traffic controllers.

The FAA logistics center is a huge warehouse of FAA spare parts. When a radar antenna, for example, breaks at Chicago's O'Hare Airport, it is the logistics center's job to get a replacement to the site quickly. When Hurricane Hugo devastated FAA facilities in the Caribbean, logistics center personnel responded swiftly, sending an FAA DC-9 jet transport loaded with vital parts to the damaged site.

The CAMI and the logistics center are important activities. But most people identify the Aeronautical Center with the FAA Academy. Here the students must prove themselves in the weeks of rigorous training before they are assigned to an operating facility. About 60 percent of candidates entering en route/terminal controller training at the FAA Academy pass the training and are sent to facilities such as centers, towers and approach controls for the years of developmental training on the job.

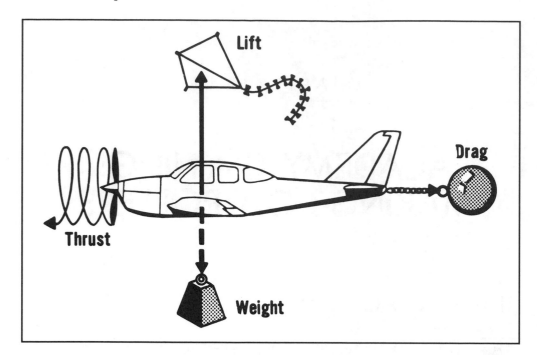

At the FAA Academy controller trainees learn forces acting on an airplane in flight. Lift is the upward acting force; weight (or gravity) is the downward acting force; thrust pulls the airplane forward; and drag is the rearward acting, or retarding force.

Trainee controllers graduating from the en route/terminal program at the academy are assigned to facilities according to the FAA's needs and their test scores. The best students go to the higher activity facilities, generally a center. Individual interests are considered in making assignments, but the needs of the FAA come first. The training for Flight Service Specialists is separate from the en route/terminal program. Its pass rate is approximately 95 percent. Scores are not a factor in place of assignment.

STEPS IN TRAINING

The phases of instruction at the FAA Academy are steps along a candidate's road in progressing from entering trainee to achieving status as a full-performance level (FPL) controller in three or four years. The early phases are taught at the Academy, and provide the foundation for the developmental controller to become a functioning member of the team in the field. The rest of the training toward full-performance level is conducted at the facility of first assignment. All phases except the first, orientation, are taught on a pass/fail basis.

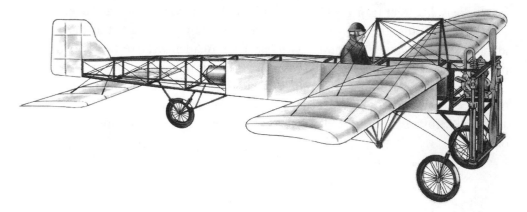

Bleriot XI, 1909. Louis Bleriot flew first across the English Channel, July 25, awakening the world to the potential of aircraft. Louis Bleriot.

The FAA Academy trains controller candidates and screens them at the same time. Therefore, it requires that all students after orientation take the toughest course first. That is the Air Traffic Controller Screen course. Persons who complete that course are ready for assignment to an en route center or a tower/approach control terminal facility for further developmental training in that area of specialization.

Depending on the option assigned, developmental controllers complete three to six weeks of additional training at the academy after passing the Screen. The additional training may be further expanded in the future, to match developmental controllers better with the operational needs of facilities in the field.

ORIENTATION: THE BEGINNING

Orientation takes up most of the first week at the FAA Academy. During this initial 24-hour phase students are now on duty as GS-7 controller trainees. In the 24 hours of instruction they are introduced to the FAA organization, policies, services, and functions. Also, the Civil Aeromedical Institute administers an examination early in the indoctrination phase which assists in its research on human factors in air traffic control.

Students receive instruction on the following topics:

1) Briefings by representatives of offices responsible for employment, civil rights, student travel, security, and credit union;

2) The FAA Academy policy letter, which discusses procedures such as student conduct, repeating the course, and other pertinent subjects;

3) The FAA Handbook. This is the basic reference for FAA employees. It covers subjects such as the history and functions of the FAA; the workweek and hours of duty; the pay and allotment system; procedures for absences and leave; policies for career development and training; policies concerning performance, promotions, and award programs; and life insurance and retirement benefits. Students are required to have a grasp of the material covered in the Handbook and, without reference to it, be able to explain the details of the FAA Drug Awareness Program.

The instruction in the orientation phase is rudimentary but necessary. As government employees, students have responsibilities, rights, and benefits and should understand them from the outset. This phase also serves as a brief transition period. During the three days of orientation, students begin to adjust from their former lives to a new one. They become ready to cope with the demands and stresses of the classroom and the laboratory training program in the succeeding phases.

AIR TRAFFIC CONTROLLER SCREEN

This course is required of all students and lasts about eight weeks, with instruction divided into a combination of classroom and laboratory work. The instruction consists of 160 hours of classroom and 168 hours of laboratory work.

This is the student's first introduction to actual air traffic control duties. It is based on en route nonradar air traffic control rules. Nonradar, as the name implies, is a set of rules and procedures in an environment without radar.

Students are first required to learn the "aeronautical center" area chart. That is a fictitious center area developed specifically for the course. On the chart are all of the symbols and bits of information just as in a real air traffic area. The "aeronautical center" aero chart is used throughout the nonradar and radar phases of Academy training.

As is the standard procedure in the facility out in the field, the first step is to identify the aids to navigation and the facilities on the map.

In the academic portion of this phase, students learn the fundamentals of recording clearances on pieces of paper called flight progress strips. They also learn and practice correct phraseology and how to issue clearances to provide vertical, longitudinal, or lateral separation distance between aircraft. Instruction also includes how to issue clearances according to priority and other control functions.

Instruction is divided into four blocks. Multiple-choice tests are given at the end of each block. A comprehensive test is administered when the academic portion is completed, before students begin the laboratory portion of the course.

Using a smoke tunnel demonstration rig Jim Webster, an FAA Academy engineering instructor, demonstrates how the flow of air over an airfoil generates lift. (FAA)

Controllers and pilots need to be aware of wake turbulence. Wake turbulence is caused by the vortices that trail behind an aircraft in flight. Vortex circulation is outward, upward, and around the wing tips. Heavy aircraft generate the strongest vortices and turbulence in their wake. Wake begins when an aircraft leaves the ground, and ends when it touches down.

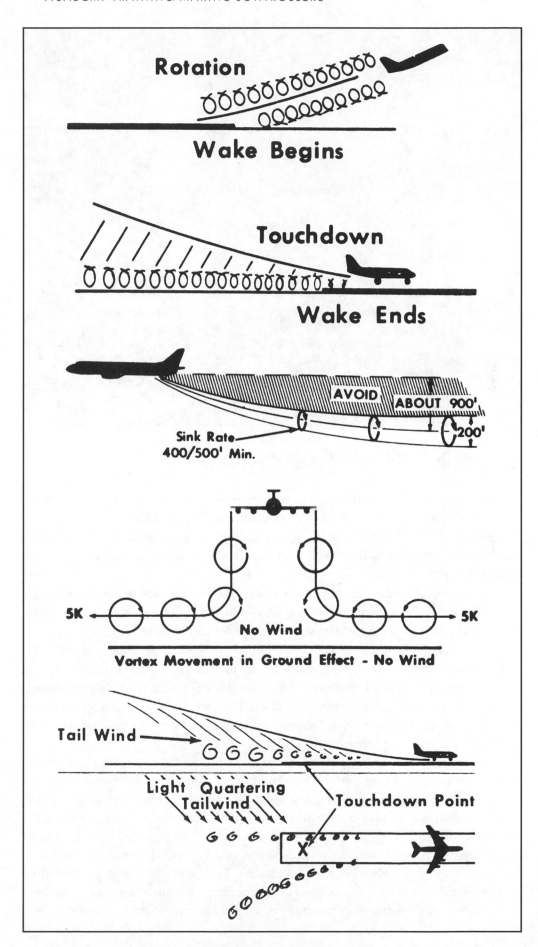

Don Arnoldy, an instructor at the FAA Academy, describes airport approach procedures to developmental controller students. (FAA)

LEARNING IN THE LABORATORY

In the laboratory part of this phase students receive 26 practice control problems of increasing complexity and six graded problems. The problems require students to perform all the functions of air traffic control. These exercises test everything the student has learned until now and stretch the student's ability to cope with ever-increasing pressure.

Skills practiced and tested in the laboratory part include estimating the times aircraft take to fly between fixes (geographical positions); marking the flight progress strips with the correct information; issuing clearances to departing, arriving, and holding aircraft; providing vertical, longitudinal, or lateral separation; and using the correct radio and interphone communications procedures. These problems worked against time truly separate those who have controller potential from those without.

Students work on 26 ungraded exercises. The fact that they are ungraded does not make them any less intense. Students know they are working against the clock, the situation, and each other.

Students are tested in six graded laboratory problems of increasing complexity. The first two graded exercises are conducted after 17 practice problems. After the remaining nine practice problems the last four graded exercises are administered. Each problem is evaluated by a different instructor. Technical assessments are made solely on the number of errors. Technical assessments are recorded in each of three areas: separation, coordination or procedural, and "other." These evaluation areas are then given a weighted score and totaled. Each student is also evaluated on potential exhibited during each graded problem. This instructor assessment is based solely on the amount of training received at the time of the evaluation.

The laboratory grades for the best five of the six graded problems are computed. They make up 60 percent of the final grade.

A controller skills test (CST) is administered at the end of the Screen course. The CST is a written, timed, multiple-choice exam designed to test the student's ability to apply laboratory procedures and identify and resolve air traffic situations. The CST is valued at 20 percent of the total score. Students must attain a final score of 70 percent to complete satisfactorily the Academy nonradar air traffic control screening phase. Students who fail to meet the established criteria are removed from the Academy.

Successfully completing this training marks another major milestone. It indicates that a student possesses the basic aptitude to be a controller and that the odds are almost three to one that he or she will become a full-performance level (FPL) controller. In fact, about 72 percent of students who succeed in the training and graduate from the academy work up to full-performance level status at the facility of first assignment. Approximately another 18 percent who graduate and report to the facility of first assignment ultimately fail or resign before achieving full-performance status, and about 10 percent switch to another option.

PLACEMENT COMES AFTER SCREENING

Students who have passed the Air Traffic Controller Screen instruction and testing are placed in centers or towers. That is, they are assigned by name to the place (the facility) to which they will report for actual work and developmental training. However, they remain at the FAA Academy for additional training that is specific to the option to which they have been assigned.

Two days (16 hours) of Placement instruction give the developmental controller a knowledge of job-related subjects in preparation for the skill-oriented training that follows. At this time each person is placed in either the En Route or Terminal option.

TRAINING FOR THE TERMINAL OPTION

This training is specific to individuals assigned to the terminal option. Its purpose is to provide knowledge of and a solid grounding in terminal procedures. This readies them to begin training at the facility to which they have been assigned, so that they are functional upon arrival there. In addition, this period allows instructors to evaluate the individuals early in their prospective careers.

The number of hours of instruction and testing on a specific subject may vary from time to time, as the training at the FAA Academy evolves to meet the needs of the facilities in the air traffic control system. However, certain fundamental skills and knowledge are essential in all situations, and are covered in the progression of instructional and laboratory phases that follow.

Students are tested at the completion of each segment of the terminal training. Ultimately, they must achieve 70 percent or better to move on to a field facility to continue training and development.

TERMINAL FUNDAMENTALS

This phase consists of 48 hours of instruction. Its goal is to provide the developmental controller with a basic understanding of ATC-related subjects. The "fundamentals" section builds a basic understanding of aviation subjects, and serves as preparation for subsequent skills training. It is important that individuals attain established minimum levels of competence at each step; therefore, their progress is closely monitored.

Highlights of subject areas covered:

1) **The Principles of Flight.** Students learn how an airplane flies. You do not have to be a pilot to be a controller. But a controller must know the capabilities and limitations of aircraft, most importantly that an airplane in flight can't stop! Although simplistic, this fact influences a great deal of what controllers do.

2) **Aircraft Identification and Performance.** A good deal of material on aircraft identification was taught in the Screen training, already completed. In this segment, the developmental controller uses and expands upon that knowledge.

When working in a control tower, it is helpful for a controller to look out the window and be able to identify aircraft immediately. It is invaluable to spot quickly a Cessna 172 or a Piper Apache or a Beech King Air, or other make or model.

At the same time a controller knows the performance characteristics of each of those aircraft. Different flying speeds can make a difference in a controller's decisions about directing aircraft.

In addition the FAA classifies aircraft under different categories, based on weight and number of engines. For example, a lightweight, single-engine, propeller-driven personal aircraft is in category II. Each category has specific and different runway separation standards, and controllers have to be able to differentiate among them.

To make it more interesting, aircraft are grouped in three classes according to weight. Aircraft capable of taking off weighing more than 300,000 pounds are classified as "heavy." Those weighing between 12,500 and 300,000 pounds are in the "large" class. Aircraft weighing less than 12,500 are "small." These class designations correspond to wake turbulence criteria.

LZ 7 Deutschland, 1910. First civil transport began passenger service Oct. 1909. In five years, flew 33,722 passengers safely. Count Ferdinand von Zeppelin.

Westinghouse advanced ASR-9 radar antenna is the most visible part of the FAA's newest airport surveillance radar. It is the first radar to show controllers local storms and aircraft at the same time. First ASR-9 went into service at Huntsville, Alabama, in mid-1989. The system monitors itself and alerts maintenance specialists if a fault occurs. (Westinghouse)

Wake turbulence results from the passage of an aircraft through the atmosphere—the air in its wake is turbulent and disturbed. The term "wake turbulence" includes vortices, thrust stream turbulence, jet blast, jet wash, propeller wash, and rotor wash both on the ground and in the air. The larger the aircraft, the greater the wake turbulence. Smaller aircraft are affected by the swirling forces in the wake turbulence of larger aircraft. Thus, wake turbulence criteria are used to determine the required separation (or distance) between aircraft. For example, a tower controller will warn a pilot of a Cessna 172 approaching to land to be aware of wake turbulence from a Boeing 747 airliner that has just landed on the same runway. The Cessna pilot will pick a touchdown point that avoids the wake turbulence the larger airplane created.

3) **Aviation Weather.** Controllers need to be familiar with the environment in which aircraft operate: the atmosphere. They must know the effects of certain atmospheric conditions on aircraft operations, especially weather that is potentially hazardous to the aircraft. Examples include thunderstorms, icing, and fog, among others. Students will not become meteorologists, but they will learn the essentials of aviation weather, and also what services the National Weather Service provides for controllers.

Also, they will learn how controllers themselves make weather observations. Some are obvious, such as reading the wind direction and speed from measuring instruments and passing the information to pilots, or using the landmarks for determining visibility. Under certain specified conditions tower controllers take visibility readings to determine how far one can see with the naked eye. Such information is essential to pilots and controllers alike.

4) **Navigation.** Again, one need not be a navigator to be a controller. But controllers do have to have a basic knowledge of how the pilot of an aircraft finds his way through the air. The simplest way is by pilotage; that is, navigating by referring to landmarks on the ground to proceed from point "A" to point "B." Pilotage was necessary in the early days of aviation, and is still an essential skill practiced by pilots. However, with the advent of radio and radar and their application as aids to navigation, aircraft crews navigate most often by using such aids. Controllers must know what kinds of navigation aids are used in the system, and how they work. They must also be able to interpret the various aeronautical charts and publications available to pilots.

5) **Federal Aviation Regulations (FARs).** As with aircraft identification, students were introduced to the Federal Aviation Regulations during the Screen segment. Now they begin to understand how to apply the FARs.

The FAA is responsible for ensuring the safe and efficient use of the nation's airspace. Writing and distributing the Federal Aviation Regulations (FARs) is one way in which the FAA executes its responsibilities. The FARs are rules and regulations issued in the interests of air safety. They are comprehensive and detailed. Everyone operating aircraft within the national airspace is required to know and abide by the parts of the regulations that apply to them. In this section of the training the students will become familiar with regulations for controlled airspace and the flight requirements for VFR flight and IFR (instrument flight rules) flight.

6) **Air Traffic Communications.** Students were taught the basics of clear air traffic communications in the Screen segment. Now they develop more practice in using proper procedures so they become second nature.

In the ATC environment, control instructions have to be concise and understandable. In using radio to communicate it is easy for letters, words, and phrases to be misunderstood. Pilots expect clear communications from controllers and controllers expect the same from pilots. Clear instructions using words and phrases with precise meanings help pilots understand what controllers are saying. Such good communication practices conserve time on radio frequencies that often become overcrowded. Students learn early to use the phonetic alphabet to prevent misunderstanding of letters that sound alike.

A range of standardized phrases has been developed over the years for use between controllers and pilots. Students will learn and be required to use the correct phraseology. The Pilot/Controller Glossary issued by the FAA is in Appendix III. Terms used frequently between controllers and pilots are highlighted for ready reference.

7) **Air Traffic Services.** Students will learn the history, purpose, and responsibilities of flight service stations, airport traffic control towers, and air route traffic control centers. That short sentence covers a hefty diet of information that students must absorb and begin to use in a very brief time

THE PHONETIC ALPHABET

CHARACTER		PRONUNCIATION
A	Alfa	(AL-Fah)
B	Bravo	(BRAH-Voh)
C	Charlie	(CHAR-Lee) or (SHAR-Lee)
D	Delta	(DELL-Tah)
E	Echo	(ECK-Oh)
F	Foxtrot	(FOKS-Trot)
G	Golf	(GOLF)
H	Hotel	(Hoh-TEL)
I	India	(IN-Dee-Ah)
J	Juliett	(Jew-Lee-ETT)
K	Kilo	(KEE-Loh)
L	Lima	(LEE-Mah)
M	Mike	(MIKE)
N	November	(No-VEM-Ber)
O	Oscar	(OSS-Cah)
P	Papa	(Pah-PAH)
Q	Quebec	(Keh-BECK)
R	Romeo	(ROW-Me-Oh)
S	Sierra	(See-AIR-Rah)
T	Tango	(TANG-Go)
U	Uniform	(YOU-Nee-Form) or (OO-Nee-Form)
V	Victor	(VIK-Tah)
W	Whiskey	(WISS-Key)
X	Xray	(ECKS-Ray)
Y	Yankee	(YANG-Key)
Z	Zulu	(ZOO-Loo)
1	One	(Wun)
2	Two	(Too)
3	Three	(Tree)
4	Four	(FOW-Er)
5	Five	(Fife)
6	Six	(Six)
7	Seven	(SEV-En)
8	Eight	(Ait)
9	Nine	(NINE-Er)
0	Zero	(ZEE-Ro)

8) **Flight Assistance Service.** This generalized heading includes a range of topics. The subjects are all designed to help the pilot.

Examples include pilot reports of weather conditions that are given to other pilots. They are known as Pilot Reports or (PIREPs). For example, a pilot who encounters icing conditions or heavy turbulence during a flight will radio that information to air traffic controllers. That becomes a PIREP. The controllers will enter the PIREPs into the ATC database, where it is immediately available to other

controllers and pilots. Another service to airmen provides alerts about significant meteorological conditions (SIGMETs), creating reports that are passed on to pilots and controllers and used in flight planning and operations.

Notices to airmen on matters of significance are abbreviated as NOTAMs. NOTAMs contain information about changes in any component of the national airspace system that is essential knowledge for people concerned with flight operations. Changes to components in the system eventually are distributed as routine changes to aeronautical charts or other publications. However, NOTAMs are disseminated quickly, so the essential knowledge reaches persons operating in the system ahead of routine publication.

Search and rescue services for aircraft in distress are also covered in this segment. For example, a pilot who is uncertain of his aircraft position can ask air traffic controllers to help him determine it. They can do so by using radar, by radio direction finding equipment, or by other means. Pilots with in-flight emergencies notify controllers of the situation and receive assistance from them.

In the FAA Academy's radar training laboratory, student Susan Hale ponders her next action under the watchful eye of instructor John Newman. Students Theresa Reingruber and Kevin Sullivan are equally absorbed. Larry Bicknell, chief of the radar training facility, observes. (FAA photo by Bob Mikkelson)

In the en route laboratory, students Ken Wisner (foreground) and John Talley work on flight data while instructors Bob Davis (left) and Charles Maitland (back to camera) observe. (FAA)

9) **Overview of the National Airspace System and the Development of Automation.** This is the "Big Picture," taught near the end of this phase. It is presented to students to enable them to place their own roles in the context of the existing system as well as the improvements planned for the near future.

In addition, individuals learn the instructional methods used in on-the-job-training (OJT), factors affecting learning, and the benefits of OJT. They also learn about the human elements that contribute to operational errors in air traffic control.

TOWER CAB TRAINING

This course consists of classroom and laboratory instruction conducted over 168 hours. It guides students through the instruction so they become proficient in the following operating positions in the control tower cab:

Flight Data. In this section students become familiar with various equipment, such as the electrowriter, the telephone system, standby radio equipment, recorder equipment, automatic terminal information system (ATIS), and flight data entry printout (FDEP) equipment.

Clearance Delivery. This controller reads the departure and en route clearances to pilots and ensures that they are correct when the pilots read them back.

Flight progress strips are used by air traffic controllers to post current data on air traffic and clearances required for control and other services. This example is from the FAA air traffic procedures handbook. It is for Delta Airlines flight 542. Highlights of information on the strip:

DC9/A (Douglas DC-9 equipped with transponder with altitude encoding);

T468 G555 (true airspeed of 468 knots filed by the captain, G555 estimated ground speed);

330 is the airplane's altitude in hundreds of feet (it is flying at 33,000 feet);

FLL J14 ENO OOD212 OOD PHL (flight originated at Fort Lauderdale, is using jet airway J14, passing over Kenton, Delaware (ENO), then along the 212-degree radial of the VOR at Woodstown, New Jersey (OOD), over the Woodstown VOR, and then landing at its destination of Philadelphia).

1 DAL542 DC9/A T468 G555 16 16 486 09	7HQ 1827 PXT	30 18	330	FLL J14 ENO 00D212 OOD PHL	2575 *ZCN

Tower controller students in the FAA Academy laboratory look down on a simulation of the Will Rogers World Airport. Other students move aircraft and ground vehicles in response. (FAA)

Ground Control. This controller is in charge of the activity on the ground, primarily the aircraft taxiing from the ramp to the runway and from the runway to the ramp. Students describe ground traffic procedures and the use of instruments in the tower and explain traffic clearances pertaining to aircraft and vehicles.

Local Control. Students will be responsible for the aircraft in the air and the aircraft landing and departing. They will have to be able to describe separation standards, procedures for assigning runways, landing sequences, wake turbulence advisories, operation of the radar, and operation of airport and runway lighting systems and emergency procedures.

Proficiency is measured during performance on laboratory problems. They determine if the student has met course objectives at each position.

Testing in this course is similar to that in the other phases of instruction. In addition, students take the tower visibility exam during the phase. A passing grade of 80 percent or better is required on this examination.

"Ghost pilots" Frank Ruth (foreground) and Sterling Parks navigate their "aircraft" via electronic input in the FAA Academy laboratory. Information they generate is displayed on video terminals being used by students. (FAA photo by Don Tullous)

Working in the tower is the only controller option that requires a federal license, which is called the Control Tower Operator Certificate. Passing the Control Tower Operator (CTO) exam with a score of 70 percent or better earns students this certificate.

TOWER SIMULATION

After tower cab training with its mix of classroom and laboratory instruction, students move into situations closer to the real operating environment. They learn via "hands-on" experience in a realistic, dynamic tower cab environment using modern simulators. The simulators enable FAA Academy instructors to raise the procedural skills of students to levels not attained by earlier methods.

The simulator situations are so real that students quickly develop sound operating habits and sensible reactions. As a result they become far more competent in a shorter time. When they report to their facility of assignment they are nearer the full-performance level and are able to handle arriving and departing air traffic earlier than in the past.

TERMINAL NONRADAR PROCEDURES

Very few terminal facilities in the national airspace system are without radar. However, all controllers in the terminal option are required to know and be able to apply proper procedures for controlling aircraft without radar. This is useful not only at the few nonradar facilities. It makes sense for controllers at all facilities to be able to continue to operate in the event of power failure or radar malfunction. Knowing nonradar procedures is a sensible form of operating insurance against the defects of machinery and nature.

TERMINAL RADAR

This phase of training in the terminal option instructs developmental controllers in the fundamentals, procedures, and techniques of terminal radar air traffic control. It qualifies them for advancement into subsequent phases of radar control position qualification and certification. Those phases are conducted in the field, at the facility of assignment. They are highlighted in Chapter Six.

This segment of terminal training is conducted over a 17-day period of academics and laboratory instruction, including examinations. Multiple-choice tests follow the blocks of instruction, and laboratory problems are also graded. In addition a comprehensive phase test is administered to evaluate students' radar qualifications.

The training mixture enables students to learn procedures in the classroom, apply them in the laboratory, and be graded to ensure their competence. Proficiency is based on laboratory performance. Laboratory evaluations comprise 70 percent of the grading in this course, the multiple-choice tests make up 12.5 percent; and the comprehensive phase test comprises the remaining 17.5 percent of the total.

During the course of this segment students solve 23 radar demonstration control problems. They begin as fairly simple situations but develop quickly into more complex situations that stretch student capabilities and demonstrate how well they have absorbed all of the instruction. Five of these lab problems are graded and make up 70 percent of the total composite score, as mentioned above. Students also solve 10 more radar control problems, again of increasing complexity, in a simulated, nongraded environment.

When students complete this phase they leave the FAA Academy and report to the facility they have been assigned to. That is the place where they begin work in the field as developmental controllers.

EN ROUTE FOLLOW-ON TRAINING

The follow-on training for developmental controllers who have been assigned to en route facilities in the system is similar to that for those in the terminal option.

It is shorter than the terminal follow-on training covered just above, occupying 96 hours of training. Many of the same fundamentals are taught, of course. They include subjects that make controllers familiar with what pilots and their aircraft are doing. Instruction covering those topics includes basic aerodynamics and flight controls and instruments, plus aircraft operational characteristics and identification features. Also included are basic navigation and use of various charts and publications.

Fundamentals of aviation weather are taught, as well as how to obtain current weather, to know about hazardous weather conditions, and the weather services available in the system.

Of course, the Federal Aviation Regulations (FAR) are covered, and students learn how the FARs are applied in practice in the en route part of the system.

Students are oriented on national en route training programs, and how Air Route Traffic Control Centers (ARTCC) are organized and operated.

En route controller students also learn the principles of radar and how to use radar in en route activities. They perform the functions at en route positions, and learn how to present position relief briefings. In addition, they learn how to process flight plans, and how the information on flight plans is disseminated through the system.

An important part of any controller's job is communication, and listening is a vital half of the task. Training is given on operational remembering and listening, with the goal of improving communications and getting it right the first time.

Air carrier operations are covered, because en route controllers will spend much of their working time dealing with air carrier aircraft passing through their center's airspace.

Finally, the en route developmental controllers learn about the National Airspace System as it is and how it will be as modernization plans go into effect in the field.

At the end of this phase of training the en route developmental controllers, like their counterparts in the terminal option, are ready to report to their facility of assignment. There they begin functioning as key elements of the system while they continue their developmental training and certification.

STUDENT COUNSELING

Counseling is an important part of the FAA Academy program and timely counseling is crucial. When a student has problems dealing with the instruction the counseling process begins. Student weaknesses are identified and then the lead instructor will counsel the student and attempt to resolve problems getting in the way of progress.

After discussion with the student the instructor will offer suggestions. They could include improving study habits and classroom participation. If either the student or the instructor deems it necessary the student may be referred to the instructor's first-line supervisor.

The first-line supervisor works with both the instructor and student to identify the problems and work out solutions. If the first-line supervisor is unable to resolve the situation the student will be referred to higher authorities at the FAA Academy or to other organizations. Among them are the Air Traffic Branch, CAMI, Civil Rights, or other appropriate offices.

The objective of the FAA Academy is to produce qualified controllers, and the agency will do all it can to have students successfully complete the course. It's all up to you.

CONCLUSION

The Academy course helps trainees make a transition. It develops a student's aptitude as measured in the initial written test to its real-world application in an ATC facility.

To reach this point students will have invested more than three months, and probably have quit the jobs that sustained them previously. Therefore, before beginning this process be sure that this is the occupation for you. It is the kind of job that requires commitment.

To help you make the commitment you should first visit an FAA air traffic control facility near you. Call ahead for an appointment and tell the supervisor your intentions. When you get to the facility, talk to the controllers. Get a feel and a sense of what they really do.

Now that the application process is over and you have seen how the training at the FAA Academy is conducted, you are ready for the next step. The following chapters will give you some appreciation for what the job is like, what it is likely to evolve into, and the environment in which controllers operate. The information should provide a solid basis for choosing to become a controller and for successfully completing the training program with its associated hurdles.

CHAPTER FIVE

THE AIRWAY SCIENCE PROGRAM

COLLEGE STUDY FOR AVIATION-RELATED CAREERS

An innovative project called the Airway Science Program began in 1981. It is another way for a person to prepare for an aviation career, including air traffic controller.

The Airway Science Program offers college students the opportunity to prepare for future administrative and management positions in the aviation field. Besides air traffic controllers, the positions include aviation safety inspectors, electronic technicians, and computer specialists. It is a demonstration project sponsored by the Office of Personnel Management (OPM), and is offered at a number of accredited four-year universities. The program was developed to explore the impact of a specialized background on a candidate's ability to cope with the constantly changing technological and human resource requirements within the world of aviation.

The project began in 1981. J. Lynn Helms, then the Administrator of the Federal Aviation Administration (FAA), formed an Airway Science Task Force to design a curriculum for the program. First, standards were set. Then the FAA, working with the University Aviation Association (UAA), established an academic review committee to standardize the airway science curricula submitted by interested colleges and universities.

LeGrand, 1913. World's first multi-engine (four) and heavy transport. First with copilot, washroom, lounge, and observation deck. Igor Sikorsky.

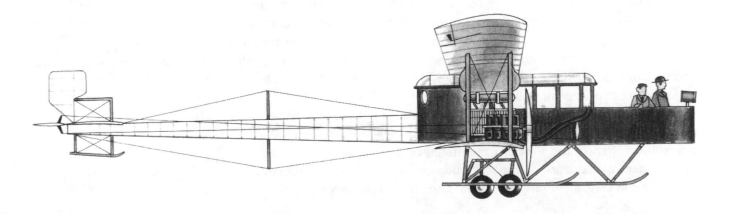

The FAA's Airway Science Register lists men and women who have received an airway science degree from a recognized institution. Their combination of academic credit and specialized aviation knowledge helps to qualify them for entry into the air traffic control field. Of course, individuals with comparable education and/or work experience can be considered for controller candidacy. Those qualifications were explained in Chapter Two.

The airway science curriculum includes five areas of concentration: airway science management, airway computer science, aircraft systems management, airways electronic systems, and aviation maintenance management. The airway science management concentration prepares students for several aviation-related administrative and management positions, including air traffic control.

Instructor and student in an airway science school practice control procedures on an AT Coach system of UFA, Inc., Newton, Massachusetts. (UFA via FAA)

REQUIRED COURSES

Students take a combination of required courses and electives totaling 120 semester hours. They include a minimum of 80 semester hours in core requirements and 40 semester hours in the area of concentration. The core subject areas are as follows:

GENERAL STUDIES

Courses	Semester Hours
English composition	3
Oral communications	3
Psychology	3
Humanities and social science electives	15-21
Total credits	**24-30**

Coursework in the general studies area teaches oral and written communication skills and includes instruction in the following subjects:

—The social, cultural, political, and economic development of American and/or Western civilization

—Human behavior

—Cultural studies such as philosophy, art, drama, music, literature, religion, or language.

MATH/SCIENCE/TECHNOLOGY

Courses	Semester Hours
Introduction to calculus	3
Physics with lab	6
Statistics	3
Electives:	9-16
—Chemistry (required for aviation maintenance management)	
—Chemistry, calculus II, and math analysis (required for airway electronic systems)	
—Calculus II (required for airway computer science)	
Total Credits	**21-28**

This study area familiarizes students with mathematical concepts that may be essential to an individual's success in a high-technology environment.

Airway science graduates can pursue careers in aviation ranging from controllers to pilots to managers. (FAA)

COMPUTER SCIENCE

This core area requires nine hours of coursework in computer sciences or demonstrated equivalent study taken outside of the program, which also satisfies the requirements listed for the aviation computer science area of concentration. The coursework exposes students to the following computer concepts:

—Knowledge and use of a computer language and its applications
—Database management
—Typical hardware configurations in use with micro and minicomputers
—Software applications, such as graphics or simulations.

MANAGEMENT

Courses	Semester Hours
Principles of management	3
Organizational behavior	3
Electives	3-6
Total credits	9-12

Instruction in this area focuses on basic management topics and concerns, including organizations, employee motivation, interpersonal relations, and general leadership concepts. Students must take a minimum of six credits in upper-division management courses.

AVIATION

Courses	Semester Hours
Introduction to aviation or private pilot course	3
Aviation legislation	3
Aviation safety	3
Aviation electives	6
Total credits	15

This core area provides an overview of aviation, covering flight problems, aircraft systems, the legal environment, and safety. At least six of the 15 credits must be taken in upper-division aviation courses.

CONCLUSION

The airway science curriculum is designed as a baccalaureate program. The FAA does not recognize an associate degree conferred by a community college. However, the FAA encourages community colleges to enter into agreements with four-year colleges to facilitate student transfers with a minimal loss of credits.

The FAA does not guarantee employment to any graduate of an airway science program. But it follows a policy to hire 500 graduates—and not exclusively for air traffic control positions—each year. The curriculum does not teach students to be controllers. It will produce more productive employees in aviation. At the same time, persons who have been successful in the airway science programs are excellent controller candidates.

Appendix II lists the institutions offering the airway science curriculum.

No matter their origin or experience candidates learn how to become controllers at the FAA Academy. Their next step is the "facility of first assignment." That is the operating location where a new graduate of the FAA Academy is sent upon graduation. There, they embark upon the training and job experience needed to become full-performance level controllers. The next chapter discusses the developmental training phases.

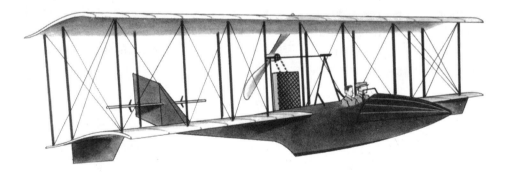

Benoist Flying Boat, 1914. World's first airline to carry passengers in an airplane, St. Petersburg-Tampa Airboat Line. Benoist Aircraft Co.

CHAPTER SIX

TRAINING AT EN ROUTE AND TERMINAL FACILITIES

INTO ACTION IN THE REAL WORLD

Fokker D.VII F, April 1918. Germany's best fighter of WW I enters service; maneuverable at high altitude and slow speeds. Fokker Flugzeuge-Werke.

Air traffic control work is far from ordinary. The job is full of satisfaction. There are also terrifying moments, some boredom and occasional frustrations, highs, lows, laughs, and even pain. Controllers work around the clock, all days of the week. They work hardest when it rains and snows. Often, the only time controllers are noticed is when something goes wrong.

Nonetheless, the job has it own special moments. You could be in the tower on a clear day when out of the south comes a stratus cloud layer. Here is a low-altitude cloud very much like fog that literally unrolls, like a spectacular carpet, across the sky. Or you could see a fluffy little cumulus cloud, caught stationary in a natural vise. You watch it bump and bubble until it stretches thousands of feet straight up—a newborn thunderstorm. You will surely see sunsets and sunrises. You may even develop a fondness for the sight of a 747 in a banking turn, framed against the skyline of Manhattan, Chicago, or Los Angeles, just as the sun sinks below the horizon on a clear evening.

Controllers almost always derive a certain aesthetic pleasure from directing a sequence of evenly spaced aircraft toward the runway. They find satisfaction in working a particularly hectic night, even though they can't fall asleep later because the adrenaline is still flowing. They take pride in the fact they have been equal to the task. They have brought order to chaos; they have guided all of their aircraft down safely without any delays.

You do not have to be a genius to be a good controller. You do not have to be college-educated, but a degree helps if you choose to advance to management ranks. But to be a successful controller you do have to possess a solid intellect, an intuitive feel for things, and an awareness of the three-dimensional world around you.

Controllers must have the right aptitude and the right attitude. If they do not have a certain type of character, personality, and skill level, they will not enjoy doing the job, they will not perform very well, and they will not last long.

EN ROUTE FACILITY TRAINING

Controllers, their equipment, and the types of air traffic users they service. (FAA)

The controllers who graduate from the FAA Academy's stressful training environment have demonstrated that they perform well under pressure. Trainees chosen for an en route facility upon graduation can then progress through every phase of the training program. Eventually they will gain the top full-performance level (FPL) grade of GS-14 at that same facility. Terminal controllers, on the other hand, usually are assigned first to less-active facilities. As they gain experience they transfer once or twice before they reach GS-14. Some controllers, however, elect to stay at less-active facilities throughout their careers.

ASSISTANT CONTROLLER TRAINING

En route facility training consists of up to eight weeks of classroom work and ends with a pass/fail evaluation. Instruction covers these six areas of study:

1) **Learning the Center Area.** Trainees label navigational aids and intersections, depict airways and jet routes, depict and identify sector boundaries and restricted and prohibited areas, and identify adjacent center sectors for the entire center area.

2) **Learning an Area of Specialization.** Trainees receive charts for their respective areas of specialization. They perform the same tasks mentioned in Study Area 1 above, but they also must learn to indicate the mileage between the critical points (such as navigational aids) and depict and label the following: intersections;

restricted and prohibited areas; warning areas; other special-use airspace; approach control airspace; visual flight rule (VFR) towers; and locations of flight service stations and control zones.

3) **Computing Fix Postings.** Trainees learn how to pass flight data or how to compute "fix postings." Fix postings is a phrase unique to centers. Each position in a center has an associated area in which to stack flight progress strips (pieces of paper on which clearance information is written). It is called a "strip bay." Center controllers keep track of a multiple number of fixes in their airspace using strip bays. They assume an aircraft will pass two of these fixes while in the sector, they estimate times for each aircraft to reach each fix, and then move the strip as the aircraft progresses along its flight.

4) **Operating the Telephone Switching System.**

5) **Training on the Flight Data Position (Nonautomated and Automated).** The latter encompasses simple instruction on how to use the computer keyboard

At the Baltimore-Washington terminal radar control center, air traffic assistants John Terenyi and Patti Exum arrange flight progress strips at the Arrival Data position. (FAA photo by Lance Strozier)

and display. Once trainees are familiar with their computer and the map of the area they are responsible for, the coursework is not particularly exotic.

6) **Taking the Pass/Fail Exam.** If trainees fail to pass the test, an additional eight hours of training is given and the test is given again. If trainees fail the second time, they are removed from the program, or moved to a less-active facility. The decision is based on the facility management's evaluation of a trainee's potential.

Navy-Curtiss NC-4, 1919. First aerial transatlantic crossing, May 8-13 from Rockaway, NY, to Lisbon, Portugal. Curtiss Aeroplane and Motor Co.

ASSISTANT CONTROLLER POSITION
QUALIFICATION OF CERTIFICATION

Developmental controllers are given 80 hours of on-the-job training to qualify in the flight data duties of their respective areas of specialization. First-level supervisors are responsible for certifying trainees on the position.

PRELIMINARY RADAR-ASSOCIATED/NONRADAR
CONTROL TRAINING AND ASSISTANT CONTROLLER TRAINING

Classroom instruction prepares developmental controllers for the associate radar controller position. It requires background knowledge of special military operations, letters of agreement (between facilities), phraseology, strip making, and charts. Trainees depict specialized terms and activities on the chart. These include standard instrument departures (SIDs) from the terminal and standard terminal arrivals (STARs), and label minimum en route altitudes (MEAs), minimum reception altitudes (MRAs), minimum obstruction clearance altitudes (MOCAs), and minimum crossing altitudes (MCAs). In addition, trainees depict the approach procedures for every airport in the area and must work through some simulated, nonradar problems.

RADAR-ASSOCIATED/NONRADAR
CONTROLLER TRAINING

Developmental controllers receive simulated control problems and classroom training. Instruction is flexible and depends upon the nonradar control requirements of the person's area of specialization. If at least one sector requires extensive use of nonradar techniques, then the training involves 56 hours of classroom instruction and adequate laboratory time. The object is to administer 15 familiarization problems and 17 nonradar control problems per sector. The radar training consists of 56 hours of classroom instruction and adequate time in a dynamic simulator (DYSIM)—a simulator with moving parts—to administer 15 familiarization problems and 16 control problems.

There are several alternatives in this phase. One reduces nonradar time and adds more radar instruction. Another eliminates the nonradar problems altogether, and includes as many as 30 radar problems (each taking 60 minutes to complete), designed along six increasing levels of complexity. Pass/fail evaluations are given at each level.

On-the-job training at the Houston Flight Service Station. Diane Weidmeier administers a problem to Gary Rizer under the eyes of Hollis Fowler, a certified instructor. (FAA)

INITIAL RADAR-ASSOCIATED/NONRADAR
CONTROL POSITION QUALIFICATION AND CERTIFICATION

At a busy terminal radar position, a controller watches a screen display whose brightness has been enhanced for clarity. (Unisys)

In the handoff position individuals receive as many as 180 hours of on-the-job training per operating position. The goal is to be certified on two positions of operation in preparation for the next phase.

EN ROUTE BASIC RADAR TRAINING

Developmental controllers are expected to gain certification on all remaining radar associate positions. The prerequisite for phase ten training is certification on two manual positions. (A manual position is one that does not involve working airplanes on radar.) This instruction prepares individuals for extensive radar training. It is presently taught at the FAA Academy, but plans are underway to increase the radar simulation capability at large facilities so that more of the training can be done there.

RADAR CONTROLLER TRAINING

This phase is administered in two parts. Depending upon the number of sectors in a person's area of specialization, it requires different levels of classroom and lab instruction and problem solving.

INITIAL RADAR CONTROL QUALIFICATION AND CERTIFICATION

During this phase, trainees are certified on two radar positions. This instruction involves as many as 180 hours of on-the-job training per position, and must be completed within 18 weeks.

FINAL RADAR CONTROL QUALIFICATION AND CERTIFICATION

This phase completes on-the-job instruction of all the required radar positions in the individual's area of specialization.

The training program offers controllers more than training time. As developmental controllers earn more certifications, they inevitably acquire more experience by working independently. Controllers who gain FPL status in three to four years have done well in all areas.

TERMINAL FACILITY TRAINING

Now we cover the training done by developmental controllers who have been assigned to terminal facilities. The terminal training program prepares trainees for positions in the tower cab and the radar room, which are unique to terminal facilities. Instruction is divided into three sections. The first two sections in each phase involve classroom work and deal with the basic knowledge of the position and facility procedures. The third section provides on-the-job training for position qualification.

One problem of terminal training is that facilities vary greatly in size. Consequently, the numbers of support staff are often limited and so are trainers. Some smaller facilities do not have any dedicated training staff. Terminal Area Training facilities are often established to help these smaller facilities develop necessary training plans and procedures. Often the classroom work for two or more positions (for example, flight data and clearance delivery; or ground control and local control) is conducted simultaneously.

FLIGHT DATA TRAINING

Section one takes the individual through the following subjects: tower operating positions and equipment; the airways and route structure; location identifiers (three-character alpha-numeric codes identifying airports, such as MIA for Miami International); tower logs and statistical records; using flight progress strips; receiving and relaying weather information; emergency procedures; operating the automatic terminal information service (ATIS); and operating the automated flight data equipment.

Section two reviews local procedures and operations. And section three, which takes 80 hours, provides on-the-job training.

CLEARANCE DELIVERY

Section one examines the elements of an IFR clearance and other areas such as phraseology, transponder codes, gate hold procedures, and the use of abbreviated clearances. Section two applies these principles to local conditions. Section three, 70 hours in length, provides on-the-job experience.

On-the-job training in the control tower at Washington Dulles International Airport. James Stephenson (foreground), is the area supervisor placing a flight progress strip in the bay for runway 1R. Developmental controller Andy Papageorge is behind Stephenson. On the right is David Arnold, who is training Papageorge on ground control. (FAA)

GROUND CONTROL

Section one requires that students identify aircraft and aircraft categories, draw the airport and identify the movement areas where aircraft can operate, and develop an understanding of console equipment and emergency procedures.

In section two, individuals apply these principles to their specific airport. This is followed by 150 hours of on-the-job training per position. (Note: some facilities operate two ground control positions during busy periods.)

LOCAL CONTROL/CAB COORDINATOR

Trainees must know the local terminal area and be familiar with the various letters of agreement and facility directives that affect their respective positions. Training also covers airport lighting, separation minima, heavy jet and wake turbulence separations, and other control procedures. After the local application is taught in section two, individuals receive 180 hours of on-the-job training before earning certification.

NONRADAR SEPARATION

Chances are that the last time controllers will use nonradar terminal procedures to any degree will be at the Academy. But this phase provides instruction that would be necessary should a controller ever be assigned to one of the few nonradar facilities still in existence.

RADAR

Radar simulation training for most terminal controllers will be conducted at the Academy. Few terminal facilities have simulation capabilities.

Section two of the radar phase is taught at the facility on real equipment. It includes classroom training on the following subjects: labeling the radar map with minimum vectoring altitudes; significant terrain and obstructions; radio frequencies used for radar positions; and other items determined by the facility.

Developmental controllers will also learn about their equipment. They will learn how to align the radar scope, use the computer, and use the radios and telephones. The on-the-job training portion includes instruction and practice on the first radar position and on each additional position. A facility can have anywhere from two to five radar positions working on a particular airport.

Since facilities vary widely, controllers who transfer to other facilities must first complete the new facility's training program before they attain the FPL status at their location. Terminal controllers usually start at lower activity locations and consequently reach FPL status much quicker than their en route facility counterparts. However, it might take five or six years and require two or three moves before a terminal controller reaches GS-14.

Individuals receive a pass/fail evaluation at the end of each phase. Those who fail to certify on the positions will be removed from the facility. That might mean dismissal or transfer to another facility. This is a local management decision.

As the standing controller converses over the radio with an aircraft off to the right, another seated controller is busy with the aircraft taxiing in front of the control tower. (FAA)

LEARNING FROM EXPERIENCE

Controllers work in a dynamic environment. New and untested situations develop constantly, and controllers have to draw upon the skills they have developed and adapt them to the scenario at hand. Sometimes it works well, sometimes not—but they learn. The process is called seasoning. Young controllers often can get by on reflexes; older controllers use experience. Seasoned controllers usually have a plan "B," for use when things begin to go wrong. They know the strengths and weaknesses of the controllers around them. (One I knew, for instance, always started humming when he was in trouble.) The experienced controller knows when to call for help. The experienced supervisor knows how to tell when a controller needs help.

To be good at what they do, controllers have to know the system. They have to talk to pilots, ride in the cockpit, and see what is happening on the other end of the radio. They have to go to other facilities and learn about their unique concerns and problems. They have to read trade publications and go to aviation seminars to anticipate changes in the industry. Controllers cannot just sit at their scopes for a few hours each day, go home, and think they are doing the job to the fullest extent of their capabilities.

PART II

DOING THE JOB

CHAPTER SEVEN

TRANSCONTINENTAL FLIGHT

THE PRESSURES OF THE JOB

It has always been difficult to describe the controller's job. The system of air traffic control is complex and riddled with acronyms and jargon. Controllers and pilots talk in a code all their own. These professionals often do not use complete sentences or elaborate on their subjects. They usually do not need to. Everyone in the system is expected to speak the same language.

To understand fully how controllers work within the system, you almost need to be there. Pressures of the moment cannot be captured entirely by tape recordings. It is impossible to hear what controllers think, or to see the options they evaluate and discard to resolve developing situations. They may be coordinating operations with their supervisors while still listening to the pilots on the radio and updating information on flight progress strips. With experience, controllers become sensitive to inconsistencies in an otherwise smooth and predictable system. They must translate what pilots say incorrectly into the proper terminology so that communication is clear. When something doesn't sound quite right, controllers can replay the conversation to identify the problem.

One thing to remember is that controllers do not work alone. If situations deteriorate rapidly, controllers at adjacent stations will clear the way and assist with the tight spots.

Most controllers like to be busy. Most controllers believe that they are the best. Some are more conservative than others. Some have greater capabilities than others. But to be there in the first place, they have to have confidence in their own ability. They know they can handle anything the system can throw at them—and they prove it every working day.

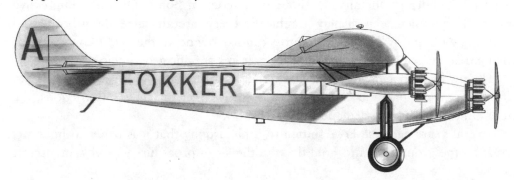

Fokker F. VIIa-3m, 1925. Trimotor transport, the first civil transport to be employed by many early airlines. Sturdy and reliable. Fokker A.G. and Fokker (USA).

BACKSEAT RIDE

On the following pages, we will highlight a simulated flight from Los Angeles to New York's Kennedy Airport. The old saying in aviation, "not for navigational purposes" (which roughly translated means that the accuracy of the document you are reviewing should be used only for illustration) applies to this narration. It is a simplified illustration that is intended to help develop your appreciation for the ATC system. Before we begin, let's look at a part of the system that is essential to our flight.

THE TRAFFIC FLOW MANAGEMENT UNIT

This relatively little-known facility used to be called "Flow Control" or "CF Squared," for Central Flow Control Facility. It is located in Washington, D.C., and oversees the smooth and efficient flow of aircraft in the ATC system. Facility computers, using information from proposed flight plans, as well as the flight plans in the system for aircraft actually in the air, generate the number of aircraft flying into a particular airport for any one hour or a series of hours. One very impressive piece of equipment can display graphically every aircraft currently airborne and working with an FAA center. Operators can narrow down the field to only aircraft flying to a particular airport, or only aircraft in a specific geographic area.

The traffic management unit ensures that an airport does not get overwhelmed. If an airport's capacity is reduced because of weather or runway restrictions, the unit limits the airborne demand for that airport.

Several years ago, the FAA shifted to a philosophy that it is better to hold aircraft on the ground than to hold them in the air (a procedure whereby an aircraft

FAA traffic management officers working in the Central Flow Control Facility, surrounded by communications equipment, computer terminals, and display equipment. (FAA)

is kept at either a specified point on the ground or in a particular chunk of airspace until further clearance is given). It is more economical for the airlines to remain on the ground because fuel is saved and airborne congestion is reduced. The problem with holding is that the airlines schedule flights tightly. Any excessive delays tend to reverberate through the system because the plane is not where it is needed when it is scheduled to be.

Consequently, the traffic flow managers at this facility must balance demands delicately to ensure that the airborne system does not get overloaded. Likewise, they must ensure that when there is a landing slot, an airplane will be on station to use it.

Every weekday at 8:00 a.m, senior air traffic management personnel in the FAA's Traffic Management Unit (TMU) are briefed on how well the system operated on the previous day. They are alerted to what can be expected for the rest of the day. On one particularly bad day, for example, the system recorded 2,864 delays. A delay is logged when an aircraft is detained 15 or more minutes. This figure was out of 104,782 operations logged by the centers and 48,112 operations at the selected busiest airports on that same day.

Weather was the problem that day—rain and fog. In fact, landing minimums at several airports forced aircraft to wait or to go to other airports. One center had trouble with two of its radar systems, but managed to handle the traffic using backup systems.

Flow control specialist Jim Bellamy receives detailed information on traffic flow in one of the en route centers. The jet stream over the northwestern USA is blowing at 90 knots at 39,000 feet. The stream diminishes to 70 knots over Minnesota. (FAA)

The average number of daily delays nowadays approaches 1,000. Weather is the primary cause for about 60 percent of them. Other causes include FAA equipment problems (about 3 percent), the volume of traffic at the airport (around 25-30 percent), closed runways (about 5 percent), and excessive traffic volume in the centers (about 6 percent).

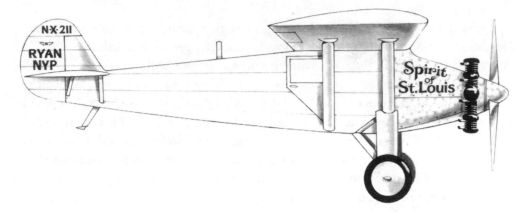

Ryan NYP "Spirit of St. Louis," 1927. Charles A. Lindbergh made first solo nonstop transatlantic crossing, May 20-21, New York to Paris. Ryan Aircraft Co.

THE FLIGHT CONDITIONS

On the day of our simulated flight, the weather at Kennedy International Airport (JFK) in New York is forecast to be rain and fog from about 4:00 p.m. to midnight, local time. Those times need to be translated into Universal Coordinated Time (UTC was formerly called Greenwich Mean Time). The air traffic control system worldwide uses UTC for operations. UTC is simple to use as an international measure. It is based on the Greenwich Meridian, zero degrees longitude, and not on variable time zones or such variables as daylight saving time.

UTC time is plus five hours Eastern Standard Time. When the local time in New York City is 1:00 p.m., it is 1800 hours, UTC. (On the 24-hour clock system, 6:00 p.m. is expressed as 1800 hours.) Thus the weather problem will settle in at JFK between 2100 hours and 0500 hours, UTC.

The normal capacity for visual approaches into JFK is 50 aircraft per hour. Pilots use visual approaches in good, visual flight rule (VFR) weather, when they can see the aircraft around them and provide their own separation. When the weather makes it difficult to see with the naked eye, controllers apply standard separations, which use up much more airspace.

With the weather as forecast, Kennedy Airport's capacity narrows to 30 aircraft per hour. This is not necessarily a problem except from 8:00 p.m. to 11:00 p.m. local time (0100 to 0400 UTC). That is a time when the hourly demand for Kennedy is 55 flights. This means that 25 aircraft will not have access during the first hour alone. The congestion is compounded during the second, third, and forth hours. Fortunately, Kennedy's traffic drops off sharply after that time, so the system can catch up.

With this in mind, the Traffic Management Unit decides to institute a flow-control program for Kennedy. It tells ATC facilities across the country to hold aircraft bound for Kennedy on the ground until a specific release time. Given the possibility of changes in the weather, the unit decides to keep a little pressure on the system. It allows for a rate of 35 aircraft per hour to ensure that any potential capacity is fully exploited.

Cockpit of the Gulfstream IV executive jet aircraft. Called the "glass cockpit," because essential information is displayed on electronic display screens, not by mechanical instruments. Gulfstream IV is flown by a crew of two, and can carry up to 19 passengers, depending on how its interior is fitted out. It cruises at Mach 0.8. (Gulfstream Aerospace)

FILING THE FLIGHT PLAN

Our aircraft is a Gulfstream G-IV executive jet transport owned by a private company. Its radio call sign is N1234. Its pilot files his flight plan over the phone with the FAA flight service station (FSS) and gets his weather briefing from the specialist on duty. The pilot tells the FSS specialist that he is planning to fly nonstop from Los Angeles International Airport to John F. Kennedy International Airport. He plans on departing at about 8:00 a.m. local time in Los Angeles and arriving five hours and 45 minutes later. (That translates to departing at 1600 hours UTC and arriving in New York at 2145 hours UTC. The specialist advises the pilot that the weather forecast for the time of his arrival at JFK is for rain and fog with reduced visibility, but adds that he can expect a smooth ride en route.

The specialist also gives the pilot the preferred instrument flight rules (IFR) routing to New York. It reads like this: J146, DVC, J197 GLD, J146 SBN, J554 JH2, J70 AVP, LENDY STAR to Kennedy.

Translated: after departure from Los Angeles International (LAX), the flight route begins with the aircraft flying on Jet Route 146. Jet routes serve aircraft operations from an altitude of 18,000 feet (flight level 180) to flight level 450. Then the flight passes over Dove Creek, Colorado, VOR. A VOR (for VHF Omnidirection Range) provides the primary en route navigational aid or guidance instructions to aircraft. Next, the aircraft flies along jet route number 197 to the

VOR at Goodland, Kansas (GLD). There it picks up jet route number 146 again to South Bend, Indiana (SBN), and thence along jet route 554 to the VOR at Johnstown, Pennsylvania (JST); then jet route 70 (J70) to the VOR at Wilkes-Barre, Pennsylvania (AVP). LENDY STAR means the Standard Terminal Arrival Routing (STAR) for landing at JFK. It provides the transition for the flight from the en route environment into the terminal area according to standard procedures.

The cross-country route for N1234 flies along the high-altitude jet airways, Los Angeles to New York.

Airways are routes through the sky. They are divided into two categories. One is measured from ground level to, but not including, 18,000 feet. Those routes are identified with a "V" followed by a number (for example, V124). The other category of airways is measured at 18,000 feet and higher, where altitudes are referred to as flight levels; that is, levels of constant atmospheric pressure, related to a standard setting of 29.92 inches of mercury. Flight levels are represented by three digits, representing hundreds of feet; for example, flight level 200 represents 20,000 feet at an altimeter setting of 29.92. Routes in this structure are called jet or "J" routes. Navigational aids used to designate jet airways are located much farther apart. That is because aircraft that use them fly much higher and their onboard instruments can detect the nav aids at greater distances.

Operations and planning specialists and meteorologists discuss weather conditions at several key airports. The ceiling at Boston is 3,000 feet; at JFK, it is 4,000 feet, expected to drop to 3,000 over the next few hours. (FAA)

GETTING CLEARANCE

Once our pilot files his flight plan for N1234, the FSS specialist wishes him a good flight and then transmits the information to the Los Angeles Center. About 30 minutes before the Gulfstream G-IV's proposed departure, the Los Angeles Center computer transmits a flight clearance and any other control instructions to the Los Angeles Tower for our aircraft, call sign N1234.

A note on radio call signs for aircraft. The radio call sign corresponds with the aircraft registration number, called "tail number" in aviation slang. Tail numbers of U.S. registered aircraft begin with the letter N. The N is followed by numerals and possibly other letters. Examples seen at Dulles Airport recently include N1IAM, N400GN, and N522CF.

In Los Angeles Tower, the flight data person places the clearance information, which is presented on a long, narrow piece of heavy paper called a flight progress strip, at the appropriate control position. In this case, it is the clearance delivery position. This controller reads the en route clearance to the pilot and makes sure that the pilot reads back the clearance correctly. In this instance, the controller has the added chore of informing the pilot that his departure will be delayed 30 minutes because of the weather at Kennedy. The delay, of course, reflects the program implemented by the Traffic Flow Management Unit in Washington.

The pilot hears this over his radio, the clearance delivery controller speaking:

N1234 is cleared to Kennedy Airport as filed; maintain flight level 180, FLIPR3 departure, squawk code 2145.

Translation: N1234 is cleared to Kennedy via the route he filed, which was not changed by the Center. Flight level 180 is his initial altitude. He will be given a higher altitude when he talks to the Center. Controllers are required to give a clearance to the requested altitude, or to advise the pilot when he might expect a higher altitude. The FLIPR3 departure is a standard instrument departure (SID) from Los Angeles. A SID is the departure counterpart of the STAR. The Standard Instrument Departure provides the transition from the terminal to the en route environment. The squawk code 2145 is a code which the pilot sets on the transponder in his aircraft. When the Air Traffic Control Radar Beacon System (ATCRBS) interrogates the aircraft transponder, the transponder broadcasts 2145. That identifies the aircraft to ATC computers across the country.

At precisely 8:45 a.m. local time (1645 hours UTC) the clearance delivery controller contacts N1234 and tells the pilot to start his engines and to call ground control when he is ready to taxi.

Los Angeles Airport is really two airports disguised as one. Two sets of parallel runways (runways 25 left and right and runways 24 left and right) are located on either side of the airport's terminal buildings and operate almost independently.

Runways are identified by their magnetic heading (their direction in relation to magnetic north), with the last digit omitted. So the magnetic heading of runway 25L might be 252 degrees. The other end of the runway would then be a heading of 072 degrees magnetic or runway 7 Right.

The active runway is the one aircraft are using for landing and departure. Generally, aircraft land into the wind. However, if the wind speed is less than five knots, aircraft can use a "calm wind runway." In heavily populated areas, noise reduction programs can also influence the selection of an airport's active runway. Flights out of Los Angeles usually depart to the southwest, because of prevailing winds. Aircraft fly over the ocean until they gain altitude and turn eastbound.

TAKING OFF

N1234 calls Los Angeles ground control on his radio to ask for taxi instructions. The ground controller separates aircraft on the ground, provides a smooth flow to the runway, and gets arrival aircraft to the ramp as quickly as possible. He also communicates with airport vehicles that frequently cross runways and proceed along taxiways.

When this photo was taken in 1970, runway 24L was in use, and 24R and the taxiways were under construction. View is from east of the airport looking toward the Pacific Ocean in distance. Airport terminal buildings are on the left. One jet is taking off from runway 24L, another is taxiing into position for takeoff, and a third approaches along the taxiway from the terminal area. (Los Angeles Department of Airports)

On occasion, when an arriving aircraft does not have a scheduled arrival gate, the ground controller takes the aircraft to a part of the airport where it can wait for room on the ramp, which is an area that can be used for parking aircraft as well as loading and unloading passengers. This task can severely complicate a ground controller's day. In the past, controllers have shut off approaches to airports because they have run out of possible surfaces on which to park the craft.

N1234 calls ground control and advises that he has information "Yankee," and that he is ready to taxi. By saying he has information Yankee, the pilot is using the code that says he has listened to the current automated terminal information service (ATIS) broadcast.

ATIS is a recording of pertinent information about operations at Los Angeles International. It is broadcast continuously over an assigned radio frequency, 133.8 MHz. Information includes the active runway, wind direction and speed, ceiling and visibility, and altimeter setting. It also includes the departure controller's radio frequency. At Los Angeles International, a separate ATIS broadcast is also made available for inbound aircraft.

The ground controller then gives N1234 instructions to maneuver on specific taxiways to reach the end of the runway. As the pilot leaves the ramp, he is told to

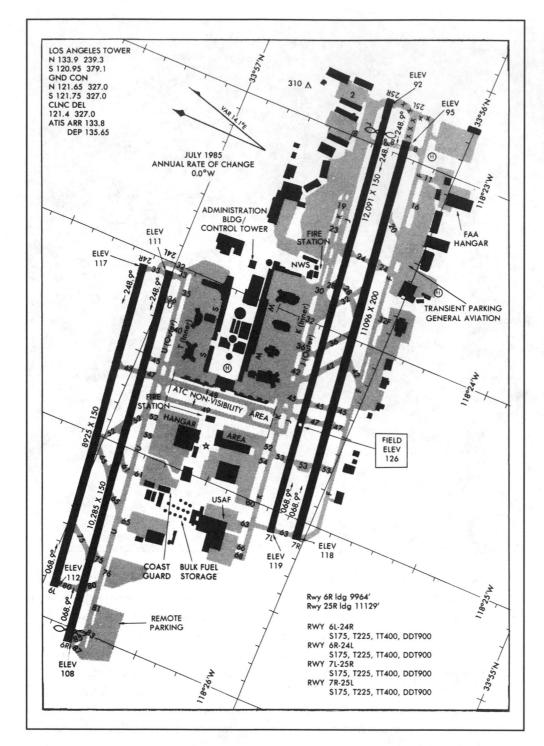

LOS ANGELES TOWER
N 133.9 239.3
S 120.95 379.1
GND CON
N 121.65 327.0
S 121.75 327.0
CLNC DEL
121.4 327.0
ATIS ARR 133.8
     DEP 135.65

JULY 1985
ANNUAL RATE OF CHANGE
0.0°W

VAR 14.1°E

310 ∧

ELEV
92

ELEV
95

ADMINISTRATION
BLDG/
CONTROL TOWER

FIRE
STATION

NWS

ELEV
111

ELEV
117

FAA
HANGAR

TRANSIENT PARKING
GENERAL AVIATION

ATC NON-VISIBILITY AREA

FIRE
STATION

HANGAR
AREA

FIELD
ELEV
126

USAF

COAST
GUARD

BULK FUEL
STORAGE

REMOTE
PARKING

ELEV
112

ELEV
119

ELEV
118

ELEV
108

Rwy 6R ldg 9964'
Rwy 25R ldg 11129'

RWY 6L-24R
    S175, T225, TT400, DDT900
RWY 6R-24L
    S175, T225, TT400, DDT900
RWY 7L-25R
    S175, T225, TT400, DDT900
RWY 7R-25L
    S175, T225, TT400, DDT900

Two sets of parallel runways are apparent on this diagram of present-day Los Angeles International Airport. Terminal area is in the center; runways 24L and 24R are above; and runways 25L and 25R are below. (Instrument Approach Procedures)

give way to a United Airlines DC-10 and follow it to the runway. As N1234 gets a little closer to the runway, the sequence is changed again. The pilot is told to wait for and follow an American Airlines 747.

Changes in sequencing are usually made on the basis of a first come, first served policy or to ensure a particular airborne separation by spreading out aircraft departure paths. Controllers do not favor certain aircraft over others.

Clearance to the runway is not a clearance to enter onto the runway. The N1234 Gulfstream pilot is told to hold short of the runway and to contact the tower on the radio frequency of 119.1 MHz. The local controller, standing next to

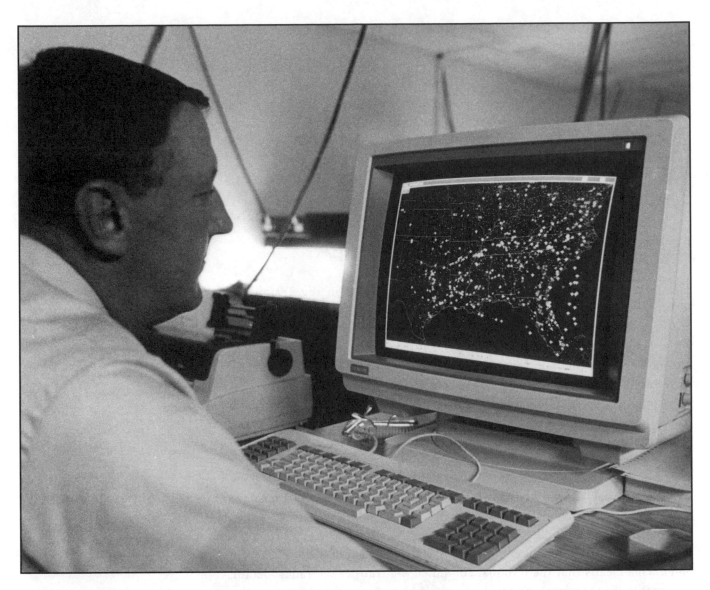

At the traffic management unit (formerly Central Flow Control Facility) in Washington, a special aircraft situation display screen enables traffic control specialists to predict airspace congestion. The system scans all flight plans in air traffic control computers nationwide, plots proposed routes, and issues an alert when the projected flight paths will result in sector saturation. Seeing this, flow controllers can reroute or slow down aircraft to prevent overload. (FAA)

the ground controller in the Los Angeles Tower, receives the flight progress strip in the sequence that the airplane is in the lineup for the departure runway. N1234 is number four in line for takeoff. Ahead of him are the American, the United, and America West airliners. America West is first for takeoff, followed by United, American, and our G-IV business jet.

The controller clears America West for takeoff, and it begins its takeoff roll after the pilot advances power and releases the brakes. The United pilot is told to taxi into position and hold. As America West passes his taxiway, the pilot of an arriving aircraft is instructed to taxi across the departure runway and to contact ground control. The second departure aircraft cannot begin to roll until the first is beyond the far end of the runway or has turned away from the runway. Once that happens, United is cleared for takeoff and it rolls. American then moves into position, another arrival crosses the runway, United turns away, and American starts its takeoff roll. N1234 now moves into position on the runway, ready for takeoff.

When things are going well, a controller's work takes on an almost musical rhythm that actually helps to drive the operation. A discordant note signals that something might be wrong and needs closer attention.

N1234 cleared for takeoff Runway 25 Left, the controller radios.

N1234's pilot acknowledges the instruction over the radio. He releases his brakes and starts his takeoff roll. Controllers do not like pilots to linger on the runway at a busy airport, whether at Los Angeles, O'Hare, or Atlanta. Others are waiting to cross the runway, or to move into position for takeoff.

N1234 contact departure control, good day.

The flight is on its way.

LEAVING THE AIRPORT FACILITY AREA

The Los Angeles departure controller actually works in the Terminal Radar Approach Control (TRACON) facility, which is located on the edge of the airport property. Usually, the controller identifies the aircraft when he sees a radar target within a mile of the end of the runway. This is the most common method of identification. The departure controller informs N1234 that TRACON has radar contact with him. This relieves the pilot of the requirement to report his position over certain compulsory points en route, because the TRACON controller sees him at a known position on his radar scope. The aircraft will remain in radar contact with the air traffic control system during the flight, and will be passed from controller to controller along the way.

The Los Angeles departure controller will handle N1234 for only a short time. The aircraft has acquired a data block, which includes its call sign, its altitude (automatically received from the aircraft's transponder), and its ground speed, which is determined by the air traffic computer. When the aircraft reaches a certain point in space, the terminal computer will initiate a "handoff" to the center computer. This means that the terminal computer will transfer the radar identification information to the center computer.

When the handoff occurs, the data block for the target will appear on the center controller's scope. That controller acknowledges the handoff, and the departure controller will instruct N1234's pilot to contact Los Angeles Center. If a problem arises, or if something unusual happens, controllers can use a direct telephone line between them to talk over the situation.

In the next two chapters, N1234's cross-country flight to New York will continue, guided by the en route ATC system and then the terminal controllers at the destination.

CHAPTER EIGHT

EN ROUTE PHASE CROSS-COUNTRY

LOS ANGELES CENTER—EN ROUTE CONTROL

Our Gulfstream IV business jet, radio call sign N1234, has taken off from Los Angeles International Airport. The tower handed off the flight to the departure controller. The departure controller established radar contact with N1234, and soon after handed control off to Los Angeles Center.

Los Angeles Center is typical of the 20 ARTCCs around the country. Let us look at its setup and then resume following N1234 on the flight.

Most of the centers look alike. One exception is in Houston where airport building requirements dictate a different architecture. Each has a large brick structure with a glass section, a big parking lot, and numerous antennae on and around the building. The glass section houses the administrative quarters where the facility manager and staff have their offices. The windowless building is where the operators work. These quarters include the controllers' operating positions as well as large equipment rooms. In the equipment rooms are the computers, switching equipment (to switch from one frequency to another), and miles of wires that keep the system going. Also in this area are training rooms, break rooms for relaxing, a cafeteria, and a small medical clinic.

The main operating room where the controllers perform their tasks is large, about as big as a football field. It houses two or three long rows of consoles and multiple radar scopes, radios, telephone lines, monitors, strip printers, and row upon row of strip bays for the thousands of flight progress strips passed through the center each day. The ceiling is 30 feet high. The lighting is subdued, though not as much as in a terminal radar room, and the noise level is kept to a kind of low rumble —never intrusive but always present.

Twenty centers control the airspace of the continental United States. Each center subdivides its geographic responsibility into five or six areas. Each area is further subdivided into 6 to 8 sectors. Every sector has a lateral, geographic dimension and a vertical dimension. In other words, one sector might extend from the ground to 17,000 feet; and the sector above it from flight level 180 to flight level 330; and another above that from flight level 350 to flight level 600. Few aircraft, except military aircraft and the Concorde, soar at flight level 600 and above. Centers assign one controller team to each sector.

Lockheed Vega I, 1927. It set new aerodynamic low-drag standards with cantilevered wing, stretched skin, monocoque fuselage. Lockheed Aircraft Co.

FEDERAL AVIATION AGENCY

AIR ROUTE TRAFFIC

CONTROL CENTER

Controllers sit along the rows of consoles watching and talking. Controllers talk on phones, they talk into microphones connected to their headsets, talk to the person next to them, talk to the person across the aisle, and talk to the supervisor. A few work with their headsets off and listen to the radio receiver over a speaker. Most sit hunched over their control positions with one hand on the microphone button and the other methodically working the computer keyboard.

A radar scope is located every 10 feet or so. The scope is the center of attention for the two (and sometimes three) persons on each controller team. One controller monitors the aircraft on the radar; the other coordinates and monitors the control frequency when workload permits.

Operations in a center might be likened to a state of organized chaos. Although the place may seem at first intimidating—even overwhelming—it is possible to master operations within the system. The system is organized and complex. However, once its parts are understood, its operations make sense. As with most complex endeavors, success comes one step at a time.

Buildings at Air Route Traffic Control Centers operated by the FAA look like these at the Washington Center, situated on the east edge of the city of Leesburg, Virginia. Administrative and support activities are in the windowed sections; the ARTCC operations are conducted in the windowless buildings. (FAA)

Inside an Air Route Traffic Control Center. Interior layouts of all the ARTCCs are similar to this one, the center at Fort Worth, Texas. (FAA photo by S. Michael McKean)

Down on the floor at an FAA Air Route Traffic Control Center. Controllers work at their consoles with supervisors standing behind. This photo of Fort Worth Center was taken by S. Michel McKean. (FAA)

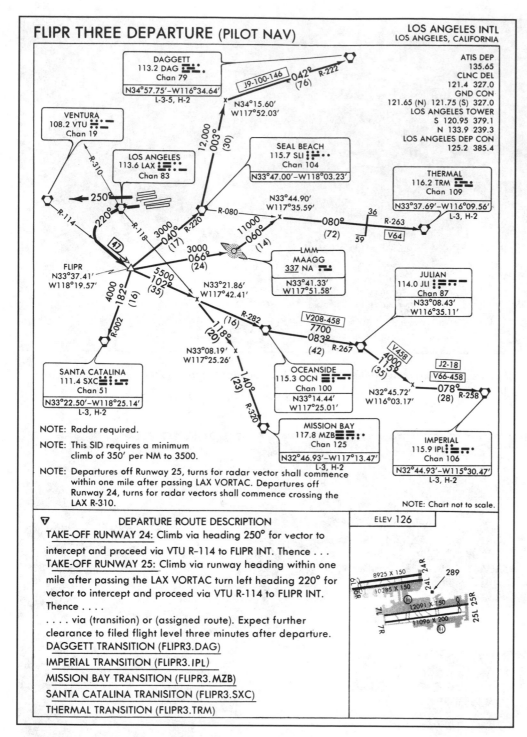

FLIPR THREE departure diagram is taken from the FAA's Standard Instrument Departure (SID) charts. N1234 takes off from Los Angeles International, climbing and heading over the ocean, then turns southeastward; he soon turns northeastward, then north, and ends up aligned properly on J146, the jet airway he is assigned.

The LEGEND describes the symbols that appear on the departure charts.

N1234 CONTINUES ITS FLIGHT

When we left N1234, the aircraft had just been handed off to Los Angeles Center. We will pick up its story from there. Using the chart on page 102, you can follow the route.

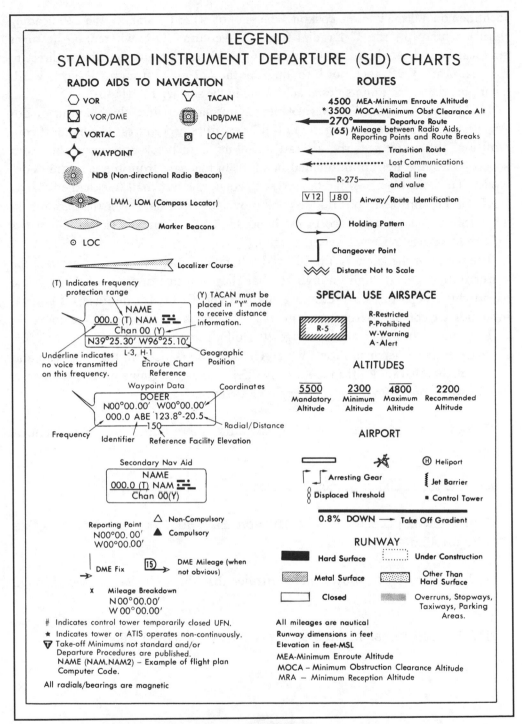

LEGEND
STANDARD INSTRUMENT DEPARTURE (SID) CHARTS

RADIO AIDS TO NAVIGATION

VOR

VOR/DME

VORTAC

WAYPOINT

TACAN

NDB/DME

LOC/DME

NDB (Non-directional Radio Beacon)

LMM, LOM (Compass Locator)

Marker Beacons

LOC

Localizer Course

(T) Indicates frequency protection range

NAME
000.0 (T) NAM
Chan 00 (Y)
N39°25.30' W96°25.10'

L-3, H-1

(Y) TACAN must be placed in "Y" mode to receive distance information.

Underline indicates no voice transmitted on this frequency.

Enroute Chart Reference

Geographic Position

Waypoint Data

Coordinates

DOEER
N00°00.00' W00°00.00'
000.0 ABE 123.8°-20.5
150

Frequency

Identifier

Reference Facility Elevation

Radial/Distance

Secondary Nav Aid

NAME
000.0 (T) NAM
Chan 00(Y)

Reporting Point
N00°00.00'
W00°00.00'

△ Non-Compulsory
▲ Compulsory

DME Fix

15 DME Mileage (when not obvious)

X Mileage Breakdown
N00°00.00'
W 00°00.00'

\# Indicates control tower temporarily closed UFN.
★ Indicates tower or ATIS operates non-continuously.
▽ Take-off Minimums not standard and/or Departure Procedures are published.
NAME (NAM.NAM2) – Example of flight plan Computer Code.

All radials/bearings are magnetic

ROUTES

4500 MEA-Minimum Enroute Altitude
* 3500 MOCA-Minimum Obst Clearance Alt
270° Departure Route
(65) Mileage between Radio Aids, Reporting Points and Route Breaks

Transition Route

Lost Communications

R-275 Radial line and value

V 12 J80 Airway/Route Identification

Holding Pattern

Changeover Point

Distance Not to Scale

SPECIAL USE AIRSPACE

R-5

R-Restricted
P-Prohibited
W-Warning
A-Alert

ALTITUDES

5500 Mandatory Altitude

2300 Minimum Altitude

4800 Maximum Altitude

2200 Recommended Altitude

AIRPORT

Arresting Gear

Displaced Threshold

H Heliport

Jet Barrier

■ Control Tower

0.8% DOWN Take Off Gradient

RUNWAY

Hard Surface

Metal Surface

Closed

Under Construction

Other Than Hard Surface

Overruns, Stopways, Taxiways, Parking Areas.

All mileages are nautical
Runway dimensions in feet
Elevation in feet-MSL
MEA-Minimum Enroute Altitude
MOCA – Minimum Obstruction Clearance Altitude
MRA – Minimum Reception Altitude

Douglas DST (DC-3), 1935. Most versatile airplane, it opened the era of economical mass travel by air. More than 1,000 are still flying and working. Douglas Aircraft Co.

The "FLIPR 3 departure" (a standard routing), instructed N1234's pilot to fly runway heading 250 (the direction in degrees in relation to north that an airplane is travelling). Then, within one minute after passing the Los Angeles VOR (VHF omnidirectional range), the aircraft is to turn left to a heading of 200 degrees. The 200-degree heading separates N1234 from the aircraft taking off from runway 24 and flying the 250 heading.

The pilot flies his aircraft over a series of navigational aids in the Los Angeles area called VORs. Each VOR has a name, and each one radiates signals through a 360-degree circle. Each radial is a certain number of degrees from north, and can be identified on a display in the cockpit. The pilot of N1234 maintains the 220 heading until he intercepts the 114 radial from the Ventura VOR, whereupon he turns southeastbound. At the Santa Catalina VOR, the aircraft turns northeast direct to the Seal Beach VOR, then north to intercept the 222 radial from the Daggett VOR. That puts the aircraft on its designated route in the sky, Jet 146 (J146).

N1234 is now flying just west of the California shoreline, climbing out of Los Angeles Airport and executing the FLIPR3 departure procedures. The handoff controller at the center sees the aircraft's blinking data block appear on the radar scope. That indicates an automated handoff, in this case from the departure controller. The controller uses his fingertips to rotate the trackball (nicknamed "slewball") on his console to position a small movable dot of light over the data block. That tells his computer to accept the handoff. A few seconds later, N1234 checks in with Los Angeles Center over the radio.

The name of the game is altitude and separation. Aircraft climb away over the water until they are high enough so that they will not disturb local residents. Meanwhile, departures are crossing the inbound flightpath because, of course, inbounds are coming in from the same places to which the outbounds are going.

The center controller acknowledges the pilot's initial call, but lets him fly the standard FLIPR3 departure for a while. He is still working with the American and United flights that took off in front of N1234, and eight or nine other airplanes as well. Instructions from the controller flow rapidly:

United, turn left heading 040; expedite your climb out of ten thousand.

American, proceed direct Seal Beach.

Continental, proceed direct Mission Bay, and contact Los Angeles Center on 118.45.

N1234's data block shows the controller that the G-IV has passed through 5,000 feet and is climbing.

N1234, Los Angeles, turn left, proceed direct Seal Beach.

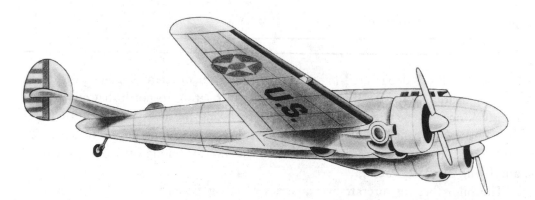

Lockheed XC-35, 1937. First successful pressurized flight deck and cabin, making high-altitude flight practical. Lockheed Aircraft Co.

The aircraft must reach 6,000 feet or higher to be clear of the Los Angeles arrivals. The controller anticipates that N1234 will easily make that altitude, and turns it on course. The data block rolls through 6,000 feet, and the time comes to hand off the aircraft to the next sector in Los Angeles Center. The plane might be worked by three or four sector controllers within the same center as it crosses the country.

CONTROL SECTORS AND HANDING OFF

Sector dimensions differ. They are tailored to accommodate particular situations. Some, like this one, are relatively small because of the high concentration of aircraft to be worked. Some are narrow, working only inbound aircraft being directed into a sequence to land at a major airport. Some sectors are large because they deal mostly with aircraft at cruising altitude, usually requiring few control decisions. But each sector, whatever its dimensions, has an equivalent team of controllers.

N1234's data block flashes. That indicates the automated handoff is made.

N1234 contact Los Angeles on 120.05, the controller says.

The aircraft leaves 10,000 feet and levels off slightly. At 10,000 feet and below, airspeed is restricted to 250 knots; but as the aircraft leaves that altitude, the pilot lowers the airplane's nose somewhat to pick up cruising speed.

Los Angeles, N1234.

The pilot checks in with the next sector controller, still in Los Angeles Center. That controller responds.

N1234, this is Los Angeles Center, climb and maintain flight level 350.

Another aircraft approaches N1234 in the opposite direction, but one thousand feet below. Los Angeles center contacts the pilot of N1234 to let him know the two flights do not conflict.

N1234, traffic at 12 o'clock, 10 miles southwest bound, out of 11,000 descending.

As N1234 leaves 17,000 feet, still climbing, the pilot changes the setting on his altimeter dial to 29.92, the standard setting for high-altitude flight. The aircraft is shifted to a high-altitude sector in the Los Angeles Center. N1234 passes south of Edwards Air Force Base and is established on airway J146, northeastbound. Most aircraft are procedurally separated at this point. Climbing aircraft are assigned to one airway, and descending aircraft to another. As N1234 flies beyond Las Vegas, it is passed to the last sector in the Los Angeles Center. The airway over the high terrain of the Rockies has a minimum altitude of 19,000 feet. About 170 miles east of Las Vegas, N1234 is switched to Denver Center.

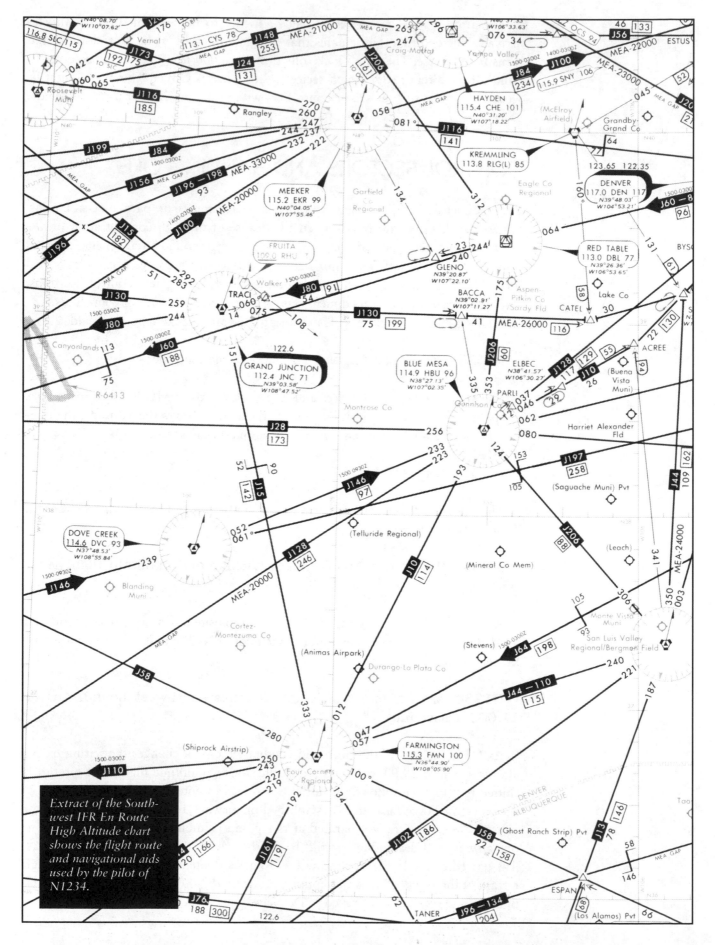

Denver Center has several large sectors, because it handles many en route aircraft flying from the West Coast to Chicago and New York. It also has busy smaller sectors which work the large number of aircraft inbound to Denver's Stapleton Airport. N1234 is being handled by one of the large sectors. Even though as many as 25 aircraft might be on the controller's frequency, the system is working well, and the radio indicates only moderate activity. As he approaches the Dove Creek VOR, N1234's pilot asks the center for a higher altitude. The controller advises him that there is northbound traffic on J15 at flight level 370, and that N1234 will have to stay at flight level 350 for a little while. The pilot acknowledges and remains at FL 350.

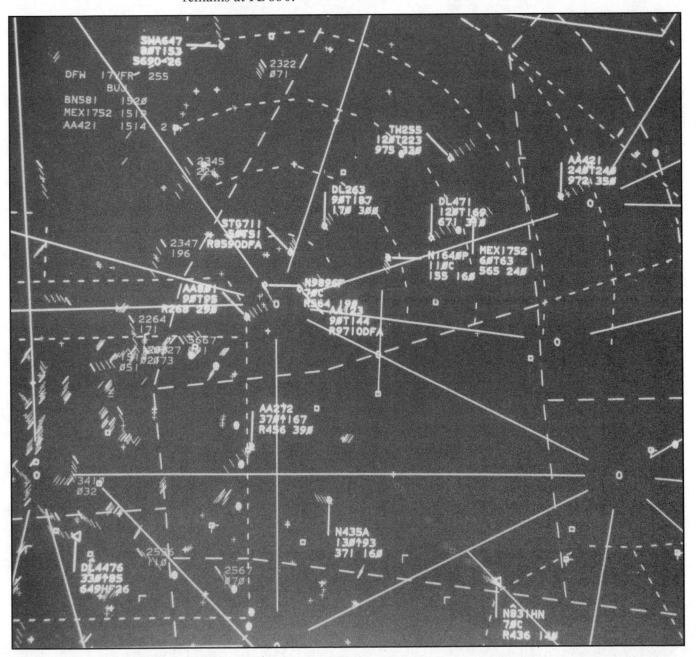

Scope at an en route center depicts airways (straight lines), and shows multiple aircraft data blocks. The slashes behind each data block show where the aircraft was in the past several minutes. For example, Delta Airlines 263, in center, is flying in a northeast to southwest direction. Below the center, American Airlines 272 is flying in a southwest to northeast direction. (FAA, S. Michael McKean)

At Dove Creek (actually over the Dove Creek VOR) the aircraft turns onto J197. It will fly along J197 for the next 400 miles or so. Five minutes after passing Dove Creek, N1234 is clear of J15 so a climb to 41,000 feet is safe. The controller clears N1234 to flight level 410 and hands it off to the next sector in Denver Center.

THE CHICAGO SECTOR

The aircraft's route continues over Colorado Springs to Goodland, Kansas, where it joins J146 again. About 125 miles east of Goodland, N1234 is passed to the center at Minneapolis.

At Minneapolis Center, the activity picks up somewhat since controllers are placing aircraft in sequence for entering the Chicago O'Hare Airport area. As they issue headings and speed restrictions, dialogue is getting a bit more crisp. Controllers can almost hear the pilots sitting up straighter in their cockpit chairs, stowing unnecessary articles, and checking approach plates (the charts for making the approach into the airport). Aircraft approaching Chicago from this direction have to fly 10 miles in-trail (or apart), and they have to fly almost in a line. Aircraft approaching from another direction have similar restrictions, and somewhere along the way a controller will fit the two streams together for a five-mile sequence, or daisy chain, for the closer approach to the airport.

But this activity does not affect N1234's pilot, as he sits comfortably at flight level 410, enjoying the show. He communicates with two sectors in Minneapolis Center and then, near Des Moines, changes to the Chicago Center.

At one time, Chicago Center was part of what used to be called the "golden triangle." That was airspace inside a line that ran from New York to Chicago to Boston and back to New York, which had the highest air traffic density in the world. Since airline deregulation, however, "hub" airports such as Atlanta, Denver, Charlotte, Raleigh, St. Louis, and Kansas City have become much busier than they were before. The "golden triangle" is no longer the only busy chunk of airspace.

N1234 passes through several sectors in Chicago Center. As the aircraft approaches Chicago, the pilot notices diminishing activity on the radio frequency. He is flying in an "ultra-high" sector at flight level 410. Most Chicago traffic is well below him, chattering on a myriad of other frequencies. Here, N1234 passes over the Joliet VOR, about 40 miles south of the O'Hare Airport.

After Joliet, N1234 continues almost due east to the South Bend VOR. At South Bend, the aircraft proceeds via the J554 airway and joins the flow of traffic heading to New York. The pilot has about 30 minutes or so before he, too, has to sit up straight and stow his extraneous gear.

A little more than 50 miles east of South Bend, N1234's pilot is instructed to contact the Cleveland Center. Cleveland is a very busy center. It not only communicates with all the "golden triangle" aircraft, it also handles a number of busy airports of its own, including Detroit and Cleveland. There is much climbing and descending of aircraft in the Cleveland Center airspace, and that makes things complex.

N1234 proceeds over the Carleton VOR, continuing on J554 just south of Windsor, Ontario, in Canadian airspace. The United States and Canada have an international agreement that allows facilities to ignore international borders and to assign airspace according to operational needs.

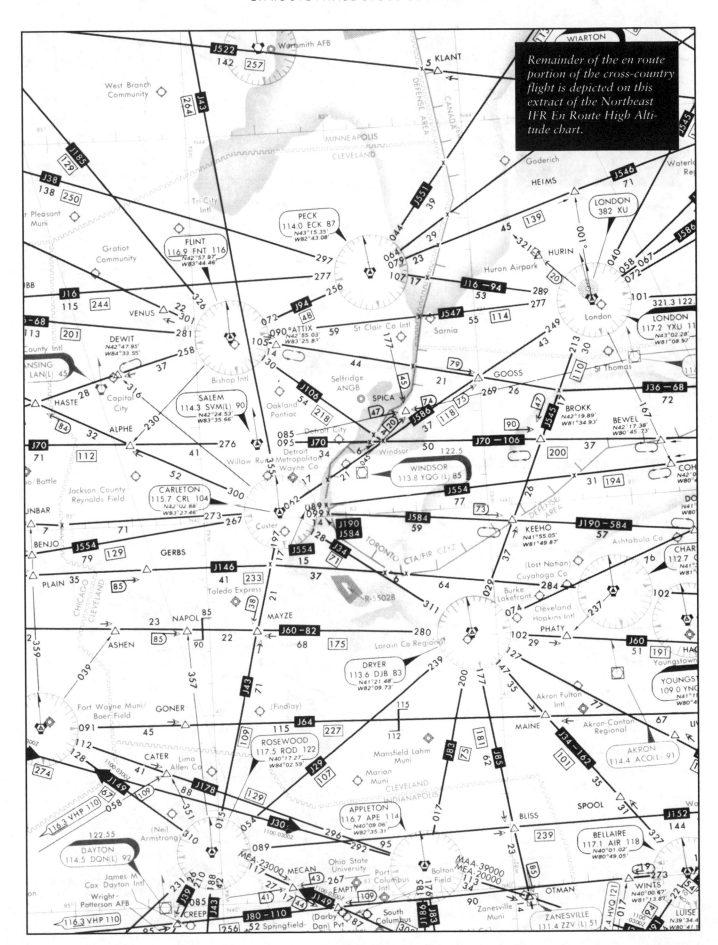

Remainder of the en route portion of the cross-country flight is depicted on this extract of the Northeast IFR En Route High Altitude chart.

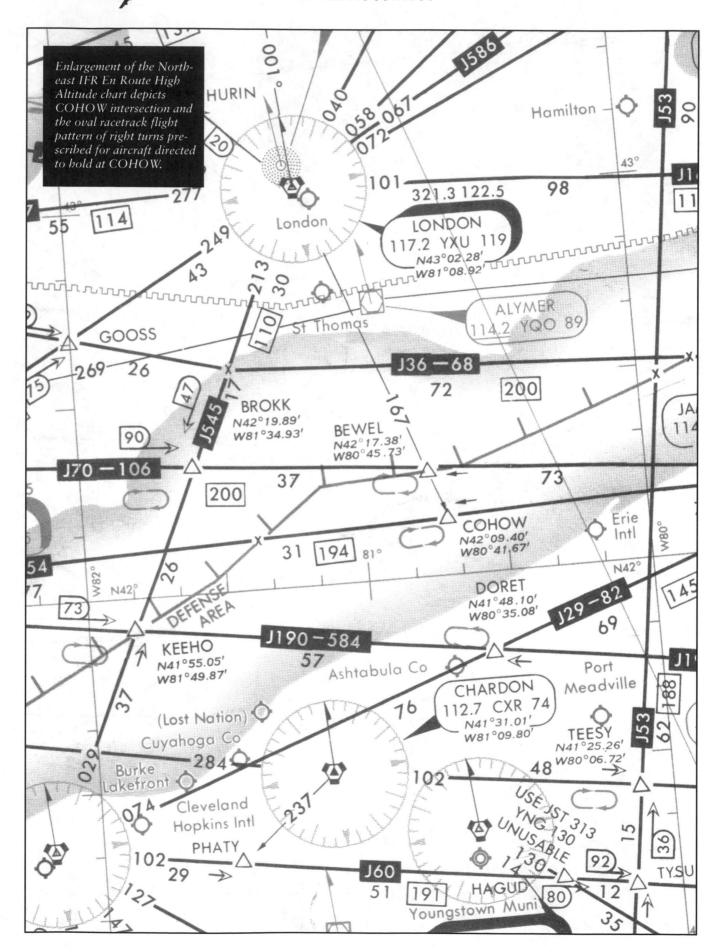

Enlargement of the Northeast IFR En Route High Altitude chart depicts COHOW intersection and the oval racetrack flight pattern of right turns prescribed for aircraft directed to hold at COHOW.

DELAYS AND HOLDING

All is not well, however. The weather forecast for Kennedy has moved in early, and the airborne demand is exceeding airport capacity. About 40 miles east of Carleton, at an intersection labeled "COHOW," the chart shows a small, racetrack-like symbol. It is a published holding pattern where aircraft circle when it is necessary to absorb a delay.

N1234, hold COHOW intersection as published; 20 mile legs; expect further clearance (EFC) 2005 UTC.

This message comes from the Cleveland sector controller. Intersections are made up of two crossing radials. These are usually the airway an aircraft is on, and another that is easily identifiable. COHOW intersection is a spot in the air over Lake Ontario. Its location is defined by J554 and a radial from the VOR at London, Ontario. Every intersection's name is based on a five-letter, pronounceable combination. The combination does not, necessarily, mean anything. Computers assign the designations on a worldwide basis. A combination is not used more than once within a 6,000-mile area to prevent a single aircraft from encountering two different intersections with the same name.

The published pattern for holding at COHOW intersection instructs N1234's pilot to turn right over the intersection, reverse course, fly for 20 miles, then reverse course to return to the intersection via J554. The time is now 1950 hours UTC, so the expected clearance time of 2005 hours UTC indicates a 15-minute delay.

At 2000 hours UTC, N1234 turns outbound over the intersection to begin his second circuit. Then the controller's voice comes again.

N1234, Cleveland, cleared to Kennedy Airport. Turn left heading 030; intercept J554; descend and maintain flight level 290.

N1234 is now inbound to the JFK airport and starting its descent. The radio frequency is congested with control instructions. The radar controller in Cleveland is hunched over his scope. His colleague has abandoned the phone and is talking on a headset plugged into the telephone line to New York Center.

New York, Cleveland, we're starting off the stack with three, 20 miles in-trail. What does it look like?

Keep them coming, Cleveland. Pilots are making the approach okay, but the ceiling and visibility are close to minimums, so who knows how long we'll last.

Okay, New York, we'll keep some altitude between them just in case they close the door on you.

The aircraft are landing, but the weather threatens to deteriorate to the point that some pilots might elect not to land. The "they" who might close the door are the controllers at the New York TRACON facility, who might ask that the planes go back into a holding pattern.

N1234, reduce speed to 220 knots and descend and maintain 15,000.

N1234 is turning onto the J70 airway over the Jamestown VOR. The pilot opens the appropriate charts, starting with the standard terminal arrival (STAR) book, which describes the LENDY TWO arrival. The LENDY TWO begins at the Wilkes-Barre VOR. Then the aircraft flies by way of the Wilkes-Barre 124 radial and the Stillwater VOR. After that, via the Stillwater 109 radial to the LENDY intersection, which is defined by the La Guardia 315 crossing radial. At LENDY, the pilot can expect vectors into Kennedy.

N1234, contact New York Center on 125.1.

The New York Center controller working with aircraft inbound to New York is receiving them as they approach from three different directions and fitting all of them into a smooth-flowing, single line. Three are coming from the same direction, 20 miles apart, each travelling at 200 knots and descending. It is the start of the Kennedy "rush," and the transmissions are nonstop.

American, turn right heading 150, slight delaying turn.

Eastern, turn right heading 120; proceed via the LENDY TWO. Keep the speed up to 250, please.

United, descend to 12,000.

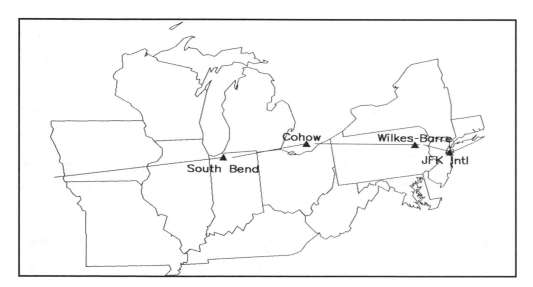

Schematic of eastern part of trip.

U.S. Air, turn left heading 090; descend to 13,000.

N1234, descend to 14,000.

American, turn left heading 100; proceed via the LENDY TWO.

FINAL LEG OF EN ROUTE FLIGHT

The New York Center radar controller is hunched over the radar scope; one hand is at the keyboard, the other at the microphone key. He is in charge of this little chunk of the world's airspace, and his job is to get these planes lined up and properly spaced. His handoff man is talking to Cleveland Center and the New York TRACON. Handoffs are still being made automatically, but information on aircraft spacing and the conditions at the field are being passed to all players. The TRACON is also taking planes from three different directions and fitting them into a single landing line. The New York Center controller does not have the complete picture. But he knows from experience that this is also the busy period for the flights from Europe, arriving by way of the northeast fix into Kennedy, and this new string might cause the TRACON to shut the door on him.

N1234's pilot has gotten the automatic terminal information service (ATIS) information Alpha. It tells him that Kennedy is landing aircraft on runway four right (4R), that the visibility is three-quarters of a mile, and that the runway's visual range is more than 6,000 feet. This is "okay" for an approach, but if conditions worsen, the situation could become tricky.

American, make a 360 to the right.

N1234, turn right heading 300.

New York needs some more space between the aircraft, so the American Airlines flight will circle to the right once and come back on course and N1234 will fly in the opposite direction for a few minutes to ensure added spacing.

N1234, turn right heading 100; intercept J70.

N1234 (back on course) descend and maintain 12,000.

The aircraft is flying over Wilkes-Barre now, about 75 miles from LENDY intersection. At this speed, it will take the pilot another 20 minutes to reach LENDY. Other planes are coming on the frequency now, flying above and behind N1234. For controllers, the stream seems never to end.

N1234 (now over Stillwater) descend and maintain 11,000.

On the controller's scope, N1234's data block starts to blink, then steadies again. TRACON accepts the handoff.

N1234, contact New York approach on 128.5; good evening.

N1234 is passing from the en route world back into the terminal world; in this case, New York TRACON.

N1234, New York Approach, good evening. Fly heading 090 vectors for a (runway) 4 right ILS (instrument landing system) approach; altimeter 29.95. Understand you have information Alpha.

The pilot acknowledges and complies with the instructions.
Next: the busy terminal phase of the flight.

CHAPTER NINE

THE ARRIVAL PHASE OF FLIGHT

Three TRACON controllers work with aircraft flying in their area of responsibility, while a supervisor monitors and stands ready to assist if needed. This scene at the Dallas TRACON, with supervisor Bill Fedowitch observing three of his controllers, is typical of a TRACON operation. (FAA)

TRANSITION TO NEW YORK TRACON

O ur Gulfstream IV airplane—N1234—is now in the hands of the busiest terminal in the world: the New York Terminal Radar Control (TRA-CON) facility at Garden City on Long Island. This facility is located near Roosevelt Field, where Charles A. Lindbergh began his historic transatlantic solo flight on May 20, 1927. It handles 1.5 million take-offs and landings in and out of New York's major and minor airports each year.

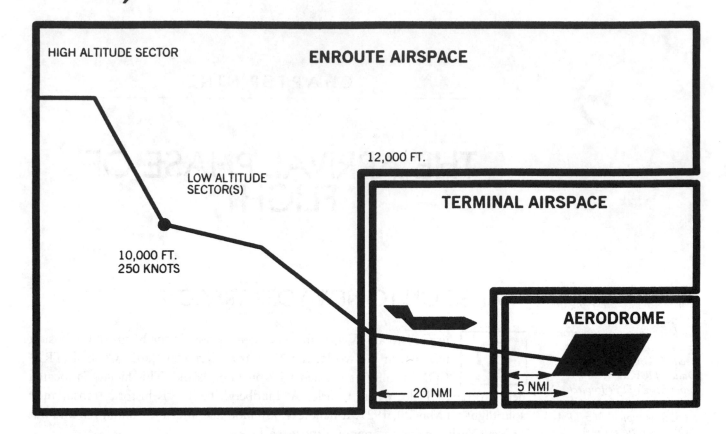

HIGH ALTITUDE SECTOR

ENROUTE AIRSPACE

LOW ALTITUDE
SECTOR(S)

12,000 FT.

TERMINAL AIRSPACE

10,000 FT.
250 KNOTS

AERODROME

20 NMI   5 NMI

Profile view of a typical commercial aircraft descent from en route altitude into the terminal airspace and then landing. (Unisys)

The TRACON, as it is known, is a large terminal control complex more like a center. Inside its large control room, radar scopes line the walls, and a supervisor's "island" dominates the center portion. The room has a high ceiling and subdued lighting. Each radar scope has a position available for a handoff controller, but it is not always staffed. A sector coordinator, usually a supervisor, brings the aircraft into the final approach course by giving the radar controllers instructions on how many aircraft to direct toward the airport and what distances they should be kept apart.

As the TRACON takes over, N1234 is heading eastbound, toward the Deer Park VOR. Overseas flights also use the Deer Park VOR as they complete their six-plus hour flights across the ocean. Controllers must join the two "streams" into a smooth flow before any of the aircraft proceed southwest toward the airport.

The LENDY intersection is about 24 miles northwest of Kennedy Airport. As it passes LENDY, N1234 is just north of Newark Airport. Below it, arriving flights for Newark are maneuvering to get into a similar sequence, and departures are beginning their climbing turns westbound. A few minutes later, N1234 passes north of La Guardia airport, and its pilot spots a departure from that airport break through the clouds on its way northeastbound.

The aircraft is now in airspace assigned to the Kennedy sector and is still flying at 11,000 feet because of departures climbing out of that airport. The Deer Park controller sees that the inbound sequence will work better if he can bring N1234 southeastbound and put it ahead of a TWA airliner approaching the VOR. He points at the target and asks the LENDY controller, who coordinates with the departure controller, the following question:

140 heading and down to 7,000?

The departure controller acknowledges the request and approves it. The instructions are transmitted immediately to the pilot.

N1234, turn right heading 140; descend and maintain 7,000. Contact New York Approach on 127.35.

N1234 acknowledges, makes the turn to a heading of 140 degrees, and begins descending to 7,000 feet.

Vought-Sikorsky VS-300, 1939. Forerunner of modern helicopters. Single main rotor, practical tail rotor. Vought-Sikorsky Aircraft Co.

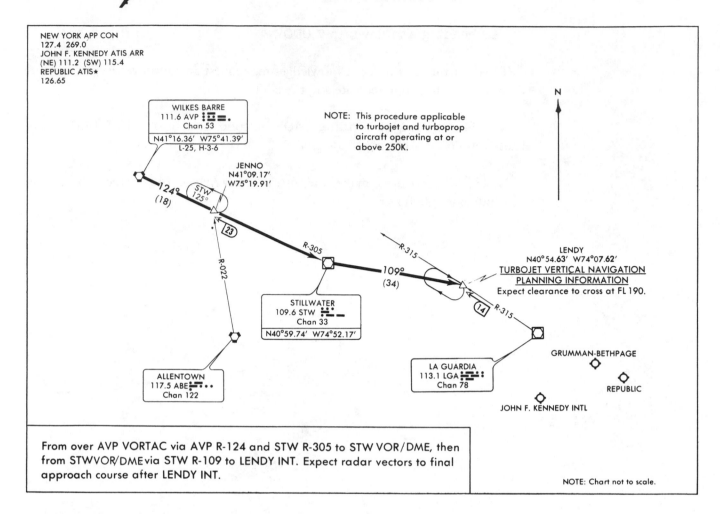

NEW YORK APP CON
127.4 269.0
JOHN F. KENNEDY ATIS ARR
(NE) 111.2 (SW) 115.4
REPUBLIC ATIS★
126.65

WILKES BARRE
111.6 AVP ▪▪▪ ▪▪ ▪
Chan 53
N41°16.36′ W75°41.39′
L-25, H-3-6

JENNO
N41°09.17′
W75°19.91′

STW
125°

124°
(18)

23

R-022

R-305

R-315

109°
(34)

R-315

14

LENDY
N40°54.63′ W74°07.62′
TURBOJET VERTICAL NAVIGATION
PLANNING INFORMATION
Expect clearance to cross at FL 190.

STILLWATER
109.6 STW
Chan 33
N40°59.74′ W74°52.17′

ALLENTOWN
117.5 ABE
Chan 122

LA GUARDIA
113.1 LGA
Chan 78

GRUMMAN-BETHPAGE ◇

REPUBLIC ◇

JOHN F. KENNEDY INTL ◇

N

NOTE: This procedure applicable
to turbojet and turboprop
aircraft operating at or
above 250K.

From over AVP VORTAC via AVP R-124 and STW R-305 to STW VOR/DME, then
from STW VOR/DME via STW R-109 to LENDY INT. Expect radar vectors to final
approach course after LENDY INT.

NOTE: Chart not to scale.

SEPARATING INBOUND TRAFFIC

N1234 now appears to be on a heading which will meet the TWA aircraft, south-westbound and about ten miles from the Deer Park VOR. The TWA aircraft is at 11,000 feet; N1234 has left 11,000 for 7,000 feet. As soon as N1234 is out of 10,000, the controller will have vertical separation, and he can let the situation ride until five miles separate the two aircraft.

TWA, reduce to 200 knots.

The controller estimates that N1234 will turn southwestbound about three miles in front of the TWA. But, to ensure a five-mile spacing, he establishes a 20-knot speed differential. N1234 is now out of 10,000 and separation is assured.

N1234, turn right heading 190; intercept the Deer Park 221 radial.

N1234 is out of 9,000, still descending to 7,000 feet.

TWA, descend and maintain 9,000.

The LENDY TWO arrival procedure for an approach into JFK International Airport begins over the Wilkes-Barre VOR (AVP, on 111.6 MHz). The aircraft flies along the 124 degree radial from AVP to JENNO intersection, thence to Stillwater VOR, and off the 109-degree radial from Stillwater to LENDY intersection. From LENDY, the pilot expects to receive radar vectors from approach controllers to bring him onto the final approach course for landing at JFK.

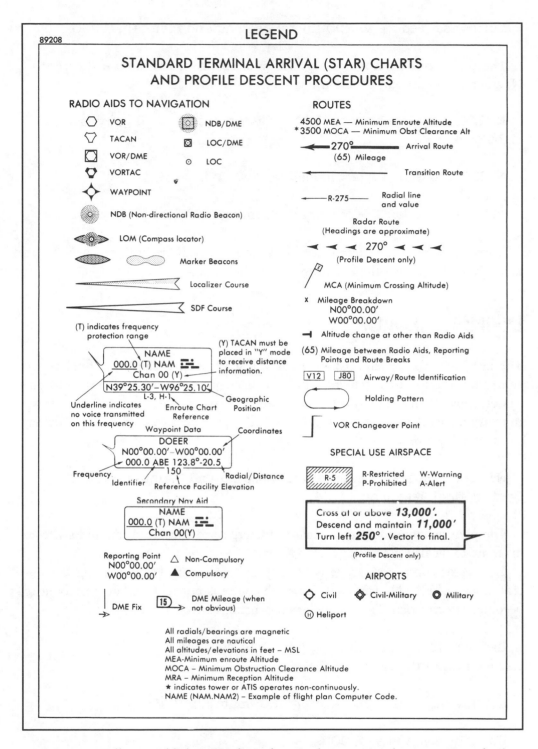

89208

LEGEND

STANDARD TERMINAL ARRIVAL (STAR) CHARTS AND PROFILE DESCENT PROCEDURES

RADIO AIDS TO NAVIGATION

⬡ VOR
▽ TACAN
▢ VOR/DME
⬡ VORTAC
◇ WAYPOINT

◉ NDB/DME
◉ LOC/DME
◦ LOC

◉ NDB (Non-directional Radio Beacon)

◈ LOM (Compass locator)

◖◗ ⬭ Marker Beacons

◁ Localizer Course

◁ SDF Course

(T) indicates frequency protection range

```
      NAME
  000.0 (T) NAM ▪▪▪
     Chan 00 (Y)
  N39°25.30'-W96°25.10'
        L-3, H-1
```

(Y) TACAN must be placed in "Y" mode to receive distance information.

Underline indicates no voice transmitted on this frequency

Enroute Chart Reference

Geographic Position

Waypoint Data

Coordinates

```
       DOEER
  N00°00.00'-W00°00.00'
   000.0 ABE 123.8°-20.5
          150
```

Frequency

Identifier

Reference Facility Elevation

Radial/Distance

Secondary Nav Aid

```
      NAME
  000.0 (T) NAM ▪▪▪
     Chan 00(Y)
```

Reporting Point
N00°00.00'
W00°00.00'

△ Non-Compulsory
▲ Compulsory

| DME Fix

[15] DME Mileage (when not obvious)

ROUTES

4500 MEA — Minimum Enroute Altitude
*3500 MOCA — Minimum Obst Clearance Alt

◀——270°———— Arrival Route
(65) Mileage

◀———————— Transition Route

——R-275—— Radial line and value

Radar Route
(Headings are approximate)

◀ ◀ ◀ 270° ◀ ◀ ◀
(Profile Descent only)

⚑ MCA (Minimum Crossing Altitude)

x Mileage Breakdown
N00°00.00'
W00°00.00'

◢ Altitude change at other than Radio Aids

(65) Mileage between Radio Aids, Reporting Points and Route Breaks

[V12] [J80] Airway/Route Identification

⬭ Holding Pattern

⌐ VOR Changeover Point

SPECIAL USE AIRSPACE

[▨ R-5] R-Restricted   W-Warning
         P-Prohibited   A-Alert

```
Cross at or above 13,000'.
Descend and maintain 11,000'
Turn left 250°. Vector to final.
```
(Profile Descent only)

AIRPORTS

◇ Civil   ◈ Civil-Military   ◉ Military
Ⓗ Heliport

All radials/bearings are magnetic
All mileages are nautical
All altitudes/elevations in feet – MSL
MEA-Minimum enroute Altitude
MOCA – Minimum Obstruction Clearance Altitude
MRA – Minimum Reception Altitude
★ indicates tower or ATIS operates non-continuously.
NAME (NAM.NAM2) – Example of flight plan Computer Code.

Once controllers establish 1,000 feet of vertical separation between aircraft, they can clear the higher aircraft to the altitude the lower aircraft has left. Finally, the five-mile horizontal separation is established between the two aircraft.

N1234, reduce to 200 knots.

TWA, descend and maintain 7,000.

KLM descend and maintain 7,000; proceed via the Deer Park 221 radial.

Lufthansa, reduce to 200 knots; descend and maintain 7,000.

The sector coordinator decides that he needs to fit two aircraft in front of N1234 and two aircraft behind it.

N1234, turn left heading 190, delaying vector; we'll get you right back in.

N1234 turns left to the new heading.

TWA, make a left 360 for traffic coming up from the south.

Below these aircraft, aircraft departing from Kennedy delay their climb for an extra five miles to clear those on approach.

LINING THEM UP

The last radar controller N1234's pilot will work with is called the final vector controller. His job is to integrate the two lines of approaching aircraft into one smooth flow to the runway. In good weather, it is sometimes possible to use two runways for landings. But the weather is bad on this occasion, and everybody has to use runway 4 right.

N1234, turn right heading 250; descend and maintain 4,000. Contact final vector on 118.4.

The pilot acknowledges the instructions, begins to execute them, and switches his radio to the new frequency, 118.4 MHz.

The vector controller's scope is literally full of aircraft. He is working five aircraft ahead of N1234. The final approach course is now empty, but it is about to become very crowded. The controller's instructions are concise and clear.

Eastern, turn right heading 010; intercept the localizer. Descend and maintain 1,500.

Northwest, turn right heading 350; maintain 2,000.

U.S. Air, descend to 2,000.

United, turn left heading 300.

American, turn left heading 300; reduce to 200 knots.

N1234, traffic—an American 727, one o'clock and three miles level at 3,000.

Controllers in the TRA-CON absorb the picture on their scopes and relate it to the requirements of the air-craft, the weather situation, and the density of air traffic operating into and out of the terminal facility they serve. Controller S. Michael McKean works at a console in the Dallas-Fort Worth TRACON. (FAA photo by Michael McKean and Warren Kneis.)

Five other aircraft approaching from the south are beginning a sweeping left turn to intercept the instrument landing system (ILS) at the airport. The pattern resembles a question mark with the top half of the hook missing. N1234 will over-fly the American flight, separated by 1,000 feet, then join the sweeping flow to the airport.

N1234, turn right heading 290.

The 10-degree difference from the American flight's heading will give the controller the desired five-mile separation. The sequence of instructions continues.

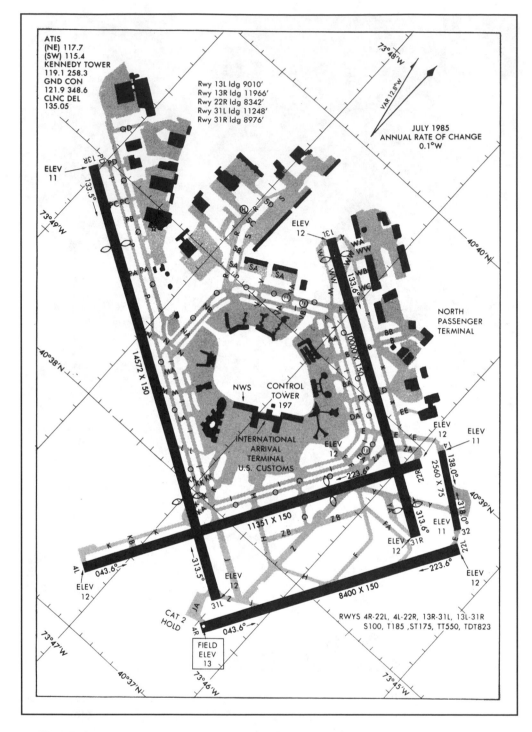

The right-angled sets of parallel runways at New York/John F. Kennedy International Airport show up clearly on this diagram. The flight we have been following will land on runway 4R, at the bottom of the diagram. Runway 4R is 8,400 feet long, and 150 feet wide. (Instrument Approach Procedures)

Northwest, turn right heading 010; intercept the localizer.

Eastern, cleared ILS [runway] 4 right approach. Contact Kennedy Tower on 118.4.

Northwest, descend and maintain 1,500.

U.S. Air, turn right heading 020.

United, turn right heading 360; descend and maintain 2,000.

Northwest, reduce to 180 knots, and hold it for as long as you can; cleared ILS 4 Right approach.

Other approach controllers are holding onto their aircraft for a few extra miles to ease the load on the final vector controller. The line of aircraft, nonetheless, is swinging up to the airport, separated by five miles each.

N1234, descend and maintain 3,000.

American, turn right heading 360; reduce to 180 knots. Descend and maintain 2,000.

U.S. Air, cleared ILS 4 right approach.

Northwest, contact the tower 119.1.

U.S Air, reduce to 160 knots if able.

N1234, reduce to 180 knots; descend and maintain 2,000.

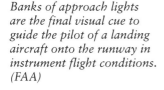

Banks of approach lights are the final visual cue to guide the pilot of a landing aircraft onto the runway in instrument flight conditions. (FAA)

Other aircraft are coming on the frequency now, with the approach chain stretching back to the Deer Park VOR. The controller announces to all aircraft that the Kennedy Airport weather is now "sky obscured," with one-quarter mile visibility; the runway visual range (RVR) for runway 4 right is 4,500 feet. The weather is deteriorating. But an instrument approach is still feasible. The controller issues the next instruction.

United, cleared ILS 4 right approach. Contact the tower on 119.1.

American, turn right heading 060; cleared ILS 4 right approach.

The controller lets the American Airlines plane fly slightly through the localizer course to add an extra mile of spacing and now has turned it back.

N1234, turn right heading 010; reduce to 160 knots.

The once curved line of approaching aircraft is now a straight line, methodically heading toward the airport.

N1234, descend and maintain 1,500; cleared ILS 4 right approach.

American, contact the tower on 119.1.

N1234, contact the tower on 119.1.

Our pilot acknowledges, and continues down the precise path to the runway. He switches his radio to Kennedy Tower frequency, 119.1 MHz.

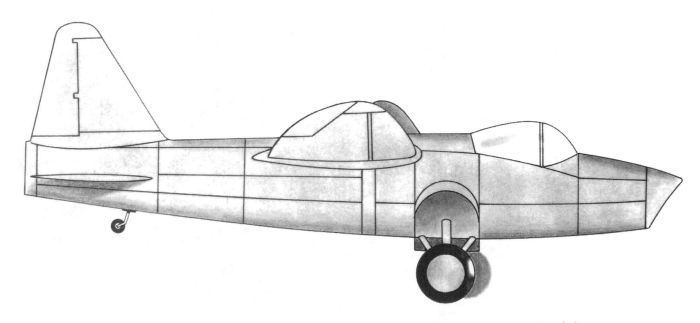

Heinkel He. 178, 1939. First aircraft to fly on turbojet power, using Dr. Pabst von Ohain's HeS engine of 1,100 lb. thrust. Ernst Heinkel A.G.

CONTACT THE TOWER

Kennedy Tower rises 160 feet above the huge airport parking lot. It is probably one of the most photographed towers in the world. It provides a dramatic contrast to the sweeping arch that identifies the airport's international arrival building. Inside the glass enclosed cab, just below the large white ball that protects the "ground" radar antenna, between seven and nine controllers work in semi-darkness. Here, as in Los Angeles, the local controller is in charge of the landing aircraft. On this particular runway alignment, landing runway 4 right and departing runway 4 left, only one local controller is handling operations. His instructions bring arriving aircraft onto the runway.

American, report the outer marker—wind 070 at 10 knots; runway 4 right RVR 4,000.

United, left turn off 4 right, hold short of 4 left, and remain this frequency.

To get to the terminal, landing aircraft have to cross runway 4 left. The local controller holds those aircraft on his frequency until they clear the runway.

Continental, cleared for takeoff runway 4 left.

After lift-off, departing aircraft turn right to a heading of 100 degrees, across the landing runway. Since the weather is deteriorating, the local controller must time departures so they do not conflict with any arrivals that miss their approaches.

American, cleared to land.

United, cross runway 4 left; contact ground on 121.9.

N1234, report the outer marker—wind 060 at 10; runway 4 right RVR 4,500.

Clipper, cleared for takeoff runway 4 left.

American, left turn off, hold short of 4 left; remain this frequency.

BAD WEATHER LANDING

With the visibility at one-quarter of a mile, the controller cannot see runway 4 right, which is 1.5 miles away. He must rely on the ground radar, called the airport surface detection equipment (ASDE). The ASDE shows everything that is moving on the airport, even automobiles. The controller observes the landing aircraft as they descend below the tower and roll out on the runway. He sees the inbounds on the TRACON's radar display, and uses strips to keep track of the aircraft.

Tower, N1234, turn down the lights, please.

Controllers must also regulate airport lighting requirements, including edge lights, touchdown lights, centerline lights, approach lights, and sequence flashers. All except the last can be dimmed. N1234's pilot is probably referring to the high-intensity approach lights. They sometimes can bother pilots with an uncomfortable glare in a fog.

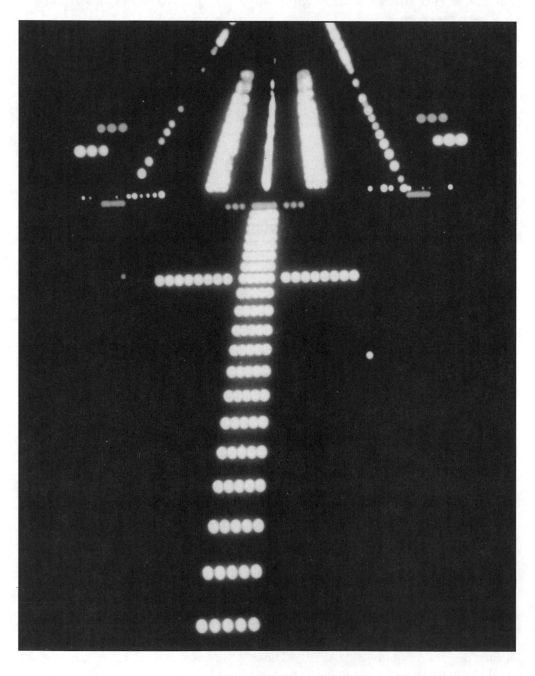

The sequenced flashing strobe lights in center of photo are nicknamed "the rabbit," because they seem to keep chasing the touch-down point on the runway, in top third of the photo. (FAA)

Do you want the approach lights down, sir? asks the controller.

No, the rabbit, replies N1234's pilot.

The controller turns off the sequence flashers (a series of high-intensity lights that appear to race toward the runway) called "the rabbit."

N1234, cleared to land runway 4 right.

American, cross runway 4 left; contact ground on 121.9.

N1234, left turn, cross runway 4 left; contact ground on 121.9 when clear of runway 4 left.

The surface of Kennedy Airport, as with other large international terminals, can be an awesome sight to behold in the evening. Boeing 747s are everywhere. DC-10s and Airbuses are engaged regularly in round-trip, transoceanic flights within a 24-hour period—miraculous testimony to how far aviation has come since Lindbergh flew from New York to Paris in 1927.

Ground control directs all aircraft clear of the active runways. This includes aircraft being towed from hangars to gates and from customs gates to departure gates—as well as the movements of hundreds of vehicles scurrying around the airport, performing support functions while sending streams of light everywhere, creating almost an "ocean" of light reflections.

American, make a right turn on the outer perimeter taxiway; cleared to the ramp.

Clipper, taxi straight out, a right on the parallel; follow the TWA to 4 left.

TWA, down taxiway Papa; give way to company leaving the ramp.

N1234, right on the outer; left at Alpha to the General Aviation ramp.

Former Kennedy controllers have their fair share of horror stories. One reported that he once had more than 100 planes monitoring his frequency waiting for clearance to taxi. On another occasion, the tower had to stop the arrivals because controllers ran out of places to put the aircraft on the ground.

For N1234, however, things worked out better. N1234 pulls into the ramp area, and the pilot shuts down its engines.

A relatively uneventful transcontinental trip has been completed. That is thanks to the skills of the aircraft manufacturer, the aircrew members, and the several controllers who worked with the pilot as the aircraft made its way across the country.

Gulfstream IV executive jet in landing attitude, a few feet above the runway and touchdown point after a cross-country flight. (Gulfstream Aerospace)

CHAPTER TEN

HEROES AND MIRACLES

SAGA OF UNITED FLIGHT 232

T he United Air Lines accident at Sioux City, Iowa on the afternoon of July 19, 1989 is an outstanding example of extraordinary skill and coordination among professional aircrew members in the air and professional air traffic controllers assisting them from the ground.

The time was 3:05 p.m. Central Daylight Time (2005 hours UTC). United Air Lines flight 232 (UAL#232), a 168-ton DC-10 bound from Denver, Colorado for Chicago, had just contacted Minneapolis Air Route Traffic Control Center (ZMP). The center was also in contact with UAL flights 126 and 774. All three center controllers were moving the flights around the sky to put more distance between them as they prepared for their approaches into Chicago's O'Hare airport, more than 400 miles away.

The text that follows are recordings of radio transmissions between controllers and UAL#232's pilot, Captain Alfred C. Haynes, and his cockpit crew. They worked together skillfully to land the aircraft after it was crippled by serious mechanical failures during flight. Some transmissions have been omitted to simplify the story. All times are expressed in Universal Coordinated Time (UTC).

Mitsubishi A6M2 Reisen (Zero-Zen), 1940-45. Japan's principal fighter aircraft of WW II, first flown April 1, 1939 as Navy Type Zero. Mitsubishi Jukogyo K.K.

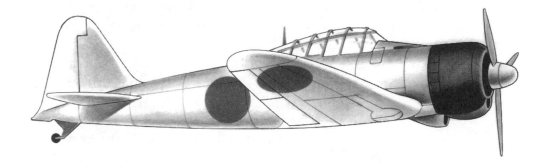

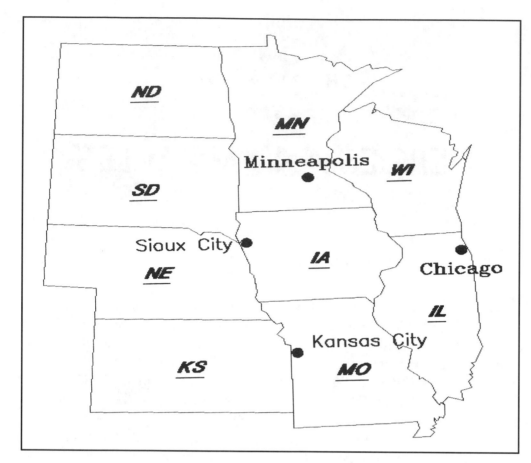

Schematic of Midwest region, highlighting Sioux City area, and showing Minneapolis.

Time	Source	Transmission
2005:40	ZMP	United Heavy, for spacing to O'Hare, turn left heading zero-one-zero.
2005:46	UAL#232	Zero-one-zero, United 232 Heavy.
2006:22	ZMP	United 126 Heavy, for spacing to O'Hare, turn right heading one-three-zero.
2006:27	UAL#126	One-three-zero heading, United 126.
2012:20	ZMP	United 126 Heavy, cleared direct Dubuque, rest of route unchanged.
2012:24	UAL#126	Direct Dubuque, United 126.
2013:55	ZMP	United 774, for Spacing to O'Hare, turn right heading of one-two-zero.
2014:04	UAL#774	Right to one-two-zero, United 774.

North American P-51D Mustang, 1940-45. Mustang prototype first flew, Oct. 26, 1940. Best long range fighter of WW II; 15,469 produced. North American Aviation Co.

2014:18	ZMP	United 232 heavy, cleared direct Dubuque, rest of route unchanged. Thanks for your help.
2014:21	UAL#232	Cleared direct Dubuque, United 232.
2014:24	UAL#232	I can't quite pick it up. What'd be good heading to start for it (Dubuque)?
2014:27	ZMP	United 232, zero-nine-five and direct Dubuque when able.

United 232 is now about 50 miles northeast of Sioux City, Iowa. The flight has been heading north. Now the controller has told the pilot he can turn east to resume his intended route for landing at Chicago. The controller observes that the aircraft is not turning.

2016:43	UAL#232	Minneapolis, United 232.
2016:46	ZMP	United 232, go ahead.
2016:47	UAL#232	We just lost number-two engine. We'd like a lower altitude, please.

United 232, a three-engine DC-10, lost power from its tail engine. It is not necessarily an emergency when a multi-engine aircraft loses one of its engines, but the controller will usually do everything possible to accommodate the pilot's requests. The pilot's tone of voice on the radio does not indicate the severity of the problem developing in the cockpit. He is calm, and remains calm throughout the crisis.

2016:56	ZMP	United 232 descend and maintain flight level two-nine-zero.
2017:00	UAL#232	Down to two-nine, United 232.
2017:23	ZMP	United 232 Heavy, do you plan on proceeding direct to O'Hare on your present routing?
2017:29	UAL#232	United 232, we've just lost number two and some hydraulics. Ah,... airplane is, ah, marginally controllable here.

The aircraft has started a sweeping right turn.

2018:08	UAL#232	What's the altitude again for 232? We're heading one eight zero.
2018:11	ZMP	United 232 descend and maintain flight level two-nine-zero.
2018:14	UAL#232	Nine-zero and okay; we got some controllability back. We had no control in the aircraft or very little; ... ah, but we don't have much yet we're gonna start a slow left turn back toward, ah, Dubuque.
2018:23	ZMP	United 232, roger.

But United 232 doesn't start back to the left, it continues slowly to the right.

2020:12	UAL#232	And Center, United 232, we're declaring an emergency here... and request landing at the nearest suitable airport.
2020:23	ZMP	United 232 you're cleared to Des Moines via fly heading one-three-zero. Descend and maintain flight level two-four-zero.
2020:32	UAL#232	Two-four-zero and that's...say again the heading.
2020:39	ZMP	United 232 cleared to Des Moines via fly heading of one-two-zero... and descend and maintain flight level two-four-zero.
2020:47	UAL#232	One-two-zero and descend to two-four-zero United 232 Heavy.
2020:58	ZMP	United 232 Heavy, are you requesting any assistance on the ground, sir?
2021:03	UAL#232	Sure we need the works, 232 we're just, ah, ...havin' trouble controlling the airplane right now.

2022:07	ZMP	United 232, your present heading looks a little better for Sioux City. Would you like to go to Sioux City?
2022:13	UAL#232	Affirmative.
2022:15	ZMP	United Heavy, roger. Fly heading of two-seven-zero...and direct Sioux City when able.
2022:19	UAL#232	Seven-zero, direct Sioux City when able, United 232.

While this exchange is going on, other areas are being informed to clear the airspace for the emergency aircraft.

2022:23	UAL#232	We have very little rudder control, ah,...no aileron control.
2022:31	UAL#232	There was an explosion and unable to shut down number two engine.
2022:36	ZMP	United 232, roger.

At this point, the controller informs the FAA traffic management unit in Washington, D.C., that the aircraft is having control problems and wants to land at Sioux City (SUX). The adjacent radar sectors have cleared the area of conflicting traffic, and Sioux City is told to have the emergency equipment standing by.

2023:16	ZMP	Sioux City, got an emergency for you.
2023:18	SUX	Alright.
2023:19	ZMP	I got a United aircraft coming in - lost number-two engine; having a hard time controlling the aircraft right now. He's out of 29 thousand and descending to Sioux City. Right now, he's east of your VOR, but he wants the equipment standing by right now.
2023:30	SUX	Alright, is he a two-seven-six-one code?

| 2023:32 | ZMP | I believe so... He's 40 miles east - 44 miles east, right now. Zero-nine-one radial, a two-seven-six-one code. |
| 2023:39 | SUX | Radar contact. |

The aircraft has been handed off to the controller working at the radar in the tower at Sioux Gateway Airport in Sioux City, Iowa. The airport lies on Missouri River bottom land six miles south of the city in the far northwest corner of Iowa.

W. Kevin Bachman is the air traffic control specialist on the radar at Sioux City tower. He passes the word to activate the fire and rescue crews. They roll into action. Many of their members are also part of the 185th Tactical Fighter Wing, Iowa Air National Guard, based at Sioux Gateway airport.

Terry Dobson, the FAA Air Traffic Manager, is in the tower. He notifies the Sioux City communication desk of the emergency. Col. Denny Swanstrom, commander of the Air Guard's 185th Tactical Fighter Wing, alerts his people to be ready to assist with the emergency.

United 232's pilot is now communicating with a second sector in Minneapolis Center. That controller will get him to a lower altitude and closer to the Sioux City airport.

2023:51	ZMP	United 232 Heavy, Minneapolis Center, roger. Descend and maintain one-one-thousand. The Sioux City altimeter is three-zero-zero-seven. Ah, you need a heading at all or any assistance getting to Sioux City?
2024:00	UAL#232	Say again the altitude.
2024:02	ZMP	Maintain one-one-thousand.
2024:05	UAL#232	One-one-thousand, roger. And we're trying to maintain a heading and (the airplane's) nearly uncontrollable... We're going through three-fifteen now.

The aircraft's flight path to Sioux City is a series of circles and curves through the skies of northwestern Iowa. The farmers working their fields below the stricken aircraft are not aware of its plight.

| 2024:12 | ZMP | Okay, you can maintain any heading at all you want. If you want any navigational assistance to Sioux City, just let me know there. |

		Right now I'm showing Sioux City off to your eleven o'clock position and about 40 miles.
2024:21	UAL#232	Roger, and we're tryin' to maintain present heading. We're into a slow right turn.
2025:09	ZMP	(To Sioux City) Okay, he's having a hard time controlling the plane right now and trying to slow down and get steady on a heading. As soon as I get comfortable, I'll ship him over to you...and he'll be your control.
2025:09	UAL#232	Give us the frequencies for Sioux City VOR, please.
2025:15	ZMP	Okay, Sioux City VOR is one-six-teen-five. One-sixteen-five for the VOR.
2025:24	ZMP	At Sioux City, (the weather) is four thousand broken, 25 thousand broken visibility, fifteen...showing a temperature 88 degrees, the winds zero-one-zero at one-four, altimeter three-zero-zero-eight.

This means that clouds are covering more than half the sky at 4,000 feet and that the visibility below the clouds is essentially unrestricted. The wind is blowing from 10 degrees east of north.

2025:44	ZMP	United 232, if you want to contact Sioux City approach right now, you can contact them on 124.6 and advise them what kind of equipment you need... They are getting the equipment ready for you.
2025:52	UAL#232	Twenty-four, roger.

United 232 has switched radio frequencies to work with Sioux City approach control. The supervisor in the Minneapolis center is keeping the airspace free of conflicting aircraft. He notifies the Air Force search and rescue center at Scott Air Force Base, Illinois, of the emergency. Mark Zielezinski, Area Supervisor in the SUX tower, activates a second radar position exclusively to handle UAL#232.

2026:19	UAL#232	Sioux City approach, United Air lines 232 Heavy with you out of twenty-six. Heading right now is two-nine-zero, and we've got about a 500 foot rate of descent.
2026:25	SUX	United Airlines 232 Heavy, Sioux City approach. Sioux City weather VFR: wind, three-five-zero at one-one, altimeter, three-zero-zero-seven. Fly heading two-five-five for vectors for a visual approach to runway 31.

W. Kevin Bachman (foreground) and Mark Zielezinski of the Sioux City, Iowa air traffic control team. Kevin Bachman handled United Airlines flight 232 for the final 36 minutes of its flight, in constant communication with Capt. Al Haynes and his flight crew. Mark Zielezinski, area supervisor in the Sioux City tower, activated a second radar position in the tower. (Office of Personnel Management photo by Terry Dobson, Air Traffic Manager at Sioux Gateway Airport)

2026:35	UAL#232	Okay, so you know we have almost no controllability—very little elevator and almost no aileron. We are controlling the turns by power. I don't think I can turn right, but I think we can only make left turns. We are starting a little bit of a left turn I mean we can only turn right, but we can't turn left.
2026:52	SUX	United 232 Heavy, understand, sir, you can only make right turns.
2026:58	UAL#232	That's affirmative.
2027:00	SUX	United 232 Heavy, roger. Your current, your present track puts you about eight miles north of the airport, sir. And the only way we can get you around to (runway) three one is a slight left turn with differential power, or if you can like jockey it over.
2027:14	UAL#232	Okay, we're in a right turn now. That's about the only way we can go. We'll be able to make very slight left turns on final, but right now just going to make right turns to whatever heading you want.
2027:24	SUX	United 232 Heavy, roger. Right turn heading two-five-five.
2027:29	UAL#232	Two-five-five.
2027:46	SUX	United 232 Heavy, when you roll out on the right turn, stop your heading on about a two-four-zero heading.

Since United 232 can only make right turns, the flight path will take him back into Minneapolis Center's airspace. The Sioux City controller coordinates that fact with the Minneapolis controller and he is told that he can use the airspace for whatever he needs. The wind has shifted to a bit west of north. The Sioux City approach controllers are aiming UAL#232 for the airport's active runway 31.

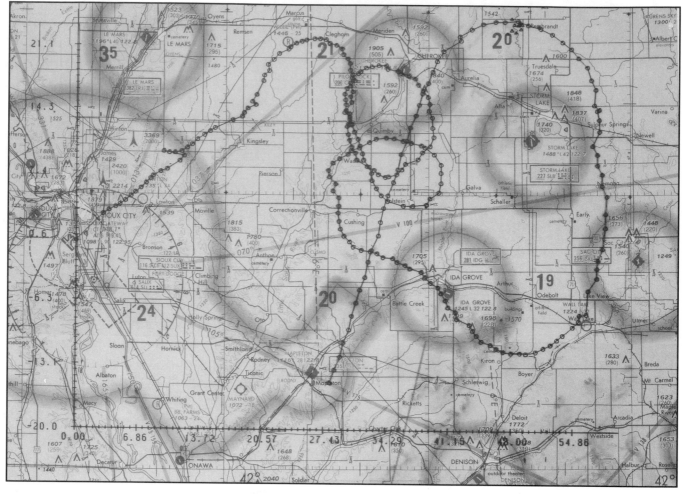

2028:04	SUX	United 232 Heavy, fly heading two-four-zero and say your souls on board.
2028:08	UAL#232	Say again.
2028:09	SUX	Souls on board, United 232 Heavy.
2028:12	UAL#232	We're getting that right now.
2028:27	SUX	United 232 Heavy, can you continue your turn to heading two four zero?
2028:31	UAL#232	I don't know. We'll try for it.
2029:04	SUX	United 232 Heavy, say souls on board and fuel remaining.
2029:07	UAL#232	We have thirty-seven six fuel, and we are counting the souls, sir.

The meandering path of United Airlines flight 232 over northwestern Iowa was portrayed in this drawing, built up from FAA recorded radar data as the drama unfolded. Because of extensive damage to the aircraft and inoperative flight controls, Captain Haynes and his crew could turn only to the right. Occasionally, by adept maneuvering of their remaining engine controls, they managed a turn to the left. Final approach into Sioux Gateway airport was straight in, to land on the inactive runway 22. (FAA)

2032:18	UAL#232	Sioux City United 232.
2032:21	SUX	United 232 Heavy, Sioux City.
2032:22	UAL#232	We have no hydraulic fluid, which means we have no elevator control almost none, and very little aileron control. I have serious doubts about making the airport. Have you got some place near there that we might be able to ditch unless we get control of this airplane? We're going to put it down wherever it happens to be.
2032:42	SUX	United 232 Heavy, roger. Ah, standby one.
2033:02	SUX	United 232 Heavy, can you hold that present heading, sir?
2033:22	UAL#232	Where is the airport now for 232, as we're turning around in circles?
2033:28	SUX	United 232, say again.
2033:30	UAL#232	Where is the airport for us, now, as we come spinning down here?
2033:32	SUX	United 232 Heavy, Sioux City airport is about twelve o'clock and three six miles.

The airport is 36 miles straight ahead, but the aircraft cannot fly straight. Iowa State Police, alerted by Sioux City police, have notified the Iowa Emergency Operation Center in the state capital of Des Moines. Their report confirms the earlier flash alert from the 185th Tactical Fighter Wing at Sioux City. Maj. Gen. Warren G. Lawson, the Adjutant General of Iowa, alerts National Guard emergency action teams, and passes the word to neighboring states.

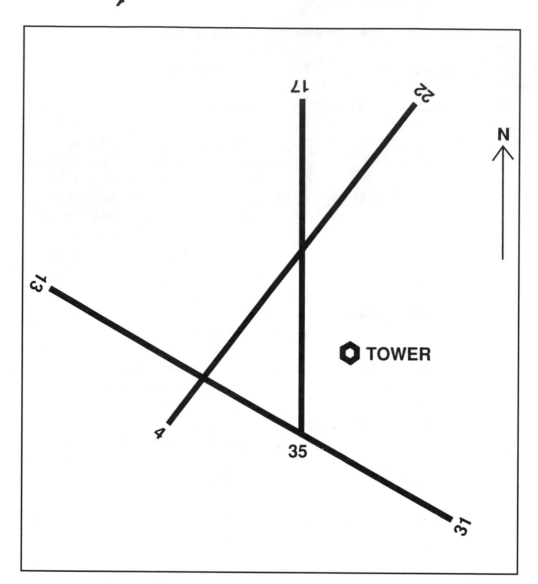

Sioux Gateway Airport runway and taxiway alignments. At the time of the emergency for United 232, runway 31 was in use. However, when Captain Haynes in the aircraft and Kevin Bachman in the tower realized that the stricken DC-10 could not maneuver for an approach to runway 31, both knew that runway 22 would have to do. Captain Haynes picked it out from 12 miles away, and in a superb display of airmanship guided his aircraft to touchdown precisely at the beginning of the runway.

2033:36	UAL#232	Okay, we are trying to go straight; we're not having much luck.
2034:35	UAL#232	Sioux City United 232 could you give us, please, your ILS frequency, the heading, and the length of the runway.
2034:43	SUX	United 232 heavy, affirmative. The localizer frequency is 109.3, and you're currently about 35 miles to the northeast. It'll take about two-three-five, two-four-zero heading to join it.
2035:00	UAL#232	We'll see if we can come up with that.

2035:03	UAL#232	Two thirty-two, we're going to try and put it in at Sioux City.
2035:08	SUX	United 232 Heavy, understand you're going to try to make it into Sioux City... There is no airport out that way that can accommodate you, sir.
2035:16	UAL#232	Okay, we'll head for Sioux City. We got a little bit of control back now. How long is your runway?
2035:21	SUX	United 232 heavy, the airport - the runway is 9,000 feet long and 150 foot wide.
2035:25	UAL#232	Okay, thank you.
2036:02	SUX	And United 232, did you get the souls on board count?

The souls on board count is vital information for the crash and rescue crew, as is the amount of fuel on board. The information helps fire and rescue crews estimate what kind of fire may result from an impact, and the number of people who may have to be treated for injuries.

2036:08	UAL#232	Standby; tell you right now, we don't even have time to let go and call the gal, ah...
2036:13	SUX	Roger.
2036:23	UAL#232	Two hundred ninety two souls on board United Two Thirty...
2036:27	SUX	United 232, say again.
2036:30	UAL#232	Ah, 292.
2036:32	SUX	Roger, thank you.
2036:53	UAL#232	Two thirty-two, we are just going to have to keep turning right, not much we can do about left. We're going to have to come back around to the heading.

2036:57	SUX	United 232, roger. Need you about a two-three-five heading, sir, if you can manage that and hold that.
2037:03	UAL#232	We'll see what happens.
2037:38	UAL#232	Where is Sioux City from my present position, United 232?
2037:29	SUX	United 232, it's about two twenty on the heading and 37 miles.

The aircraft has flown two miles further away in the last three minutes.

2039:10	SUX	United 232 Heavy, your company just called. They want you to try to contact them one twenty-nine forty-five, one twenty-nine forty-five for Chicago.

The airlines have a company radio network, which they use to talk directly to their own crews. UAL#232 has at least three radios on board, so the pilot retained communications with Sioux City while he talked to his company.

2039:56	SUX	United 232 Heavy, do you think you'll be able to hold about a two-forty heading?
2040:00	UAL#232	We'll try and turn it right now.
2040:03	SUX	Roger... When you get turned to that two-forty heading, sir, the airport will be about, oh twelve o'clock and 38 miles.
2040:06	UAL#232	Okay, we'll try to control it by power alone now. We have no hydraulics at all, so we're doing our best here.
2040:15	SUX	Roger. We have notified the equipment out in that area, too, sir. The equipment's here on the airport, standing by, and they're sending some out to that area.

2040:26	UAL#232	Okay, you got one twelve five for the localizer, and what's the heading?
2040:26	SUX	Localizer is 109.3 - 109.3 is the localizer for one three and two forty on the heading.
2040:34	UAL#232	Okay, 109.3 and two-forty.
2043:02	UAL#232	United 232, we're going to have to continue one more right turn. We've got the elevators pretty much under control, within three or four hundred feet, but we still can't do much with the steering.
2043:12	SUX	United 232 Heavy, roger. Understand you do have the elevators possibly under control. Will you be able to hold your altitude?
2043:15	UAL#232	Negative, we don't have it, we are better, that's all.
2043:39	UAL#232	How far is the field now?
2043:44	SUX	United 232 Heavy, you're currently 33 miles northeast.

The controller points out two small airports closer to United's position, but the pilot elects to continue to Sioux City.

2046:09	UAL#232	Okay, United 232, we're starting a left turn back to the airport. Since we have no hydraulics, braking is really going to be a problem. We suggest the equipment be toward the far end of the runway, and I think under the circumstances, regardless of the condition of the airplane when we stop, we're going to evacuate. So you might want to notify the ground crew equipment that we're going to do that.

2046:28	SUX	United 232 Heavy, wilco; and if you can continue that left turn to about a two-twenty heading, sir, that will take you right to the airport.
2046:42	UAL#232	Your ceiling right now?
2046:45	SUX	The ceiling is 4,000, broken, and the visibility is one five underneath it.
2046:47	UAL#232	The airport elevation?
2046:51	SUX	One thousand ninety-eight, ten ninety eight.
2048:48	SUX	United 232 Heavy, your present heading looks good.

The controller continues to give United 232 slight course adjustments. In the cockpit of the damaged aircraft, Captain Haynes and his colleagues are performing control feats never envisioned by the designers of the DC-10 aircraft. In the passenger cabin, the crew of flight attendants are preparing the passengers for the emergency landing that is now only a few minutes ahead.

2051:08	SUX	United 232, the airport is currently twelve o'clock and one-two miles.
2051:15	SUX	United 232 Heavy, you are going to have to widen out just slightly to your left, sir, to make the turn to final and also to take you away from the city.
2051:24	UAL#232	Whatever you do, keep us away from the city.
2051:46	SUX	United 232 Heavy, fly heading one-eight-zero.
2052:21	SUX	United 232, there's a tower five miles off your right side that's, ah, three thousand four hundred MSL is the height.
2052:37	SUX	United 232, how steep a right turn can you make, sir?

2052:40	UAL#232	About a 30 degree bank.
2052:43	SUX	United 232 Heavy, roger. Turn right heading one-eight-zero.
2053:02	SUX	United 232 Heavy, been advised there's a four lane highway up in that area, sir, if you can pick that up.
2053:08	UAL#232	Okay, we'll see what we can do here. We've already put the gear down, and we're going to have to put it down on something solid if we can.

The controller continues to give the aircraft headings toward the field and away from the city. He also tries to point out roads that might be used as a last resort.

2057:37	SUX	United 232 Heavy, roger. The airport is currently at your one o'clock position one-zero miles.
2057:56	SUX	And, ah, United 232 Heavy, if you cannot make the airport, sir, there is an interstate that runs north to south to the east side of the airport; ah . . . it's a four lane interstate.
2058:06	UAL#232	We're just passing it right now. We're going to try for the airport.
2058:12	SUX	United 232 Heavy, roger and advise when you get the airport in sight.
2058:20	UAL#232	Have runway in sight. We'll be with you shortly, thanks a lot for your help.
2058:23	SUX	United 232 Heavy, the wind is currently three six zero at one-one, three sixty at eleven. You're cleared to land on any runway.
2058:30	UAL#232	(laughter) You want to be particular and make it a runway, huh?

| 2058:49 | SUX | (Wind) zero-one-zero at one-one and, ah, there is a runway that's closed, sir, that could probably work too. It runs northeast to southwest. |

The controller is pointing out runway 4-22 at Sioux Gateway airport. Since UAL#232 is northeast of the airport, that runway is the best for a straight-in approach. Although 4-22 is closed for normal operations, it is the logical choice for UAL#232.

| 2058:59 | UAL#232 | We're pretty well lined up on this one, or we think we will be. |

| 2059:06 | SUX | United 232 Heavy, roger sir. That, ah, closed runway—that will work sir. We're getting the equipment off the runway and they'll line up for that one. |

The fire and rescue crews move quickly into new positions near runway 22. All of Sioux City's public safety and emergency organizations are alerted and ready. The community stands by as UAL#232 approaches from the northeast.

| 2059:14 | UAL#232 | How long is it? |

| 2059:33 | SUX | Sixty-six hundred feet - six thousand six hundred, and the equipment is coming off. |

| 2059:33 | SUX | At the end of the runway, it's just a wide open field, sir, so the length won't be a problem. |

| 2059:37 | UAL#232 | Okay. |

| 2059:45 | UAL#232 | (The ground proximity warning horn sounds) *Pull up. Pull up...* |

Throughout the emergency, Captain Haynes and his cockpit crew had controlled the aircraft solely by varying power from the two engines remaining. At one point as he approached the runway, he had to reduce his power so that he could land. At that instant, the right wing dipped and touched the approach end of runway 22. The aircraft cartwheeled down the runway, stopping finally in a cornfield off the right side of the runway.

Capt. Alfred C. Haynes (left) and two of his fellow crew members from United 232 receive the Aviation/Space Writers Association and US News & World Report "Newsmaker of the Year" award. Capt. Denny Fitch is in the center. He is an instructor at United's Denver training center. As a passenger aboard United 232, he volunteered to help Captain Haynes when the emergency arose. On the right is First Officer Bill Records. Second Officer Dudley Dvorak was the fourth man in the cockpit during this emergency. He could not be present for the AWA award. (Aviation/Space Writers Association photo)

One hundred and eighty-five people, including the cockpit crew, survived the crash. Many persons survived because of Captain Haynes's skills and the coordinated efforts of many individuals, trained and working skillfully within the system. The pilots did a masterful job of flying the plane to the airport and landing the stricken bird. The controllers did all they could to get flight 232 safely to the runway. Emergency crews, medical personnel, and volunteers helped rescue and treat the injured after the crash. The entire Sioux City community, as well as Iowa National Guard resources, took part in the rescue effort.

In the months after the emergency landing of flight 232, both the flight crew and FAA controllers were honored with awards for valor, professionalism, and courage. Kevin Bachman and Mark Zielezinski both received the Department of Transportation Award for Meritorious Service, presented at an award ceremony on October 19 in Washington, D.C. President Bush welcomed Bachman to his White House office, and lauded him for his professionalism.

Captain Alfred Haynes, the pilot-in-command of UAL flight 232, and his fellow aircrew members exhibited extraordinary airmanship in the incident. Capt. Haynes singled out Bachman for special mention, saying:

"There is nothing like a calm, soothing voice talking to you, giving the information you want to know. The gentleman (Bachman) was right on the money with everything we wanted to know—very calm, very professional. And I want to make sure the controllers' names get mentioned, because they certainly deserve a lot of credit for keeping us calm and getting us there."

United 232's 40-minute ordeal over Iowa is a dramatic example of the potential situations that all controllers must face. Pilots get in trouble and frequently need help from the ground.

CONTROLLER ACTIONS IN EMERGENCIES

Sometimes the FAA receives cheering news. One pilot sent the FAA a letter about a flight he made in his small plane to a family Christmas celebration with his young wife and small child. He had relatively few flight hours and experience when he made the trip. He became lost in stormy weather. Running low on fuel, he called on an air traffic facility. The facility located the aircraft and directed the pilot to the nearest airport, where he made a safe landing. The young man told us that the controller had made it one of his happiest Christmases.

In one recent three-month period, the FAA reported 252 flight assists, involving 457 people on board the assisted aircraft. Of that number 119 were lost aircraft. One typical flight assist occurred at Waco, Texas, on November 21, 1989.

James L. Brown, a controller at Waco approach, observed an unidentified aircraft squawking code 7700. That is a four-digit emergency code broadcast by the transponder in the aircraft. The 7700 code shows up brightly on radar scopes. The target was approximately 35 miles north of the Waco VOR and was southbound. Brown attempted to contact the aircraft but was unsuccessful. Another controller, Gregory A. Studer, thought he heard the call sign N150R on the emergency frequency. He recognized the call sign as belonging to a local flight school aircraft. (The call sign is the combination of letters and numbers used in radio conversation to identify the aircraft.)

After contacting the flight school, the controllers determined that the pilot of N150R was a student on a solo cross-country flight. Brown handed control of the emergency to the supervisor, David C. Lambert, so that the effort could be better focused and isolated from other traffic. Controllers failed in their attempts to relay instructions through another aircraft. However, Lambert directed the second aircraft to the vicinity of the aircraft in distress. Unfortunately, radar contact with both aircraft was then lost.

Based on the last seen radar position, Lambert instructed the second aircraft that the aircraft in distress should be at his 12 o'clock position, approximately one mile. The pilot saw the distressed aircraft and was able to lead him to Hillsboro Airport. N150R landed at Hillsboro with less than 10 minutes of fuel remaining.

Controllers are called upon to think quickly, to make decisions, and to act upon them. Flight assists are just one aspect of the job. Most of the time, controllers ensure that aircraft don't get into dangerous situations. But when such situations occur, controllers react to assist.

PART III

KNOWING THE SYSTEM

CHAPTER ELEVEN

THE HISTORY OF AIR TRAFFIC CONTROL

HERITAGE OF THE PAST

T he field and profession of air traffic control (ATC) is entering a 21st century that promises almost unlimited technological opportunities. But before looking at what marvels may lie ahead, it is important to look back through the evolution of air traffic control in the USA.

The following milestones serve as a tribute to the many people who have worked and sacrificed to make the system more safe and efficient. Their efforts remain the controller's heritage.

Messerschmitt Me. 262A-1a, 1943. First operational turbojet fighter. First flown, Jul. 18, 1942. 1,430 built before WW II ended. Messerschmitt A.G.

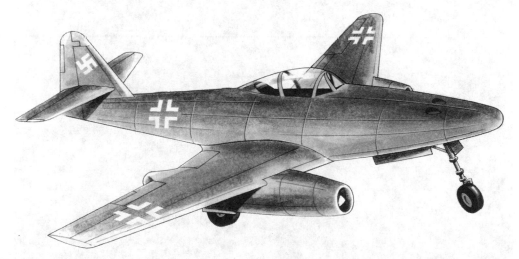

EARLY DAYS

In May 1918, the U.S. Army established the first airmail service in the United States. In August 1918, the U.S. Post Office took over the operation and began providing their own planes and other equipment. By September 1920, with the inauguration of service between Omaha, Nebraska and San Francisco, the Post Office was operating a transcontinental airmail route. However, air traffic control did not exist in those days.

Archie League, the nation's first air traffic controller, with his signal flags and wheelbarrow at Lambert Field, St. Louis in 1929. Archie was an airplane mechanic hired by the city to organize the air traffic into the busy airport. Lambert Field was also Charles Lindbergh's home base. (FAA)

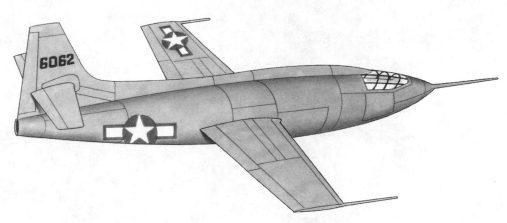

Bell X-1, 1947. First super-sonic airplane. Capt. Chuck Yeager, USAF, passed through Mach 1.0 in level flight on Oct. 14, 1947. Bell Aircraft Co.

Airplanes operated only in good weather and only in the daytime. At night, trains carried the mail. As operations expanded, the Post Office established airports every 200 miles or so and set up communications stations at each field to report on the mail planes' progress. Those stations were the direct ancestors of today's flight service stations.

CHRONOLOGY

LATE 1920s

On May 20, 1926 President Calvin Coolidge signed the Air Commerce Act of 1926. The Act instructed the Commerce Secretary to foster air commerce; designate and establish airways; and to establish, operate, and maintain aids to air navigation.

August 11, 1926—William P. MacCracken became the first Assistant Secretary of Commerce for Aeronautics, and the first head of the Aeronautics Branch.

December 31, 1926—The first air commerce regulations of the Aeronautics Branch entered into effect. The regulations included safety rules applying to air traffic.

June 30, 1927—The transcontinental airway was transferred from the Post Office Department to the Aeronautic Branch. Extending from New York to San Francisco, the airway was 2,612 miles long, with 2,041 of those miles "lighted." By this time, the Post Office had overcome the night flying problem by lighting the airway with beacon lights placed every 10 miles or so. This did not solve the problem of bad weather, however. Its air navigation facilities included 92 intermediate fields, 101 electric beacons, 417 acetylene beacons, and 17 radio stations. Personnel included 43 radio operators, 14 maintenance mechanics, and 84 caretakers.

July 1, 1928—Teletype machines began transmitting aviation weather information.

1928—Radiotelephone or voice communication with aircraft in flight became available on U.S. airways.

1929—The first seven radio-range beacons appeared on the airways. These emitted radio signals, and were a major step forward in air navigation.

September 24, 1929—James H. Doolittle made the first recorded successful instrument landing, using a system developed in 1928 by the Bureau of Standards for the Aeronautical Branch. Receiving directional guidance from a radio range course aligned with the airport runway and distance from the airport by means of radio markers, he controlled his airplane's altitude with the aid of a sensitive altimeter. Two other special instruments, a directional gyro and artificial horizon, aided Doolittle in controlling the aircraft solely by reference to the instruments.

Stanley Seltzer of American Airlines wrote about the early days of air traffic control. He described the situation in 1929 this way:

"While most of the world remembers 1929 as the year of the big stock market crash, ATC buffs will also remember that St. Louis' Lambert Field in 1929 was a thriving airport. Not only was it Lindbergh's home base, but it was here that a gentleman named Archie League became the nation's very first historically authenticated air traffic controller.

Customs officer checks baggage of passengers arriving aboard a Fokker F-10 transport of Western Air Express at Alhambra, California, 1929. Compare the smiles on the passengers in those uncrowded days with the throngs going through Customs in the jet age. (FAA)

"Archie was an airplane mechanic at St. Louis in 1929, when he was hired by the city to organize the traffic that frequented the busy airport. It was Archie who came up with the idea for what we believe was the first U.S. air traffic control facility. It consisted of a wheelbarrow containing two flags used to signal aircraft at the end of the runway, either that it was okay to take off, or that they should hold their position. Archie also had a huge sun umbrella and a portable chair. Archie called it a "mobile tower," and he moved from runway to runway, as dictated by wind conditions, hauling with him his trusty wheelbarrow containing the flags, his chair and the umbrella. He also took along a large cloth wind tee which he laid out on the ground to indicate the direction of landing. To keep it from blowing away, the cloth tee had sleeves around the edges, into which iron rods were inserted (another reason why Archie needed a wheelbarrow)." (*Journal of Air Traffic Control*, September 1985)

Archie League at Lambert Field tower in 1933, now working inside. He aims his light gun to signal an aircraft, in this case probably to taxi or take off. (FAA)

INTO THE 1930s

In 1930, Cleveland Municipal Airport established radio control of airport traffic. During the next five years, approximately 20 cities followed Cleveland's lead.

September 5, 1931—The first instrument landing using a glide slope transmitted by radio was made at College Park Airport, Maryland.

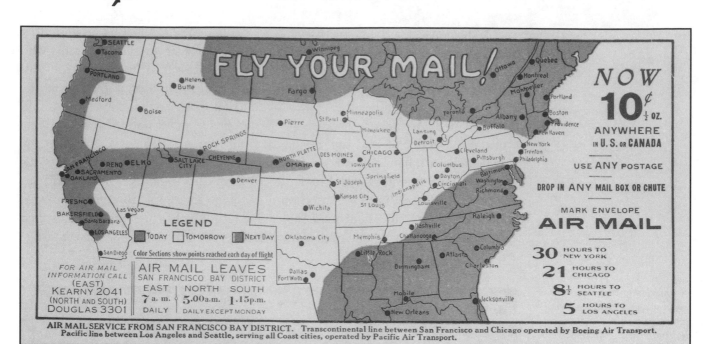

FLY YOUR MAIL!

NOW 10¢ ½ OZ.
ANYWHERE IN U.S. OR CANADA

USE ANY POSTAGE

DROP IN ANY MAIL BOX OR CHUTE

MARK ENVELOPE **AIR MAIL**

30 HOURS TO NEW YORK
21 HOURS TO CHICAGO
8½ HOURS TO SEATTLE
5 HOURS TO LOS ANGELES

LEGEND
TODAY — TOMORROW — NEXT DAY
Color Sections show points reached each day of flight

FOR AIR MAIL INFORMATION CALL (EAST) KEARNY 2041 (NORTH AND SOUTH) DOUGLAS 3301

AIR MAIL LEAVES
SAN FRANCISCO BAY DISTRICT
EAST | NORTH | SOUTH
7 a.m. | 5.00 a.m. | 1.15 p.m.
DAILY | DAILY EXCEPT MONDAY

AIR MAIL SERVICE FROM SAN FRANCISCO BAY DISTRICT. Transcontinental line between San Francisco and Chicago operated by Boeing Air Transport. Pacific line between Los Angeles and Seattle, serving all Coast cities, operated by Pacific Air Transport.

May 9, 1932—Captain A. F Hegenberger made the first "blind" solo flight using only instruments.

March 21, 1933—The first cross-country test of all-instrument (or blind) flying was made from College Park, Maryland to Newark, New Jersey.

All-weather flying created an untenable situation for pilots. They could not separate their aircraft from others, because they could not see them. This created an operational requirement for air traffic controllers, but three years would pass before the federal government began to operate an air traffic control system.

May 8, 1935—Senator Bronson M. Cutting was killed in the crash of a Transcontinental and Western Air (predecessor of TWA) airliner near Atlanta, Missouri. (The incident fueled existing efforts to improve passenger transportation conditions.)

November 12-14, 1935—Government and user representatives met and drafted methods for controlling airport and airway traffic.

December 1, 1935—The first airway traffic control center began service at Newark, New Jersey. It was organized and manned by airline companies, and it provided information to airline pilots on the whereabouts of other planes in the Newark area under instrument weather conditions. Two other centers opened months later in Chicago (April 1936) and in Cleveland (June 1936).

Lee Warren, one of the airline controllers, wrote:

"The airlines had agreed to do the job only until it could be assumed by the Feds. To do this, the participating airlines formed a company, 'Air Traffic Control, Inc.' to operate Newark, Cleveland and Chicago. In Newark it was administered by TWA, in Cleveland by United, and in Chicago by American. The controller pay was $200 per month. The fifteen controllers were selected from volunteers recommended by the airlines. Since no one was sure this new idea would fly, each con-

Air mail of the 1930s was considerably faster than today's mails, even though the aircraft were much slower. Rates were lower, too. (FAA)

Glen Gilbert (right), is considered the father of air traffic control. In this 1936 photo, Gilbert and J.V. Tighe use the tools of their trade at the Newark (NJ) Airway Traffic Control Station, the first in the nation. Tighe developed the first "shrimp boat" pieces to depict aircraft in the control center. The men use a set of dividers and circular slide rule to calculate the next positions of the aircraft they are controlling. The Glen Gilbert Award is the highest tribute the Air Traffic Control Association can bestow on an honoree. The award is presented by ATCA to the person who has demonstrated a long-term commitment to, and achievement of excellence in, aviation in the USA. (FAA)

troller had a promise that he could return to his old airline job, if he so wished. The total cost of each facility was about $6000 per month with a staff of five or six. To open Chicago, a staff of five was picked at Newark. On a Monday morning they boarded the airlines for Chicago. On the following Monday morning, they opened the Chicago Center. Needed decisions were not long in coming.

"It was urgent from several aspects that federal control of all traffic (not just airlines), system expansion, organizational stability and operational responsibility, begin as soon as possible. The Federal government responded quickly. The Bureau of Air Commerce scraped up $175,000 for the takeover. On June 3rd, the U.S.

Solicitor reaffirmed his earlier ruling that air traffic control was 'absolutely necessary to foster air commerce, prevent disasters and protect lives and property.'" (*Journal of Air Traffic Control*, July-September 1985)

On the eve of World War II, controllers at the busy Oakland center plot aircraft positions and calculate the next position for one that is outbound to the northeast. (FAA)

March 2, 1936—The federal government appointed an Airway Traffic Control Supervisor.

July 6, 1936—The government took over operation of the three airway traffic control centers at Newark, Cleveland, and Chicago. (This marked the birthday of a federally provided air traffic control separation service.)

Lee Warren described the situation:

"There were a few glitches in the transfer. Pay was one. In the ATC corporation we were all paid $200 per month. When our Federal appointments were made, on July 6, 1936, the salaries were $2000 per year ($167 per month) for controllers. Since we were not yet convinced the whole thing was a good idea, this was it. In Chicago, we all decided to quit at the end of the pay period and return to our old airline jobs. It took a lot of long distance calls and cajoling for the leaders to convince us to stay. The argument was that this was only the beginning; that the pay scale was Controllers $2000, Assistant Managers $2900, Managers $3500, and that we would all move up rapidly because of the expansion. And we did." (*Journal of Air Traffic Control*, July-September 1985)

November 1, 1937—The main part of the Civil Air Regulations went into effect. They constituted a thorough revision and codification of the earlier Air Commerce Regulations.

In 1937 it was decreed that all tower controllers should be federally certificated. The first batch of certificates was awarded alphabetically. For example, Lonnie Dietrich of Cleveland Tower received certificate No. 1; Tirey Vickers (at the other end of the alphabet) got No. 29.

January 1, 1938—The government created an Airport Traffic Control Section. Its job: to standardize airport control tower equipment, operational techniques, and personnel standards. By June 30 of that year, 40 airport control tower operators had been certified.

June 23, 1938—President Franklin Roosevelt signed the Civil Aeronautics Act into law. The law created the Civil Aeronautics Authority (CAA). It was a new kind of federal agency with quasi-legislative and quasi-judicial functions regarding safety and economic regulation of civil aviation.

1938—The teletype network "schedule B" was established. It connected the airway traffic control centers with Army and Navy air bases and airway communications stations of the Department of Commerce.

During World War II, civil and military air traffic control operations were combined. At the Washington (DC) center in 1943, a mixture of uniformed and civilian controllers worked the traffic into and out of the busy national capital area. Pneumatic tubes overhead carried paper messages throughout the center. (FAA)

May 1, 1939—A $7 million airways modernization and improvement program was completed, expanding the Federal Airways System to cover a total of 25,500 miles and to include 231 radio-range stations.

FORWARD INTO THE 1940s

March 26, 1940—This date marked a full year during which U.S. commercial air carriers flew without a fatal accident or a serious injury to passengers or crew.

April 1941—With U.S. involvement in the global war looming, the War Department sponsored the formation of the Interdepartmental Air Traffic Control Board (IATCB). The IATCB included representatives from the Army, Navy, CAA, and the CAB. It helped to establish many of the procedures that evolved during World War II for the control and regulation of air traffic.

November 1, 1941—The government began operating airport traffic control towers. The towers were taken over later by the CAA for national defense purposes. By November 15, the CAA operated eight towers.

July 1943—The CAA established a flight communications service. It required communicators, when contacted by aircraft, to volunteer information of essential interest, such as important changes in weather or the location of inoperable navi-

Even after World War II ended, civilian and military controllers worked together in the transition period to peacetime aviation operations. In the Kansas City center in mid-1945, banks of flight strips dominated the room, a hint of the busy air traffic over the Midwest region. (FAA)

gational facilities.

1945—Developmental work began on adapting radar to civil aviation. The work was done at the Indianapolis Experimental Station with equipment supplied by the armed forces.

April 1, 1946—The government published Standards for the Control of Instrument Flight Rule Traffic. This was a manual officially approved by the operations executives of the Army Air Forces, Navy, Coast Guard, and the CAA. Its adoption recognized the need for common procedures in the control of civil-military air traffic.

May 24, 1946—Indianapolis Airport unveiled the first radar-equipped control tower for civilian flying.

March 15, 1947—The CAA established airport traffic control zones having radii of three or five miles around certain airports.

A decade after World War II ended, radar was more prevalent in air traffic control centers, but the ubiquitous flight strips were still very much in evidence. In the foreground of this photo of the Washington (DC) Air Route Traffic Control Center in 1955, controllers move "shrimp boats" across the surface of a "battleship type" horizontal radar scope. (FAA)

April 1, 1947—The CAA tested the ground controlled approach (GCA) radar systems. The GCA was modified radar precision landing equipment developed originally for military use. Tests were conducted at Washington National and Chicago Municipal Airports.

February 17, 1948—Requirements for a common civil-military communications system, were issued in the report, *Air Traffic Control.*

May 1, 1948—The Air Force, Navy, Coast Guard, and CAA officially adopted a manual of air traffic control procedures (the ANC manual) to standardize the operation of air traffic controller procedures.

June 1948—The Soviet Union stopped rail and road traffic between Berlin and the West. The Western powers began airlifting vital supplies to the beleaguered city. Controllers used radar to deliver aircraft to the runway at intervals as brief as one per minute. This rate is matched today only at the busiest U.S airports.

THE BUSY FIFTIES

October 15, 1951—The CAA put into operation the first very high frequency omnidirectional range (VOR) airways. Although 271 omniranges had already been commissioned in different parts of the United States, this marked the first designation of a chain of these ranges as a controlled airway.

January 7, 1952—The Washington Air Route Traffic Control Center inaugurated radar departure procedures. Use of radar for approach procedures began a few months later, on July 1, 1952.

December 21, 1955—The CAA and the U.S. Air Force announced an agreement under which the CAA would, for the first time, use U.S Air Force Defense Command radar for civil air traffic control.

1956—The Air Traffic Control Association (ATCA) was formed.

It was the first organization of professional civil controllers in the world. After a rocky beginning, it mushroomed to an unprecedented 9,000 members by 1960. The major thrust of the Association was toward early retirement and reclassification standards commensurate with a controller's responsibilities.

June 30, 1956—A TWA Constellation and a United Airlines DC-7 collided over the Grand Canyon, killing all 128 occupants. Congressional hearings probed the relationship between the tragedy and more general problems of airspace and air traffic control. This tragedy did more to stimulate action to modernize the air traffic control system than any other single occurrence.

Clifford Burton, FAA retired, told about a significant organizational action taken at that time.

"On July 1, 1956, the Office of Air Traffic Control was established. Selected to head the new office, as Director of Air Traffic Management, was the competent and highly articulate David D. Thomas, a former controller, with experience in budget and planning, then occupying the position of Deputy Director of Federal Airways. Dave Thomas had the unusual ability to wend his way through the mine fields of special interests, and congressional committees, without triggering off an explosion.

"The industry, as well as personnel of the Air Traffic and Communications Service, hailed his appointment. It was the beginning of a period of long and steady improvement. At long last, air traffic control now had an authoritative voice where it was needed.

"The decision to upgrade the ATC service and appoint Dave Thomas as Director was made by the CAA Administrator, Charles 'Chuck' Lowen. Unfortunately Mr. Lowen died a few months later and would never fully realize the impact his decision had on the future of Air Traffic Control." (*Journal of Air Traffic Control*, October-December 1985)

November 20, 1956—The CAA announced that a $9 million contract had been awarded for 23 long-range radars. The new radars were to be used primarily for en route air traffic control.

May 10, 1957—The Curtis Report recommended an independent federal aviation agency.

December 1, 1957—The CAA instituted a continental control area above 24,000 feet. Use of the air traffic control service was optional with the pilot in clear weather, but mandatory under conditions of restricted visibility. Previously, the CAA had offered such service only on the 100,000 miles of federal airways.

May 28, 1958—Positive control route segments were designated on portions of the airspace between 17,000 and 35,000 feet. Only instrument flight operations with prior approval of air traffic control were permitted in such space.

June 15, 1958—The CAA began using Greenwich Mean Time for all domestic air traffic control operations.

June 30, 1958—File computers were installed at the New York and Washington centers. Automatic strip printing machines were installed at four centers.

August 23, 1958—President Dwight D. Eisenhower signed into law the Federal Aviation Act establishing the Federal Aviation Agency (FAA). The FAA became an independent agency with complete responsibility for domestic airspace.

David D. Thomas was Director of Air Traffic Management. He described the situation this way.

"The era of The Federal Aviation Agency—November 1, 1958 to March 31, 1967—was one of the brightest in ATC history. The three Administrators of that era, General Elwood R. Quesada, Mr. Najeeb E. Halaby, and General William F. McKee, had the support and respect of their respective Presidents, the Congress, and FAA employees. Each one was different from the other two in many respects, but they had the common attribute of a burning desire to improve the system, and each left lasting imprints. There were excellent administrators before and after these three, but none before or since had the freedom to act that is granted to the head of an independent agency reporting directly to the President.

"The new agency now controlled the rules (formerly CAB), controlled R&D (formerly Airways Modernization Board, CAA, DOD), were free of a layer of ritualistic budget review (Commerce) and could determine policies based on aviation needs. The challenge was to use these new powers wisely." (*Journal of Air Traffic Control*, October-December 1985)

September 23, 1958—The CAA certified the Boeing 707 jet transport, the commercial version of the military C-135. The 707 ushered in the true jet age for mass air travel.

January 29, 1959—American Airlines began transcontinental jet airliner service. High-altitude radar advisory service was established using FAA-military radar teams, based at 17 military installations.

May 15, 1959—New procedures for allocating airspace to meet civil and military requirements became effective. In keeping with the authority vested solely in the FAA administrator, the revised rules superseded procedures under which airspace matters were processed through a joint civil-military coordination committee.

THE JET-AGE SIXTIES

August 25, 1960—The FAA commissioned the first improved airport surveillance radar (ASR-4) at Newark, New Jersey.

September 1960—The first airport surveillance detection equipment (ASDE) was commissioned at Newark.

September 11, 1961—The Project Beacon Report was issued, recommending modernization of the air traffic control system.

November 1, 1963—At New York's Idlewild Airport (later John F. Kennedy Airport), the FAA began operational tests of automatic broadcasts of routine, noncontrol information using the voice channel of the navigational aid serving the airport. It was named Automated Terminal Information Service, or ATIS.

December 1965—All previous aviation regulations were codified into a single body of rules, the Federal Aviation Regulations (FARs).

October 1966—President Lyndon B. Johnson signed the Department of Transportation Act. It brought the FAA into the newly created Department, and renamed it the Federal Aviation Administration.

July 19, 1968—This was civil aviation's "Black Friday." A total of 1,927 aircraft were delayed, some for as long as three hours, in New York.

December 30, 1968—The data-processing capability of the en route computer system went into operation at Jacksonville (Florida) Center.

January 15, 1969—The FAA adopted a method of regulating the flow of traffic into the metropolitan New York area. The new procedures took effect each time the delay forecast for IFR aircraft flying into New York exceeded one hour. When this happened, the flow of traffic into New York was limited by keeping New York-bound aircraft on the ground at the points of departure.

June 1, 1969—A rule limiting the number and type of IFR operations between the hours of 6:00 a.m. and midnight at Kennedy, La Guardia, Newark, O'Hare, and Washington National Airports went into effect.

December 30, 1969—The Boeing 747 with a passenger capacity of 490 was certified by the FAA. Pan American Airways scheduled daily 747 service between New York and London beginning on January 21; however, because of mechanical problems, the 747's inaugural flight did not depart until early on January 22. The delay was one of life's small blessings. A few hours before the scheduled departure time, the FAA released a series of complex, special separation minima based on the significantly increased threat of wake turbulence generated by the huge aircraft. The controllers had a hard time figuring out exactly what to do with the new procedures, but by the time the plane actually departed it was the only aircraft in the neighborhood and caused no problems.

CROWDED SKIES OF THE 1970s

March 19, 1970—Denver and Los Angeles computers linked up to establish air traffic control capability for coast-to-coast automated flight data processing.

April 27, 1970—The Central Flow Control Facility was established at FAA headquarters as a permanent part of the air traffic control system.

May 21, 1970—President Richard M. Nixon signed Public Law 91-258. It included Title I, the Airport and Airway Development Act of 1970; and Title II, the Airport and Airway Revenue Act of 1970. The new law gave the FAA dedicated tax revenues for the development of aviation facilities.

June 25, 1970—A major new safety rule established the concept of terminal control areas (TCAs). The TCAs were designed to minimize the possibilities of mid-air collisions near major airports.

October 4, 1971—The automated radar terminal system (ARTS) III was commissioned at Chicago's O'Hare Airport.

Calendar year 1973—All 20 air traffic control centers required full flight data processing, using the NAS Stage A automation program. By September, 10 centers were operational in radar data processing.

December 4, 1974—A TWA jet airliner on final approach to Washington's Dulles Airport crashed into Mount Weather, Virginia. The accident was attributed to the aircrew's misapplication of the instrument approach procedure.

August 3, 1975—ARTS III radar systems became operational in all 63 air traffic control terminals.

January 1976—Conflict Alert, a software program to give controllers a warning of loss of separation, became operational in the centers.

June 1, 1976—The air traffic control system received the first prototype microwave landing system (MLS).

October 3, 1977—The minimum safe altitude warning (MSAW) system became operational at all ARTS III locations. It was a terminal automation enhancement developed as a result of the 1974 TWA crash into Mount Weather.

July 30, 1979—The first direct access radar channel (DARC) became operational.

September 30, 1979—Contracts were let for $12.8 million to design computer systems for automating flight service stations.

1980s: CONTROLLER STRIKE AND MODERNIZATION

April 1980—Conflict Alert became operational at all ARTS III locations.

August 3, 1981—More than 11,000 controllers responded to a strike call by the Professional Air Traffic Controllers Organization (PATCO) Union and walked off the job.

August 5, 1981—The controllers failed to respond to an order by President Ronald Reagan to return to work and were fired.

January 28, 1982—The National Airspace System Plan was published. Usually referred to as the "Brown Book," it is a plan for the comprehensive modernization of the air traffic control system and has an estimated price tag of more than $11 billion.

1984—The Operational Error Detection Program became operational in air traffic control centers. This software patch automatically records loss of aircraft separation between aircraft.

July 1988—The IBM Corporation was awarded the contract for the advanced automation system.

CHAPTER TWELVE

OPERATIONAL ENVIRONS

AIRSPACE: THE CONTROLLER'S ENVIRONMENT

Airspace is the controller's basic operating arena. It is the place where aircraft operate and require control for the system to remain safe and efficient. Since regulated airspace is the environment in which the work is done, controllers must master the regulations in order to operate competently in the dynamic air traffic control environment.

The places in the United States where pilots can operate their aircraft without being involved with some form of air traffic control are becoming scarce. Alaska, of course, has plenty of airspace and fewer aircraft per cubic mile of air than do the states in the continental USA. In the contiguous 48 states and Hawaii and Puerto Rico, aircraft operations are more numerous and regulated, in the interests of safety and best use.

Viscount V.630, 1950. First turboprop civil transport inaugurated intermediate speed medium range commercial flight. Vickers-Armstrong Ltd.

FEDERAL AVIATION REGULATIONS

The Federal Aviation Act of 1958 empowered the FAA to promulgate certain regulations governing the safety of flight. Consequently, the Federal Aviation Regulations (FARs) have the force of law and are generally enforced by the agency through its licensing power.

In other words, pilots who violate a Federal Aviation Regulation can expect an FAA investigation of the violation. If warranted, the FAA may suspend their licenses for a specified time. The FAA also has the power to levy fines. Also, some violations of the Federal Aviation Regulations can be considered criminal offenses, such as flying under the influence of alcohol or using an aircraft to traffic in drugs.

Airspace regulations that we will review are established by the FARs, and pilots must comply with those regulations. It is, for instance, a violation of the FARs for a pilot, not in an emergency condition, to disregard an ATC clearance.

Airspace designations have developed through the years as reactions to circumstances. Improvements to the system have served the industry well. However, the cumulative result has been ever-increasing complexity that is often difficult to explain, even to pilots. Efforts to simplify the system began several years ago. They were based on work originally performed in Canada. When the study efforts are converted into simplified airspace designation, the result should be a great improvement. The new series of designations is expected to be in place by 1995.

Aircraft operate in airspace, and the FAA has instructors to teach operations within the national airspace. Three FAA instructors in Air Carrier Operations constituted the first all-female crew to fly the FAA's Boeing 727 aircraft in 1986. Debbie Dunfee (left) is the captain; Bonnie Kankaala (right) is the co-pilot, and Valerie Ticer (center) is the flight engineer. (FAA)

CONTROLLED AIRSPACE: AN OVERVIEW

In the United States, the term "controlled airspace" has a specific meaning. It means that controllers can issue an air traffic control clearance for the airspace, and that planes flying under instrument flight rules (IFR) in the airspace must have a clearance. Planes flying under visual flight rules (VFR) can fly in most controlled airspace without a clearance. However, they must observe the provisions of the regulations that specify safe operation of their aircraft. This is not the case in many other countries, which do not have as many pilots who want to fly visually.

Originally, controlled airspace was confined to the airways and the airspace needed for pilots to depart the airport and get to the airway. Then the system created the alternate airway. It was a route that diverged from the main airway then rejoined it at the next navigational aid. The airspace between these airways became controlled airspace. Alternate airways have been relegated to the archives, but primary routes have proliferated to such an extent that today, most of the eastern United States is controlled airspace. It is only in such areas as Nevada, New Mexico, and Arizona that pilots can find any large areas of uncontrolled airspace.

Air traffic control clearances are effective only in controlled airspace. Other airspace is considered "uncontrolled." Aircraft also can fly in uncontrolled airspace without contacting a controller. In such a situation, the pilot is essentially on his own, with the exception of the FAR that specifies altitudes to be flown, providing some separation from crossing and opposing aircraft.

Definitions of the several kinds of controlled airspace are depicted in this profile drawing. (FAA)

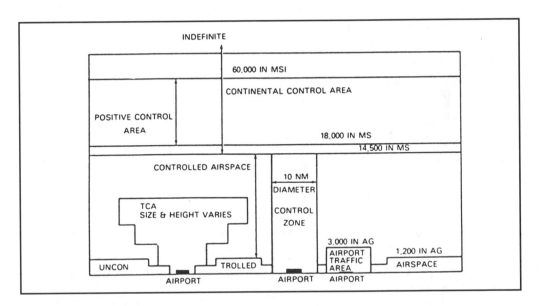

CONTROL ZONE

A control zone is a chunk of designated controlled airspace within a five statute-mile radius centered on a primary airport. Almost every distance in aviation is measured in nautical miles, except for control zones and airport visibilities, which are determined in statute miles. The airspace extends from the surface to the continental control area. It also includes extensions necessary to include instrument departure and arrival paths. To qualify for a control zone, an airport is required to have communications and weather observation reporting capabilities.

Transition Area. Aircraft use a transition area to get from the control zone to the airway. The base of a transition area is either 700 feet above ground level (AGL) when there is an instrument approach procedure involved, or 1,200 feet AGL otherwise.

AIRWAYS

Airways are specified routes through the sky, just as highways are designated routes over the ground. Airways have names, just as highways do. By using airways to specify flight routes, both pilots and controllers know precisely what the other person means.

Low-altitude Airways. These airways have defined dimensions. A radial from a VOR is established as the airway centerline. The airspace four miles either side of that radial is included. At a point 51 miles from the VOR the outer boundary of the airspace diverges at an angle of 4.5 degrees. These dimensions are based on the accuracy of the VOR signal and the likelihood of pilot and airborne equipment error.

The Continental Control Area. This area begins at 14,500 feet mean sea level (MSL), with the exception of certain special-use airspace, and extends upward without defined boundary (that is, above 14,500 feet, virtually all airspace is controlled).

Terminal Control Area (TCA). The TCA is often referred to as an upside down wedding cake, although recent designs are graphically more complex. The area is a controlled airspace around very active airports in which all aircraft are controlled. VFR aircraft have somewhat reduced separation criteria, but they are separated, nonetheless. The simplest TCAs are centered on a primary airport, with an inner ring that approximates the control zone. As the zone extends toward the outer boundary, successive rings comprise higher floors until reaching the edge, which is about 30 miles from the airport.

The early TCAs extended to 7,000 feet; however, the top altitudes in TCAs tend to be higher today. The TCA is designed to contain high-performance IFR aircraft until they reach a higher altitude. Pilots must adhere to an extensive set of requirements when operating in a TCA, and they are all discussed in the Airman's Information Manual (AIM).

Airport Radar Service Area (ARSA). This region usually consists of two rings centered on an airport. The inner ring has a radius of five nautical miles, and extends from the surface to 4,000 feet AGL. The outer ring has a 10 nautical mile-radius which starts at 1,200 feet AGL and extends to 4,000 feet AGL. In addition, an outer area, with a 20 nautical mile radius, begins at the lower limits of the facility's radar/radio coverage and extends to the ceiling of the approach control's delegated airspace. The operating requirements for ARSAs are also outlined in the AIM.

Positive Control Airspace (PCA). Although this term is not used in the FARs to define controlled airspace, regulations have imposed definite operational requirements for its use.

The low-altitude "Victor" airways extend up to but not including 18,000 feet MSL. Above 18,000 feet, pilots change their altimeters to the standard pressure setting of 29.92 and start using flight levels instead of altitudes. Once in PCA, pilots also begin navigating on jet airways. In PCA, aircraft are required to operate with air traffic control clearances, and they receive standard separation service from controllers.

Airport Traffic Area. This airspace belongs to the airport traffic control tower. It is defined by a five-statute-mile radius around the geographic center of the airport, extending to, but not including 3,000 feet AGL.

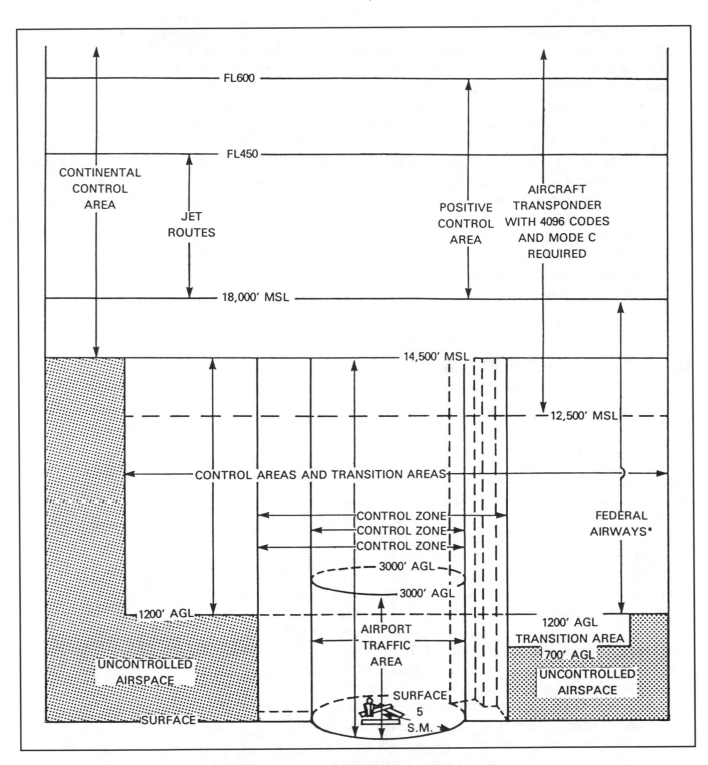

MILITARY REQUIREMENTS

The Federal Aviation Act of 1958 gave the FAA total and complete responsibility for navigable U.S. airspace. On a worldwide basis, this is a unique situation. In other countries, the military either takes predominance or shares joint responsibility. Here, the FAA does its best to accommodate the needs of the military, and it does so in part by establishing "special-use" airspace.

Special-use categories vary, but generally are designed to support the military mission while minimizing the impact on civilian traffic.

Prohibited areas, for example, define airspace where the flight of aircraft unattached to an operation is prohibited. These areas are very few in number. Most are connected with efforts to protect the President.

Restricted areas. Generally, the military has first call on airspace within restricted areas, but if units are not using the airspace, an ATC facility can direct aircraft through the area. Other special categories include warning areas, which are restricted areas in international waters; military operations areas (MOA); alert areas; and controlled firing areas. Each of these is less restrictive, but each necessitates caution on the part of pilots and controllers alike.

This introductory discussion on controlled airspace is an overview, and has avoided the various operating rules associated with particular airspace segments; for example, when distance measuring equipment or transponders are required. But, the overview is a start. Controllers must take it upon themselves to become familiar with the subject before they can consider themselves well-qualified in their profession.

TOMORROW'S AIRSPACE

When the new, "simplified" airspace system is fully developed and incorporated, airspace will be designated by letters. That should go into effect before 1995.

In brief:

Airspace A. For airspace at 18,000 feet and above; replaces positive control airspace.

Airspace B. Identical to current Terminal Control Areas.

Airspace C. Identical to current Airport Radar Service Areas, typically covering airspace from the surface to 4,000 feet above the surface.

Airspace D. This replaces current Airport Traffic Areas and Control Zones. All Class D airspace will have a common ceiling at 4,000 feet above the surface.

Airspace E. It replaces all other control airspace previously mentioned, including transition areas, controlled areas (airways), and the continental control area. It will be shown on charts. Covers the airspace between the surface and Flight Level 180, or the ceiling of uncontrolled airspace and FL 180.

Airspace G. Corresponds to uncontrolled airspace. Reaches from the ground to the indicated floor of controlled airspace.

The Canadian Government developed this new system several years ago, and it has worked quite well. In fact, the International Civil Aviation Organization (ICAO), a technical organization of the United Nations, recommends adopting the system worldwide. U.S. adoption will mark the first time that this country has moved in synchronization with the rest of the world in an airspace matter; quite an accomplishment, indeed.

GETTING OUT THE WORD

With a basic understanding of the system's evolution in hand, the following discussion will focus on the tools available to controllers and the environment in

Proposed Airspace Reclassification

FL 600

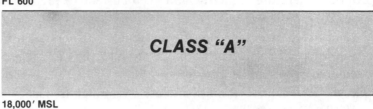

CLASS "A"

18,000' MSL

OPERATIONS:
- IFR Only
- Two-way Radio Communications
- ATC Clearance

SERVICE:
- Aircraft Separation
- Safety Advisories

CONFIGURATION:
Replaces Positive Control Area, FL180 to FL600.

OPERATIONS:
- IFR, VFR and SVFR Allowed
- Transponder and Mode C
- Two-way Radio Communications
- Student Pilot Certificate*
- ATC Clearance
- VFR—Clear of Clouds/3 Miles

SERVICE:
- Aircraft Separation
- Safety Advisories

CONFIGURATION:
Identical to Current TCA's, as Shown on Charts.

*Except at some airports, CFI endorsements.

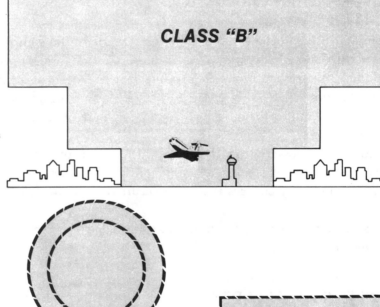

CLASS "B"

OPERATIONS:
- IFR, VFR and SVFR
- Two-way Radio Communications
- VFR—2000/1000/500 and 3 Miles

SERVICE:
- Aircraft Separation: IFR-IFR/SVFR/VFR
- Conflict Resolution: IFR-VFR
- Safety Advisories
- Traffic Advisories

CONFIGURATION:
Identical Current ARSA's, as Shown on Charts, Typically Surface to 4,000' AGL.

CLASS "C"

OPERATIONS:
- IFR, VFR and SVFR
- Two-way Radio Communications
- VFR—2000/1000/500 and 3 Miles

SERVICE:
- Aircraft Separation: IFR, IFR/SVFR
- Safety Advisories
- Traffic Advisories—Workload Permitting

CONFIGURATION:
Replaces Current ATA's and Control Zones (with Federal Towers), Common Ceiling at 4,000' AGL.

4000' AGL

CLASS "D"

which they operate. Keep in mind, however, that air traffic control functions in a dynamic setting in which things change everyday. Therefore, controllers must consult the appropriate literature regularly, and keep current to prepare for tomorrow's technology.

The FAA administers a comprehensive system of dispersing information, designed to ensure that all participants are operating by the same regulations and all know the required and essential information.

For example, the FAA cannot establish and use a very high frequency omnidirectional range (VOR) without telling pilots its location and assigned frequency. In another instance, a procedural change may be implemented that only interests controllers at particular facilities, but they may number 300, and all of them have to be informed before the change goes into effect. Most often, procedural changes are disseminated to pilots as well, through a facility letter.

THE AIRMAN'S INFORMATION MANUAL

The most comprehensive document describing current air traffic control procedures for use in the national airspace system is the Airman's Information Manual (AIM). It is sold by subscription from the Superintendent of Documents, U.S. Government Printing Office. The AIM is updated by the FAA on a regular basis every 112 days during the year. It is the official guide to basic flight information and air traffic control procedures.

The Pilot/Controller Glossary from the AIM is included in Appendix III of this book. However, this Appendix is not a substitute for the most recent AIM publication, which will include any changes that have occurred since the publication of this book.

The following material reviews parts of the air traffic control system that, generally, are less likely to change.

AERONAUTICAL CHARTS

The National Ocean Service, a part of the Commerce Department, produces a series of aeronautical charts (based on information furnished by the FAA) designed for individual users. They provide the official notification of navigational changes to the system, and include information on topographical features, hazards and obstructions, navigational aids and routes, designated airspace, and airports. Charts are described in detail in Chapter 14.

All changes to charts are made on one Thursday a month. This date, called an "airac date," is keyed to a 28-day cycle, based on an international standard. Thus, all significant changes involving standards go into effect on the same day of the month around the world. This procedure is essential since the U.S. air traffic control system interfaces with others worldwide. The United States actually uses a 56-day cycle to publish its charts, skipping every other airac date to reduce the cost of producing the charts.

NOTICES TO AIRMEN

Occasionally, the system undergoes immediate or unexpected changes. For example, a VOR might go out of service for an extended period for maintenance reasons. The FAA disseminates this information using the "notices to airmen" (NOTAMs) system. Pilots are required to check current NOTAMs prior to their departure as part of their flight planning activity.

DECISION-MAKING

Most major changes to the system are developed in consultation with system users. An informal infrastructure of aviation user interests has grown up during the years. This grouping of interests provides the FAA with advice and counsel (sometimes more than is desired) on the health of the system. These interests are often referred to as "the alphabet groups."

The groups include:

Air Traffic Control Association (ATCA), concerned with continuing safety, reliability, and efficiency of the air traffic control system,

Air Transport Association (ATA), a grouping of many of the domestic airlines,

Airline Pilots Association (ALPA) and Allied Pilots Association (APA), whose members are most of the airline pilots in the United States,

Aircraft Owners and Pilots Association (AOPA), speaking for general aviation pilots,

National Business Aircraft Association (NBAA), which represents the corporate aircraft operations.

Several other aviation interest groups contribute to operational discussions, but these are the major players involved. A more comprehensive listing of aviation-related organizations is in Appendix IV.

When the FAA contemplates a major airspace or procedural change, it gathers a group of controllers to develop the plan and asks for representatives from the alphabet groups to either participate in project development or to offer briefings on a frequent basis as work progresses. When the plan is formulated, the pilots are informed of impending changes. No decisions are made in a vacuum; very few things are dictated from Washington.

deHavilland D.H.106 Comet I, 1952.First commercially operated turbojet civil transport. Prototype first flew Jul. 27, 1949. deHavilland Aircraft Co., Ltd.

AIR TRAFFIC PROCEDURES ADVISORY COMMITTEE

The Air Traffic Procedures Advisory Committee (ATPAC) is a standing group that meets each quarter to discuss problems (great and small) in the system, and to suggest remedies. Senior air traffic officials from the FAA meet with industry representatives frequently to answer questions and to hear views on how the system is working. Although these representatives often advance parochial views—lobbying for improvements that would benefit their constituency, perhaps at the expense of other users of the system—the FAA remains open and responsive to their ideas. The Administration's job is to balance the benefits and the potential penalties and come up with the best solution for all users, including the passengers.

The challenge for controllers is to keep up with the changes, to stay informed on the work that is being done, and to participate in developing improvements to the overall system. Air traffic officials in Washington rely heavily on the expertise of working controllers to bring positive change to the system.

CHAPTER THIRTEEN

TOOLS OF THE TRADE

EQUIPMENT FOR CONTROLLERS

Bell Small Rocket Lift Device (SRLD), 1961. First rocket belt, world's smallest human-flight apparatus. Bell Aircraft Corp.

Much of the hardware used by controllers has been mentioned in previous chapters. This chapter offers some background on the tools themselves. It is not a technical description of how systems work; rather, it will help readers become familiar with some of the technical aspects that controllers will learn during training.

EQUIPMENT IN THE TOWER

Windows—The most important tool in the tower is the array of windows encircling it. Controllers are supposed to look out the tower windows to service aircraft within visual range, and to observe what is happening on the ground and in the air within their domain. But often, poor visibility impairs their view. Then, radar presentations extend the controller's "eyesight."

Flight Strip Printer and Computer Input Device (Interfaced with Center Computer)—Aircraft en route clearances are printed automatically on flight strips several minutes before estimated departure times, so the clearance delivery controller has the strip and its information on hand when pilots call.

Telephone Lines—Several lines are available at each position, depending upon requirements. For example, the flight data controller can call the center flight data operator to inquire about a specific aircraft's clearance. The local controller has a line to coordinate operations with the radar departure controller. The supervisor has a line to the airport operations people in case questions arise about the airport itself.

Controllers also have access to a red-colored telephone that serves as a hot line to airport emergency crews. The tower alerts the fire and rescue crews when an aircraft is in trouble and becomes a focal point for action.

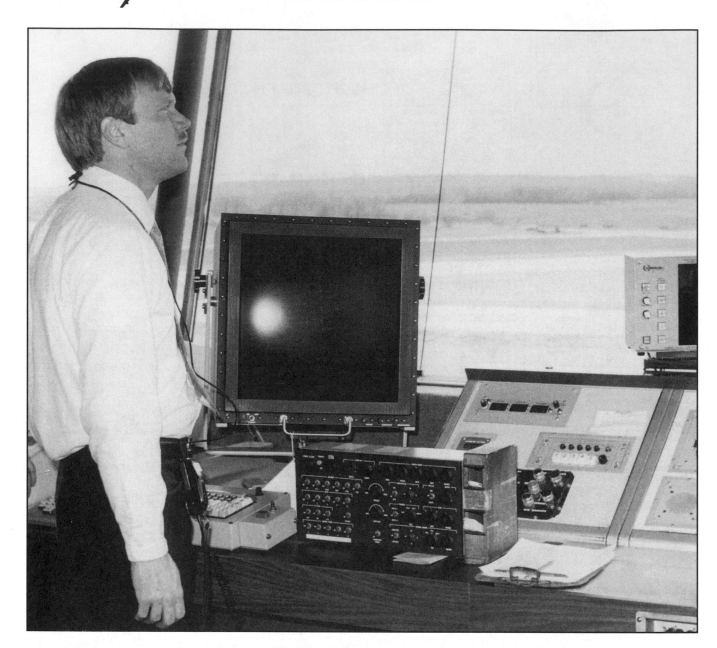

Radio Frequencies—The clearance delivery, ground, and local controllers each have a very-high frequency (VHF) radio channel at their disposal. They may share one or two ultra-high frequency (UHF) channels. Frequencies in the VHF band range from 30 to 300 MHz. Navigational aids such as VORs use frequencies between 108 to 118 MHz. Frequencies between 118 and 136 MHz are used for civil air-to-ground voice communications. The UHF band is between 300 and 3,000 MHz, and is used for military air-to-ground voice communications. In some instances it may dip as low as 225 MHz and still be called UHF. The UHF emergency channel is 243.0 MHz. The VHF emergency channel is 121.5 MHz.

Basic tools for a tower controller range from clear windows to keyboard input devices, radios and telephones and the switches to operate on several of each, flight progress strips, and a clear space to operate. (FAA)

Wind Speed and Direction Indicators and Altimeter Setting Indicator—Ground and local controllers each have these indicators. The altimeter setting indicator works differently from an aircraft's altimeter because the height of the tower is fixed. The indicator is based on that altitude setting. Pilots, on the other hand, who fly at varying altitudes, adjust their pressure altimeters based on barometric pressure readings for variations in existing atmospheric pressure or to the standard altimeter setting (29.92).

Runway Visual Range (RVR) Indicators—Many towers have one or more RVRs. The RVR is a transmissometer located at the approach end of the runway. It measures the distance that can be seen down the runway. The readings are calculated in hundreds of feet with a maximum reading of 6,000 feet. Some airports install transmissometers at both ends of the runway. Occasionally, under poor conditions such as patchy fog, it is necessary for controllers to give pilots the roll-out RVR; that is, the distance they can see as their aircraft rolls down the runway after landing.

The Low-Level Wind Shear Alert System (LLWAS)—This relatively new piece of equipment consists of five wind measuring stations. Four are located on the airport perimeters and one at midfield. The system detects variations in wind direction and speed, providing a warning of a possible wind shear. A wind shear is a sudden change of wind direction and speed which, at low altitudes, can be extremely hazardous to an aircraft. Several major airline accidents have been attributed to wind shears.

The low level wind shear phenomenon can be extremely hazardous to unwarned aircraft. Four wind measuring stations on the airport perimeter and one at midfield automatically transmit wind readings into the Low Level Wind Shear Alert System (LLWAS) in the tower. In this situation, the strong and variable wind directions and speeds alert tower controllers to potential wind shear problems. (FAA)

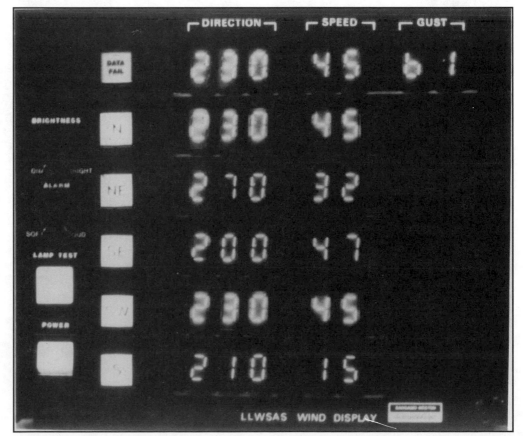

Navigational Aids—The tower also monitors the operation of significant navigational aids. For example, if the instrument landing system (ILS) at the airport fails for some reason, an alarm sounds in the tower, signaling the local controller to advise pilots of the problem. The pilots will ascertain the situation from their own instruments, but the alert assists in a coordinated recovery, with both pilots and controllers cooperating.

Brite Display—A video presentation of the local radar situation, the display usually extends to a 15- or 20-mile radius. It enables the local controller to ensure separation between aircraft, both arrivals and departures, close to the airport.

Airport Surface Detection Equipment (ASDE)—Some towers also employ ASDEs. They are radars that detect objects below the level of the tower. The ASDE is used during periods of reduced visibility when controllers cannot see the aircraft outside their windows.

Lighting Panels—These panels allow controllers to turn on taxiway lights, runway lights, approach lights, and other airport lighting systems. The runway lights and the approach lights usually have several intensity settings to be used under various visibility conditions.

Tower controller at Patrick Henry Airport, Virginia, working with airmen over the radio. Clear, uncluttered radio conversations are essential for smooth air operations. (FAA)

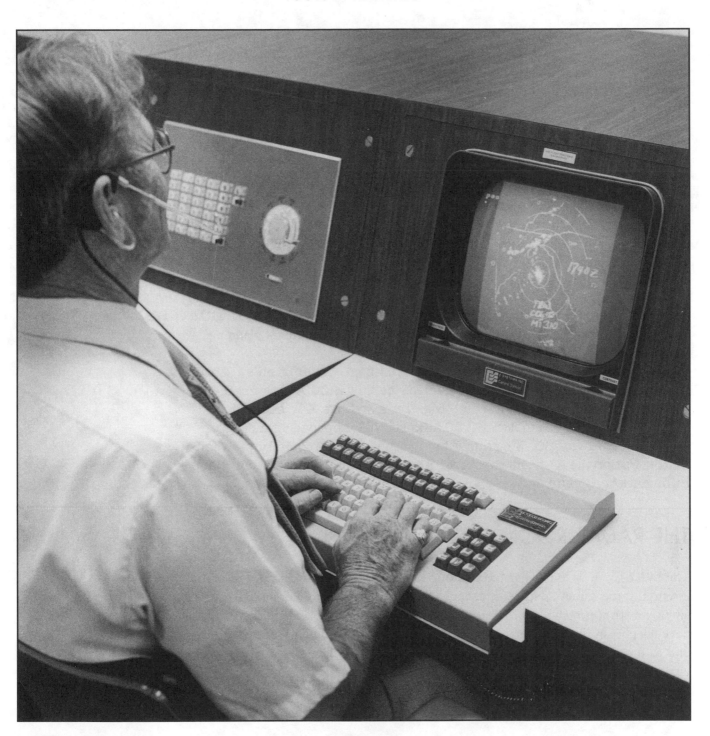

Specialist in a Flight Service Station calls up current weather display onto the screen and conveys the information in a preflight briefing to an interested pilot over the radio via his headset. (E-Systems via FAA)

Light Guns—Towers still are equipped with red, green, and white light guns for use in the event of an aircraft radio failure. Each color has a defined meaning. Generally speaking, green indicates go, red means stop, and white conveys caution. Since radio failures happen rarely these days, most pilots and controllers may need to be reminded of the exact meanings. The military still uses flares for the same purpose on some airfields, but the FAA does not.

National Weather Service Telewriter or Video Hookup—The meteorological information fed to tower controllers includes cloud heights, visibility, significant weather (such as rain, snow, or fog), wind speed and direction, and the altimeter setting. As noted previously, controllers have separate wind and altimeter indicators that are used directly. If the visibility is reduced below three miles, the tower controller assumes responsibility for making the official visibility observation as well. The only exception to this procedure is when, on rare occasions, the tower is actually above a fog layer. It can be quite disconcerting for controllers to have a clear sky above and unrestricted forward visibility when they themselves cannot see the ground because of fog.

Automated Terminal Information Service (ATIS)—This is a simple, continuous-loop tape recorder. It broadcasts a message over an assigned VHF frequency. The message tells pertinent information such as departure and arrival runways, wind speed and other essentials. It is updated every hour. Use of the ATIS message saves controllers from having to repeat the information to every pilot. Broadcasting the ATIS on a separate frequency removes clutter from the controller frequencies.

Here is an example of an actual ATIS broadcast for Washington National Airport. Pilots can hear the information by tuning to the frequency of 132.65 MHz. The ATIS is also available over the telephone for pilots' use in preflight planning.

Washington National information November. Washington's 1150Z observation. 1,200 scattered, measured ceiling 3,300 broken, 8,000 overcast. Visibility 6, light rain, fog. Temperature 41, dewpoint 41. Wind 050 at 12. Altimeter 30.00. Expect ILS approach landing and departing Runway 36. Migratory bird activity in the vicinity of Washington National has been reported. Advise on initial contact you have information November.

THE RADAR ROOM

The radar room is somewhat more exotic looking than the tower cab, but offers essentially the same equipment, except for windows. Controllers in this setting employ a strip printer for information about arriving and departing aircraft. They have telephones linked to the tower, to the center, to the National Weather Service, and to other airport operations; dedicated VHF bands and the shared UHF band emergency frequencies; wind indicators; the altimeter setting; the RVR indicator; and current weather information hookups. The major difference is the presence of the radar scopes.

Terminal Radar—This system has a range of 60 nautical miles and completes an antenna rotation (that is, it updates the picture) about every five seconds.

Automated Radar Terminal System (ARTS) III—Major facilities employ the ARTS III. It uses primary radar returns created by bouncing the radar signal off the surface of the aircraft, and secondary radar signals generated by a transponder in the aircraft. The prototype system was ARTS I, which was tested in Atlanta and New York. The first operational system was ARTS III, which went to 63 facilities. A less sophisticated system was called ARTS II and was the third system to go operational. It went to less active facilities.

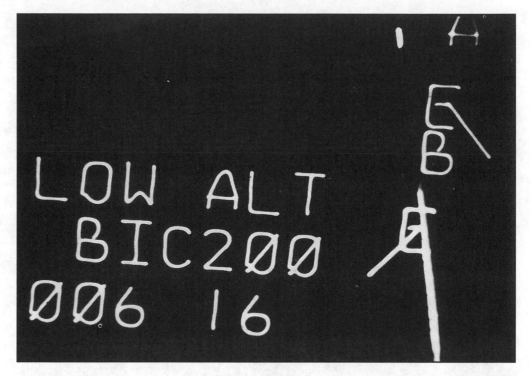

A data block on the display at the Jacksonville ARTCC shows the aircraft identity (Pan American flight 987), altitude (33,000 feet), and that the aircraft is equipped with an automatic altitude-reporting unit operating on Mode C. (FAA)

Transponder and Interrogator—The transponder is the part of the radar system carried on board the aircraft. The other half is an interrogator, which is usually attached to the radar antenna on the ground. The ground equipment interrogates the transponder on board the aircraft, which responds with a signal that is set to one of 4,096 possible codes. For example, if a pilot is told to dial in (squawk) code 2016 on his transponder, the equipment will reply to the interrogator with a signal that will be interpreted as 2016. In most operational transponders, part of the signal to the ground will include the aircraft's altitude in hundreds of feet as well.

Computer Data Blocks—The target derived from the transponder signal overlies the primary target so that they are almost indistinguishable. The computer identifies the discrete transponder code 2016 as one assigned to a specific aircraft, say American 124, and generates a data block for AA124. The aircraft's position is identified by a position symbol indicating which controller is working the plane. A short leader line connects the data block with the position symbol. The full data block contains the aircraft identification, its altitude, and its ground speed, which is calculated by the computer based on target movement.

Trackball ("Slewball")—Controllers have a computer input device called a trackball (nicknamed "slew ball") at each console. The trackball is a plastic sphere that spins beneath the controller's fingers. Manipulating the trackball moves a cursor on the display screen to the position the controller designates. This allows controllers to communicate with the computer. The ball-like device is capable of rotating in any direction.

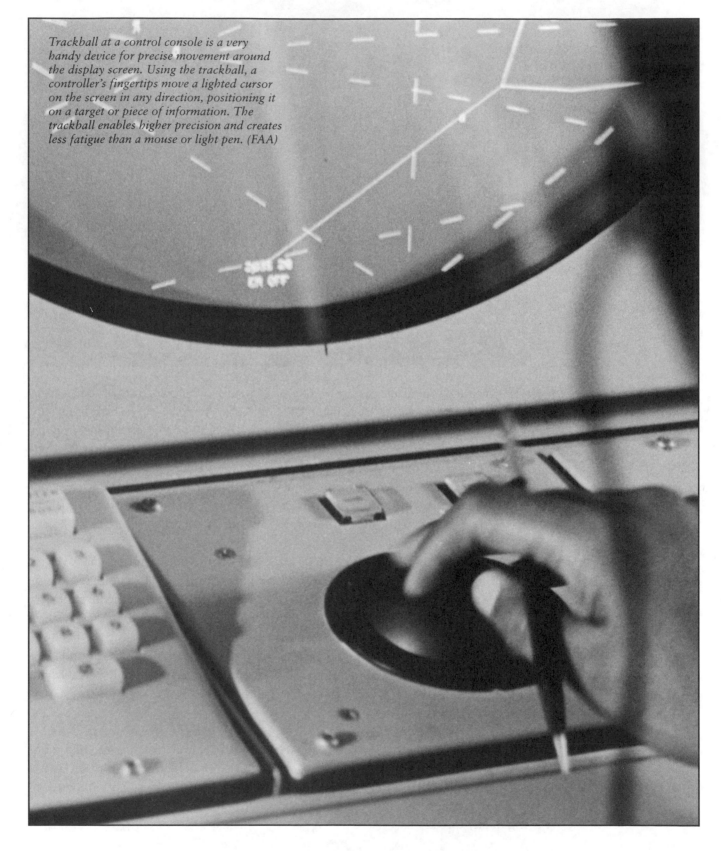

Trackball at a control console is a very handy device for precise movement around the display screen. Using the trackball, a controller's fingertips move a lighted cursor on the screen in any direction, positioning it on a target or piece of information. The trackball enables higher precision and creates less fatigue than a mouse or light pen. (FAA)

The trackball is similar to the "mouse" input device, familiar to many computer users. Rotating the trackball moves the cursor on the radar scope to a target or piece of information the controller wants to identify to the computer. This is one of several ways that information is sent into the computer. Data also can be identified by using the aircraft's identification number or the computer track number in the data block.

A keypad is also at each control position for controllers to use to key information into the computer system.

When a departure aircraft reaches a predetermined point after takeoff the computer initiates an automatic handoff to the center. When the handoff is accepted by the center computer and control of the aircraft is turned over to the next facility, the data block drops off the departure scope. Inbound aircraft are handed off to the approach controller from the center in a similar fashion.

ARTS III Software—The ARTS III software incorporates two significant enhancements. The first is conflict alert. It warns the controller that aircraft are about to lose separation; that is, move too close to each other. In the terminal area, aircraft operate so closely together that the parameters for this software program are set virtually at the minimum. Therefore, when the alert goes off, it is usually too late to maintain the legal separation, but the warning allows sufficient time for controllers to avert a potentially dangerous situation.

The second enhancement to the ARTS III software is the minimum safe altitude warning (MSAW) system. It sounds an alarm when the aircraft descends below the minimum safe altitude for the terrain in question. The crash of TWA mentioned in Chapter 11 was caused by the pilot's mistaken impression that when cleared for the approach to Dulles Airport it was all right to descend to the initial approach altitude. The pilot should have followed the vertical profile on the printed approach diagram for Washington Dulles. That would have kept the aircraft above Mount Weather. The controller at Dulles did not notice the airplane's excessive descent and the aircraft crashed into the mountain, claiming 92 lives. The incident generated the requirement for the MSAW as well as the pilot-controller glossary (included in Appendix III). The glossary is designed to ensure that both pilots and controllers are interpreting operating terms in the same way.

Video Map—An integral part of any terminal radar system is the video map. It features a seemingly incomprehensible series of solid, dashed, and curved lines, boxes, and circles. Each symbol means something to the controller. After a little orientation, it is possible to identify the primary and secondary airports, the runway center lines, and the aids to navigation serving the airport and the local area. Also seen are the boundary of the facility's airspace and subdivisions of that airspace, which play a part in the segregation of traffic, as well as prominent landmarks used as reporting points by visual flight rules (VFR) aircraft. The video map seems as real to controllers as the picture they see out of their windows.

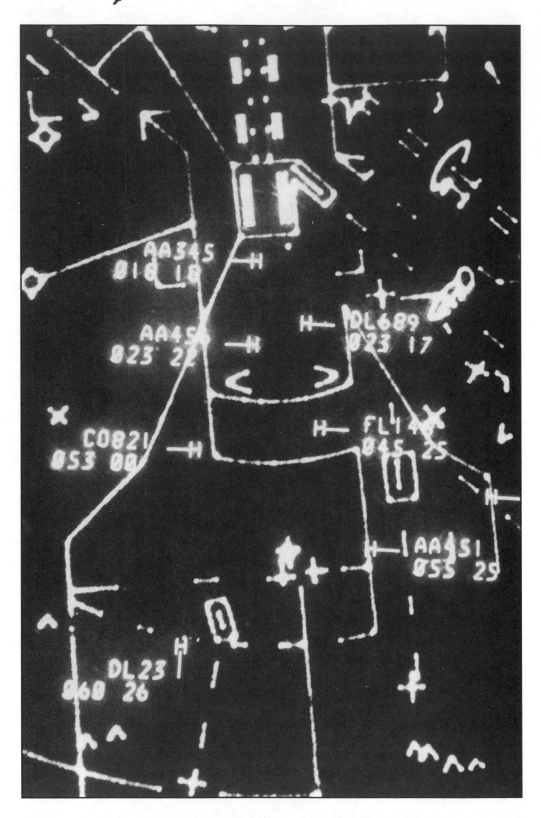

Progression of aircraft taking off from Dallas-Fort Worth can be seen clearly in this photo of an ARTS III scope. On the left, Continental Flight 821 is at 5300 feet; behind it, American 456 is climbing out at 2300 feet; and American 345 is just taking off at 1800 feet.

By using modular components such as common display screens, consoles, and input devices, different functions can be performed by changing the software involved. This two-screen model was created by E-Systems to demonstrate the concept. (E-Systems via FAA)

THE CONTROL ROOM

The control room will likely house other aids, such as charts mounted above the radar positions; a status board which displays the aids to navigation and indicates whether or not they are operating normally; and, of course, the flight strips. Controllers have been using strips since 1936. Efforts to develop an adequate replacement for the strips have met with little or no success. One reason, perhaps, is the concern that if the computer shuts down suddenly and all of the electronically provided information disappears, at least the strips will provide a reminder of which airplanes are being worked and where they are headed. The system is something of a security blanket for controllers.

Air Traffic Control Specialist Larry Kempton has a clear view of the various airways around Fort Worth (shown in straight lines on the scope). Distances from the airport are depicted by dashed circles. A few aircraft data blocks can be seen on his scope. (FAA photo by S. Michael McKean.)

EQUIPMENT AT THE CENTER

Centers have a similar operational setup to terminals, but on a much larger scale. They have phone lines to facilities in their area and in adjacent areas; to adjacent centers; between sectors in the facility; and to the Traffic Management Unit, or "Flow Control," in Washington, D.C. The individual control position has every line needed, and maybe a few extra. Each control position has radios for communication on the VHF band and UHF band.

Some centers have added a traffic position controller, who monitors the control position and assists the radar controller with any necessary coordination. In addition, this controller monitors the traffic situation for potential conflicts. The position has a telephone and radio capability. In busy periods, a sector may have a third controller to assist with the flight data. The third position has a telephone but no radio capability.

THE CENTER COMPUTER

This computer is the focal point of the center's ATC system. Originally, the National Air Space (NAS) Stage A 9020 system comprised an array of IBM computers. It was installed in centers during the 1970s. It served well for nearly 15 years, but began to show its age by the time the new Host computer was installed. The Host is a larger, faster, and more capable computer. It is an interim replacement and a building block for the advanced automation system that is approaching. The changeover to the Host system did not alter the way controllers in any of the 20 centers performed their duties. It has ensured a smooth transition to the future system now being developed.

Flight plans for aircraft operating within the center area come to the center computer. The center then generates clearances for each and sends them back to the originating terminal. The computer creates appropriate flight progress strips for the sectors which the aircraft will fly through and informs the adjacent center of the proposed flight. When the aircraft is airborne, the computer updates the estimated flight times, if necessary, and provides current information for all sectors where required.

The computer makes no decisions on separating aircraft; these are made by controllers. A conflict alert system gives the center controller a little more time to take corrective action than in the terminal, but these controllers have no device for resolving conflicts.

THE OPERATIONAL ERROR DETECTION PATCH (OEDP)

Affectionately called the "snitch patch" by some controllers, the OEDP "blows the whistle" when a controller has lost the required minimum separation between two aircraft. In essence, it is the automatic detection of an operational error. When OEDP first became operational in 1984-85, the number of reported errors increased significantly because the program was capable of detecting 4.9-mile separations when the stated requirement is five miles. Controllers could not discern the one-tenth-of-a-mile loss of separation with the naked eye, so they became more conservative, increasing the usual separation to seven miles.

Initially, controllers did not greet the OEDP with a great deal of enthusiasm. But now that they have grown used to it and the system is accommodating slightly increased distances between aircraft, most everyone agrees that the "snitch patch" has made the system safer.

PROCESSING INFORMATION

The center automation system is slightly different from the terminal's system when it comes to radar data processing. The center radar display is entirely digitized. The center computer transforms the primary radar return into a digital signal for display on the controller's scope. Consequently, the center scope can be adjusted to display only those aircraft known to be in the altitude levels controlled by the sector and those whose altitude is unknown. This clears clutter off the screen. The center controller's scope displays a data block connected to the radar target, which includes aircraft identification and altitude. The controller operates a computer input device as well as a trackball. A small cathode ray tube located to the side of the scope displays information such as the weather at specific airports, and beacon codes that can be assigned to an aircraft.

Center controllers use facilities located many miles from the center building to control their aircraft. Remote communication air-to-ground (RCAG) facilities use microwave links to get the signal to controllers. Center radar equipment has a 200-mile radius and an antenna rotation cycle of 10-12 seconds. Today, most centers have access to two or more radars covering much of the same airspace. The computer takes the best target presentation from the available sources and displays it on the controller's scope (a process called "mosaicking"). The culmination of these technological advances is that center controllers routinely "see" and control aircraft flying through the air hundreds of miles from the center building.

Controllers' work spaces are compact and well-equipped. But in exercising the air traffic control function, they project their minds and voices far out of the space into the four-dimensional situation of aircraft in flight. (FAA)

Typical displays and equipment at a work position for a specialist operating at an Automated Flight Service Station. Four-color weather graphic is above, and lower screen conveys weather observations for several reporting points in the region. (E-Systems via FAA)

Strip printers and strip bays are sprinkled liberally throughout center facilities. Charts placed above each position show specific areas of responsibility.

Each center has a meteorologist on duty to inform controllers about significant weather in their area. Facilities also have their own traffic management unit, which coordinates with the Washington, D.C. facility to ensure the optimum flow of traffic into sectors.

Centers may field an impressive array of lights, buzzers, voice calls, scopes, telephones, strip bays, and teletypes. However, the key ingredient is the human one, the controller. Controllers work with the pilots of aircraft. A partner in an adjacent sector will help a fellow controller in a bind, or a supervisor will get somebody to share the workload, and will impose restrictions to help moderate the number of aircraft coming into an overloaded controller's airspace. These are the human aspects of the tools of the trade.

Boeing 707-120, 1957. Civil production prototype flew Dec. 20. PanAm began commercial service New York-Paris, Oct. 26, 1958. Boeing Aircraft Co.

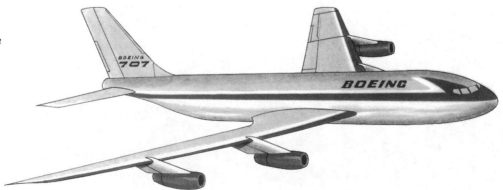

CHAPTER FOURTEEN

AERONAUTICAL INFORMATION SOURCES

CURRENT INFORMATION IS ESSENTIAL

North American X-15, 1967. World's fastest airplane. Holds absolute speed record of Mach 6.72, set on Oct. 3, 1967. North American.

A ir traffic controllers must be able to get and use all available aeronautical information that is pertinent to the area in which they work. Information is vital to their jobs, just as it is essential to pilots operating aircraft. But information by itself is not useful unless it is up to date. Also, information should be available in formats that are easy to use. The Federal Aviation Administration spends millions of dollars each year to produce information resources for controllers, pilots, and other users of the national airspace.

Consider the size of the aviation interests and activities in the United States. Nearly 17,000 airports are dotted across the country (not counting assorted rural grass strips). Of those, nearly 3,500 are included in the FAA's national plan for integrating airport systems. Approximately 400 of those airports operate FAA-regulated towers, which handle more than 64 million landings and takeoffs each year.

As for pilots, 715,800 are licensed in the U.S., and 276,000 of them are instrument-rated. Student pilots number nearly 130,000, and 60,000 pilots are certified instructors.

The number of general aviation aircraft in the United States is nearly 217,000, of which 4,000 are jet propelled and 7,100 are rotary wing (helicopters). More than 35,000 aircraft are classified as being used for business purposes, 123,000 are designated for personal flying use, and 5,600 are certified as air carriers. According to FAA estimates, general aviation aircraft alone fly more than 34 million hours a year.

The number of passengers carried by the airlines continues to zoom upward. The FAA estimates that more than 483 million persons will be carried as passengers on the airlines and commuter carriers this year. That's almost twice as many as in 1980.

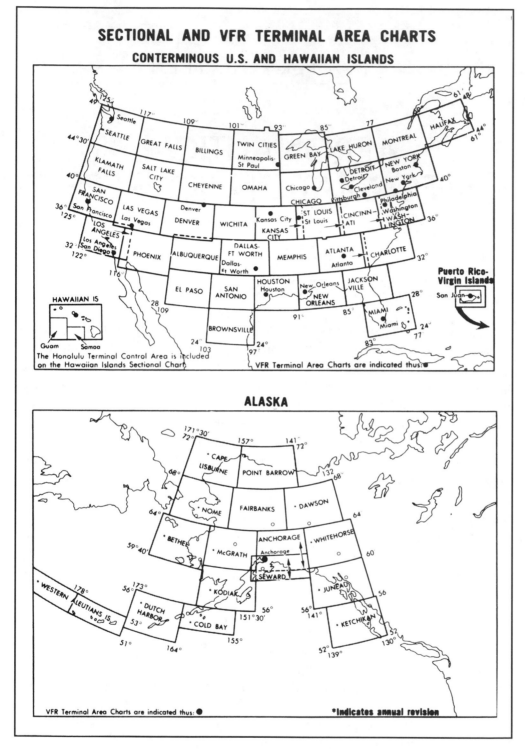

Fewer than 30 Sectional Aeronautical Charts (Sectionals) are required to cover the entire 48 contiguous states. Terminals having their own Terminal Area Charts (TCA) are denoted with a bullet.

Given those numbers, it is easy to see why the FAA and its controllers need accurate and current information. Basic regulatory information is carried in the Federal Aviation Regulations (FARs), already described. Pilots and controllers need to know the information in the FARs as a foundation for operating. For flight operations, however, pilots need information about the countryside, the airports, navigational aids, and other essentials. For a person driving cross-country in his car, that information requirement is satisfied by a highway map. For pilots and controllers, aeronautical charts are the aviation counterpart to the highway map.

AERONAUTICAL CHARTS

Pilots rely upon several different types of charts. Each is designed for specific purposes and users. On some flights, pilots may refer to more than one type of chart or to more than one chart in a series. The choice of charts and related publications is dictated by the needs of a particular flight. Pilots in rural areas who do not plan to fly into busy metropolitan airports need only the most basic charts. However, pilots of business jets such as the Gulfstream G-IV on the cross-country flight depicted earlier, need many more charts and publications to operate efficiently and safely.

The following discussion provides a general description of the charts available. Controllers as well as pilots should become familiar with these charts and how to interpret the invaluable information they offer.

One might think that controllers will not need the information contained in these publications. But the more information that controllers have at their fingertips, the better they can perform their special jobs. The controller at Sioux City working with the crew of United 232 in their emergency used his knowledge of the charts and the surrounding terrain throughout that tense time. He was able to offer choices to the crew, such as airports and a four-lane highway; he also pointed out potential obstructions on their final flight path. Controllers never know what information they will need; so they need to know where to look for options and answers before an emergency arises.

SECTIONAL CHARTS AND VFR TERMINAL AREA CHARTS

Sectional charts are designed for the visual navigation of slow and medium-speed aircraft. The 38 sectional charts cover the entire United States. Their scale is fairly large, 1:500,000. That is, one inch on the chart equals 500,000 inches (6.86 nautical miles) on the ground. The VFR terminal area charts (TCA charts) are at even larger scale, 1:250,000. At that scale, one inch on the chart equals 3.43 nautical miles on the ground.

Since the sectional and TCA charts are used for visual navigation, they are designed to highlight information a pilot will see from an aircraft. Topographic information on the charts portrays the terrain and elevations. Also highlighted are visual checkpoints used for VFR flight. They include populated places; drainage such as lakes, rivers, and creeks; roads and railroads; and other distinctive landmarks.

Of course, airports are highlighted. Essential information about each airport is shown next to its symbol, so a pilot has immediate ready reference to the information. The sectional and TCA charts also depict visual and radio aids to navigation, controlled airspace, restricted areas, obstructions and other related data. Different colors highlight essential information such as boundaries of Terminal Control Areas.

Sectional charts are drawn at a scale of 1:500,000. Information essential for pilotage under visual flight rules (VFR) is highlighted. Airport runway patterns are shown. In this extract from the Washington (DC) sectional chart, Washington National Airport (location identifier "DCA") is in the center. Parallel runways at Washington Dulles (IAD) and Andrews AFB (ADW) are clear. Legend provides users with a clear reference on symbols used. NOTE: This extract is not to be used for navigation.

Key information can be spotted quickly on the extract of the Washington (D.C.) sectional chart, even on the black and white extract pictured here. The Potomac River flows past Washington National Airport, then widens as it flows southward into Chesapeake Bay. Immediately north of the symbol for Washington National (which shows the runway pattern), appears an "H" inside a circle. That is the Pentagon Heliport, operated by the U.S. Army. Just above the Pentagon Heliport and across the Potomac, the Prohibited Area P-56 is marked. P-56 is actually two areas close to each other. The rectangular part, oriented east-west, includes the U.S. Capitol, the Mall, and the White House. One mile north and slightly west is the circular part of P-56, encompassing the Naval Observatory and the Vice President's mansion on the observatory grounds.

TCA CHARTS AT LARGER SCALE

Terminal Control Area charts are at twice the scale of sectional charts so that more detail may be included. That is because the pilots using them are flying in a Terminal Control Area, with its high density of aircraft traffic.

Compare the presentation of information on the Washington (D.C.) TCA chart with the sectional chart of the same area. Now the finer details of topography, obstacles, road networks, and navigational aids are spotted more easily because they appear at twice the scale. Note the Prohibited Area P-56 and the Pentagon Heliport, and how easily they are perceived. Also see how obstacles such as radio station broadcast towers are highlighted. The towers north and west of Prohibited Area P-56 all protrude into the sky to the same elevation above mean sea level (MSL), 1,049 feet. That elevation is proclaimed in bold type, hard to miss. Beneath the MSL altitude the actual height of each tower above ground level is stated in parentheses. One tower is 809 feet above ground level, while others rise to 705 and 761 feet.

Speaking of obstacles to flight, pick out the Washington Monument, whose tip rises 596 feet above mean sea level. Its height above the ground is 555 feet; therefore, the gentle hill on which it is erected must be 41 feet above mean sea level.

In planning a flight under visual flight rules, a pilot will draw the route on a sectional chart, and then devote careful study to the information presented on it. He benefits from careful study of the charts by identifying obstacles, locating potential emergency landing sites, highlighting navigational aids, and becoming familiar with all aspects of the flight route before flying it.

To use these charts, knowledge of basic map reading skills and symbols is helpful. Each chart has a very comprehensive legend, which explains the symbols used on it.

Information in the legend of these VFR charts constitutes a handy refresher in map reading, as well as being a useful source of information on airports, aids to navigation, and airspace restrictions. The information is presented from the viewpoint of a pilot of a fairly slow-flying aircraft. For example, power lines are shown. Although a pilot's eyesight will not perceive the power cables, the cleared area that marks their right of way and the pylons holding them up are spotted quickly from the air and are useful visual aids to navigation. Race tracks, with their distinctive oval shape, are also spotted easily from the air.

The scale for charts for use in Terminal Control Areas (TCA) is 1:250,000, twice as large as for sectionals. In this extract from the Washington (DC) TCA chart, more detail of the topography, obstacles, and restricted and prohibited areas can be seen. Prohibited Area P-56 covers the U.S. Capitol, White House, and the circular area is around the Naval Observatory. Not to be used for navigation.

Note the different types of airport symbols and the wealth of airport data available on the legend of a Sectional Aeronautical Chart. The reference material is handy and available when a pilot needs to consult it.

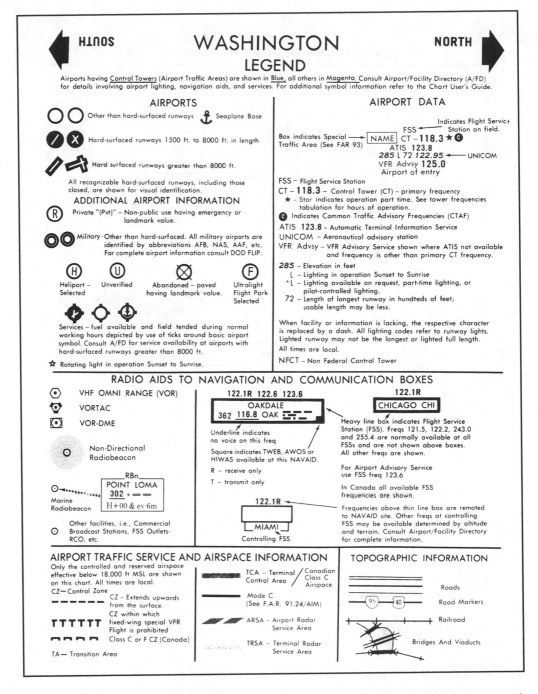

Sectional and TCA charts are revised semiannually. Several Alaskan sectional charts and the Puerto Rico, Virgin Islands TCA are revised annually.

WORLD AERONAUTICAL CHARTS (WACS)

World Aeronautical Charts are drawn to a scale that is half that of the sectionals; 1:1,000,000. At that scale, one inch equals 13.7 nautical miles. They are convenient for navigation by moderate-speed aircraft. The charts show less detail than either the sectionals or the TCA charts because the scale is smaller.

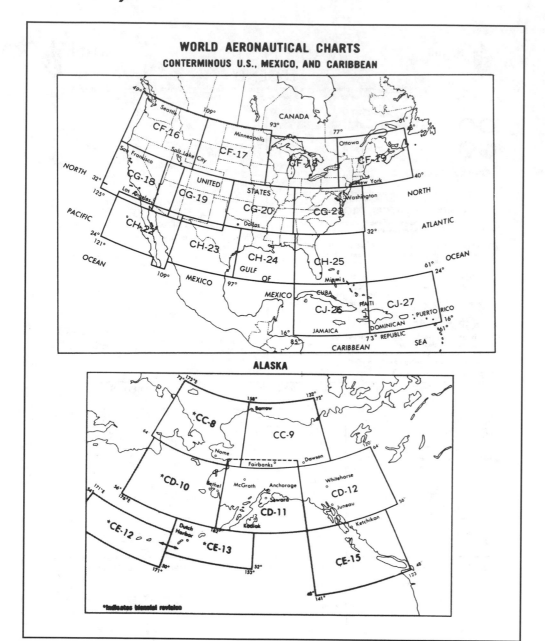

Fewer World Aeronautical Charts, at much smaller scale than sectionals, are necessary for total coverage of the United States. They are useful for planning and for navigation by moderate-speed aircraft.

Topographical information on the World Aeronautical Charts includes cities and towns, principal roads, railroads, distinctive landmarks, drainage, and relief features (indicated by spot elevations, contours, and gradient tints). Aeronautical information includes visual and radio aids to navigation, airports, airways, restricted areas, and obstructions. These charts are revised annually, with the exception of several Alaskan and Mexican/Caribbean charts, which are revised every two years.

EN ROUTE LOW-ALTITUDE CHARTS

These charts are designed for flight under instrument flight rules (IFR) in the low altitude stratum (that is, the "victor" airways beneath 17,000 feet). The series also includes en route area charts. The area charts furnish terminal data in a large scale format for congested areas such as Washington, Los Angeles, New York, Chicago, and several others.

Topographic information is not depicted on these charts. Instead, they highlight information essential to an IFR pilot. Examples of the information include: airways, limits of controlled airspace, position, identification and frequencies of radio aids, selected airports, minimum en route and obstruction clearance altitudes, airway distances, reporting points, special use airspace, and related information.

Look at the extract from the Low Altitude chart, and see how the radio aids to navigation are highlighted. So are the "victor" airways clearly shown. The designation of a victor airway is in a box astride the airway line, which is drawn between two identifiable points. Below the airway designation box is a figure that expresses the distance in nautical miles between the two points. Above the designation is a figure for the Minimum En Route Altitude (MEA) between the two points.

As with the VFR charts, the legends for these en route low altitude charts are bursting with useful information. A pilot who cannot recall the exact meaning of a symbol can consult the legend and be refreshed immediately.

Revisions to these charts are made every 56 days. Obsolete charts should be discarded; only the current chart should be used for flight.

EN ROUTE HIGH-ALTITUDE CHARTS

These charts are designed for flight in the high-altitude stratum, the jet route structure at flight level 180 and higher. They contain essentially the same type of information as the low altitude charts. The charts are noticeably less cluttered, however, as navigational aids are usually spread farther apart in the high-altitude environment. That is because the navigational aids can be received and radio transmissions received over longer ranges from the higher altitudes. Pilots flying in the high-altitude stratum need low altitude charts for the departure and arrival phases of flight and high altitude charts for the en route phase. These charts also are revised every 56 days.

For an appreciation of the difference between types of charts, examine the extract from High Altitude Chart H-6, which includes Washington, D.C. Now Washington National Airport is no longer the focal point; its VOR identification and radio frequency are shown (DCA, 111.0 MHz), and its location on the Potomac River. More important to the high altitude pilot are the jet airways and radio navigational aids used to define them, and the boundaries of restricted and warning areas.

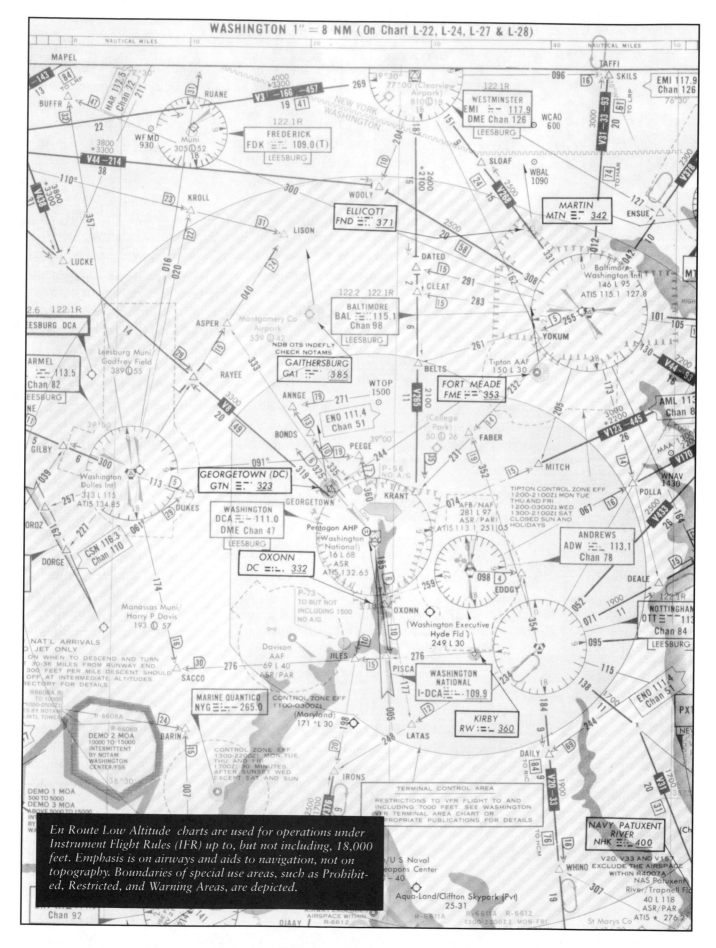

En Route Low Altitude charts are used for operations under Instrument Flight Rules (IFR) up to, but not including, 18,000 feet. Emphasis is on airways and aids to navigation, not on topography. Boundaries of special use areas, such as Prohibited, Restricted, and Warning Areas, are depicted.

Legend for Low Altitude Chart (below 18,000 feet) is printed on every chart for ready reference.

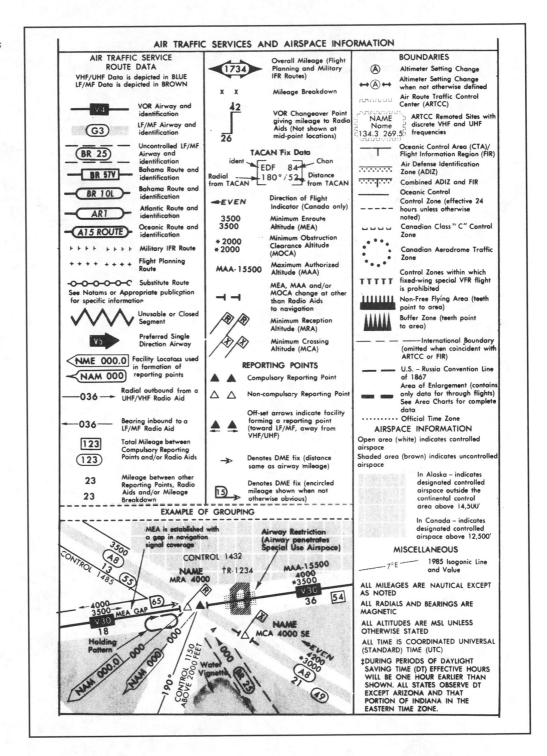

ALASKA EN ROUTE CHARTS (LOW- AND HIGH-ALTITUDE)

Produced in a low-altitude and high-altitude identical to the low and high altitude charts previously described, these charts also are revised every 56 days.

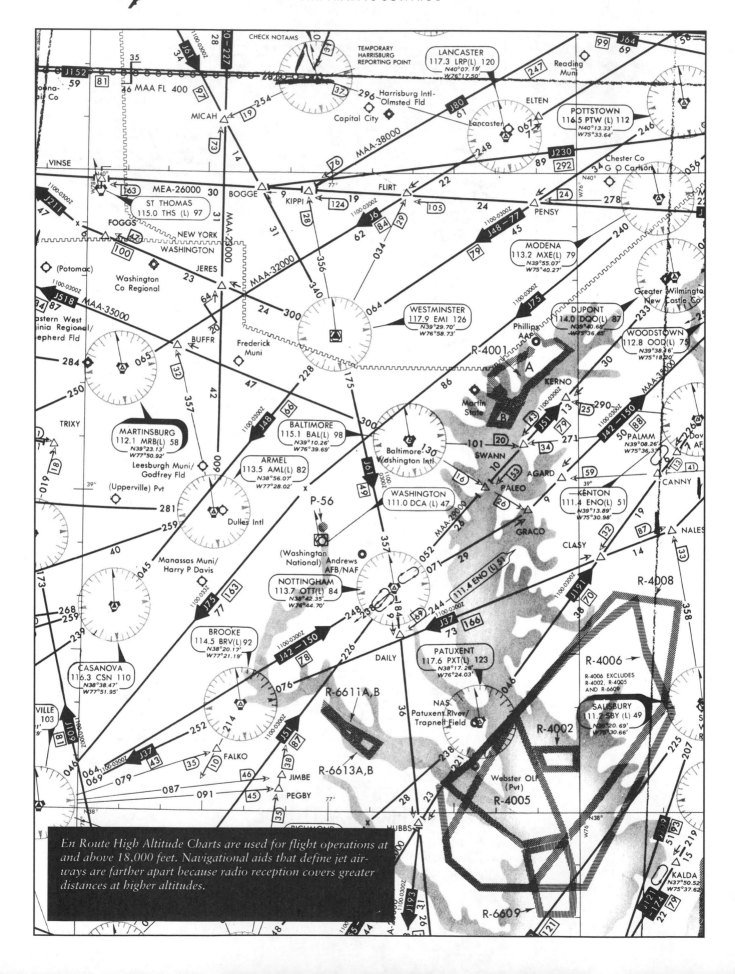

En Route High Altitude Charts are used for flight operations at and above 18,000 feet. Navigational aids that define jet airways are farther apart because radio reception covers greater distances at higher altitudes.

CHARTED VFR FLYWAY PLANNING CHARTS

These publications show multiple VFR routings through high-density traffic areas, which may be used as an alternative to flight within the major controlled traffic flows. The charts provide ground references as guides for improved visual navigation, using a scale of 1:250,000, or one inch for every 3.43 miles. They are not intended to discourage VFR operations within terminal control areas, but are designed to inform and to facilitate planning. The charts, published semiannually, are printed on the back of the existing VFR terminal charts.

Inside terminal control areas, VFR flying is restricted unless pilots contact and receive a clearance from a controller. The restriction is designed to keep aircraft separated. But the procedure can cause delays if the controller is busy with other aircraft.

VFR pilots usually have three alternatives in dealing with a terminal control area (TCA). They can fly around the TCA, which could add a considerable distance to the flight. Or they can fly below the floor or above the ceiling of the TCA. However, flying beneath the TCA floor may restrict them to an altitude that is too low for comfort and safety. Flying above the TCA ceiling might force them to a higher altitude than they care to go and also might put them into the realm of high-performance aircraft climbing out of the terminal control area. Or they can fly in the VFR corridor through the terminal control area, if one is designated. That is kept clear of IFR aircraft and often cuts through the center of the area. VFR flyway charts help pilots make this decision.

PLANNING CHARTS

When one needs a long-range perspective for a flight, then the flight planning charts are useful. They help a pilot visualize a long cross-country flight, to make decisions on the choices of routes to fly, and then to go to the larger-scale charts for detailed flight planning.

The following charts are used for flight planning:

VFR/IFR (Preflight) Planning Chart—The chart is produced at a small scale of 1:2,333,232, or one inch for every 32 nautical miles. It is printed in two parts so that, when assembled, it forms a composite VFR planning chart on one side and an IFR planning chart on the other. The IFR chart depicts low-altitude airways and mileages, navigational facilities, special-use airspace, time zones, airports, isogonic lines, and related data. Information on the VFR chart includes selected populated places, large bodies of water, major drainage, shaded relief, navigational facilities, airports, special-use areas, and military training routes.

Flight Case Planning Chart—This publication is designed for preflight and en route flight planning for VFR flights. The chart covers the entire contiguous 48 states. It is produced at an even smaller scale of 1:4,374,803, or one inch for every 60 nautical miles. It depicts basically the same information as the VFR/IFR planning chart, with the following additions: selected flight service stations and Weather Service offices, located at airport sites; parachute jumping areas; a tabulation of special use airspace areas; a mileage table listing distances between 174 major airports; and a city/aerodrome location index.

Gulf of Mexico and Caribbean Planning Chart—This chart is designated for preflight planning for VFR flights in the region. It is printed on the reverse side of the Puerto Rico-Virgin Islands TCA chart. Produced on a scale of 1:6,270,551, or one inch for every 86 nautical miles, it depicts mileages between airports of entry; a selection of special-use airspace; and a directory of airports, which lists available facilities and servicing capabilities.

North Atlantic Route Chart—This four-color chart is designed for air traffic controllers to use in monitoring transatlantic flights.

North Pacific Oceanic Route Chart—This chart series similarly is designed for FAA controllers who monitor transoceanic traffic.

En Route High Altitude Planning Chart—This one is designed specifically for IFR en route planning at or above 18,000 feet mean sea level (MSL). The chart also may be used for preflight planning. It has a scale equivalent to that of the flight case planning chart and features published jet routes, restricted areas, a navigation aid location index, and a special-use airspace index. Information is revised every 56 days. It is published in four colors; green shading is used for water areas, blue for special-use airspace, black for high-frequency jet routes, and brown for low-frequency routes. This chart, along with the five described previously, is printed on a large, single sheet and folded in a pocket-sized format. Controllers are most familiar with the charts used for IFR flight, but they also frequently use the VFR flight charts.

INSTRUMENT APPROACH PROCEDURES (IAP) CHARTS

IAP charts are published in 15 bound volumes, each measuring 5.375 x 8.25 inches. They display the aeronautical data that is required to execute instrument approaches to airports in the United States, Puerto Rico and the Virgin Islands.

Also included are airport diagrams of the major airports located within the coverage area of each of the titles in the series. Again, essential information is highlighted. For Washington National Airport (location identifier DCA), for instance, the three runways and all connecting taxiways are depicted and identified. Also, spot elevations are shown, as are the latitude and longitude, down to tenths of a nautical mile.

Airports with several instrument approach procedures (IAP) are depicted in large scale drawings as part of the Instrument Approach Procedure chart books. This drawing of Washington National Airport not only shows and labels the runways and taxiways; useful radio frequencies and ground activities are also depicted.

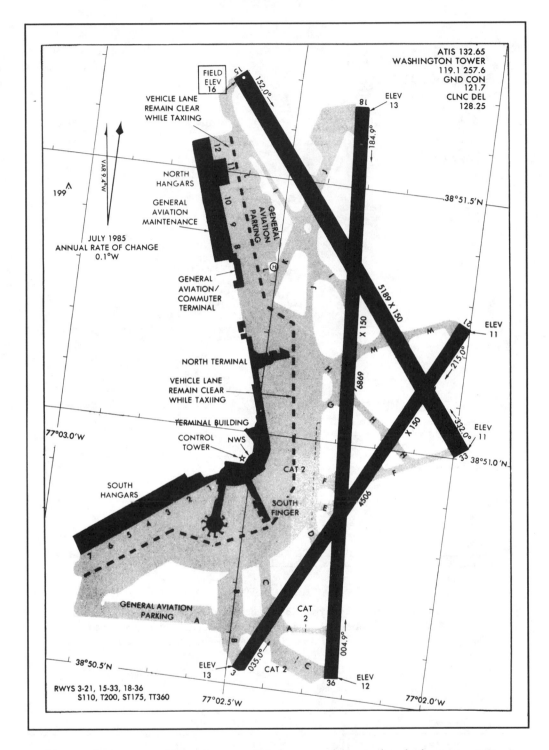

New volumes are released every 56 days, and procedural changes occurring within the 56-day cycle are reflected in one volume issued at mid-cycle. Each page in each volume depicts one instrument approach procedure. That includes all related navigational data, communications information, and an airport sketch, or large airport diagrams, where available. Large airports might have ten or more IAPs, so these volumes contain considerable data.

The basic airport diagrams included on each chart generally show only the runways. The larger charts printed on a separate page, show runways, taxiways, and terminals. Procedures are designated for use with specific electronic navigational aids, such as instrument landing systems, VOR stations, or nondirection beacons.

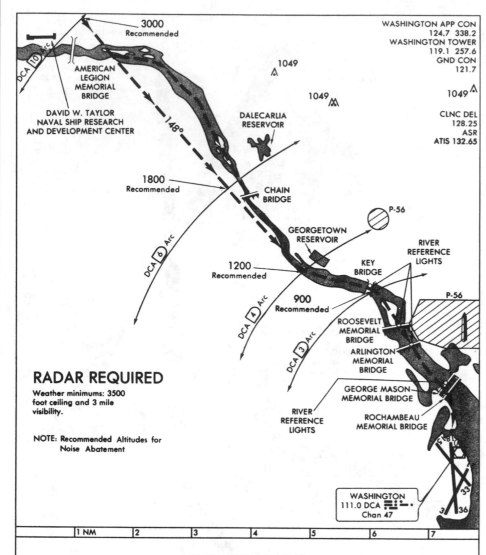

3000
Recommended

WASHINGTON APP CON
124.7 338.2
WASHINGTON TOWER
119.1 257.6
GND CON
121.7

1049

AMERICAN
LEGION
MEMORIAL
BRIDGE

DAVID W. TAYLOR
NAVAL SHIP RESEARCH
AND DEVELOPMENT CENTER

1049

DCA 10 Arc

148°

1049

CLNC DEL
128.25
ASR
ATIS 132.65

DALECARLIA
RESERVOIR

1800
Recommended

CHAIN
BRIDGE

P-56

GEORGETOWN
RESERVOIR

DCA 6 Arc

1200
Recommended

KEY
BRIDGE

RIVER
REFERENCE
LIGHTS

900
Recommended

P-56

DCA 4 Arc

DCA 3 Arc

ROOSEVELT
MEMORIAL
BRIDGE

ARLINGTON
MEMORIAL
BRIDGE

RADAR REQUIRED

Weather minimums: 3500
foot ceiling and 3 mile
visibility.

NOTE: Recommended Altitudes for
Noise Abatement

GEORGE MASON
MEMORIAL BRIDGE

ROCHAMBEAU
MEMORIAL BRIDGE

RIVER
REFERENCE
LIGHTS

WASHINGTON
111.0 DCA
Chan 47

| 1 NM | 2 | 3 | 4 | 5 | 6 | 7 |

RIVER VISUAL RWY 18

Aircraft may visually follow the river to the airport, or may proceed via the DCA
VOR/DME R-328 (148° inbound) or via the Rosslyn LDA Rwy 18 Approach to
abeam Georgetown Reservoir or the DCA 4 NM DME fix, then follow the river to
the airport.
NOTE: Clearance for visual approach does not authorize penetration of P-56.

Where special approaches are required, as at Washington National, then a graphic depiction is used for clarity. The "River Approach (Visual)" for landing to the south is a sightseer's delight, but requires precise navigation and airmanship from pilots.

STANDARD INSTRUMENT DEPARTURE (SID) CHARTS

Standard Instrument Departure procedures mean just that; standard procedures for departing from a given airport. These charts are published in two bound volumes issued every 56 days. They help expedite clearance delivery and ease the transition between takeoff and en route operations. They furnish pilots departure routing clearance information in graphic and textual form.

STANDARD TERMINAL ARRIVAL (STAR) CHARTS

Again, the charts depict just what the title says. These charts expedite ATC arrival route procedures and facilitate transition between en route and instrument approach operations. They give pilots preplanned IFR ATC arrival route procedures in graphic and textual form. Each STAR procedure is presented as a separate chart and may serve a single airport or more than one airport in a given geographic location. One bound volume of STAR charts for the United States, excluding Alaska, is issued every 56 days.

ALASKA TERMINAL PUBLICATION

This document contains charts depicting instrument approach procedures, standard instrument departures, standard terminal arrivals, airport diagrams, and radar minimums for use by all civil and military aircraft in the state of Alaska. The publication covers supplementary supporting data, which includes IFR takeoff and departure procedures, IFR alternate minimums, a rate of descent table, and an inoperative components table.

HELICOPTER ROUTE CHARTS

Aviators operating in major metropolitan areas with large concentrations of helicopter activity need these charts. They are designed to make helicopter traffic safe and efficient, within the constraints of a big city. Scale is 1:125,000, twice as large as the TCA charts above. The charts are very readable, even in a vibrating helicopter.

Topographical information includes urban tint, principal roads, railroads, pictorial symbols, and spot elevations. Aeronautical information includes named routes for helicopters to fly, four classes of heliports, aids to navigation, special-use airspace, obstacles, control tower frequencies, and terminal control area surfaces.

Examine the extract from the Washington (D.C.) Helicopter Route Chart. Note the named helicopter routes, as well as spotting prominent landmarks such as the Washington Monument, the Capitol, Pentagon, and others. Also see how clearly the Prohibited Area P-56 is marked.

A high volume of helicopter traffic flies through the airspace of the nation's cap-

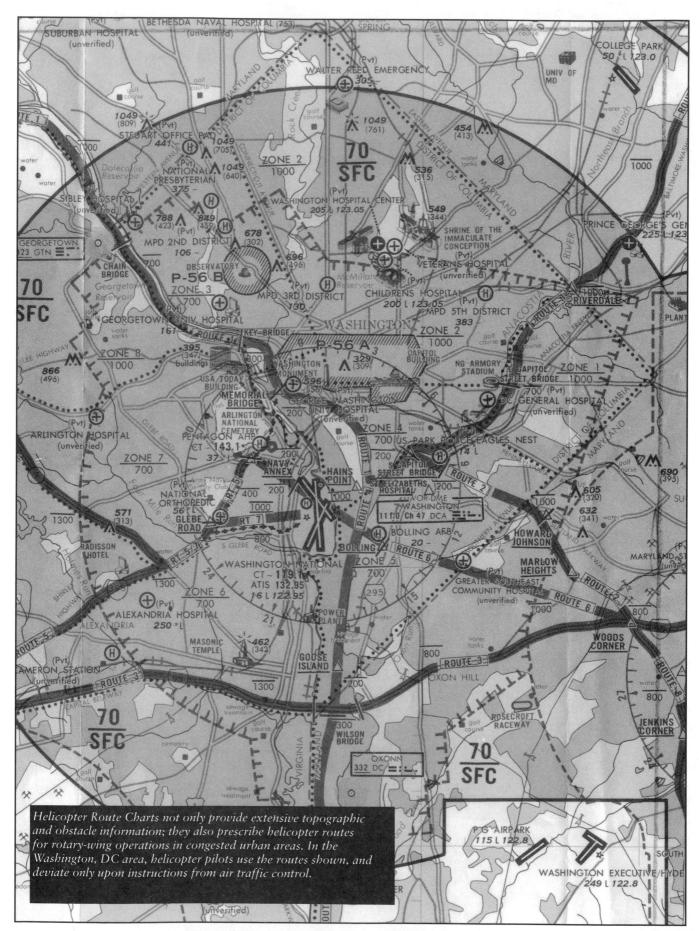

Helicopter Route Charts not only provide extensive topographic and obstacle information; they also prescribe helicopter routes for rotary-wing operations in congested urban areas. In the Washington, DC area, helicopter pilots use the routes shown, and deviate only upon instructions from air traffic control.

ital. With Washington National Airport so close to downtown, and the heavy fixed-wing traffic there and at Washington Dulles and Andrews AFB, helicopter pilots must adhere precisely to the published routes and to air traffic controllers' instructions.

These charts are revised every two years unless earlier revision is needed because of significant aeronautical information changes or safety-related events.

Coverage diagram informs operators which charts to order for operations in different parts of the country.

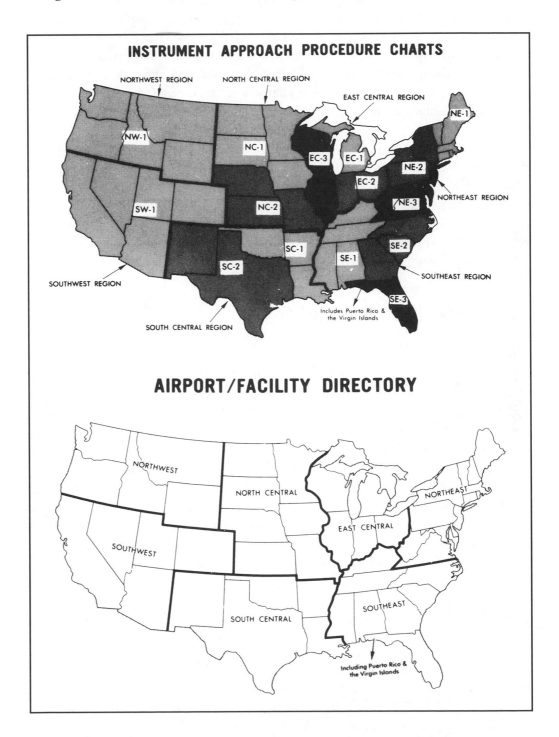

INSTRUMENT APPROACH PROCEDURE CHARTS

AIRPORT/FACILITY DIRECTORY

RELATED PUBLICATIONS

The Airport Facility Directory is issued in seven volumes. Each volume covers a specific geographic area of the United Station, including Puerto Rico and the U.S. Virgin Islands. The directory is reissued in its entirety every 56 days. A wealth of information about airports and air traffic control facilities is included. The information is indexed alphabetically by state and by airport, navigational aid, and air traffic control facilities for the area covered.

The Alaska Supplement is a joint civil and military flight information publication published and distributed every 56 days. It contains an airport/facility directory of all airports shown on en route charts, and those requested by appropriate agencies, communications data, navigational facilities, and special notices and procedures.

The Pacific Supplement is a civil flight information publication, published and distributed every 56 days by the National Ocean Service (NOS). The supplement is designed for use with the flight information en route publication charts and the sectional aeronautical chart covering Hawaii and the Pacific areas served by U.S. facilities. It contains an airport/facility directory of all public airports; and those requested by appropriate agencies; communications data; navigational facilities; and special notices and procedures

INFORMATION SOURCES

The publications cited previously are produced by NOS from information and funds, about $15 million annually, provided by the FAA. The numbers and types of charts being published are continually increasing in response to a constant give and take between desired information and available space. On charts that cover congested areas, it is sometimes difficult to discern particular elements. That is called chart clutter, with so much information depicted in a small area.

Most charts are published on a regular basis. That can be 56 days, or semiannually, or annually, even though the information presented may not have changed. Regular publication dates are necessary, however, to give users confidence that the data in hand is up-to-date information. Controllers or pilots who pick up an en route low-altitude chart that is more than 56 days old know that the information on it is suspect. Before flying or controlling, they should obtain a current chart.

A vertical aerial photo of Washington (D.C.) National Airport. Runway 18-36 points north and sorth. The Potomac River flows past on the east. (FAA)

DEFENSE DEPARTMENT, ANOTHER SOURCE

The Defense Mapping Agency Aerospace Center also produces a series of aeronautical publications. They are intended primarily for military use, but some are available to the general public. The center also releases to the military services some publications that are not available to the general public. Examples include:

> **Pilotage charts**
> **Jet navigation charts**
> **LORAN (long-range navigation) and consol LORAN charts**
> **Continental entry chart aerospace planning chart**
> **Air distance/geography chart**
> **LORAN C chart**
> **Department of Defense weather plotting chart**
> **Flight information publications**
> **World aeronautical and operational navigation charts**
> **Jet navigation charts**
> **Global navigation charts**

The address and telephone number for requesting DMA charts and obtaining information about prices and payment procedures is:

> **Director**
> **DMA Combat Support Center (DMACSC)**
> **ATTN: PMSA**
> **Washington, DC 20315-0010**
> **Phone, toll-free: 1-800-826-0342**

THE "JEPP" CHARTS

In addition to these government charts, commercial suppliers produce several different types. The most well known is the series produced by the Jeppesen-Sanderson Company. It was founded by Mr. Elray Jeppesen when he was flying passengers and mail in the Mountain States in the early 1930s. Mr. Jeppesen built up a series of notebooks based on his own observations and experience, as well as what he learned from other pilots. Soon, pilots began asking him for a copy of his notes, and he began producing them. As the word spread, so did the demand. By the time of World War II, the Jeppesen Company charts covered the nation.

The Jeppesen charts are produced in a slightly different format and scale from the government charts. The scale is often preferred by pilots who may fly in rather cramped cockpits that do not lend themselves to the larger, unfolding government charts.

The range of charts and information sources cited in this chapter may seem formidable at first glance. But as one begins using the system or controlling in it, the charts become familiar tools. They are invaluable resources, and the prudent pilot consults them and keeps them current and ready for use.

Now you can understand why pilots carry those big leather cases. The cases are needed to carry the number and variety of charts and books a pilot must have ready for immediate use.

CHAPTER FIFTEEN

CLEARANCES AND AIRCRAFT SEPARATION

CLEARANCES PREVENT COLLISIONS

C ontrollers issue air traffic control clearances to provide separation between aircraft. In fact, an air traffic clearance is defined as "an authorization by air traffic control, for the purpose of preventing collision between known aircraft . . . " For convenience, the term is shortened to clearance. That is a relatively simple mission statement. But to achieve the desired results can lead to some complex situations that can tax a controller's skill as well as character. Keeping aircraft separated is difficult enough at the best of times in crowded airspace. When the weather turns bad or the skies become overcrowded, the task is formidable, but can be done. In short, clearances are tools to achieve separation.

WHAT CLEARANCES ARE

Controllers issue clearances based on known traffic and known physical airport conditions. Pilots flying under instrument flight rules (IFR) are required to provide their own separation from visual flight rules (VFR) aircraft that are unknown to the controller. It is not the controller's fault if a taxiing aircraft hits a barrier that the controller did not know was there.

An air traffic control clearance, authorized by air traffic control for the purpose of preventing collision between known aircraft, allows an aircraft to proceed under specified conditions within controlled airspace. The separation of responsibility that exists between the pilot and the controller is one that in definition seems almost unworkable, but in operation has worked for many years. FAR 91.3(a) states:

"The pilot in command of an aircraft is directly responsible for, and is the final authority as to, the operation of that aircraft."

In other words, if the controller issues a clearance that would cause a pilot to deviate from a rule or regulation or, in the pilot's opinion, would place the aircraft in jeopardy, it is the pilot's responsibility to request an amended clearance.

Pilots may not deviate from an air traffic control clearance or instruction without first notifying the controller. If the situation is such that the pilot has to act immediately, he must notify the controller as soon as possible.

In practice, controllers are in charge of the movement of all IFR aircraft. Their decisions are guided by an understanding of the physical limitations of the aircraft, the Federal Air Regulations, and operational procedures that have been developed through the years. The controller has the total picture of the traffic situation; the pilot does not. The pilot knows what the airplane can do, and acts accordingly. If either one deviates from this working framework, each had better have a good reason. The division of responsibility is usually not a problem. If a clearance is relayed by a third party, for example by a flight service station, the instruction is preceded by "ATC clears."

CLEARANCE ELEMENTS

Clearances contain specific elements. An example is provided by the en route clearance delivered to the pilot by the tower prior to taxi:

Jet Star one four two four cleared to Atlanta airport, South Boston two departure then as filed except change route to read South Boston Victor 20 Greensboro, maintain one seven thousand.

Clearance Limit—The traffic clearance issued prior to an aircraft's departure will normally authorize flight to the airport of intended destination. Under certain circumstances and at some locations, a short range clearance procedure is used, whereby a clearance is issued to a fix within or just outside of the terminal area. Pilots then are advised of the radio frequency on which they will receive the long-range clearance direct from the center controller.

Departure Procedure—Controllers may issue headings and altitude restrictions to separate a departing aircraft from other air traffic in the terminal area. Where the volume of traffic warrants, standard instrument departures have been developed.

Route of Flight—Clearances normally are issued for the routes that pilots request, including altitude and flight level. However, traffic conditions frequently require controllers to specify a route or an altitude or flight level different from that requested by the pilot. In certain congested areas or between congested areas, traffic is cleared to preferred routes and established flow patterns. Pilots usually request those routes. If they do not, their request is usually modified to a clearance that uses those routes.

If the controller can approve the route filed by the pilot, he uses the statement, "cleared . . . as filed." When this procedure was first introduced, skeptics made dire predictions that planes would fly off in unexpected directions, because pilots had filed two flight plans and chose to follow the wrong one. This situation has happened rarely, and the procedure has worked well.

Altitude Data—Normally, controllers issue an altitude to be maintained by aircraft. If the initial cleared altitude is not in the stratum filed by the pilot (for example, the jet routes), the controller provides a time or location when a pilot can expect a clearance to a higher altitude. After departure, if a pilot desires a different altitude than the one assigned, the pilot must request the change from the controller. If the requested altitude would conflict with other aircraft traffic, the controller will either advise the pilot when he can expect the altitude change, or suggest that he request it from the next sector along the flight route.

Generally, altitudes are assigned according to the direction of flight. If an aircraft's heading is in the half-circle from 360 to 179 degrees and its altitude is 29,000 feet or less, the aircraft will be assigned an odd altitude. If the heading is from 180 to 359 degrees, the aircraft will be assigned an even altitude. Controllers can coordinate a nonstandard altitude if there is reason to do so.

The term "cruise" is occasionally used in connection with altitude instead of "maintain." Cruise means that the pilot can go no higher, but can go lower, than the stated altitude. If a pilot reports leaving the cruise altitude in descent, he may not return to that altitude unless he gets a clearance from the controller. This type of clearance is often issued to a pilot who intends to land at an airport that is outside of controlled airspace.

AIR TRAFFIC CONTROL CLEARANCE AND INSTRUCTION

The Pilot/Controller Glossary included in Appendix III provides the following definitions:

AIR TRAFFIC CLEARANCE/ATC CLEARANCE—An authorization by air traffic control for the purpose of preventing collision between known aircraft, for an aircraft to proceed under specified traffic conditions within controlled airspace.

ATC INSTRUCTIONS—Directives issued by air traffic control for the purpose of requiring a pilot to take specific actions; e.g., "Turn left heading two five zero," or "Go around," or "Clear the runway."

Pilots are required to follow both air traffic control clearances and air traffic control instructions unless they are exercising their emergency authority. More and more, this is a distinction without a difference since air traffic control instructions are often given to separate aircraft. Clearances usually start with the word "cleared." Controllers clear aircraft for takeoff, clear them for approaches, and clear them to land. Most of the rest of what is said are instructions.

In the past, air traffic controllers cleared aircraft to taxi, to cross runways, and to turn off runways, until a disastrous incident changed the procedure.

Tenerife is a relatively quiet airport in the Canary Islands, off the coast of North Africa. On March 27, 1977, the airport was loaded with 747 airliners that had been diverted from their European destinations because of bad weather on the continent. Eventually the continental weather improved. By the time the aircraft were ready to depart for their original destinations, fog had settled on Tenerife. The fog restricted visibility somewhat, but not enough to stop departures.

The Tenerife airport was not built to accommodate this degree of activity. One consequence was that aircraft had to taxi halfway down the single runway before they could turn off onto a taxiway that would take them to the departure point. A KLM 747 was in position on the runway waiting for a departure clearance to take off. The tower controller cleared a taxiing Pan American 747 for a left turn off the runway. The KLM pilot apparently heard the word "cleared." He understood it to be his takeoff clearance and began accelerating down the runway. The KLM was just barely airborne when it collided with the taxiing Pan Am 747. More than 400 people were killed in the collision.

The KLM pilot was a top pilot, known for his care and precision. No one will ever know what mental process caused such a mistake. Shortly thereafter, to prevent misunderstanding, the air traffic control system stopped using the word "cleared" with taxiing aircraft.

A COOPERATIVE SYSTEM

Air traffic control depends upon clear, concise, and understandable communications between pilots and controllers. Pilots should read back to the clearance delivery controller the clearance or instruction that the controller gives them. If a pilot reads back the information incorrectly and the controller fails to catch it, it is the controller's error. On the other hand, controllers expect pilots to react to instructions within a reasonable time, and often base separation instructions on that expectation. So if a pilot is told to "Turn left heading 250" and acknowledges it but is slow in starting the turn for a minute or two, the delay is the pilot's error.

If a clearance or instruction is not acknowledged, the situation is different. That is considered to be a clearance that has not been issued. In addition, pilots are required to fly along the centerline of airways. The protected airspace on either side of the centerline is to allow for equipment and pilot error, not for aircraft to wander off the centerline. Pilots are also required to fly exactly at the altitude assigned, not somewhere near it.

It is important for controllers to anticipate the unexpected, and to make sure the pilot knows what is going to happen and to be prepared for it. For example, a controller informs a pilot well in advance of the approach to be expected at the airport. If conditions change, requiring a different approach procedure, the controller should pass along that information to the pilot as soon as possible. The pilot will need time to change approach plates, reset frequencies, and become familiar with the new procedure. If the weather deteriorates significantly, the pilot might choose not to attempt the approach at all. If a windshear develops on the final approach, ample warning to prepare for it should be given. Communication is the lifeblood of the system.

Holding aircraft on the ground while awaiting clearance to take off for a flight is more efficient than holding them in the air, circling and burning up fuel and congesting airspace. Occasionally, aircraft already in the air may have to hold briefly because of unforeseen delays. (FAA)

HOLDING: COOPERATION AT WORK

Holding aircraft, not allowing them to proceed as planned, creates a situation as complex as any in air traffic control. Before the 1981 controllers' strike, the U.S. air traffic control philosophy allowed as much holding in the air as the system could accommodate, so that aircraft were in a position to match airport capacity. The strike prompted new procedures to be developed that slashed holding in the air and reduced the strain on the airborne system. Aircraft were held on the ground until they could be released for an uninterrupted flow into the airport of destination. This system has proven more efficient and safer, and also saved fuel, and has been continued to the present time.

Some holding still occurs, however. It is caused either by unanticipated weather conditions, or a slightly over-subscribed inbound traffic flow.

Holding Instructions—Whenever an aircraft is cleared to a navigation fix other than the destination airport and a delay is expected, the controller is responsible to inform the pilot. The controller issues complete holding instructions (unless the pattern is charted), states a time at which the pilot can expect further clearance, and the best estimate of any additional en route or terminal delay. These instructions include the fix the pilot is expected to use for holding, the direction from the fix where the hold should take place, the turn over the fix, and the length of the outbound leg in time or distance. For example, a controller might say:

American 124, hold southwest of the South Bend VOR, right turns, ten-mile legs (or two-minute legs), expect further clearance at 1014.

If the holding pattern is depicted on the appropriate chart, the controller merely says, "Hold as published," adding an "expect further clearance" time. Again, the controller has to anticipate these conditions. It is inappropriate to tell a pilot to enter a holding pattern when the aircraft is only a mile from the fix. The aircraft

Wondered what a VOR looks like? The acronym stands for Very High Frequency Omnidirectional Range station. It is a basic ground-based electronic navigation aid that transmits VHF signals in all directions, 360 degrees, oriented from magnetic north. This VOR station is at Washington National Airport, DC. The VOR identifies itself by Morse Code signals; it may also have an additional voice identification feature. (FAA)

has to slow down well in advance of entering a holding pattern, or go flying past the fix and possibly cause a conflict. It would be like applying the brakes in your automobile only a few feet from an intersection, but then not being able to stop until after you pass through the intersection.

In today's air traffic control environment, center controllers usually maintain radar contact with the aircraft during a hold, and provide radar separation between it and other aircraft. However, if traffic conditions are too heavy to allow this, established criteria for a holding pattern or protected airspace exist. Under these conditions the controller protects the entire airspace at the holding aircraft's altitude.

AIR TRAFFIC CONTROL SEPARATION

Keeping aircraft separated is a controller's prime responsibility. Separations vary according to conditions, but usually are discussed in three dimensions, or planes: vertical, longitudinal, and lateral. Vertical is the separation between aircraft at different altitudes. Longitudinal is the separation between aircraft following one another in trail. Lateral is the separation between aircraft at the same altitude, most often to the left or right side. In some respects, with today's use of radar, separation could be thought of as either vertical or horizontal.

Conflict alert modifications to controller's scopes render early warnings if aircraft flight paths have a potential for collision. In this situation, both aircraft are at the same altitude, 17,000 feet, and their flight paths are converging. The system alerts the controller, who takes action to prevent the conflict. (FAA)

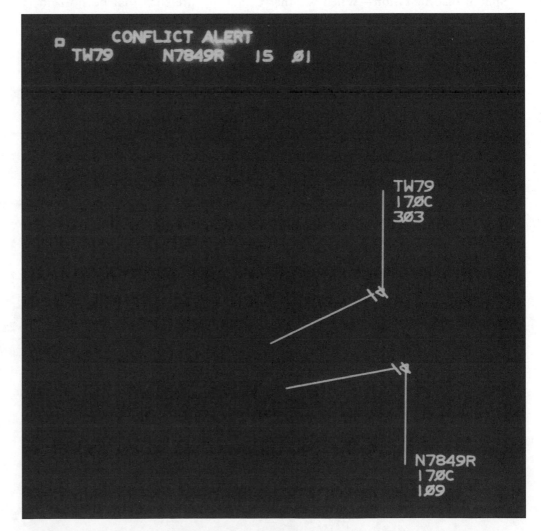

VERTICAL SEPARATION

Vertical separation between IFR aircraft is 1,000 feet up to and including flight level (FL) 290. Above flight level 290, vertical separation is 2,000 feet. So controllers can assign aircraft to fly at 10,000, 11,000, and 12,000 feet up to 29,000 feet. But up where the jets like to travel, the altitudes are at flight levels such as 310, 330, and 350.

Recall the altitudes for direction of flight rules outlined previously. To provide 2,000 feet of vertical separation above 29,000 feet, only odd altitudes (flight levels) are used. Aircraft at the higher altitudes flying on courses of 360 to 179 degrees fly at FL 330, 370, 410, etc. Aircraft flying courses of 180 to 359 use FLs 310, 350, 390, etc.

According to the Federal Aviation Regulations, VFR aircraft fly at an altitude plus 500 feet. Thus, for example, they use 10,500, 11,500, and 12,500 feet. VFR aircraft in terminal control areas also are provided 500 feet of separation.

The 2,000-foot separation minimum above FL 290 is based (among other things) on altimeter accuracy problems at those altitudes. During the last several years, an extensive study on altimeter accuracy has investigated the possibility of reducing the separation to 1,000 feet. The study is still going on.

Spatial disorientation—When weather conditions are such that no horizon is visible, it is often difficult for pilots to determine the relative altitude of other aircraft. Two incidents that occurred at John F. Kennedy Airport during the 1970s illustrate the problem. In those days, aircraft inbound to Kennedy from the northeast proceeded at 6,000 feet. This kept them 1,000 feet above departing aircraft, which flew outbound at 5,000 feet. On one occasion, two aircraft were positioned over the ocean east of the airport. One was outbound, the other inbound. The inbound pilot saw the departure airplane, thought that it was at his altitude, and dove to avoid it. He just managed to recover before hitting the water.

On the other occasion, with a different runway setup, the departing aircraft was flying above the inbound. As the departure banked to the right to turn southeastbound, the inbound aircraft, flying in the opposite direction, banked to the left to turn inbound. Looking out the cockpit window, the pilot of the departing aircraft perceived that both aircraft were at the same altitude, and dove to avoid it. This time, unfortunately, the pilot was unable to pull out of the dive before hitting the water.

Minimum En Route Altitude (MEA)—This is the lowest altitude that can be assigned along a route. It is a published altitude that assures acceptable navigational signal coverage, and at the same time meets obstacle clearance requirements between fixes.

Minimum Vectoring Altitude (MVA)—This is the lowest altitude at which an IFR aircraft will be vectored by a controller. It meets IFR obstacle clearance criteria, but may be lower than the MEA because the controller is providing the navigational guidance and the pilot does not require signals from aids to navigation.

Wing tip vortices appear off the wingtips of a Boeing 747 as it takes off. Vortices are circular patterns of air created by the movement of the wing through the air as it generates lift. Such vortices are the most predominant parts of wake turbulence. Controllers and pilots are careful to maintain separation behind a heavy aircraft generating wake turbulence. (FAA)

LONGITUDINAL SEPARATION

In today's environment most aircraft are separated by three nautical miles in terminal areas and five nautical miles when under control of the centers. But again, separation criteria are not always so simple.

Wake Turbulence Separation Minima—Several years ago, the FAA discovered wake turbulence. Wake turbulence is a violent disturbance of the air behind an aircraft, resembling a pair of horizontal tornadoes. The bigger and heavier the aircraft, the more violent the disturbance. The phenomenon was well known. However, it had not been a consideration in aircraft separation criteria until the introduction of the Boeing 747.

For wake turbulence purposes, aircraft are divided into three categories: heavy, large, and small. (A 747 is a heavy aircraft, a 727 is a large aircraft, and a Cessna 421 is a small aircraft.) For aircraft flying directly behind, and less than 1,000 feet below a preceding aircraft, the following separation minima apply:

1) **Heavy behind a heavy**—four nautical miles

2) **Small or large behind a heavy**—five nautical miles.

Near the runway, when the preceding aircraft is over the landing threshold:

3) **Small behind a large**—four nautical miles

4) **Small behind a heavy**—six nautical miles.

Parallel runway pattern of Washington Dulles International enables controllers to operate aircraft on both runways, yet maintain the required separation between them. Dulles' two main runways, 11,500 feet long, are oriented north-south and are separated laterally by more than a mile. The third runway, designated 12-30, is oriented northwest-southeast and is 10,001 feet long. At busy times, Dulles controllers are able to have aircraft operating from all three runways.

Visual separation under instrument flight rules—In selected cases, carefully applied visual separation can be used to separate IFR aircraft. In one case the tower controller can apply visual separation between aircraft in direct view, provided at least one of the aircraft is under the controller's direct control. In another case, if a pilot has another aircraft in sight, the controller can instruct the pilot to maintain visual separation from the other aircraft.

Aircraft can be cleared for visual approaches using radar, when the airport weather facilitates visual flight and when the ceiling is at least 500 feet above the minimum vectoring altitude (MVA). The visual approach can be made to the airport if the pilot has reported the field in sight and is first in the sequence, or if the pilot has reported the preceding aircraft in sight and the controller instructs the pilot to follow the first aircraft to the airport. This type of approach can be used for simultaneous approaches to parallel runways. Aircraft on one runway can be making instrument approaches, while aircraft on the other runway are making visual approaches. This significantly increases the number of aircraft that can land and take off in a given time. Many of the country's busiest airports simply could not accommodate the daily demand without using this procedure.

Contact Approaches—The grandfather of the visual approach, a contact approach does not involve the pilot's separation from other aircraft. It is simply approval for the pilot to proceed to the airport using visual references to the ground. The controller still has to provide separation from other IFR aircraft.

NONRADAR SEPARATION

After initial departure, nonradar separation is just what it says, separation based entirely on the pilot's position reports. Nonradar separation incorporates time and, in some cases, distances determined by distance measuring equipment (DME). It also relies upon protected airspace. The following separation standards are taken from the Controller's Handbook (7110.65):

INITIAL SEPARATION OF SUCCESSIVE DEPARTING AIRCRAFT

Par. 6-10 Minima on Diverging Courses

Separate aircraft that will fly courses diverging by 45 degrees or more after departing the same or adjacent airports by use of one of the following minima:

> *a. When aircraft will fly diverging courses:*

>> *1. Immediately after takeoff—one minute until courses diverge*

>> *2. Within five minutes after takeoff—two minutes until courses diverge.*

>> *3. Within 13 miles DME after takeoff—three miles until courses diverge.*

Longitudinal Separation
Par. 6-31 Minima on Same, Converging, or Crossing Courses

Separate aircraft on the same, converging, or crossing course by an interval expressed in time or distance, using the following minima:

> *a. When the leading aircraft maintains a speed at least 44 knots faster than the following aircraft—five miles between aircraft using DME and/or area navigation (RNAV); or three minutes between other aircraft.*
>
> *b. When the leading aircraft maintains a speed at least 22 knots faster than the following aircraft—ten miles between aircraft using DME and/or RNAV; or five minutes between other aircraft.*
>
> *c. When an aircraft is climbing or descending through the altitude of another aircraft:*
>
> > *1. Between aircraft using DME—ten miles.*
> >
> > *2. Between other aircraft—five minutes.*
>
> *d. When the conditions of paragraph 6-31a, b, or c cannot be met—20 miles between aircraft using DME and/or RNAV; or ten minutes between other aircraft.*

Lateral Separation
Par. 6-40 Separation Methods

Separate aircraft by one of the following methods:

> *a. Clear aircraft on different airways or routes whose widths or protected airspace do not overlap.*

This explanation of separation criterion has not discussed several conditions that are tied to these separations. But it does provide a sense of the complexity of nonradar separation and its relative inefficiency. In nonradar operations, controllers can accommodate two aircraft within 20 miles. By using radar, they can control five in the same distance.

RUNWAY SEPARATION MINIMA

Generally, only one aircraft can use the runway at a time. That is, a second departing aircraft cannot start its takeoff roll until a first departure aircraft has taken off and cleared the end of the runway or turned away from the runway. The separation minima used between departures vary depending upon aircraft categories. Three category definitions are used: Category I is a light-weight, single-engine aircraft; Category II is a light-weight, twin-engine aircraft; and Category III encompasses all other aircraft. Using these categories, the following standard separations apply:

- **When only Category I aircraft are involved**—3,000 feet

- **When a Category I is preceded by a Category II**—3,000 feet

- **When either the preceding or both are Category II aircraft** - 4,500 feet

- **When either is a Category III aircraft**—6,000 feet

Wake turbulence also factors into runway separations. For example, when another aircraft takes off behind a heavy jet, the standard separation is two minutes. Similar separation minima have been established for landing aircraft.

Applying separation minima is the most delicate component of the controller's job. Applying the criteria is an art, not a science. The process is the end product of years of training, but not an end in itself. Controllers never actually reach the optimum; they must always strive to get the job done better. The standards ensure a safe distance between aircraft and take into account equipment limitations, the controller's limitations, and the pilot's limitations. Therefore, if a controller loses required separation, the aircraft probably will not collide, but the controller can expect to get some extra training to sharpen necessary skills. After all, separating aircraft is the name of the game.

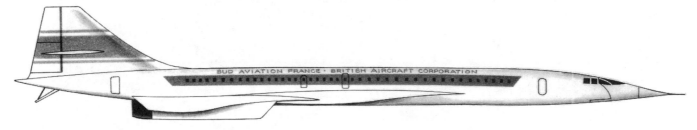

Concorde Supersonic Transport, 1969. First flight of first supersonic civil transport. Aerospatiale and British Aircraft Corp.

CHAPTER SIXTEEN

IMPROVING THE SYSTEM

IMPROVEMENTS NOW AND INTO THE 21ST CENTURY

T he U.S. National Airspace System (NAS) is the busiest and most complex in the world. Earlier chapters have described the system as it is today. By the year 2000 the system will be improved still more. Actually, the National Airspace System (NAS) is undergoing continuous refinement every year.

The basis for improvements made since 1982 and out to the year 2000 is an FAA document called the National Airspace System (NAS) Plan. It is nicknamed the "Brown Book," for the color of its cover. As a plan for capital investment, it contemplated improvements totaling $11 billion when first issued in 1982. For improvements beyond the year 2000, another comprehensive planning document sponsored by the FAA already exists. It is called the Advanced Aviation System Design. Both will be covered in this chapter.

Both forward planning documents are comprehensive. That is, they integrate all elements to be improved. This is significant in comparing prospects for the future with those made in the past. In the past, improvements to the air traffic control system often were considered piecemeal. For example, the need to improve radar might be the focus of attention in one year, and better controller training might receive top priority in the next year. Improvements provided remedies for localized operational problems, but the system was not treated as a whole. Consequently, by 1980, the National Airspace System was expensive to operate and maintain. Its capability for expansion was limited. Worse, the system's ability to adapt to changing requirements was difficult. Recall also that airline deregulation began in 1978. Expected demands on the system were expected to double in 20 years. All of those factors created a situation where piecemeal corrections would not work.

Congress plays a significant oversight role in how the FAA operates. Improvements to the National Airspace System are planned and put into practice with taxpayer funds authorized and appropriated by Congress. As with planning by the FAA, in the past Congress tended to deal with each part of NAS improvements by itself, not as a comprehensive package. But Congress approved the National Airspace System (NAS) Plan as an inclusive and thorough document late in 1981.

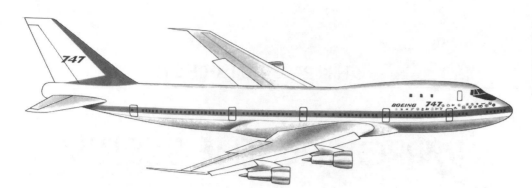

Boeing 747-100, 1969. First wide-body jumbo-jet civil transport. PanAm began commercial operations in 1970. Boeing Commercial Airplane Co.

NATIONAL AIRSPACE SYSTEM PLAN

The FAA's creation of the National Airspace System Plan and its approval by Congress as a package was an important achievement. J. Lynn Helms was the FAA Administrator when the plan was adopted. He deserves credit for his leadership in bringing the plan together and in convincing Congress of the merits of the comprehensive approach. The plan involved making a commitment to major capital investments over a long period of time, $11 billion to start. The prospect of such investments created opportunities for industry to develop new equipment to meet new demands. Industry, Congress, and the FAA have cooperated in putting the plan into practice since it was first issued in December 1981.

Both the FAA and Congress recognized that even the most farsighted plans must evolve and be modified as conditions change. For its part, Congress required the FAA to report regularly, and to provide an annual update on the plan. The FAA has seen the plan evolve over the past few years. At first, it concentrated on system design and buying hardware. Then, on executing the design and putting the hardware to work. In 1990, FAA Administrator James B. Busey developed a new capital investment plan. His plan incorporated changes in approach and format, and built on the achievements of the "Brown Book" as it evolved.

GOALS OF THE NAS PLAN

Goals of the National Airspace System (NAS) Plan are simply stated. Its central objective is to provide for the safe and efficient use of the Nation's airspace, while minimizing constraints on its use. Within that central goal, the FAA identified specific objectives. They include:

1) Having an operating National Airspace System in place that meets the national aviation demand at the time it is required. This objective recognizes that demands on the system are expected to become more intense as time passes. Aircraft operations at airports are expected to grow by more than 45 percent between 1982 and 2000. At the same time, demand on terminal control facilities is projected to increase by 92 percent. Demands on other parts of the system are expected to grow in similar fashion.

2) Accommodating increasing demand in a way that allows airspace users to operate with a minimum of artificial constraints and with fuel efficiency.

3) Reducing operational errors by controllers by 80 percent between 1984 and 1995.

4) Reducing risks of midair and surface traffic collisions, landing and weather related accidents, and collisions with the ground.

5) Increasing air traffic controller and flight specialist productivity. The objective: to improve productivity by a factor of at least two by the year 2000, compared with 1980. In numbers, the productivity goal by 2000 is 10,982 operations per controller position per year.

6) Reducing the technical staff required to maintain and operate the modernized and expanded system by one-third by the year 2000 compared to 1980. That means cutting the technical staff to 7,735 by 2000.

7) Holding maintenance costs of the system to 1980 levels.

HOST COMPUTER SYSTEM INSTALLED

The most significant project already completed is called the Host Computer system. A host computer is a replacement computer which uses existing software from another computer system. The Host system was designed to replace the IBM 9020 computers in the centers. They were old and tired and operating too close to their capacity.

The Host computer replacement worked out on time, with the first one becoming operational in Seattle in mid-1987. The system was operational in all 20 centers by June 1988 as planned. It has been performing at expectation, if not better.

Voyager, 1986. First non-stop, unrefuelled aerial circumanvigation of the earth, Dec. 23, 1986. Voyager Aircraft Co.

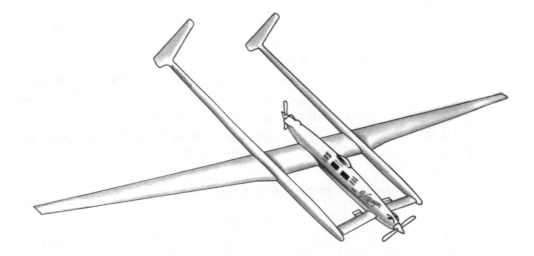

COMMON CONSOLE
Operational Features

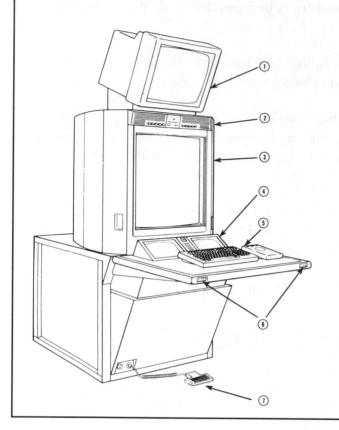

① **Auxiliary Display** accommodates support data products such as manuals, checklists, plates and maps/charts on a high resolution graphics monitor. These products are also available on the main display.

② **Power and communications controls**
  • Ground-to-ground speaker with volume and chime control and left headset jacks (2). Volume controls on the left.
  • Air-to-ground speaker with volume control and right headset jacks (2). Volume controls on the right.
  • VSCS and common console power switches are in center.

③ **Main Display Monitor** 20" x 20" with 100 lines per inch. Very high resolution and multi-color. May be used for radar or data display.

④ **Voice Switching and Control System (VSCS)** components include Display Modules and Indirect Access Keypad.
  • Each display is
    – multi-function   – multi-color
    – touch-sensitive   – interchangeable with the others
  • Displays provide access to and assignment of communication functions within the sector (intercom/interphone lines and up to 24 simultaneous frequencies).

⑤ **Keyboard and trackball** are movable to accommodate individual preferences.

⑥ **Headset jacks** (4) accommodate both left and right-hand operation and make provisions for trainee and supervisor access.

⑦ A **push-to-talk footswitch** is available for each console.

ELEMENTS OF THE NAS PLAN

The comprehensive National Airspace Plan includes major elements which correspond to the basic breakdown of the air traffic control functions and supporting field activities. Knowledge already gained in earlier chapters makes these plans easier to understand.

Take the category of "Air Traffic Control," for instance. The plan addresses improvements in the familiar functional areas of terminal systems, en route systems, and flight service and weather systems.

Supporting systems are broken down into categories of ground-to-air, interfacility communications, and maintenance and operations support systems. Finally, the plan addresses other capital needs that have become apparent but have not been accommodated in the planning, as well as a plan for making the transition into using the new systems, and also considering how military activities interact with the National Airspace System.

Highlights of the major categories follow in the next several pages.

Consoles are joined into a sector suite for use in the centers. Radar displays and tabular data appear on multicolor screens. (Raytheon)

AIR TRAFFIC CONTROL SYSTEMS

Three major thrusts are central to the plan for en route and terminal air traffic control improvements.

First, the FAA plans to consolidate major ATC facilities from more than 200 in 1990 to less than 30 by the year 2000. Second, the use of common modular computers and software, as well as modular controller work stations, will increase capacity and availability.

Third, the FAA expects that safety, fuel efficiency, and productivity will improve, thanks to higher levels of automation.

What will be consolidated? En route and terminal radar approach control facilities (ARTCC and TRACON) will be consolidated into area control facilities (ACF). The hardware and software elements in facilities are expected to be identical. Also, central computers will be of the same family, and sector suites will be identical.

Thanks to an advanced automation system (AAS), computer processing capability will be distributed. Thus, controllers in sector suites will have additional processing power at their fingertips. The distributed processing capability will provide a new environment in which air traffic controllers function more effectively. In a typical sector suite, multiple displays will display the air traffic and weather situation; alphanumeric flight and weather data and other aeronautical information, such as notices to airmen; and traffic planning data, including the ability to probe the system for conflict free, fuel-efficient flight paths.

The AAS will include color radar presentation. The working group of controllers who helped develop the NAS plan wanted color presentations and the designers agreed.

Distributed processing will provide high availability and backup protection from total system failure. Increased operational flexibility can be achieved since the number of controller operating positions can be reconfigured to meet changing demand based on day-to-day or hour-to-hour workload requirements.

AUTOMATED EN ROUTE ATC

Next will come automated en route air traffic control, designated by the acronym AERA. Those functions will be added in incremental steps. AERA is in fact, the most significant change to the air traffic system contained in the plan. It is the first attempt to introduce the computer into the decision-making process.

THREE PHASES OF AERA ARE PLANNED:

AERA 1 is first. In this phase, a four-dimensional flight path trajectory estimation model will be developed. (Time is the fourth dimension.) The estimation model will support such features as:

Flight plan conflict probe, which will predict potential violations of separation standards between aircraft.

Sector workload analysis, which will calculate and display controller workload measures to supervisors and specialists to assist them in balancing sector staffing levels.

Trial flight plan function, which will allow controllers to evaluate alternative clearances before issuing them to aircraft.

Reconformance aid, which will assist controllers in reestablishing aircraft conformance with their flight plan positions.

Reminder function, which will assist controllers by reminding them of planned actions.

Next comes AERA 2. It will extend AERA 1 functions. It will detect potential conflicts and provide the controller with resolutions of the conflicts before they become hazardous.

AERA 3 will extend the AERA capability even more. That includes issuing computer-generated clearances, as well as transmitting the clearances and weather and flight information direct to aircraft via data link.

AERA presents the challenge of developing very complex software for the operating program, and even more complex software to validate the system in operation. It will transform the controller's role away from active participation in separating aircraft, to that of an alert but passive monitor.

The open question, and one that must be resolved if AERA is to function as intended, is this: if the automatic system malfunctions, if something goes wrong, will human controllers be able to intervene in time?

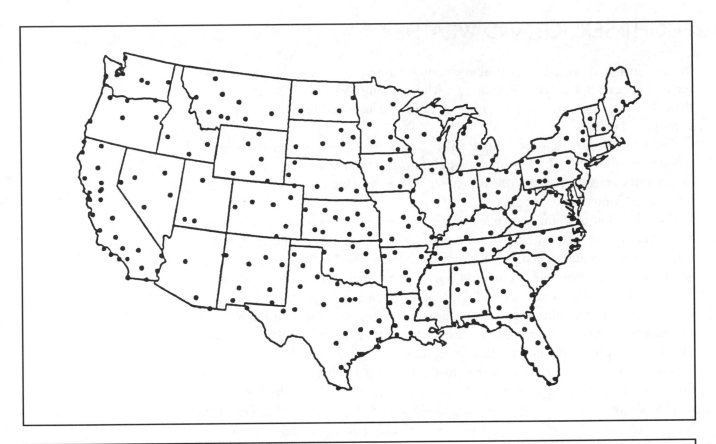

The "measles" dots across the United States show the distribution of Flight Service Stations in 1985 (top). Below, between 1990 and 2000, automation reduces the numbers to a very few. (FAA)

FLIGHT SERVICE AND WEATHER

In this functional area, automation and consolidation are expected to provide better and more complete services to airmen while holding costs down. By 1994, more than 300 nonautomated flight service stations will be consolidated into 61 new automated facilities.

The FAA intends that the automated FSS will provide pilots with "one-stop" service for weather, flight plan filing, and information about system status such as delays and outages. Also, improved weather services will increase safety and be tailored to individual pilots' needs.

Consolidation of flight service stations has been one of the most agonizing and controversial of Federal programs. The proposal to consolidate manned flight service stations into automated facilities first surfaced in the 1960s. Almost 40 years will have passed before the automation is finally accomplished.

Equipment problems have slowed the process, but generally it is a political story. Congressmen do not take too easily to closing federal facilities and cutting back on the number of federal employees in their districts. It is somewhat akin to closing the local post office, and just a little behind closing a military base.

Airmen who have been accustomed to dealing with a skilled human being at a flight service station have complained about having to adapt to dealing with a remote, anonymous machine. Over the transition period, as staffing has been held to a minimum, some facilities have been staffed only part of the time. Some only operated eight hours a days, five days a week with only one specialist on duty. On more than one occasion a female FSS specialist has had to take maternity leave, closing the facility for three months. In such cases the services were provided by a nearby Automated Flight Service Station, but not without complaints from users and Congress, and reams of FAA paper explaining the situation.

By the year 2000 the system will have the capability to provide the majority of flight services directly to pilots without specialist intervention.

An especially interesting project associated with the automated flight service stations is the Automated Weather Observing System (AWOS). AWOS will obtain critical aviation weather data through the use of automated sensors. Examples include wind speed and direction, temperature, dew point, altimeter setting, cloud height, visibility, plus the precipitation type, occurrence and accumulation. The AWOS system will process the data, and disseminate the information to pilots via computer synthesized voice.

It is clear that aviation people are going to be doing a lot of talking to computers.

GROUND-TO-AIR

Eighteen projects are listed under this heading in the NAS Plan. The plan underscores three major themes related to the ground-to-air system. Again, consolidation and modernization lead the way.

Navigation, radar, and communications facilities will be consolidated and modernized so that an integrated national network will provide the required coverage with a reduced number of separate facilities and at a reduced cost.

The older instrument landing systems (ILS) will be succeeded by microwave landing systems (MLS). The newer MLS will provide multiple, curved, and segmented approaches and selectable glide angles. The FAA is testing MLS systems at operational commercial airports.

Third, a discretely addressable surveillance capability (called Mode S) will be put into practice. The system will not only identify aircraft, it will also include an integral data link. By that data link, information will be sent directly into the aircraft for use by the pilot. This system will replace the present ATC radar beacon interrogator systems at most terminal and en route surveillance areas.

En route surveillance (radar) coverage, as traffic density requires, will be provided down to 6,000 feet msl or minimum instrument flight rules altitudes and to the surface at qualifying airports. By the mid 1990s Mode S and data link coverage will be provided down to 12,500 feet msl and to the surface at designated airports.

Data link capability is, in truth, the wave of the future. Voice communication channels are extremely cluttered at high density traffic locations. Both controller and pilot errors are attributed to communication mistakes. Just under 15 percent of all controller operational errors are attributed to the controller's failure to properly monitor a pilot's clearance readback. A survey was conducted by all 20 centers and selected terminals over a five-day period. Approximately 9,000 pilot communications mistakes were recorded by controllers. The vast majority were minor errors, but it demonstrates the weakness of voice communications. With data links, information will be transmitted between pilots and controllers precisely, without the chances of error that are inherent in voice communications.

INTERFACILITY COMMUNICATIONS

The ATC system lives and dies on reliable communications among its many facilities. The FAA is one of AT&T's best customers, using its network services to link the far-flung operations into a coherent system.

The key points in the Plan relating to interfacility communications are these. First, the system will be characterized by a reliable, efficient, integrated, interfacility network. The network will use modern equipment capable of multiplexing, automatic switching, alternate routing, high-speed digital transfer, and trunking. The goal is improved communications at significantly lower operating costs.

Both terrestrial and satellite transmission facilities will be used. Existing microwave links will be replaced with highly reliable, low-maintenance equipment. Also, while some of the equipment will be owned by the FAA, much will be leased from others.

The FAA operates on the principle that a catastrophic event in one location should not shut the system down. That is, all the telephone lines serving one air traffic control center should not go through the same switching center, and there should be backup routings. This is easier said than done. Controllers may not know that they are operating on a non-standard setup until something goes wrong. For instance, the building gets flooded and the controllers' phones go dead, as happened at a New Jersey switching center a few years ago.

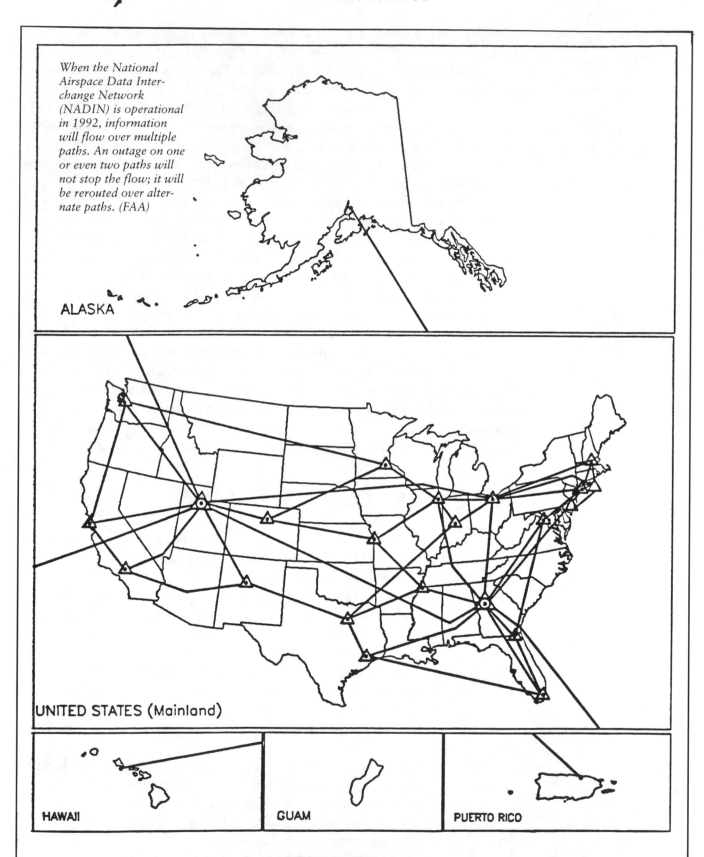

When the National Airspace Data Interchange Network (NADIN) is operational in 1992, information will flow over multiple paths. An outage on one or even two paths will not stop the flow; it will be rerouted over alternate paths. (FAA)

ALASKA

UNITED STATES (Mainland)

HAWAII

GUAM

PUERTO RICO

1992 SYSTEM
NATIONAL AIRSPACE DATA INTERCHANGE NETWORK (NADIN)

MAINTENANCE AND OPERATIONS SUPPORT

This is another area that does not sound very exciting, but whose vitality is essential for the entire system. Again, the major goals are consolidation, improving service, and containing costs.

The FAA is cutting maintenance costs by consolidating work centers and manned facilities. It is cutting staff level and improving field training. At the same time, flight inspection costs are being contained by consolidating field offices and modernizing the FAA aircraft fleet. These aircraft and skilled crews check the accuracy of the thousands of navigational aids dotted around the country. The FAA flight inspection crews fly more than 23,000 hours annually in checking navigational aids.

A concept called "remote maintenance" saves money while maintaining high standards of performance. Under this concept, an FAA maintenance expert can monitor key systems from many miles away. He can perform diagnostic checks with the same confidence that he would if he were on the scene. It is a good theory and technologically feasible. However, controllers usually like to have a technician around who is as close as "touch" and "feel," and who will get to fixing the thing and get it back on the air.

OTHER CAPITAL NEEDS

After initial development of the NAS Plan, new requirements became evident. In this category, the Brown Book lists 14 projects listed as requiring action before 1992, and 10 more after 1992. They are generally support projects and replacement systems.

Included are such things as additional ILS equipment for those airports with a requirement that must be satisfied before the MLS becomes operational. There is also a project called Automatic Dependent Surveillance (ADS). This is a data link system which will provide aircraft position information directly from the aircraft's navigational equipment. It will be used first in oceanic areas where there is no radar coverage.

The Global Positioning System (GPS) is not part of the NAS Plan because it is a Department of Defense system (although GPS monitors are included in the Plan). GPS is a system comprising 21 or more navigational satellites which will provide extremely accurate position fixing for aviation, maritime and other interests. The GPS will eventually make the current VOR system obsolete.

LORAN C is primarily a maritime system, but it has been adapted for aviation and might provide a low cost navigation system for general aviation aircraft that would give them a GPS-like capability. A gap in the maritime LORAN system exists in the middle of the USA. The "mid-continent gap" will be filled in with a system that is in the Brown Book. This will mean that a pilot will be capable of flying random routes, not bound by today's requirement to fly from point to point, passing over geographically located VORs. The question is when will the ATC system be able to accommodate such flexibility? Not until the time that AERA phase 3 is in action, probably.

RETURN ON INVESTMENT

The NAS Plan is a massive undertaking. It is complicated by its having to be put into service during continuous operation of the system. The ATC system cannot shut down for three months to accommodate a switch-over. Consequently, transition planning is crucial. For instance, centers are having whole new buildings constructed to house the new equipment. On a night when everything is ready controllers man consoles in both the old and new rooms. The new equipment is brought on-line to control traffic. But the old consoles are manned for a while. That is done to make sure that everything is wired correctly and there are no glitches in the software.

As we have said before, controllers are a conservative lot. It is in their nature, given the hazards of making mistakes. They will not embrace a new setup quickly. They will test it, see what its limits are, get used to the buttons, experiment a little bit, then make it work better and in different ways than any of us envision.

Ultimately, as the NAS Plan and its pieces are put into place and their operations integrated, its goals will be realized. That means safer and fuel-efficient flight paths, free of conflict with other aircraft. Overhead costs will be cut, and so will the number of people required to operate the system.

However, the demand for air traffic controllers is expected to remain steady for years into the future. Also, as the current NAS Plan is being put into practice, other people will be working on the next generation system. That is the system of the 21st Century. The roadmap for developing the system is a project called, "Advanced Aviation System Design."

VISION OF THE FUTURE

While improvements in the air traffic control system contained in the National Airspace Plan were coming about, a small group of aviation planners was looking further ahead. This was an advanced aviation system design team. I was affiliated with the team in the twilight of my FAA career. The team produced a report in 1989 called "Advanced Aviation System Design." Its findings and its approach create a true vision of the future for the global aviation system. FAA Administrator T. Allan McArtor called it a "planned and reasoned course for aviation."

Demand on the global aviation system will continue unabated. In the U.S. alone, revenue passenger miles will double by 2000, and double once again by the year 2015. International passengers will double and double again over the same intervals. But no major new domestic airports are expected by 2000. To keep pace with the increased demand which is expected in the next 15 years and the next century, it will be essential to exploit technology to its fullest in the global aviation system.

That was a central conclusion of the Advanced Aviation System Design group. If the future global aviation system is to work effectively, it must exploit technology to the fullest. Major elements of the design are these: Satellites, Airports, Vehicles (aircraft), Airspace, Avionics, People, Ground Facilities, Policy/Legislation/Regulation, and Support Infrastructure. Each of these elements is discussed in more detail in the paragraphs that follow.

	1982	1985	1990	1995	2000	Percent Growth 1982-2000
Large Hub Commercial Service*						
Airports	24	28	29	31	32	33.3
Operations (millions)	8.2	11.1	12.4	14.6	16.1	96.3
Enplanements** (millions)	196.3	280.3	352.3	453.0	538.8	174.5
Based Aircraft (thousands)	2.4	3.5	3.1	3.2	3.6	50.0
Other Commercial Service*						
Airports	521	518	534	537	556	6.7
Operations (millions)	53.8	40.0	48.7	57.5	66.5	23.6
Enplanements** (millions)	112.7	125.2	182.8	220.7	264.1	134.3
Based Aircraft (thousands)	61.0	60.3	57.8	58.3	60.4	(1.0)

*   Airports at which over 1 percent of total U.S. passengers are enplaned.

**   Includes scheduled and nonscheduled traffic by domestic and foreign flag carriers, commuters, and air taxis.

***   Airports receiving regularly scheduled service when 2,500 or more passengers are enplaned annually (excludes large hub commercial airports).

Extraordinary growth in commercial airport operations are forecast between 1982 and the year 2000. (FAA)

The aviation system contemplated for the early 21st century is governed by the fundamental process which applies to all systems: information is acquired, information is processed, and there is a response action.

The design may be summarized simply, using the nine elements mentioned above. Satellites provide the signals in space and the communication links necessary to enable the fundamental design premise. Vehicles, which are used to move people and goods through the airspace to and from airports, must determine their position and communicate this information to other system participants. People, in the air or on the ground, will utilize the information processed by their avionics or ground facilities to take the appropriate response action.

The underlying operating principles of the Advanced Aviation System Design are:

1) Vehicles operating in the system must determine their position and communicate their position to all participants needing that information via the appropriate links.

2) System participants process this information and react as necessary according to the system protocol for their operation.

3) People and goods are moved expeditiously and efficiently through a dynamic airspace to and from all types of airports, including superports and networks of vertiports.

4) People operate more in system management than in manipulating controls. They use advanced avionics and automated or semi-automated subsystems both in the air and at ground facilities.

5) New and revised policy, legislation, and regulations permit rapid application of new technologies for all parts of the aviation system including the necessary support infrastructure.

In a very few years, aircraft will pin down their positions precisely via satellite signals. Also, information will be transmitted automatically between aircraft and ground stations, reducing the workload on humans. (Advanced Aviation System Design)

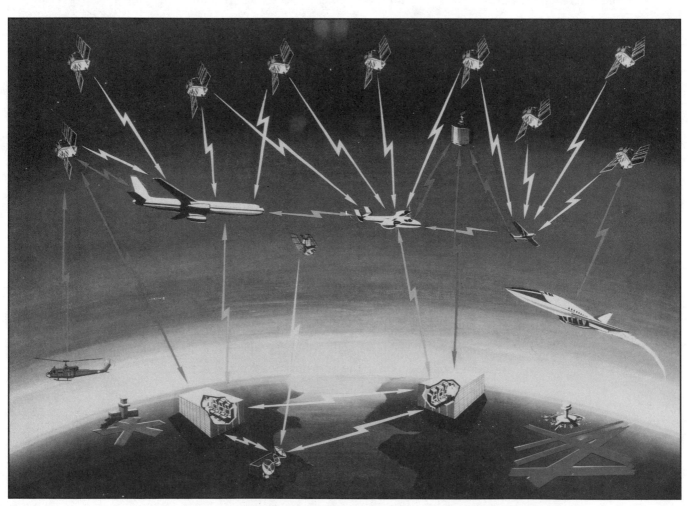

No matter how much automation occurs in the next decade, skilled air traffic control specialists will be required. The FAA Academy will adapt its training to keep pace with automation. (FAA)

KEY ROLE OF SUPPORT INFRASTRUCTURE

The Advanced Aviation System will require major changes in a number of system elements. The support infrastructure must provide the opportunity for those changes to occur.

For example, the introduction of the tiltrotor class of aircraft can be simple or complex. To keep it simple, the tiltrotor aircraft might be treated as just another aircraft. However, its introduction could become quite complex. It could result in a totally new infrastructure of vertiports, routes, new concepts for airspace utilization, relative flight, maintenance, certification, and supply support issues, ticketing, airport transfer to conventional aircraft, and more. Without the proper research and development base, the complex and certainly more desirable approach might never come to pass.

The Advanced Aviation System Design established a goal toward which future system planners can direct their efforts in strategic planning for the next decade and beyond. The design envisions the extensive exploitation of technology, such as satellites for position determination, communications, and automatic dependent surveillance; new vehicles such as the tiltrotor which would, in conjunction with a new infrastructure of airports and airspace, permit new and innovative origin/destination operations; innovative avionics which would provide information on a system basis, rather than a specific phase of flight; and new roles for people, both in the air and on the ground. While it may appear revolutionary to some, it will evolve from the aviation system which currently exists or is being implemented.

The team effort that produced the Advanced Aviation System design established a base line of reference for approaching aviation more comprehensively, more globally, and more systematically than ever before. Knowing what is ahead, you should now have a perspective to assist in your own individual planning for your involvement in aviation.

As one critic said, "The future of aviation isn't what it used to be." Indeed, the future of aviation is more exciting and promising than it ever was. So can your future be joined with the exciting prospects ahead for aviation. As a prospective air traffic controller, you are about to become a part of it.

APPENDIXES

APPENDIX I

WHERE TO GET INFORMATION

T his appendix gives the addresses and telephone numbers of the Federal Job Information/Testing Offices operated by the Office of Personnel Management (OPM) nationwide.

Also listed are the regional offices of the Federal Aviation Administration, again with addresses and telephone numbers.

Persons interested in a career as an FAA air traffic control specialist should make contact with one of these offices to request information and the appropriate government forms.

ALABAMA
Huntsville:
Southerland Building
806 Governors Dr., SW, 35801
(205) 544-5802

ALASKA
Anchorage:
Federal Building
701 C St., Box 22, 99513
(907) 271-5821

ARIZONA
Phoenix:
U.S. Postal Service Bldg.
522 N. Central Ave.,
Room 120, 85004
(602) 261-4736

ARKANSAS
Little Rock:
Federal Bldg., Rm 3421
700 W. Capitol Ave., 72201
(501) 378-5842

CALIFORNIA
Los Angeles:
Linder Bldg., 3rd Floor
845 S. Figueroa, 90017
(213) 894-3360

Sacramento:
1029 J St., 2nd floor, 95814
(916) 551-1464

San Diego:
880 Front St., 92188
Federal Bldg., Rm 459
(619) 575-6165

San Francisco:
211 Main St.,
Second Floor, Room 235, 94105
(415) 974-9725

COLORADO
Denver:
P.O. Box 25167, 80225
(303) 236-4160
Physically located at
12345 W. Alameda Pkwy.
Lakewood, CO

For job information (24 hrs. a day)
in the following states dial:

MONTANA
(303) 236-4162

UTAH
(303) 236-4165

WYOMING
(303) 236-4166
For forms and local supplements dial:
(303) 236-4159

CONNECTICUT
Hartford:
Federal Bldg., Rm. 613
450 Main St., 06103
(203) 240-3263

DELAWARE
(See Philadelphia, PA listing)

DISTRICT OF COLUMBIA
1900 E St., N.W.,
Rm. 1416, 20415
(202) 653-8468

FLORIDA
Orlando:
Commodore Bldg., Suite 125
3444 McCrory Pl, 32803-3712
(305) 648-6148

GEORGIA
Atlanta:
Richard B. Russell Federal Bldg.
Rm. 960, 75 Spring St., S.W., 30303
(404) 331-4315

GUAM
Agana:
Pacific Daily News Bldg.
238 O'Hara St., Rm. 902, 96910
472-7451

HAWAII
Honolulu:
(and other Hawaiian Islands and overseas):
Federal Bldg., Rm. 5316
300 Ala Moana Blvd., 96850
(808) 541-2791
(808) 541-2784 - Overseas jobs

IDAHO
(See Washington listing)

ILLINOIS
Chicago:
175 W. Jackson Blvd.,
Rm. 530, 60604
(312) 353-6192

INDIANA
Indianapolis:
Minton-Capehart Federal Bldg.
575 N. Pennsylvania Ave., 46204
(317) 269-7161

IOWA
(See Kansas City, Missouris listing)

KANSAS
Wichita:
One-Twenty Bldg., Rm. 101
120 S. Market st., 67202
(316) 269-6796

*In Johnson, Leavenworth and
Wyandotte Counties dial*
(816) 374-5702

KENTUCKY
(See Ohio listing)

LOUISIANA
New Orleans:
F. Edward Hebert Bldg.
610 S. Maestri Pl, Rm. 802, 70130
(504) 589-2764

MAINE
(see New Hampshire listing)

MARYLAND
Baltimore:
Garmatz Federal Bldg.
101 W. Lombard Street, 21201
(310) 962-3822

MASSACHUSETTS
Boston:
Boston Federal Office Bldg.,
10 Causeway St., 02222-1031
(617) 565-5900

MICHIGAN
Detroit:
477 Michigan Ave.,
Rm 565, 48226
(313) 226-6950

MINNESOTA
Twin Cities:
Federal Building
Ft. Snelling, Twin Cities, 55111
(612) 725-3430

MISSISSIPPI
(See Alabama listing)

MISSOURI
Kansas City:
Federal Bldg., Rm 134
601 E. 12th St., 64106
(816) 374-5720

St. Louis:
Old Post Office, Rm. 400
815 Olive St., 63101
(314) 425-4285

MONTANA
(See Colorado listing)

NEBRASKA
(See Kansas listing)

NEVADA
(See Sacramento, CA listing)

NEW HAMPSHIRE
Portsmouth:
Thomas J. McIntyre Federal Bldg.,
Rm. 104
80 Daniel Street, 03801-3879
(603) 431-7115

NEW JERSEY
Newark:
Peter W. Rodino, Jr., Federal Bldg.,
970 Broad St., 07102
(201) 645-3673
In Camden, dial (215) 597-7440

NEW MEXICO
Albuquerque:
Federal Bldg.
421 Gold Ave., S.W., 87102
(505) 766-5583
In Dona Ana, Otero and El Paso
Counties dial (505) 766-1893

NEW YORK
New York City:
Jacob K. Javits Federal Building
26 Federal Plaza, 10278
(212) 264-0422

Syracuse:
James N. Hanley Federal Bldg.
100 S. Clinton St., 13260
(315) 423-5660

NORTH CAROLINA
Raleigh:
Federal Building
310 New Bern Ave.
P.O. Box 25069, 27611
(mailing address)
(919) 856-4361

NORTH DAKOTA
(See Minnesota listing)

OHIO
Dayton:
Federal Bldg., Room 506
200 W. 2nd St., 45402
(513) 225-2720

OKLAHOMA
Oklahoma City:
(mail or phone only)
200 N.W. Fifth St.,
Second Floor, 73102
(405) 231-4948

OREGON
Portland:
Federal Bldg., Rm. 376
1220 S.W. Third St., 97204
(503) 221-3141

PENNSYLVANIA
Harrisburg:
Federal Bldg., Rm. 168
P.O. Box 761, 17108
(717) 782-4494

Philadelphia:
Wm. J. Green, Jr. Federal Bldg.
600 Arch St., Rm. 1416, 19106
(215) 597-7440

Pittsburgh:
Federal Building
1000 Liberty Ave., Rm. 119, 15222
(412) 644-2755

PUERTO RICO
San Juan:
Federico Degatau Federal Bldg.
Carlos E. Chardon St.
Hato Rey, P.R. 00918
(809) 753-4209

RHODE ISLAND
Providence:
John O. Pastore Federal Bldg.
Rm. 310, Kennedy Plaza, 02903
(401) 528-5251

SOUTH CAROLINA
(See North Carolina listing)

SOUTH DAKOTA
(see Minnesota listing)

TENNESSEE
Memphis:
200 Jefferson Ave.
Suite 1312, 38103-2355
(901) 521-3956

TEXAS
Dallas:
(mail or phone only)
Rm. 6812, 1100 Commerce St. 75242
(214) 767-8035

Houston:
(phone recording only)
(713) 226-2375

San Antonio:
(mail or phone only)
643 E. Durgano Blvd., 78206
(512) 229-6611 or 6600

UTAH
(See Colorado listing)

VERMONT
(See New Hampshire listing)

VIRGINIA
Norfolk:
Federal Bldg., Rm 220
200 Granby Mall, 23510-1886
(804) 441-3355

WASHINGTON
Seattle:
Federal Building
915 Second Ave., 98174
(206) 442-4365

WEST VIRGINIA
(See Ohio listing)
or dial **(513) 225-2866**

WISCONSIN
Residents in **Counties of Grant,
Iowa, Lafayette, Dane, Green, Rock,
Jefferson, Walworth, Waukesha, Racine,
Kenosha** and **Milwaukee** should dial
(312) 353-6189 for job information.
All other Wisconsin residents should
refer to the Minnesota listing for
Federal job information in their area.

WYOMING
(See Colorado listing)

Now follows a listing of Federal Aviation Administration Regional Headquarters. They are useful sources of information about aviation careers. Ask them for the required forms and dates of testing for the air traffic controller written examination.

ALASKAN REGION HEADQUARTERS
222 West 7th Avenue
Anchorage, Alaska 99513

CENTRAL REGION HEADQUARTERS
601 East 12th Street
Federal Building
Kansas City, Missouri 64106

EASTERN REGION HEADQUARTERS
JFK International Airport
Fitzgerald Federal Building
Jamaica, New York 11430

GREAT LAKES REGION HEADQUARTERS
O'Hare Lake Office Center
2300 East Devon Avenue
Des Plaines, Illinois 60018

NEW ENGLAND REGION HEADQUARTERS
12 New England Executive Park
Burlington, Massachusetts 01803

NORTHWEST MOUNTAIN REGION HEADQUARTERS
17900 Pacific Highway South
C-68966
Seattle, Washington 98168

SOUTHERN REGION HEADQUARTERS
3400 Norman Berry Drive
East Point, Georgia 20636
(Mail Address: P.O. Box 20636
Atlanta, Georgia 30320)

SOUTHWEST REGION HEADQUARTERS
4400 Blue Mound Road
Fort Worth, Texas 76193-0000

**WESTERN PACIFIC REGION
HEADQUARTERS**
15000 Aviation boulevard
Hawthorne, California
(Mail address: P O Box 92007
Worldway Postal Center
Los Angeles, California 90009)

EDUCATION RESOURCES

AIRWAY SCIENCE SCHOOLS

T hese Airway Science Schools all participate in the Federal Aviation Administration's airway science project.
While they all share that common characteristic, their individual criteria for admission and their specific programs will vary. Ask for admission information and course catalogues from the ones that interest you.

ARIZONA STATE UNIVERSITY
Tempe, AZ 85287

AUBURN UNIVERSITY
162 Wilmore Lab
Auburn, Al 36849

BRIDGEWATER STATE COLLEGE
Bridgewater, MA 02324

CENTRAL MISSOURI STATE UNIVERSITY
Technology Complex 210
Warrensburg, MO 64093

CENTRAL WASHINGTON UNIVERSITY
Hebeler 101
Ellensburg, WA 98926

CHADRON STATE COLLEGE
Chadron, NE 69337

DANIEL WEBSTER COLLEGE
University Boulevard
Nashua, NH 03063

DELAWARE STATE COLLEGE
1200 North DuPont Highway
Dover, DE 19901

DELTA STATE UNIVERSITY
Cleveland, MS 38733

DOWLING COLLEGE
Idle Hour Boulevard
Oakdale, NY 11769

EDWARD WATERS COLLEGE
1658 Kings Rd., Lee Admin Bldg, Rm 2
Jacksonville, FL 32209

ELIZABETH CITY STATE UNIVERSITY
ECSU Box 823
Elizabeth City, NC 27909

EMBRY-RIDDLE AERONAUTICAL UNIVERSITY
Daytona Beach, FL 32014

FLORIDA INSTITUTE OF TECHNOLOGY
150 W. University Blvd.
Melbourne, FL 32901

FLORIDA MEMORIAL COLLEGE
15800 Northwest 42nd Ave.
Miami, FL 33054

HAMPTON UNIVERSITY
Hampton, VA 23668

INTERAMERICAN UNIVERSITY OF PUERTO RICO
Metropolitan Campus, Box 1293
Hato Rey, PR 00919

JACKSON STATE UNIVERSITY
1400 John R. Lynch St.
Jackson, MS 39217

KEARNEY STATE COLLEGE
Kearney, NE 68849

KENT STATE UNIVERSITY
4020 Kent Rd.
Stow, OH 44224

LOUISIANA TECH UNIVERSITY
P.O. Box 3181 Tech Station
Ruston, LA 71270

METROPOLITAN STATE UNIVERSITY
1006 11th St.
Denver, CO 80204

MIDDLE TENNESSEE STATE UNIVERSITY
Box 67
Murfreesboro, TN 37132

NATIONAL UNIVERSITY
4141 Camino del Rio South
San Diego, CA 92108

NORTHEAST LOUISIANA UNIVERSITY
Monroe, LA 71209

OHIO STATE UNIVERSITY
P.O. Box 3022
Columbus, OH 43210

OHIO UNIVERSITY
Athens, OH 45701

PARKS COLLEGE
St. Louis University
Cahokia, IL 62206

PURDUE UNIVERSITY
West Lafayette, IN 47907

SAN JOSE STATE UNIVERSITY
One Washington Square
San Jose, CA 95192

SO. ILLINOIS UNIV. AT CARBONDALE
Carbondale, IL   52901

ST. CLOUD STATE UNIVERSITY
HH 101-SCSU
St. Cloud, MN 56301

ST. FRANCIS COLLEGE
180 Remsen St.
Brooklyn, NY 11201

SUFFOLK UNIVERSITY
8 Ashburton Place
Boston, MA 02108

TEXAS SOUTHERN UNIVERSITY
3100 Celburne Ave.
Houston, TX 77004

UNIVERSITY OF MARYLAND EASTERN SHORE
Airway Science Program
Princess Anne, MD 21853

UNIVERSITY OF NORTH DAKOTA
Box 8216 University Station
Grand Forks, ND 58202

UTAH STATE UNIVERSITY
Industrial Science 112E
Logan, UT 84322

WESTERN MICHIGAN UNIVERSITY
Kalamazoo, MI 49088

WINONA STATE UNIVERSITY
Johnson and Sanborn
Winona, MN 55987

FEDERAL AVIATION ADMINISTRATION SOURCES

At FAA headquarters and its major offices nationwide, education officers are sources of information and materials about aviation. Persons interested in the air traffic control system, air safety, and virtually any aviation topic are encouraged to contact these persons. They are designated by the term Aviation Education Officers.

AT FAA HEADQUARTERS
Phillip S. Woodruff, APA-100
Director of Aviation Education
MaryJo Byberg
Connie Housewright
800 Independence Avenue, SW
Office of Public Affairs
Aviation Education Program
Washington, DC 20591
(202) 267-3476

AT THE AERONAUTICAL CENTER
Robert Hoppers, AAC-5
Office of Public Affairs
Room 308, H-West
PO Box 25082
Oklahoma City, OK 73125
(405) 680-7500

AT THE FAA TECHNICAL CENTER
Holly Baker, ACT-5
Office of Public Affairs
Atlantic City International Airport
Atlantic City, NJ 08405

In the regional offices:

ALASKAN REGION
Ivy Moore, AAL-5A
Mary Lou Wojtalik
222 West 7th Avenue, Box 14
Anchorage, AK 99513-7587
(907) 271-5169
for: **Alaska**

CENTRAL REGION
Sandra Campbell, ACE-5
601 E 12th Street
Federal Building, Room 1501
Kansas City, MO 64106
(816) 426-5449
for: **Iowa, Kansas, Missouri, and Nebraska**

EASTERN REGION
George Briskey, AEA-15C
JFK International Airport
Federal Building
Jamaica, NY 11430
(718) 917-1056
for: **Delaware, District of Columbia, Maryland, New Jersey, Pennsylvania, Virginia, and West Virginia**

GREAT LAKES REGION
Lee Carlson, AGL-5A
O'Hare Lake Office Center
2300 East Devon Avenue
Des Plaines, IL 60018
(312) 694-7042
for: **Illinois, Indiana, Michigan, Minnesota, North Dakota, Ohio, South Dakota, and Wisconsin**

NEW ENGLAND REGION
Arlene B. Feldman, ANE-1
12 New England Executive Park
Burlington, MA 01803
(617) 273-7244
for: **Connecticut, Maine, New Hampshire, Rhode Island, Vermont, and Massachusetts.**

NORTHWEST MOUNTAIN REGION
Richard Meyer, ANM-5E
17900 Pacific Highway South
C-68966
Seattle, WA 98168
(206) 431-2008
for: **Colorado, Idaho, Montana, Oregon, Utah, Washington and Wyoming**

SOUTHERN REGION
Jack Barker, ASO-5
PO Box 20636
Atlanta, GA 30320
(404) 763-7201
for: **Alabama, Florida, Georgia, Kentucky, Mississippi, North Carolina, Tennessee, Puerto Rico, and the Virgin Islands.**

SOUTHWEST REGION
Geraldine Cook, ASW-5
4400 Blue Mound Road
Fort Worth, TX 76193-0005
(817) 624-5804
for: **Arkansas, Louisiana, New Mexico,
Oklahoma,** and **Texas**

WESTERN-PACIFIC REGION
Barbara Abels, AWP-5
Fred O'Donnell
PO Box 92007
Worldway Postal Center
Los Angeles, CA 90009
(213) 297-1431
for: **Arizona, California, Nevada,** and **Hawaii**

AVIATION EDUCATION RESOURCE CENTERS

These centers are another means of obtaining information about aviation topics. They function as information distribution centers for FAA aviation education materials and resources. They also develop their own aviation education materials. Among the types of materials they distribute are printed matter, videotapes, slides, and computer educational software.

Persons at these centers answer general information requests, provide duplication services, conduct workshops, and make aviation-related presentations.

ALABAMA

Alabama Aviation Technical College
Ms. Megan Johnson, President
PO Box 1209
Ozark, AL 36361
(205) 774-5113

University of North Alabama
Ms. Michele R. Walker
PO Box 5016
Florence, AL 35632-0001
(205) 760-4623

University Aviation Association
Gary W. Kitely, Executive Director
3410 Skyway Drive
Opelika, AL 36801
(205) 844-2432

ARIZONA

**Embry-Riddle
Aeronautical University**
Dr. Peggy Baty
Associate Dean of Academics
3200 N. Willow Creek Road
Prescott, AZ 86301
(602) 776-3802
(602) 776-3811

CALIFORNIA

National University
Mr. Emiddio Massa
University Park
San Diego, CA 92108
(619) 563-7100

San Jose State University
Dr. H. Gene Little
Chairman, Department of Aviation
1 Washington Square
San Jose, CA 95125-0081
(408) 924-3206

Museum of Flying
Mr. Harvey Ferer
2772 Donald Douglas Loop North
Santa Monica, CA 90405
(213) 392-8822

COLORADO

U.S. Space Foundation
Mr. Mike Diamond
Educational Director
1525 Vapor Trail
Colorado Springs, CO 80916
(719) 550-1000

CONNECTICUT

**Connecticut Department
of Transportation
Bureau of Aeronautics**
Mr. Edward M. Archibald
24 Wolcott Hill Road
PO Drawer A
Wethersfield, CT 06109
(203) 566-4417

FLORIDA

**Embry-Riddle
Aeronautical University**
Mrs. Patricia Fleener-Ryan
Center for Excellence
Regional Airport
Daytona Beach, FL 32014
(904) 239-6440

Florida Memorial College
Mr. Anthony Sharp, Director
15800 Northeast 42 Avenue
Miami, FL 33054
(305)623-4277

KANSAS

Kansas College of Technology
Mrs. Betty Cramton
2408 Scanlan Avenue
Salina, KS 67401
(913) 825-0275

ILLINOIS

**Parks College
of St. Louis University**
Dr. Paul A. Whelan
500 Falling Springs Road
Cahokia, IL 62206
(618) 337-7500

Southern Illinois University
Mr. Paul Harre
College of Technical Careers
Room 222
Carbondale, IL 62901
(618) 453-8821

**State of Illinois
Division of Aeronautics**
Mr. Richard M. Ware
One Langhorne Bond Drive
Capital Airport
Springfield, IL 62707-8415
(217) 785-8516

MASSACHUSETTS

Bridgewater State College
Mr. Bill Annesley
Department of Aviation Safety
Bridgewater, MA 02324
(508) 697-1395

Boston Museum of Science
Matthew Stein, Outreach Coordinator
Planetarium Science
Boston, MA 02114-1099
(617) 589-0266

MAINE

Kennebec Valley Technical College
Mr. Edgar B. Rhodes
P.O. Box 29
Fairfield, ME 04937-0020
(207) 453-9762

MICHIGAN

Oakland University
Dr. David Housel, Director
Aviation & Space Center
115 O'Dowd Hall
Room 216
Rochester, MI 48063

NEW HAMPSHIRE

**New Hampshire
Department of Transportation
Division of Aeronautics**
Mr. Ronald Wanner
65 Airport Road
Concord Municipal Airport
Concord, NH 03301-52

NEW YORK

Dowling College
Dr. Albert E. Donor
Oakdale, NY 11769-1999
(516) 244-3200

TENNESSEE

Middle Tennessee State University
Dr. Wallace R. Maples
Aerospace Department
East Main Street
P.O. Box 67
Murfreesboro, TN 37132

WEST VIRGINIA

Salem-Teikyo University
Dr. Ronald Ohl
Salem, WV 26426
(304) 782-5234

OKLAHOMA

University of Oklahoma
Dr. Virginia Duca
1700 Asp Avenue
Norman, OK 73037-0001
(405) 325-1935

WISCONSIN

Experimental Aircraft Association
Mr. Chuck Larsen
EAA Aviation Center
3000 Poberezny Road
Oshkosh, WI 54903-3065
(414) 426-4800

Department of Transportation
Bureau of Aeronautics
Mr. Duane Esse
4802 Sheboygan Avenue
P.O. Box 7914
Madison, WI 53707-7914
(608) 266-3351

VIRGINIA

Virginia Aviation Museum
Mr. Kenneth A. Rowe
Richmond International Airport
5701 Huntsman Road
Sandston, VA 23150-1946
(804) 222-8690

APPENDIX III

PILOT/CONTROLLER GLOSSARY

The Pilot/Controller Glossary is published by the Flight Information and Obstructions Branch (ATO-210) of the Federal Aviation Administration (FAA). Its purpose is to promote a common understanding of the terms used in the Air Traffic Control system. The FAA notes that the terms are applicable to both users and operators of the National Airspace System. When pilots and controllers use the terms in this glossary, they have the meaning defined here.

The terms most frequently used in communications between pilots and controllers are printed in **BOLD ITALICS** for quick recognition.

Cross references are made in many cases in this glossary to related items appearing elsewhere in it. Also, where relevant, citations are given to other documents such as the Federal Aviation Regulations (FAR) and the Airman's Information Manual (AIM).

The Pilot/Controller Glossary appears as a supplement in each issue of the Airman's Information Manual (AIM). The Airman's Information Manual is issued by the FAA every 112 days. Revisions to the Pilot/Controller Glossary appear in the AIM as necessary. Revisions or changes are highlighted in the beginning of the AIM and each revised or changed entry is highlighted within the glossary itself.

The Airman's Information Manual (AIM) is available by subscription from the Superintendent of Documents, Government Printing Office, Washington, DC 20402. Price for a one-year subscription is $20.00.

ABBREVIATED IFR FLIGHT PLANS — An authorization by ATC requiring pilots to submit only that information needed for the purpose of ATC. It includes only a small portion of the usual IFR flight plan information. In certain instances, this may be only aircraft identification, location, and pilot request. Other information may be requested if needed by ATC for separation/control purposes. It is frequently used by aircraft which are airborne and desire an instrument approach or by aircraft which are on the ground and desire a climb to VFR-on-top. (See VFR-ON-TOP) (Refer to AIM)

ABEAM — An aircraft is "abeam" a fix, point, or object when that fix, point, or object is approximately 90 degrees to the right or left of the aircraft track. Abeam indicates a general position rather than a precise point.

ABORT — To terminate a preplanned aircraft maneuver; e.g., an aborted takeoff.

ACKNOWLEDGE — Let me know that you have received my message.

ADDITIONAL SERVICES — Advisory information provided by ATC which includes but is not limited to the following:

1. Traffic advisories.

2. Vectors, when requested by the pilot, to assist aircraft receiving traffic advisories to avoid observed traffic.

3. Altitude deviation information of 300 feet or more from an assigned altitude as observed on a verified (reading correctly) automatic altitude readout (Mode C).

4. Advisories that traffic is no longer a factor.

5. Weather and chaff information.

6. Weather assistance.

7. Bird activity information.

8. Holding pattern surveillance.

Additional services are provided to the extent possible contingent only upon the controller's capability to fit them into the performance of higher priority duties and on the basis of limitations of the radar, volume of traffic, frequency congestion, and controller workload. The controller has complete discretion for determining if he is able to provide or continue to provide a service in a particular case. The controller's reason not to provide or continue to provide a service in a particular case is not subject to question by the pilot and need not be made known to him. (See Traffic Advisories) (Refer to AIM)

ADMINISTRATOR — The Federal Aviation Administrator or any person to whom he has delegated his authority in the matter concerned.

ADVISE INTENTIONS — Tell me what you plan to do.

ADVISORY — Advice and information provided to assist pilots in the safe conduct of flight and aircraft movement. (See Advisory Service)

ADVISORY FREQUENCY — The appropriate frequency to be used for Airport Advisory Service. (See Airport Advisory Service and UNICOM) (Refer to Advisory Circular No. 90-42 and AIM)

ADVISORY SERVICE — Advice and information provided by a facility to assist pilots in the safe conduct of flight and aircraft movement. (See Airport Advisory Service, Traffic Advisories, Safety Alerts, Additional Services, Radar Advisory, En Route Flight Advisory Service) (Refer to AIM)

AERIAL REFUELING/IN-FLIGHT REFUELING — A procedure used by the military to transfer fuel from one aircraft to another during flight. (Refer to VFR/IFR Wall Planning Charts).

AERODROME — A defined area on land or water (including any buildings, installations and equipment) intended to be used either wholly or in part for the arrival, departure, and movement of aircraft.

AERONAUTICAL BEACON — A visual NAVAID displaying flashes of white and/or colored light to indicate the location of an airport, a heliport, a landmark, a certain point of a Federal airway in mountainous terrain, or an obstruction. (See Airport Rotating Beacon) (Refer to AIM)

AERONAUTICAL CHART — A map used in air navigation containing all or part of the following: Topographic features, hazards and obstructions, navigation aids, navigation routes, designated airspace, and airports. Commonly used aeronautical charts are:

1. **Sectional Charts** (1:500,000) — Designed for visual navigation of slow or medium speed aircraft. Topographic information on these charts features the portrayal of relief and a judicious selection of visual check points for VFR flight. Aeronautical information includes visual and radio aids to navigation, airports, controlled airspace, restricted areas, obstructions, and related data.

2. **VFR Terminal Area Charts** (1:250,000) — Depict Terminal Control Area (TCA) airspace which provides for the control or segregation of all the aircraft within the TCA. The chart depicts topographic information and aeronautical information which includes visual and radio aids to navigation, airports, controlled airspace, restricted areas, obstructions, and related data.

3. **World Aeronautical Charts** (WAC) (1:1,000,000) — Provide a standard series of aeronautical charts covering land areas of the world at a size and scale convenient for navigation by moderate speed aircraft. Topographic information includes cities and towns, principal roads, railroads, distinctive landmarks, drainage, and relief. Aeronautical information includes visual and radio aids to navigation, airports, airways, restricted areas, obstructions, and other pertinent data.

4. **En Route Low Altitude Charts** — Provide aeronautical information for en route instrument navigation (IFR) in the low altitude stratum. Information includes the portrayal of airways, limits of controlled airspace, position identification and frequencies of radio aids, selected airports, minimum en route and minimum obstruction clearance altitudes, airway distances, reporting points, restricted areas, and related data. Area charts, which are a part of this series, furnish terminal data at a larger scale in congested areas

5. **En Route High Altitude Charts** — Provide aeronautical information for en route instrument navigation (IFR) in the high altitude stratum. Information includes the portrayal of jet routes, identification and frequencies of radio aids, selected airports, distances, time zones, special use airspace, and related information.

6. **Instrument Approach Procedures (IAP) Charts** — Portray the aeronautical data which is required to execute an instrument approach to an airport. These charts depict the procedures, including all related data, and the airport diagram. Each procedure is designated for use with a specific type of electronic navigation system including NDB, TACAN, VOR, ILS/MLS, and RNAV. These charts are identified by the type of navigational aid(s) which provide final approach guidance.

7. **Standard Instrument Departure (SID) Charts** — Designed to expedite clearance delivery and to facilitate transition between takeoff and en route operations. Each SID procedure is presented as a separate chart and may serve a single airport or more than one airport in a given geographical location.

8. **Standard Terminal Arrival (STAR) Charts** — Designed to expedite air traffic control arrival procedures and to facilitate transition between en route and instrument approach operations. Each STAR procedure is presented as a separate chart and may serve a single airport or more than one airport in a given geographical location

9. **Airport Taxi Charts** — Designed to expedite the efficient and safe flow of ground traffic at an airport. These charts are identified by the official airport name; e.g., Washington National Airport.

AFFIRMATIVE — Yes.

AIR CARRIER DISTRICT OFFICE/ACDO — An FAA field office serving an assigned geographical area, staffed with Flight Standards personnel serving the aviation industry and the general public on matters related to the certification and operation of scheduled air carriers and other large aircraft operations.

AIRCRAFT — Device(s) that are used or intended to be used for flight in the air, and when used in air traffic control terminology, may include the flight crew.

AIRCRAFT APPROACH CATEGORY — A grouping of aircraft based on a speed of 1.3 times the stall speed in the landing configuration at maximum gross landing weight. An aircraft shall fit in only one category. If it is necessary to maneuver at speeds in excess of the upper limit of a speed range for a category, the minimums for the next higher category should be used. For example, an aircraft which falls in Category A, but is circling to land at a speed in excess of 91 knots, should use the approach Category B minimums when circling to land. The categories are as follows:

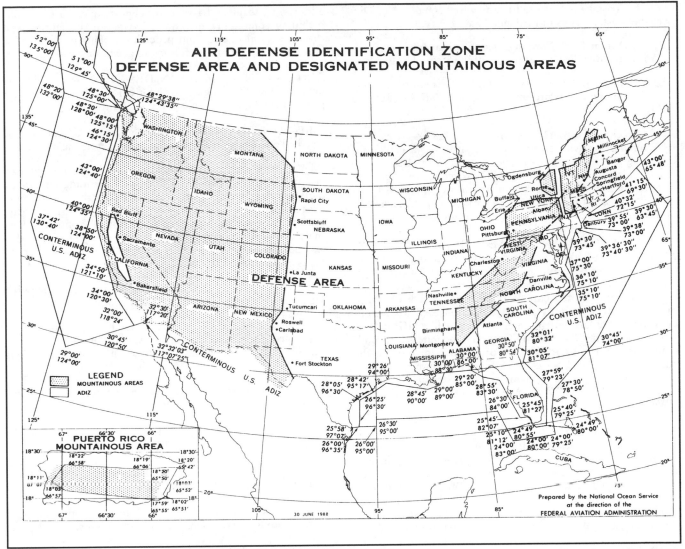

Air Defense Identification Zone (ADIZ) boundaries embrace the coastlines of the United States. Aircraft violating the ADIZ boundaries are liable to find a pair of F-15 interceptors flying alongside.

1. **Category A** — Speed less than 91 knots.

2. **Category B** — Speed 91 knots or more but less than 121 knots.

3. **Category C** — Speed 121 knots or more but less than 141 knots.

4. **Category D** — Speed 141 knots or more but less than 166 knots.

5. **Category E** — Speed 166 knots or more.

(Refer to FAR Part 1 and FAR Part 97)

AIRCRAFT CLASSES — For the purposes of Wake Turbulence Separation Minima, ATC classifies aircraft as Heavy, Large, and Small as follows:

1. **Heavy** — Aircraft capable of takeoff weights of 300,000 pounds or more whether or not they are operating at this weight during a particular phase of flight

2. **Large** — Aircraft of more than 12,500 pounds, maximum certificated takeoff weight, up to 300,000 pounds.

3. **Small** — Aircraft of 12,500 pounds or less maximum certificated takeoff weight. (Refer to AIM)

AIR DEFENSE EMERGENCY — A military emergency condition declared by a designated authority. This condition exists when an attack upon the continental U.S., Alaska, Canada, or U.S. installations in Greenland by hostile aircraft or missiles is considered probable, is imminent, or is taking place. (Refer to AIM)

AIR DEFENSE IDENTIFICATION ZONE/ADIZ — The area of airspace over land or water, extending upward from the surface, within which the ready identification, the location, and the control of aircraft are required in the interest of national security

1. **Domestic Air Defense Identification Zone** — An ADIZ within the United States along an international boundary of the United States.

2. Coastal Air Defense Identification Zone — An ADIZ over the coastal waters of the United States.

3. Distant Early Warning Identification Zone (DEWIZ) — An ADIZ over the coastal waters of the State of Alaska.

ADIZ locations and operating and flight plan requirements for civil aircraft operations are specified in FAR Part 99. (Refer to AIM)

AIRMAN'S INFORMATION MANUAL/AIM — A primary FAA publication whose purpose is to instruct airmen about operating in the National Airspace System of the U.S. It provides basic flight information, ATC Procedures and general instructional information concerning health, medical facts, factors affecting flight safety, accident and hazard reporting, and types of aeronautical charts and their use.

AIRMET/WA/AIRMAN'S METEOROLOGICAL INFORMATION — In-flight weather advisories issued only to amend the area forecast concerning weather phenomena which are of operational interest to all aircraft and potentially hazardous to aircraft having limited capability because of lack of equipment, instrumentation, or pilot qualifications. AIRMETs concern weather of less severity than that covered by SIGMETs or Convective SIGMETs. AIRMETs cover moderate icing, moderate turbulence, sustained winds of 30 knots or more at the surface, widespread areas of ceilings less than 1,000 feet and/or visibility less than 3 miles, and extensive mountain obscurement. (See AWW, SIGMET, Convective SIGMET, and CWA) (Refer to AIM)

AIR NAVIGATION FACILITY — Any facility used in, available for use in, or designed for use in, aid of air navigation, including landing areas, lights, any apparatus or equipment for disseminating weather information, for signaling, for radio-directional finding, or for radio or other electrical communication, and any other structure or mechanism having a similar purpose for guiding or controlling flight in the air or the landing and take-off of aircraft. (See Navigational Aid)

AIRPORT — An area on land or water that is used or intended to be used for the landing and takeoff of aircraft and includes its buildings and facilities, if any.

AIRPORT ADVISORY AREA — The area within ten miles of an airport without a control tower or where the tower is not in operation, and on which a Flight Service Station is located. (See Airport Advisory Service) (Refer to AIM)

AIRPORT ADVISORY SERVICE/AAS — A service provided by flight service stations or the military at airports not serviced by an operating control tower. This service consists of providing information to arriving and departing aircraft concerning wind direction and speed, favored runway, altimeter setting, pertinent known traffic, pertinent known field conditions, airport taxi routes and traffic patterns, and authorized instrument approach procedures. This information is advisory in nature and does not constitute an ATC clearance. (See Airport Advisory Area)

AIRPORT ELEVATION/FIELD ELEVATION — The highest point of an airport's usable runways measured in feet from mean sea level. (See Touchdown Zone Elevation)

AIRPORT/FACILITY DIRECTORY — A publication designed primarily as a pilot's operational manual containing all airports, seaplane bases, and heliports open to the public including communications data, navigational facilities, and certain special notices and procedures. This publication is issued in seven volumes according to geographical area.

AIRPORT INFORMATION DESK/AID — An airport unmanned facility designed for pilot self-service briefing, flight planning, and filing of flight plans. (Refer to AIM)

AIRPORT LIGHTING — Various lighting aids that may be installed on an airport. Types of airport lighting include:

1. Approach Light System/ALS — An airport lighting facility which provides visual guidance to landing aircraft by radiating light beams in a directional pattern by which the pilot aligns the aircraft with the extended centerline of the runway on his final approach for landing. Condenser-Discharge Sequential Flashing Lights/Sequenced Flashing Lights may be installed in conjunction with the ALS at some airports. Types of Approach Light Systems are:

a. **ALSF-1** — Approach Light System with Sequenced Flashing Lights in ILS Cat-I configuration.

b. **ALSF-2** — Approach Light System with Sequenced Flashing Lights in ILS Cat-II configuration. The ALSF-2 may operate as an SSALR when weather conditions permit.

c. **SSALF** — Simplified Short Approach Light System with Sequenced Flashing Lights.

d. **SSALR** — Simplified Short Approach Light System with Runway Alignment Indicator Lights.

e. **MALSF** — Medium Intensity Approach Light System with Sequenced Flashing Lights.

f. **MALSR** — Medium Intensity Approach Light System with Runway Alignment Indicator Lights.

g. **LDIN** — Sequenced Flashing Lead-in Lights.

h. **RAIL** — Runway Alignment Indicator Lights (Sequenced Flashing Lights which are installed only in combination with other light systems).

i. **ODALS** — Omnidirectional Approach Lighting System consists of seven omnidirectional flashing lights located in the approach area of a nonprecision runway. Five lights are located on the runway centerline extended with the first light located 300 feet from the threshold and extending at equal intervals up to 1,500 feet from the threshold. The other two lights are located, one on each side of the runway threshold, at a lateral distance of 40 feet from the runway edge, or 75 feet from the runway edge when installed on a runway equipped with a VASI.

2. Runway Lights/Runway Edge Lights — Lights having a prescribed angle of emission used to define the lateral limits of a runway. Runway lights are uniformly spaced at intervals of approximately 200 feet, and the intensity may be controlled or preset.

3. Touchdown Zone Lighting — Two rows of transverse light bars located symmetrically about the runway centerline normally at 100 foot intervals. The basic system extends 3,000 feet along the runway.

Airport Radar Service Area (ARSA)

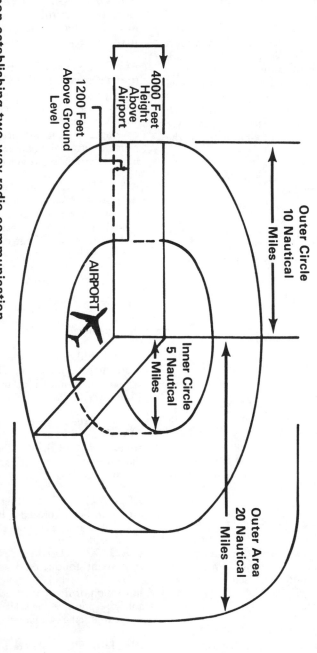

4000 Feet Height Above Airport

1200 Feet Above Ground Level

Outer Circle 10 Nautical Miles

AIRPORT

Inner Circle 5 Nautical Miles

Outer Area 20 Nautical Miles

Services upon establishing two-way radio communication and radar contact:

Sequencing Arrivals
IFR/IFR Standard Separation
IFR/VFR Traffic Advisories and Conflict Resolution
VFR/VFR Traffic Advisories

Note: The normal radius of the Outer Area, will be 20nm, with some site specific variations.

| IFR: | Instrument Flight Rules |
| VFR: | Visual Flight Rules |

As air traffic increases, more airports are being ringed with Airport Radar Service Areas. This is one type of controlled airspace whose object is keeping aircraft separated.

4. Runway Centerline Lighting — Flush centerline lights spaced at 50-foot intervals beginning 75 feet from the landing threshold and extending to within 75 feet of the opposite end of the runway.

5. Threshold Lights — Fixed green lights arranged symmetrically left and right of the runway centerline, identifying the runway threshold.

6. Runway End Identifier Lights/REIL — Two synchronized flashing lights, one on each side of the runway threshold, which provide rapid and positive identification of the approach end of a particular runway.

7. Visual Approach Slope Indicator/VASI — An airport lighting facility providing vertical visual approach slope guidance to aircraft during approach to landing by radiating a directional pattern of high intensity red and white focused light beams which indicate to the pilot that he is "on path" if he sees red/white, "above path" if white/white, and "below path" if red/red. Some airports serving large aircraft have three-bar VASIs which provide two visual glide paths to the same runway.

8. Boundary Lights — Lights defining the perimeter of an airport or landing area. (Refer to AIM)

AIRPORT MARKING AIDS — Markings used on runway and taxiway surfaces to identify a specific runway, a runway threshold, a centerline, a hold line, etc. A runway should be marked in accordance with its present usage such as:

1. **Visual.**

2. **Nonprecision instrument.**

3. **Precision instrument.** (Refer to AIM)

AIRPORT RADAR SERVICE AREA/ARSA — (See Controlled Airspace)

AIRPORT ROTATING BEACON — A visual NAVAID operated at many airports. At civil airports, alternating white and green flashes indicate the location of the airport. At military airports, the beacons flash alternately white and green, but are differentiated from civil beacons by dualpeaked (two quick) white flashes between the green flashes. (See Special VFR Operations, Instrument Flight Rules) (Refer to AIM, Rotating Beacons)

AIRPORT SURFACE DETECTION EQUIPMENT /ASDE — Radar equipment specifically designed to detect all principal features on the surface of an airport, including aircraft and vehicular traffic, and to present the entire image on a radar indicator console in the control tower. Used to augment visual observation by tower personnel of aircraft and/or vehicular movements on runways and taxiways.

AIRPORT SURVEILLANCE RADAR/ASR — Approach control radar used to detect and display an aircraft's position in the terminal area. ASR provides range and azimuth information but does not provide elevation data. Coverage of the ASR can extend up to 60 miles.

AIRPORT TRAFFIC AREA — Unless otherwise specifically designated in FAR Part 93, that airspace within a horizontal radius of 5 statute miles from the geographical center of any airport at which a control tower is operating, extending from the surface up to, but not including, an altitude of 3,000 feet above the elevation of an airport. Unless otherwise authorized or required by ATC, no person may operate an aircraft within an airport traffic area except for the purpose of landing at or taking off from an airport within that area. ATC authorizations may be given as individual approval of specific operations or may be contained in written agreements between airport users and the tower concerned. (Refer to FAR Part 1 and FAR Part 91).

AIRPORT TRAFFIC CONTROL SERVICE — A service provided by a control tower for aircraft operating on the movement area and in the vicinity of an airport. (See Movement Area, Tower)

AIR ROUTE SURVEILLANCE RADAR/ARSR — Air route traffic control center (ARTCC) radar used primarily to detect and display an aircraft's position while en route between terminal areas. The ARSR enables controllers to provide radar air traffic control service when aircraft are within the ARSR coverage. In some instances, ARSR may enable an ARTCC to provide terminal radar services similar to but usually more limited than those provided by a radar approach control.

AIR ROUTE TRAFFIC CONTROL CENTER/ ARTCC — A facility established to provide air traffic control service to aircraft operating on IFR flight plans within controlled airspace and principally during the en route phase of flight. When equipment capabilities and controller workload permit, certain advisory/assistance services may be provided to VFR aircraft. (See NAS Stage A, En Route Air Traffic Control Service) (Refer to AIM)

AIRSPEED — The speed of an aircraft relative to its surrounding air mass. The unqualified term "airspeed" means one of the following:

1. **Indicated Airspeed** — The speed shown on the aircraft airspeed indicator. This is the speed used in pilot/controller communications under the general term "airspeed." (Refer to FAR Part 1)

2. **True Airspeed** — The airspeed of an aircraft relative to undisturbed air. Used primarily in flight planning and en route portion of flight. When used in pilot/controller communications, it is referred to as "true airspeed" and not shortened to "airspeed."

AIRSTART — The starting of an aircraft engine while the aircraft is airborne, preceded by engine shutdown during training flights or by actual engine failure.

AIR TAXI — Used to describe a helicopter/VTOL aircraft movement conducted above the surface but normally not above 100 feet AGL. The aircraft may proceed either via hover taxi or flight at speeds more than 20 knots. The pilot is solely responsible for selecting a safe airspeed/altitude for the operation being conducted. (See Hover Taxi) (Refer to AIM)

AIR TRAFFIC — Aircraft operating in the air or on an airport surface, exclusive of loading ramps and parking areas.

AIR TRAFFIC CLEARANCE/ATC CLEARANCE — An authorization by air traffic control, for the purpose of preventing collision between known aircraft, for an aircraft to proceed under specified traffic conditions within controlled airspace. (See ATC Instructions)

Note 1. — For convenience, the term air traffic control clearance is frequently abbreviated to clearance when used in appropriate contexts.

Note 2. — The abbreviated term clearance may be prefixed by the words taxi, takeoff, departure, en route, approach or landing to indicate the particular portion of flight to which the air traffic control clearance relates.

AIR TRAFFIC CONTROL/ATC — A service operated by appropriate authority to promote the safe, orderly and expeditious flow of air traffic.

1) **Preventing collisions:**

a) Between aircraft; and

b) On the maneuvering area between aircraft and obstructions; and

2) **Expediting and maintaining an orderly flow of air traffic.**

AIR TRAFFIC CONTROL COMMAND CENTER/ ATCCC — An Air Traffic Operations Service facility consisting of four operational units.

1.**Central Flow Control Function/CFCF** — Responsible for coordination and approval of all major intercenter flow control restrictions on a system basis in order to obtain maximum utilization of the airspace. (See Quota Flow Control)

2. **Central Altitude Reservation Function/CARF** — Responsible for coordinating, planning, and approving special user requirements under the Altitude Reservation (ALTRV) concept. (See Altitude Reservation)

3. **Airport Reservation Office/ARO** — Responsible for approving IFR flights at designated high density traffic airports (John F. Kennedy, LaGuardia, O'Hare, and Washington National) during specified hours. (Refer to FAR Part 93 and Airport/Facility Directory)

4. **ATC Contingency Command Post** — A facility which enables the FAA to manage the ATC system when significant portions of the system's capabilities have been lost or are threatened.

AIR TRAFFIC CONTROL SERVICE — (See Air Traffic Control)

AIR TRAFFIC CONTROL SPECIALIST/CONTROLLER — A person authorized to provide air traffic control service. (See Air Traffic Control, Flight Service Station)

AIRWAY BEACON — Used to mark airway segments in remote mountain areas. The light flashes Morse Code to identify the beacon site. (Refer to AIM)

AIRWAY/FEDERAL AIRWAY — A control area or portion thereof established in the form of a corridor, the centerline of which is defined by radio navigational aids. (Refer to FAR Part 71, AIM)

ALERT AREA — (See Special Use Airspace)

ALERT NOTICE/ALNOT — A request originated by a flight service station (FSS) or an air route traffic control center (ARTCC) for an extensive communication search for overdue, unreported, or missing aircraft.

ALPHANUMERIC DISPLAY/DATA BLOCK — Letters and numerals used to show identification, altitude, beacon code, and other information concerning a target on a radar display. (See Automated Radar Terminal Systems, NAS Stage A)

ALTERNATE AIRPORT — An airport at which an aircraft may land if a landing at the intended airport becomes inadvisable.

ALTIMETER SETTING — The barometric pressure reading used to adjust a pressure altimeter for variations in existing atmospheric pressure or to the standard altimeter setting (29.92). (Refer to FAR Part 91, AIM)

ALTITUDE — The height of a level, point, or object measured in feet Above Ground Level (AGL) or from Mean Sea Level (MSL). (See Flight Level)

1. **MSL Altitude** — Altitude expressed in feet measured from mean sea level.

2. **AGL Altitude** — Altitude expressed in feet measured above ground level.

3. **Indicated Altitude** — The altitude as shown by an altimeter. On a pressure or barometric altimeter it is altitude as shown uncorrected for instrument error and uncompensated for variation from standard atmospheric conditions.

ALTITUDE READOUT/AUTOMATIC ALTITUDE REPORT — An aircraft's altitude, transmitted via the Mode C transponder feature, that is visually displayed in 100-foot increments on a radar scope having readout capability. (See Automated Radar Terminal Systems, NAS Stage A, Alphanumeric Display) (Refer to AIM)

ALTITUDE RESERVATION/ALTRV — Airspace utilization under prescribed conditions normally employed for the mass movement of aircraft or other special user requirements which cannot otherwise be accomplished. ALTRVs are approved by the appropriate FAA facility. (See Air Traffic Control Command Center)

ALTITUDE RESTRICTION — An altitude or altitudes, stated in the order flown, which are to be maintained until reaching a specific point or time. Altitude restrictions may be issued by ATC due to traffic, terrain, or other airspace considerations.

ALTITUDE RESTRICTIONS ARE CANCELED — Adherence to previously imposed altitude restrictions is no longer required during a climb or descent.

APPROACH CLEARANCE — Authorization by ATC for a pilot to conduct an instrument approach. The type of instrument approach for which a clearance and other pertinent information is provided in the approach clearance when required. (See Instrument Approach Procedure, Cleared for Approach) (Refer to AIM and FAR Part 91)

APPROACH CONTROL FACILITY — A terminal ATC facility that provides approach control service in a terminal area. (See Approach Control Service, Radar Approach Control Facility).

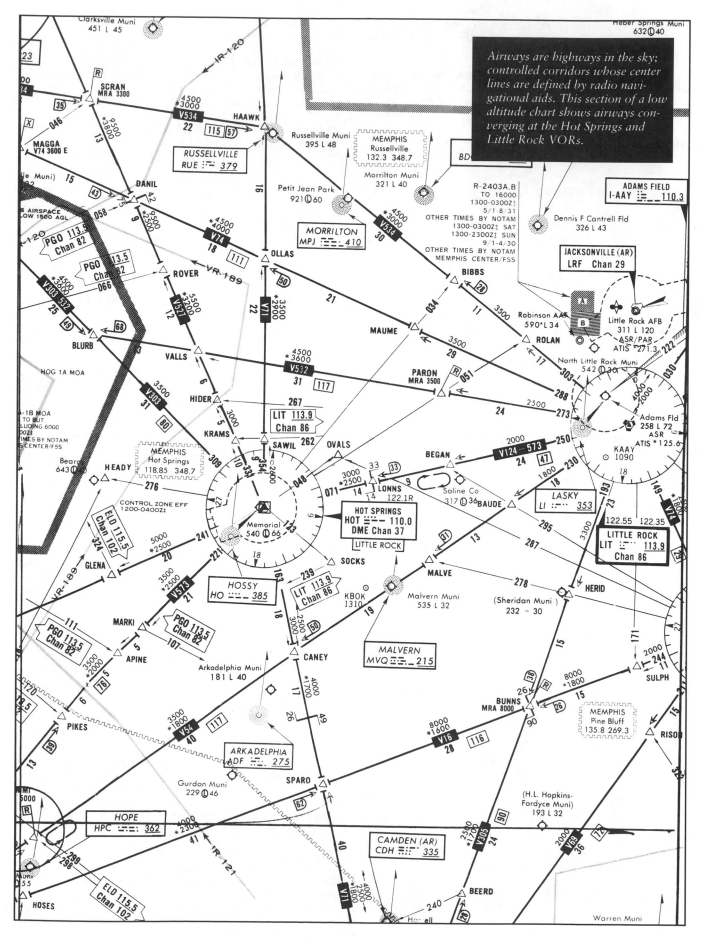

Airways are highways in the sky; controlled corridors whose center lines are defined by radio navigational aids. This section of a low altitude chart shows airways converging at the Hot Springs and Little Rock VORs.

APPROACH CONTROL SERVICE — Air traffic control service provided by an approach control facility for arriving and departing VFR/IFR aircraft and, on occasion, en route aircraft. At some airports not served by an approach control facility, the ARTCC provides limited approach control service. (Refer to AIM)

APPROACH GATE — An imaginary point used within ATC as a basis for vectoring aircraft to the final approach course. The gate will be established along the final approach course 1 mile from the outer marker (or the fix used in lieu of the outer marker) on the side away from the airport for precision approaches and 1 mile from the final approach fix on the side away from the airport for nonprecision approaches. In either case when measured along the final approach course, the gate will be no closer than 5 miles from the landing threshold.

APPROACH LIGHT SYSTEM — (See Airport Lighting)

APPROACH SEQUENCE — The order in which aircraft are positioned while on approach or awaiting approach clearance. (See Landing Sequence)

APPROACH SPEED — The recommended speed contained in aircraft manuals used by pilots when making an approach to landing. This speed will vary for different segments of an approach as well as for aircraft weight and configuration.

APRON/RAMP — A defined area on an airport or heliport intended to accommodate aircraft for purposes of loading or unloading passengers or cargo, refueling, parking, or maintenance. With regard to seaplanes, a ramp is used for access to the apron from the water.

ARC — The track over the ground of an aircraft flying at a constant distance from a navigational aid by reference to distance measuring equipment (DME).

AREA NAVIGATION/RNAV — A method of navigation that permits aircraft operation on any desired course within the coverage of station-referenced navigation signals or within the limits of a self-contained system capability. Random area navigation routes are direct routes, based on area navigation capability, between waypoints defined in terms of latitude/longitude coordinates, degree/distance fixes, or offsets from published or established routes/airways at a specified distance and direction. The major types of equipment are:

1. VORTAC referenced or Course Line Computer (CLC) systems, which account for the greatest number of RNAV units in use. To function, the CLC must be within the service range of a VORTAC.

2. OMEGA/VLF, although two separate systems, can be considered as one operationally. A long-range navigation system based upon Very Low Frequency radio signals transmitted from a total of 17 stations worldwide.

3. Inertial (INS) systems, which are totally self-contained and require no information from external references. They provide aircraft position and navigation information in response to signals resulting from inertial effects on components within the system.

4. MLS Area Navigation (MLS/RNAV), which provides area navigation with reference to an MLS ground facility.

A sensitive barometric altimeter is most accurate when the local barometric pressure is set correctly in the window on the right-hand side. In this case, it is at 30.35 inches of mercury.

5. LORAN-C is a long-range radio navigation system that uses ground waves transmitted at low frequency to provide user position information at ranges of up to 600 to 1,200 nautical miles at both en route and approach altitudes. The useable signal coverage areas are determined by the signal-to-noise ratio, the envelope-to-cycle difference, and the geometric relationship between the positions of the user and the transmitting stations.

ARMY AVIATION FLIGHT INFORMATION BULLETIN/USAFIB — A bulletin that provides air operation data covering Army, National Guard, and Army Reserve aviation activities.

ARRESTING SYSTEM — A safety device consisting of two major components, namely, engaging or catching devices and energy absorption devices for the purpose of arresting both tailhook and/or nontailhook-equipped aircraft. It is used to prevent aircraft from overrunning runways when the aircraft cannot be stopped after landing or during aborted takeoff. Arresting systems have various names; e.g., arresting gear, hook device, wire barrier cable. (See Abort) (Refer to AIM)

ARRIVAL TIME — The time an aircraft touches down on arrival.

ARTCC — (See Air Route Traffic Control Center)

ASR APPROACH — (See Surveillance Approach)

ATC ADVISES — Used to prefix a message of noncontrol information when it is relayed to an aircraft by other than an air traffic controller. (See Advisory)

ATC ASSIGNED AIRSPACE/ATCAA — Airspace of defined vertical/lateral limits, assigned by ATC, for the purpose of providing air traffic segregation between the specified activities being conducted within the assigned airspace and other IFR air traffic. (See Special Use Airspace)

ATC CLEARANCE — (See Air Traffic Clearance)

ATC CLEARS — Used to prefix an ATC clearance when it is relayed to an aircraft by other than an air traffic controller.

ATC INSTRUCTIONS — Directives issued by air traffic control for the purpose of requiring a pilot to take specific actions; e.g., "Turn left heading two five zero," "Go around," "Clear the runway." (Refer to FAR Part 91)

ATCRBS — (See Radar)

ATC REQUESTS — Used to prefix an ATC request when it is relayed to an aircraft by other than an air traffic controller.

AUTOLAND APPROACH — An autoland approach is a precision instrument approach to touchdown and, in some cases, through the landing rollout. An autoland approach is performed by the aircraft autopilot which is receiving position information and/or steering commands from onboard navigation equipment (See Coupled Approach).

Note. — Autoland and coupled approaches are flown in VFR and IFR. It is common for carriers to require their crews to fly coupled approaches and autoland approaches (if certified) when the weather conditions are less than approximately 4,000 RVR.

AUTOMATED RADAR TERMINAL SYSTEMS/
ARTS — The generic term for the ultimate in functional capability afforded by several automation systems. Each differs in functional capabilities and equipment. ARTS plus a suffix roman numeral denotes a specific system. A following letter indicates a major modification to that system. In general, an ARTS displays for the terminal controller aircraft identification, flight plan data, other flight associated information; e.g., altitude, speed, and aircraft position symbols in conjunction with his radar presentation. Normal radar co-exists with the alphanumeric display. In addition to enhancing visualization of the air traffic situation, ARTS facilitate intra/inter-facility transfer and coordination of flight information. These capabilities are enabled by specially designed computers and subsystems tailored to the radar and communications equipments and operational requirements of each automated facility. Modular design permits adoption of improvements in computer software and electronic technologies as they become available while retaining the characteristics unique to each system.

1. ARTS II — A programmable nontracking, computer-aided display subsystem capable of modular expansion. ARTS II systems provide a level of automated air traffic control capability at terminals having low to medium activity. Flight identification and altitude may be associated with the display of secondary radar targets. The system has the capability of communicating with ARTCC's and other ATRS II, IIA, III, and IIIA facilities.

2. ARTS IIA — A programmable radar-tracking computer subsystem capable of modular expansion. The ARTS IIA detects, tracks, and predicts secondary radar targets. The targets are displayed by means of computer-generated symbols, ground speed, and flight plan data. Although it does not track primary radar targets, they are displayed coincident with the secondary radar as well as the symbols and alphanumerics. The system has the capability of communicating with ARTCC's and other ARTS II, IIA, III, and IIIA facilities.

3. ARTS III — The Beacon Tracking Level (BTL) of the modular programmable automated radar terminal system in use at medium to high activity terminals. ARTS III detects, tracks, and predicts secondary radar-derived aircraft targets. These are displayed by means of computer-generated symbols and alphanumeric characters depicting flight identification, aircraft altitude, ground speed, and flight plan data. Although it does not track primary targets, they are displayed coincident with the secondary radar as well as the symbols and alphanumerics. The system has the capability of communicating with ARTCC's and other ARTS III facilities.

4. ARTS IIIA — The Radar Tracking and Beacon Tracking Level (RT&BTL) of the modular, programmable automated radar terminal system. ARTS IIIA detects, tracks, and predicts primary as well as secondary radar-derived aircraft targets. This more sophisticated computer-driven system upgrades the existing ARTS III system by providing improved tracking, continuous data recording, and fail-soft capabilities.

AUTOMATIC ALTITUDE REPORTING — That function of a transponder which responds to Mode C interrogations by transmitting the aircraft's altitude in 100-foot increments.

AUTOMATIC CARRIER LANDING SYSTEM/ACLS — U.S. Navy final approach equipment consisting of precision tracking radar coupled to a computer data link to provide continuous information to the aircraft, monitoring capability to the pilot, and a backup approach system.

AUTOMATIC DIRECTION FINDER/ADF — An aircraft radio navigation system which senses and indicates the direction to a L/MF nondirectional radio beacon (NDB) ground transmitter. Direction is indicated to the pilot as a magnetic bearing or as a relative bearing to the longitudinal axis of the aircraft depending on the type of indicator installed in the aircraft. In certain applications, such as military, ADF operations may be based on airborne and ground transmitters in the VHF/UHF frequency spectrum. (See Bearing, Nondirectional Beacon)

AUTOMATIC TERMINAL INFORMATION SERVICE/
ATIS — The continuous broadcast of recorded noncontrol information in selected terminal areas. Its purpose is to improve controller effectiveness and to relieve frequency congestion by automating the repetitive transmission of essential but routine information; e.g., "Los Angeles information Alfa. One three zero zero Coordinated Universal Time. Weather, measured ceiling two thousand overcast, visibility three, haze, smoke, temperature seven one, dew point five seven, wind two five zero at five, altimeter two niner niner six. I-L-S Runway Two Five Left approach in use, Runway Two Five Right closed, advise you have Alfa." (Refer to AIM)

AUTOROTATION — A rotorcraft flight condition in which the lifting rotor is driven entirely by action of the air when the rotorcraft is in motion.

1. Autorotative Landing/Touchdown Autorotation — Used by a pilot to indicate that he will be landing without applying power to the rotor.

2. Low Level Autorotation — Commences at an altitude well below the traffic pattern, usually below 100 feet AGL and is used primarily for tactical military training.

3. 180 degrees Autorotation — Initiated from a downwind heading and is commenced well inside the normal traffic

pattern. "Go around" may not be possible during the latter part of this maneuver.

AVIATION WEATHER SERVICE — A service provided by the National Weather Service (NWS) and FAA which collects and disseminates pertinent weather information for pilots, aircraft operators, and ATC. Available aviation weather reports and forecasts are displayed at each NWS office and FAA FSS. (See En Route Flight Advisory Service, Transcribed Weather Broadcast, Weather Advisory, Pilots Automatic Telephone Weather Answering Service) (Refer to AIM)

AZIMUTH, MLS — A magnetic bearing extending from an MLS navigation facility. Note: azimuth bearings are described as magnetic and are referred to as "azimuth" in radio telephone communications.

BASE LEG — (See Traffic Pattern)

BEACON — (See Radar, Nondirectional Beacon, Marker Beacon, Airport Rotating Beacon, Aeronautical Beacon, Airway Beacon)

BEARING — The horizontal direction to or from any point, usually measured clockwise from true north, magnetic north, or some other reference point through 360 degrees. (See Nondirectional Beacon)

BELOW MINIMUMS — Weather conditions below the minimums prescribed by regulation for the particular action involved; e.g., landing minimums, takeoff minimums.

BLAST FENCE — A barrier that is used to divert or dissipate jet or propeller blast.

BLIND SPEED — The rate of departure or closing of a target relative to the radar antenna at which cancellation of the primary radar target by moving target indicator (MTI) circuits in the radar equipment causes a reduction or complete loss of signal.

BLIND SPOT/BLIND ZONE — An area from which radio transmissions and/or radar echoes cannot be received. The term is also used to describe portions of the airport not visible from the control tower.

BOUNDARY LIGHTS — (See Airport Lighting)

BRAKING ACTION (GOOD, FAIR, POOR, OR NIL) — A report of conditions on the airport movement area providing a pilot with a degree/quality of braking that he might expect. Braking action is reported in terms of good, fair, poor, or nil. (See Runway Condition Reading)

BRAKING ACTION ADVISORIES — When tower controllers have received runway braking action reports which include the terms "poor" or "nil," or whenever weather conditions are conducive to deteriorating or rapidly changing runway braking conditions, the tower will include on the ATIS broadcast the statement, "BRAKING ACTION ADVISORIES ARE IN EFFECT." During the time Braking Action Advisories are in effect, ATC will issue the latest braking action report for the runway in use to each arriving and departing aircraft. Pilots should be prepared for deteriorating braking conditions and should request current runway condition information if not volunteered by controllers. Pilots should also be prepared to provide a descriptive runway condition report to controllers after landing.

BROADCAST — Transmission of information for which an acknowledgment is not expected.

CALL UP — Initial voice contact between a facility and an aircraft, using the identification of the unit being called and the unit initiating the call. (Refer to AIM)

CARDINAL ALTITUDES OR FLIGHT LEVELS — "Odd" or "Even" thousand-foot altitudes or flight levels; e.g., 5,000, 6,000, 7,000, FL 250, FL 260, FL 270. (See Altitude, Flight Levels)

CEILING — The heights above the earth's surface of the lowest layer of clouds or obscuring phenomena that is reported as "broken," "overcast," or "obscuration," and not classified as "thin" or "partial".

CENTER — (See Air Route Traffic Control Center)

CENTER'S AREA — The specified airspace within which an air route traffic control center (ARTCC) provides air traffic control and advisory service. (See Air Route Traffic Control Center) (Refer to AIM)

CENTER WEATHER ADVISORY/CWA — An unscheduled weather advisory issued by Center Weather Service Unit meteorologists for ATC use to alert pilots of existing or anticipated adverse weather conditions within the next 2 hours. A CWA may modify or redefine a SIGMET. (See AWW, SIGMET, Convective SIGMET, and AIRMET) (Refer to AIM)

CHAFF — Thin, narrow metallic reflectors of various lengths and frequency responses, used to reflect radar energy. These reflectors when dropped from aircraft and allowed to drift downward result in large targets on the radar display.

CHARTED VFR FLYWAYS — Charted VFR Flyways are flight paths recommended for use to bypass areas heavily traversed by large turbine-powered aircraft. Pilot compliance with recommended flyways and associated altitudes is strictly voluntary. VFR Flyway Planning charts are published on the back of existing VFR Terminal Area charts.

CHARTED VISUAL FLIGHT PROCEDURE (CVFP) APPROACH — An approach wherein a radar-controlled aircraft on an IFR flight plan, operating in VFR conditions and having an ATC authorization, may proceed to the airport of intended landing via visual landmarks and altitudes depicted on a charted visual flight procedure.

CHASE/CHASE AIRCRAFT — An aircraft flown in proximity to another aircraft normally to observe its performance during training or testing.

CIRCLE-TO-LAND MANEUVER/CIRCLING MANEUVER — A maneuver initiated by the pilot to align the aircraft with a runway for landing when a straight-in landing from an instrument approach is not possible or is not desirable. This maneuver is made only after ATC authorization has been obtained and the pilot has established required visual reference to the airport (See Circle to Runway, Landing Minimums) (Refer to AIM)

CIRCLE TO RUNWAY (RUNWAY NUMBERED) — Used by ATC to inform the pilot that he must circle to land because the runway in use is other than the runway aligned with the instrument approach procedure. When the direction of the circling maneuver in relation to the airport/runway is required, the controller will state the direction (eight cardinal compass points) and specify a left or right downwind or base leg as appropriate; e.g., "Cleared VOR Runway Three Six Approach circle to Runway Two Two," or "Circle northwest of the airport for a right downwind to Runway Two Two." (See Circle-to-Land Maneuver, Landing Minimums) (Refer to AIM)

CIRCLING APPROACH — (See Circle-to-Land Maneuver)

CIRCLING MINIMA — (See Landing Minimums)

CLEAR-AIR TURBULENCE/CAT — Turbulence encountered in air where no clouds are present. This term is commonly applied to high-level turbulence associated with wind shear. CAT is often encountered in the vicinity of the jet stream. (See Wind Shear, Jet Stream)

CLEARANCE — (See Air Traffic Clearance)

CLEARANCE LIMIT — The fix, point, or location to which an aircraft is cleared when issued an air traffic clearance.

CLEARANCE VOID IF NOT OFF BY (TIME) — Used by ATC to advise an aircraft that the departure clearance is automatically cancelled if takeoff is not made prior to a specified time. The pilot must obtain a new clearance or cancel his IFR flight plan if not off by the specified time.

CLEARED AS FILED — Means the aircraft is cleared to proceed in accordance with the route of flight filed in the flight plan. This clearance does not include the altitude, SID, or SID Transition. (See Request Full Route Clearance) (Refer to AIM)

CLEARED FOR (Type of) APPROACH — ATC authorization for an aircraft to execute a specific instrument approach procedure to an airport; e.g., "Cleared for ILS Runway Three Six Approach." (See Instrument Approach Procedure, Approach Clearance) (Refer to AIM, FAR Part 91)

CLEARED FOR APPROACH — ATC authorization for an aircraft to execute any standard or special instrument approach procedure for that airport. Normally, an aircraft will be cleared for a specific instrument approach procedure. (See Instrument Approach Procedure, Cleared for (Type of) Approach) (Refer to AIM, FAR Part 91)

CLEARED FOR TAKEOFF — ATC authorization for an aircraft to depart. It is predicated on known traffic and known physical airport conditions.

CLEARED FOR THE OPTION — ATC authorization for an aircraft to make a touch-and-go, low approach, missed approach, stop and go, or full stop landing at the discretion of the pilot. It is normally used in training so that an instructor can evaluate a student's performance under changing situations. (See Option Approach) (Refer to AIM)

CLEARED THROUGH — ATC authorization for an aircraft to make intermediate stops at specified airports without refiling a flight plan while en route to the clearance limit.

CLEARED TO LAND — ATC authorization for an aircraft to land. It is predicated on known traffic and known physical airport conditions.

CLEARWAY — An area beyond the takeoff runway under the control of airport authorities within which terrain or fixed obstacles may not extend above specified limits. These areas may be required for certain turbine-powered operations and the size and upward slope of the clearway will differ depending on when the aircraft was certificated. (Refer to FAR Part 1)

CLIMBOUT — That portion of flight operation between takeoff and the initial cruising altitude.

CLIMB TO VFR — ATC authorization for an aircraft to climb to VFR conditions within a control zone when the only weather limitation is restricted visibility. The aircraft must remain clear of clouds while climbing to VFR. (See Special VFR) (Refer to AIM)

CLOSED RUNWAY — A runway that is unusable for aircraft operations. Only the airport management/military operations office can close a runway.

CLOSED TRAFFIC — Successive operations involving takeoffs and landings or low approaches where the aircraft does not exit the traffic pattern.

CLUTTER — In radar operations, clutter refers to the reception and visual display of radar returns caused by precipitation, chaff, terrain, numerous aircraft targets, or other phenomena. Such returns may limit or preclude ATC from providing services based on radar. (See Ground Clutter, Chaff, Precipitation, Target)

COASTAL FIX — A navigation aid or intersection where an aircraft transitions between the domestic route structure and the oceanic route structure.

CODES/TRANSPONDER CODES — The number assigned to a particular multiple pulse reply signal transmitted by a transponder. (See Discrete Code)

COMBINED CENTER-RAPCON/CERAP — An air traffic facility which combines the functions of an ARTCC and a radar approach control facility. (See Air Route Traffic Control Center/ARTCC, Radar Approach Control Facility)

COMMON ROUTE/COMMON PORTION — That segment of a North American Route between the inland navigation facility and the coastal fix.

COMMON TRAFFIC ADVISORY FREQUENCY/CTAF — A frequency designed for the purpose of carrying out airport advisory practices while operating to or from an uncontrolled airport. The CTAF may be a UNICOM, Multicom, FSS, or tower frequency and is identified in appropriate aeronautical publications. (Refer to AC 90-42E)

COMPASS LOCATOR — A low power, low or medium frequency (L/MF) radio beacon installed at the site of the outer or middle marker of an instrument landing system (ILS). It can be used for navigation at distances of approximately 15 miles or as authorized in the approach procedure.

    1. **Outer Compass Locator/LOM** — A compass locator installed at the site of the outer marker of an instrument landing system. (See Outer Marker)

    2. **Middle Compass Locator/LMM** — A compass locator installed at the site of the middle marker of an instrument landing system. (See Middle Marker)

Note. — A locator usually has an average radius of rated coverage of between 18.5 and 46.3 km (10 and 25 NM).

COMPASS ROSE — A circle, graduated in degrees, printed on some charts or marked on the ground at an airport. It is used as a reference to either true or magnetic direction.

COMPOSITE FLIGHT PLAN — A flight plan which specifies VFR operation for one portion of flight and IFR for another portion. It is used primarily in military operations. (Refer to AIM)

COMPOSITE ROUTE SYSTEM — An organized oceanic route structure, incorporating reduced lateral spacing between routes, in which composite separation is authorized.

COMPOSITE SEPARATION - A method of separating aircraft in a composite route system where, by management of route and altitude assignments, a combination of half the lateral minimum specified for the area concerned and half the vertical minimum is applied.

COMPULSORY REPORTING POINTS — Reporting points which must be reported to ATC. They are designated on aeronautical charts by solid triangles or filed in a flight plan as fixes selected to define direct routes. These points are geographical locations which are defined by navigation aids/fixes. Pilots should discontinue position reporting over compulsory reporting points when informed by ATC that their aircraft is in radar "contact."

CONFLICT ALERT — A function of certain air traffic control automated systems designed to alert radar controllers to existing or pending situations between tracked targets (known IFR or VFR aircraft) that require his immediate attention/action. (See Mode C Intruder Alert)

CONFLICT RESOLUTION — The resolution of potential conflictions between IFR aircraft and VFR aircraft that are radar identified and in communication with ATC by ensuring that radar targets do not touch. Pertinent traffic advisories shall be issued when this procedure is applied. Note: This separation procedure will not be provided utilizing fully digitized radar systems. (See Controlled Airspace; Airport Radar Service Area/ARSA; Outer Area)

CONSOLAN — A low frequency, long-distance NAVAID used principally for transoceanic navigations.

CONTACT —

1. Establish communication with (followed by the name of the facility and, if appropriate, the frequency to be used).

2. A flight condition wherein the pilot ascertains the attitude of his aircraft and navigates by visual reference to the surface. (See Contact Approach, Radar Contact)

CONTACT APPROACH — An approach wherein an aircraft on an IFR flight plan, having an air traffic control authorization, operating clear of clouds with at least 1 mile flight visibility and a reasonable expectation of continuing to the destination airport in those conditions, may deviate from the instrument approach procedure and proceed to the destination airport by visual reference to the surface. This approach will only be authorized when requested by the pilot and the reported ground visibility at the destination airport is at least 1 statute mile. (Refer to AIM)

CONTERMINOUS U.S. — The 48 adjoining States and the District of Columbia.

CONTINENTAL CONTROL AREA — (See Controlled Airspace)

CONTINENTAL UNITED STATES — The 49 States located on the continent of North America and the District of Columbia.

CONTROL AREA — (See Controlled Airspace)

CONTROLLED AIRSPACE — Airspace designated as a control zone, airport radar service area, terminal control area, transition area, control area, continental control area, and positive control area within which some or all aircraft may be subject to air traffic control. (Refer to AIM, FAR Part 71)

Types of U.S. Controlled Airspace:

1. **Control Zone** — Controlled airspace which extends upward from the surface of the earth and terminates at the base of the continental control area. Control zones that do not underlie the continental control area have no upper limit. A control zone may include one or more airports and is normally a circular area with a radius of 5 statute miles and any extensions necessary to include instrument approach and departure paths.

2. **Airport Radar Service Area/ARSA** — Regulatory airspace surrounding designated airports wherein ATC provides radar vectoring and sequencing on a full-time basis for all IFR and VFR aircraft. The service provided in an ARSA is called ARSA service which includes: IFR/IFR — standard IFR separation; IFR/VFR — traffic advisories and conflict resolution; and VFR/VFR — traffic advisories and, as appropriate, safety alerts. The AIM contains an explanation of ARSA. The ARSA's are depicted on VFR aeronautical charts. (See Conflict Resolution, Outer Area) (Refer to AIM, Airport/Facility Directory, FAR Part 91)

3. **Terminal Control Area/TCA** — Controlled airspace extending upward from the surface or higher to specified altitudes, within which all aircraft are subject to operating rules and pilot and equipment requirements specified in FAR Part 91. TCA's are depicted on Sectional, World Aeronautical, En Route Low Altitude, DOD FLIP, and TCA charts. (Refer to FAR Part 91, AIM)

4. **Transition Area** — Controlled airspace extending upward from 700 feet or more above the surface of the earth when designated in conjunction with an airport for which an approved instrument approach procedure has been prescribed; or from 1,200 feet or more above the surface of the earth when designated in conjunction with airway route structures or segments. Unless otherwise specified, transition areas terminate at the base of the overlying controlled airspace. Transition areas are designed to contain IFR operations in controlled airspace during portions of the terminal operation and while transiting between the terminal and en route environment.

5. **Control Area** — Airspace designated as Colored Federal airways, VOR Federal airways, control areas associated with jet routes outside the continental control area (FAR 71.161), additional control areas (FAR 71.163), control area extensions (FAR 71.165), and area low routes. Control areas do not include the continental control area, but unless other-

wise designated, they do include the airspace between a segment of a main VOR Federal airway and its associated alternate segments with the vertical extent of the area corresponding to the vertical extent of the related segment of the main airway. The vertical extent of the various categories of airspace contained in control areas is defined in FAR Part 71.

6. **Continental Control Area** — The airspace of the 48 contiguous States, the District of Columbia and Alaska, excluding the Alaska peninsula west of Long. 1601/2 00' 00"W, at and above 14,500 feet MSL, but does not include:

a. The airspace less than 1,500 feet above the surface of the earth; or
b. Prohibited and restricted areas, other than the restricted areas listed in FAR Part 71.

7. **Positive Control Area/PCA** — Airspace designated in FAR, Part 71 within which there is positive control of aircraft. Flight in PCA is normally conducted under instrument flight rules. PCA is designated throughout most of the conterminous United States and its vertical extent is from 18,000 feet MSL to and including flight level 600. In Alaska PCA does not include the airspace less than 1,500 feet above the surface of the earth nor the airspace over the Alaska Peninsula west of longitude 160 degrees West. Rules for operating in PCA are found in FARs 91.97 and 91.24.

CONTROLLED DEPARTURE TIME (CDT) PROGRAMS — These programs are the flow control process whereby aircraft are held on the ground at the departure airport when delays are projected to occur in either the en route system or the terminal of intended landing. The purpose of these programs is to reduce congestion in the air traffic system or to limit the duration of airborne holding in the arrival center or terminal area. A CDT is a specific departure slot shown on the flight plan as an expected departure clearance time (EDCT).

CONTROLLER — (See Air Traffic Control Specialist)

CONTROL SECTOR — An airspace area of defined horizontal and vertical dimensions for which a controller or group of controllers has air traffic control responsibility, normally within an air route traffic control center or an approach control facility. Sectors are established based on predominant traffic flows, altitude strata, and controller workload. Pilot communications during operations within a sector are normally maintained on discrete frequencies assigned to the sector. (See Discrete Frequency)

CONTROL SLASH — A radar beacon slash representing the actual position of the associated aircraft. Normally, the control slash is the one closest to the interrogating radar beacon site. When ARTCC radar is operating in narrowband (digitized) mode, the control slash is converted to a target symbol.

CONTROL ZONE — (See Controlled Airspace)

CONVECTIVE SIGMET/WST/CONVECTIVE SIGNIFICANT METEOROLOGICAL INFORMATION — A weather advisory concerning convective weather significant to the safety of all aircraft. Convective SIGMET's are issued for tornadoes, lines of thunderstorms, embedded thunderstorms of any intensity level, areas of thunderstorms greater than or equal to VIP level 4 with an areal coverage of 4/10 (40%) or more, and hail 3/4 inch or greater. (See AWW, SIGMET, CWA, and AIRMET) (Refer to AIM)

COORDINATES — The intersection of lines of reference, usually expressed in degrees/minutes/seconds of latitude and longitude, used to determine position or location.

COORDINATION FIX — The fix in relation to which facilities will handoff, transfer control of an aircraft, or coordinate flight progress data. For terminal facilities, it may also serve as a clearance for arriving aircraft.

CORRECTION — An error has been made in the transmission and the correct version follows.

COUPLED APPROACH — A coupled approach is an instrument approach performed by the aircraft autopilot which is receiving position information and/or steering commands from onboard navigation equipment. In general, coupled nonprecision approaches must be discontinued and flown manually at altitudes lower than 50 feet below the minimum descent altitude, and coupled precision approaches must be flown manually below 50 feet ALG (See Autoland Approach).

Note. — Coupled and autoland approaches are flown in VFR and IFR. It is common for carriers to require their crews to fly coupled approaches and autoland approaches (if certified) when the weather conditions are less than approximately 4,000 RVR.

COURSE —

1. The intended direction of flight in the horizontal plane measured in degrees from north.

2. The ILS localizer signal pattern usually specified as the front course or the back course.

3. The intended track along a straight, curved, or segmented MLS path.

(See Bearing, Radial, Instrument Landing System, Microwave Landing System)

CRITICAL ENGINE — The engine which, upon failure, would most adversely affect the performance or handling qualities of an aircraft.

CROSS (FIX) AT (ALTITUDE) — Used by ATC when a specific altitude restriction at a specified fix is required.

CROSS (FIX) AT OR ABOVE (ALTITUDE) — Used by ATC when an altitude restriction at a specified fix is required. It does not prohibit the aircraft from crossing the fix at a higher altitude than specified; however, the higher altitude may not be one that will violate a succeeding altitude restriction or altitude assignment. (See Altitude Assignment, Altitude Restriction.) (Refer to AIM)

CROSS (FIX) AT OR BELOW (ALTITUDE) — Used by ATC when a maximum crossing altitude at a specific fix is required. It does not prohibit the aircraft from crossing the fix at a lower altitude; however, it must be at or above the minimum IFR altitude. (See Minimum IFR Altitude, Altitude Restriction) (Refer to FAR Part 91)

CROSSWIND —

1. When used concerning the traffic pattern, the word means "crosswind leg." (See Traffic Pattern)

2. When used concerning wind conditions, the word means a wind not parallel to the runway or the path of an aircraft. (See Crosswind Component)

CROSSWIND COMPONENT — The wind component measured in knots at 90 degrees to the longitudinal axis of the runway.

CRUISE — Used in an ATC clearance to authorize a pilot to conduct flight at any altitude from the minimum IFR altitude up to and including the altitude specified in the clearance. The pilot may level off at any intermediate altitude within this block of airspace. Climb/descent within the block is to be made at the discretion of the pilot. However, once the pilot starts descent and verbally reports leaving an altitude in the block, he may not return to that altitude without additional ATC clearance. Further, it is approval for the pilot to proceed to and make an approach at destination airport and can be used in conjunction with:

1. An airport clearance limit at locations with a standard/special instrument approach procedure. The FAR's require that if an instrument letdown to an airport is necessary, the pilot shall make the letdown in accordance with a standard/special instrument approach procedure for that airport, or

2. An airport clearance limit at locations that are within/below/outside controlled airspace and without a standard/special instrument approach procedure. Such a clearance is NOT AUTHORIZATION for the pilot to descend under IFR conditions below the applicable minimum IFR altitude nor does it imply that ATC is exercising control over aircraft in uncontrolled airspace; however, it provides a means for the aircraft to proceed to destination airport, descend, and land in accordance with applicable FAR's governing VFR flight operations. Also, this provides search and rescue protection until such time as the IFR flight plan is closed. (See Instrument Approach Procedure)

CRUISING ALTITUDE/LEVEL — An altitude or flight level maintained during en route level flight. This is a constant altitude and should not be confused with a cruise clearance. (See Altitude)

DECISION HEIGHT/DH — With respect to the operation of aircraft, means the height at which a decision must be made during an ILS, MLS, or PAR instrument approach to either continue the approach or to execute a missed approach.

Note 1. — Decision altitude (DA) is referenced to mean sea level (MSL) and decision height (DH) is referenced to the threshold elevation.

Note 2. — The required visual reference means that section of the visual aids or of the approach area which should have been in view for sufficient time for the pilot to have made an assessment of the aircraft position and rate of change of position, in relation to the desired flight path.

DECODER — The device used to decipher signals received from ATCRBS transponders to effect their display as select codes. (See Codes, Radar)

DEFENSE VISUAL FLIGHT RULES/DVFR — Rules applicable to flights within an ADIZ conducted under the visual flight rules in FAR Part 91. (See Air Defense Identification Zone) (Refer to FAR Part 99)

DELAY INDEFINITE (REASON IF KNOWN) EXPECT FURTHER CLEARANCE (TIME) — Used by ATC to inform a pilot when an accurate estimate of the delay time and the reason for the delay cannot immediately be determined; e.g., a disabled aircraft on the runway, terminal or center area saturation, weather below landing minimums, etc. (See Expect Further Clearance)

DEPARTURE CONTROL — A function of an approach control facility providing air traffic control service for departing IFR and, under certain conditions, VFR aircraft. (See Approach Control) (Refer to AIM)

DEPARTURE TIME — The time an aircraft becomes airborne.

DEVIATIONS —

1. A departure from a current clearance, such as an off course maneuver to avoid weather or turbulence.

2. Where specifically authorized in the FAR's and requested by the pilot, ATC may permit pilots to deviate from certain regulations. (Refer to AIM)

DF APPROACH PROCEDURE — Used under emergency conditions where another instrument approach procedure cannot be executed. DF guidance for an instrument approach is given by ATC facilities with DF capability. (See DF Guidance, Direction Finder) (Refer to AIM)

DF FIX — The geographical location of an aircraft obtained by one or more direction finders. (See Direction Finder)

DF GUIDANCE/DF STEER — Headings provided to aircraft by facilities equipped with direction finding equipment. These headings, if followed, will lead the aircraft to a predetermined point such as the DF station or an airport. DF guidance is given to aircraft in distress or to other aircraft which request the service. Practice DF guidance is provided when workload permits. (See Direction Finder, DF Fix) (Refer to AIM)

DIRECT — Straight line flight between two navigational aids, fixes, points, or any combination thereof. When used by pilots in describing off-airway routes, points defining direct route segments become compulsory reporting points unless the aircraft is under radar contact.

DIRECT ALTITUDE AND IDENTITY READOUT/ DAIR — The DAIR System is a modification to the AN/TPX-42 Interrogator System. The Navy has two adaptations of the DAIR System — Carrier Air Traffic Control Direct Altitude and Identification Readout System for Aircraft Carriers and Radar Air Traffic Control Facility Direct Altitude and Identity Readout System for land-based terminal operations. The DAIR detects, tracks, and predicts secondary radar aircraft targets. Targets are displayed by means of computer-generated symbols and alphanumeric characters depicting flight identification, altitude, ground speed, and flight plan data. The DAIR System is capable of interfacing with ARTCC's.

DIRECTION FINDER/DF/UDF/VDF/UVDF — A radio receiver equipped with a directional sensing antenna used to take bearings on a radio transmitter. Specialized radio direction finders are used in aircraft as air navigation aids. Others are ground-based, primarily to obtain a "fix" on a pilot requesting orientation assistance or to locate downed aircraft. A location "fix" is established by the intersection of two or more bearing lines plotted on a navigational chart using either two separately located Direction Finders to obtain a fix on an aircraft or by a pilot plotting the bearing indications of his DF on two separately located ground-based transmitters, both of which can be identified on his chart. UDF's receive signals in the ultra high frequency radio broadcast band; VDF's in the very high frequency band; and UVDF's in both bands. ATC provides DF service at those air traffic control towers and flight service stations listed in the Airport/Facility Directory and the DOD FLIP IFR En Route Supplement. (See DF Guidance, DF Fix)

DISCRETE CODE/DISCRETE BEACON CODE — As used in the Air Traffic Control Radar Beacon System (ATCRBS) any one of the 4096 selectable Mode 3/A aircraft transponder codes except those ending in zero zero; e.g., discrete codes: 0010, 1201, 2317, 7777; non-discrete codes: 0100, 1200, 7700. Non-discrete codes are normally reserved for radar facilities that are not equipped with discrete decoding capability and for other purposes such as emergencies (7700). VFR aircraft (1200), etc. (See Radar) (Refer to AIM)

DISCRETE FREQUENCY — A separate radio frequency for use in direct pilot-controller communications in air traffic control which reduces frequency congestion by controlling the number of aircraft operating on a particular frequency at one time. Discrete frequencies are normally designated for each control sector in en route/terminal ATC facilities. Discrete frequencies are listed in the Airport/Facility Directory and the DOD FLIP IFR En Route Supplement. (See Control Sector)

DISPLACED THRESHOLD — A threshold that is located at a point on the runway other than the designated beginning of the runway. (See Threshold) (Refer to AIM)

DISTANCE MEASURING EQUIPMENT/DME — Equipment (airborne and ground) used to measure, in nautical miles, the slant range distance of an aircraft from the DME navigational aid. (See TACAN, VORTAC, Microwave Landing System)

DISTRESS — A condition of being threatened by serious and/or imminent danger and of requiring immediate assistance.

DIVERSE VECTOR AREA/DVA — In a radar environment, that area in which a prescribed departure route is not required as the only suitable route to avoid obstacles. The area in which random radar vectors below the MVA/MIA, established in accordance with the TERPS criteria for diverse departures obstacles and terrain avoidance, may be issued to departing aircraft.

DME FIX — A geographical position determined by reference to a navigational aid which provides distance and azimuth information. It is defined by a specific distance in nautical miles and a radial, azimuth, or course (i.e., localizer) in degrees magnetic from that aid. (See Distance Measuring Equipment/DME, Fix, Microwave Landing System)

DME SEPARATION — Spacing of aircraft in terms of distances (nautical miles) determined by reference to distance measuring equipment (DME). (See Distance Measuring Equipment)

DOD FLIP — Department of Defense Flight Information Publications used for flight planning, en route, and terminal operations. FLIP is produced by the Defense Mapping Agency for world-wide use. United States Government Flight Information Publications (en route charts and instrument approach procedure charts) are incorporated in DOD FLIP for use in the National Airspace System (NAS).

DOWNBURST — A strong downdraft which induces an outburst of damaging winds on or near the ground. Damaging winds, either straight or curved, are highly divergent. The sizes of downbursts vary from 1/2 mile or less to more than 10 miles. An intense down burst often causes widespread damage. Damaging winds, lasting 5 to 30 minutes, could reach speeds as high as 120 knots.

DOWNWIND LEG — (See Traffic Pattern)

DRAG CHUTE — A parachute device installed on certain aircraft which is deployed on landing roll to assist in deceleration of the aircraft.

EMERGENCY— A *distress* or an *urgency* condition.

EMERGENCY LOCATOR TRANSMITTER/ELT — A radio transmitter attached to the aircraft structure which operates from its own power source on 121.5 MHz and 243.0 MHz. It aids in locating downed aircraft by radiating a downward sweeping audio tone, 2-4 times per second. It is designed to function without human action after an accident. (Refer to FAR Part 91, AIM)

EMERGENCY SAFE ALTITUDE — (See Minimum Safe Altitude)

E-MSAW — (See En Route Minimum Safe Altitude Warning)

EN ROUTE AIR TRAFFIC CONTROL SERVICES — Air traffic control service provided aircraft on IFR flight plans, generally by centers, when these aircraft are operating between departure and destination terminal areas. When equipment, capabilities, and controller workload permit, certain advisory/assistance services may be provided to VFR aircraft. (See NAS Stage A, Air Route Traffic Control Center) (Refer to AIM)

EN ROUTE AUTOMATED RADAR TRACKING SYSTEM/EARTS — An automated radar and radar beacon tracking system. Its functional capabilities and design are essentially the same as the terminal ARTS IIIA system except for the EARTS capability of employing both short-range (ASR) and long-range (ARSR) radars, use of full digital radar displays, and fail-safe design. (See Automated Radar Terminal Systems/ARTS)

EN ROUTE CHARTS — (See Aeronautical Charts)

EN ROUTE DESCENT — Descent from the en route cruising altitude which takes place along the route of flight.

EN ROUTE FLIGHT ADVISORY SERVICE/FLIGHT WATCH — A service specifically designed to provide, upon pilot request, timely weather information pertinent to his type of flight, intended route of flight, and altitude. The FSS's providing this service are listed in the Airport/Facility Directory. (Refer to AIM)

EN ROUTE MINIMUM SAFE ALTITUDE WARNING/E-MSAW — A function of the NAS Stage A en route computer that aids the controller by alerting him when a tracked aircraft is below or predicted by the computer to go below a predetermined minimum IFR altitude (MIA).

EXECUTE MISSED APPROACH — Instructions issued to a pilot making an instrument approach which means continue inbound to the missed approach point and execute the missed approach procedure as described on the Instrument Approach Procedure Chart or as previously assigned by ATC. The pilot may climb immediately to the altitude specified in the missed approach procedure upon making a missed approach. No turns should be initiated prior to reaching the missed approach point. When conducting an ASR or PAR approach, execute the assigned missed approach procedure immediately upon receiving instructions to "execute missed approach." (Refer to AIM)

EXPECT (ALTITUDE) AT (TIME) or (FIX) — Used under certain conditions to provide a pilot with an altitude to be used in the event of two-way communications failure. It also provides altitude information to assist the pilot in planning. (Refer to AIM)

EXPECTED DEPARTURE CLEARANCE TIME/EDCT — The runway release time assigned to an aircraft in a controlled departure time program and shown on the flight progress strip as an EDCT.

EXPECT FURTHER CLEARANCE (TIME)/EFC — The time a pilot can expect to receive clearance beyond a clearance limit.

EXPECT FURTHER CLEARANCE VIA (AIRWAYS, ROUTES OR FIXES) — Used to inform a pilot of the routing he can expect if any part of the route beyond a short range clearance limit differs from that filed.

EXPEDITE — Used by ATC when prompt compliance is required to avoid the development of an imminent situation.

FAST FILE — A system whereby a pilot files a flight plan via telephone that is tape recorded and then transcribed for transmission to the appropriate air traffic facility. Locations having a fast file capability are contained in the Airport/Facility Directory. (Refer to AIM)

FEATHERED PROPELLER — A propeller whose blades have been rotated so that the leading and trailing edges are nearly parallel with the aircraft flight path to stop or minimize drag and engine rotation. Normally used to indicate shutdown of a reciprocating or turboprop engine due to malfunction.

FEEDER FIX — The fix depicted on Instrument Approach Procedure Charts which establishes the starting point of the feeder route.

FEEDER ROUTE — A route depicted on instrument approach procedure charts to designate routes for aircraft to proceed from the en route structure to the initial approach fix (IAF). (See Instrument Approach Procedure)

FERRY FLIGHT — A flight for the purpose of:

1. Returning an aircraft to base.

    2. Delivering an aircraft from one location to another.

    3. Moving an aircraft to and from a maintenance base.

Ferry flights, under certain conditions, may be conducted under terms of a special flight permit.

FILED — Normally used in conjunction with flight plans, meaning a flight plan has been submitted to ATC.

FILED EN ROUTE DELAY — Any of the following pre-planned delays at points/areas along the route of flight which require special flight plan filing and handling techniques.

    1. **Terminal Area Delay** — A delay within a terminal area for touch-and-go, low approach, or other terminal area activity.

    2. **Special Use Airspace Delay** — A delay within a Military Operating Area, Restricted Area, Warning Area, or ATC Assigned Airspace.

    3. **Aerial Refueling Delay** — A delay within an Aerial Refueling Track or Anchor.

FINAL — Commonly used to mean that an aircraft is on the final approach course or is aligned with a landing area. (See Final Approach Course, Final Approach-IFR, Traffic Pattern, Segments of an Instrument Approach Procedure)

FINAL APPROACH COURSE — A published MLS course, a straight line extension of a localizer, a final approach radial/bearing, or a runway centerline all without regard to distance. (See Final Approach-IFR, Traffic Pattern)

FINAL APPROACH FIX/FAF — The fix from which the final approach (IFR) to an airport is executed and which identifies the beginning of the final approach segment. It is designated on Government charts by the Maltese Cross symbol for non-precision approaches and the lightning bolt symbol for precision approaches; or when ATC directs a lower-than-published Glideslope/path Intercept Altitude, it is the resultant actual point of the glideslope/path intercept. (See Final Approach Point, Glideslope/path Intercept Altitude, Segments of an Instrument Approach Procedure)

FINAL APPROACH-IFR — The flight path of an aircraft which is inbound to an airport on a final instrument approach course, beginning at the final approach fix or point and extending to the airport or the point where a circle-to-land maneuver or a missed approach is executed. (See Segments of an Instrument Approach Procedure, Final Approach Fix, Final Approach Course, Final Approach Point)

    a) At the end of the last procedure turn, base turn or inbound turn of a racetrack procedure, if specified; or

    b) At the point of interception of the last track specified in the approach procedure; and ends at a point in the vicinity of an aerodrome from which:

        1) A landing can be made; or

        2) A missed approach procedure is initiated.

FINAL APPROACH POINT/FAP — The point, applicable only to a nonprecision approach with no depicted FAF (such as an on-airport VOR), where the aircraft is established inbound on the final approach course from the procedure turn and where the final approach descent may be commenced. The FAP serves as the FAF and identifies the beginning of the final approach segment. (See Final Approach Fix, Segments of an Instrument Approach Procedure)

FINAL APPROACH SEGMENT — (See Segments of an Instrument Approach Procedure)

FINAL APPROACH-VFR — (See Traffic Pattern)

FINAL CONTROLLER — The controller providing information and final approach guidance during PAR and ASR approaches utilizing radar equipment. (See Radar Approach)

FIX — A geographical position determined by visual reference to the surface, by reference to one or more radio NAVAIDs, by celestial plotting, or by another navigational device.

FLAG/FLAG ALARM — A warning device incorporated in certain airborne navigation and flight instruments indicating that:

1. Instruments are inoperative or otherwise not operating satisfactorily, or

2. Signal strength or quality of the received signal falls below acceptable values.

FLAMEOUT — Unintended loss of combustion in turbine engines resulting in the loss of engine power.

FLIGHT CHECK — A call-sign prefix used by FAA aircraft engaged in flight inspection/certification of navigational aids and flight procedures. The word "recorded" may be added as a suffix; e.g., "Flight Check 320 recorded" to indicate that an automated flight inspection is in progress in terminal areas. (See Flight Inspection/Flight Check) (Refer to AIM).

FLIGHT FOLLOWING — (See Traffic Advisories)

FLIGHT INFORMATION REGION/FIR — An airspace of defined dimensions within which Flight Information Service and Alerting Service are provided.

1. **Flight Information Service** — A service provided for the purpose of giving advice and information useful for the safe and efficient conduct of flights.

2. **Alerting Service** — A service provided to notify appropriate organizations regarding aircraft in need of search and rescue aid and to assist such organizations as required.

FLIGHT INSPECTION/FLIGHT CHECK — Inflight investigation and evaluation of a navigational aid to determine whether it meets established tolerances. (See Navigational Aid)

FLIGHT LEVEL — A level of constant atmospheric pressure related to a reference datum of 29.92 inches of mercury. Each is stated in three digits that represent hundreds of feet. For example, flight level 250 represents a barometric altimeter indication of 25,000 feet; flight level 255, an indication of 25,500 feet.

Note 1. — A pressure type altimeter calibrated in accordance with the standard atmosphere:

a) When set to a QNH altimeter setting, will indicate altitude;

b) When set to a QFE altimeter setting, will indicate height above the QFE reference datum; and

c) When set to a pressure of 1013.2 hPa (1013.2 mb), may be used to indicate flight levels.

Note 2. — The terms height and altitude, used in Note 1 above, indicate altimetric rather than geometric heights and altitudes.

FLIGHT LINE — A term used to describe the precise movement of a civil photogrammetric aircraft along a predetermined course(s) at a predetermined altitude during the actual photographic run.

FLIGHT PATH — A line, course, or track along which an aircraft is flying or intended to be flown. (See Track, Course)

FLIGHT PLAN — Specified information relating to the intended flight of an aircraft that is filed orally or in writing with an FSS or an ATC facility. (See Fast File, Filed) (Refer to AIM)

FLIGHT RECORDER — A general term applied to any instrument or device that records information about the performance of an aircraft in flight or about conditions encountered in flight. Flight recorders may make records of airspeed, outside air temperature, vertical acceleration, engine RPM, manifold pressure, and other pertinent variables for a given flight.

Note. — See Annex 6 Part I, for specifications relating to flight recorders.

FLIGHT SERVICE STATION/FSS — Air traffic facilities which provide pilot briefing, en route communications and VFR search and rescue services, assist lost aircraft and aircraft in emergency situations, relay ATC clearances, originate Notices to Airmen, broadcast aviation weather and NAS information, receive and process IFR flight plans, and monitor NAVAIDs. In addition, at selected locations, FSSs provide Enroute Flight Advisory Service (Flight Watch), take weather observations, issue airport advisories, and advise Customs and Immigration of transborder flights. (Refer to AIM)

FLIGHT STANDARDS DISTRICT OFFICE/FSDO — An FAA field office serving an assigned geographical area and staffed with Flight Standards personnel who serve the aviation industry and the general public on matters relating to the certification and operation of air carrier and general aviation aircraft. Activities include general surveillance of operational safety, certification of airmen and aircraft, accident prevention, investigation, enforcement, etc.

FLIGHT TEST — A flight for the purpose of:

1. Investigating the operation/flight characteristics of an aircraft or aircraft component.
2. Evaluating an applicant for a pilot certificate or rating.

FLIGHT VISIBILITY — (See Visibility)

FLIGHT WATCH — A shortened term for use in air-ground contacts to identify the flight service station providing En Route Flight Advisory Service; e.g., "Oakland Flight Watch." (See En Route Flight Advisory Service)

FLIP — (See DOD FLIP)

FLOW CONTROL — Measures designed to adjust the flow of traffic into a given airspace, along a given route, or bound for a given aerodrome (airport) so as to ensure the most effective utilization of the airspace. (See Quota Flow Control) (Refer to Airport/Facility Directory)

FLY HEADING — Continue on, a specific compass direction in order to comply with the instructions. The pilot is expected to turn in the shorter direction to the heading unless otherwise instructed by ATC.

FORMATION FLIGHT — More than one aircraft which, by prior arrangement between the pilots, operate as a single aircraft with regard to navigation and position reporting. Separation between aircraft within the formation is the responsibility of the flight leader and the pilots of the other aircraft in the flight. This includes transition periods when aircraft within the formation are maneuvering to attain separation from each other to effect individual control and during join-up and breakaway.

    1. A standard formation is one in which a proximity of no more than 1 mile laterally or longitudinally and within 100 feet vertically from the flight leader is maintained by each wingman.

    2. Nonstandard formations are those operating under any of the following conditions:

        a. When the flight leader has requested and ATC has approved other than standard formation dimensions.

        b. When operating within an authorized altitude reservation (ALTRV) or under the provisions of a letter of agreement.

        c. When the operations are conducted in airspace specifically designed for a special activity. (See Altitude Reservation) (Refer to FAR Part 91)

FSS — (See Flight Service Station)

FUEL DUMPING — Airborne release of usable fuel. This does not include the dropping of fuel tanks. (See Jettisoning of External Stores)

FUEL SIPHONING/FUEL VENTING — Unintentional release of fuel caused by overflow, puncture, loose cap, etc.

GATE HOLD PROCEDURES — Procedures at selected airports to hold aircraft at the gate or other ground location whenever departure delays exceed or are anticipated to exceed 15 minutes. The sequence for departure will be maintained in accordance with initial call-up unless modified by flow control restrictions. Pilots should monitor the ground control/clearance delivery frequency for engine startup advisories or new proposed start time if the delay changes. (See Flow Control)

GENERAL AVIATION — That portion of civil aviation which encompasses all facets of aviation except air carriers holding a certificate of public convenience and necessity from the Civil Aeronautics Board and large aircraft commercial operators.

GENERAL AVIATION DISTRICT OFFICE/GADO — An FAA field office serving a designated geographical area and staffed with Flight Standards personnel who have the responsibility for serving the aviation industry and the general public on all matters relating to the certification and operation of general aviation aircraft.

GLIDESLOPE/GLIDEPATH — Provides vertical guidance for aircraft during approach and landing. The glideslope/glidepath is based on the following:

    1. Electronic components emitting signals which provide vertical guidance by reference to airborne instruments during instrument approaches such as ILS/MLS, or

    2. Visual ground aids, such as VASI, which provide vertical guidance for a VFR approach or for the visual portion of an instrument approach and landing.

    3. PAR. Used by ATC to inform an aircraft making a PAR approach of its vertical position (elevation) relative to the descent profile.

GLIDESLOPE/GLIDEPATH INTERCEPT ALTITUDE — The minimum altitude to intercept the glideslope/path on a precision approach. The intersection of the published intercept altitude with the glideslope/path, designated on Government charts by the lightning bolt symbol, is the precision FAF; however, when ATC directs a lower altitude, the resultant lower intercept position is then the FAF. (See Final Approach Fix, Segments of an Instrument Approach Procedure)

GO AHEAD — Proceed with your message. Not to be used for any other purpose.

GO AROUND — Instructions for a pilot to abandon his approach to landing. Additional instructions may follow. Unless otherwise advised by ATC, a VFR aircraft or an aircraft conducting visual approach should overfly the runway while climbing to traffic pattern altitude and enter the traffic pattern via the crosswind leg. A pilot on an IFR flight plan making an instrument approach should execute the published missed approach procedure or proceed as instructed by ATC; e.g., "Go around" (additional instructions if required). (See Low Approach, Missed Approach)

GROUND CLUTTER — A pattern produced on the radar scope by ground returns which may degrade other radar returns in the affected area. The effect of ground clutter is minimized by the use of moving target indicator (MTI) circuits in the radar equipment resulting in a radar presentation which displays only targets which are in motion. (See Clutter)

GROUND CONTROLLED APPROACH/GCA — A radar approach system operated from the ground by air traffic control personnel transmitting instructions to the pilot by radio. The approach may be conducted with surveillance radar (ASR) only or with both surveillance and precision approach radar (PAR). Usage of the term "GCA" by pilots is discouraged except when referring to a GCA facility. Pilots should specifically request a "PAR" approach when a precision radar approach is desired or request an "ASR" or "surveillance" approach when a nonprecision radar approach is desired. (See Radar Approach)

GROUND DELAY — The amount of delay attributed to ATC, encountered prior to departure, usually associated with a CDT program.

GROUND SPEED — The speed of an aircraft relative to the surface of the earth.

GROUND VISIBILITY — (See Visibility)

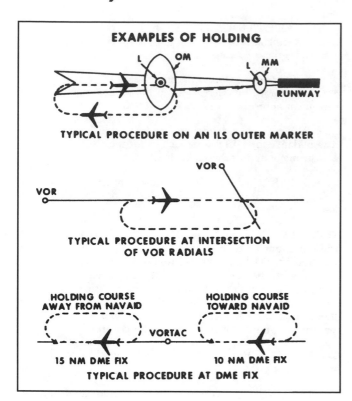

EXAMPLES OF HOLDING

TYPICAL PROCEDURE ON AN ILS OUTER MARKER

TYPICAL PROCEDURE AT INTERSECTION OF VOR RADIALS

HOLDING COURSE AWAY FROM NAVAID   HOLDING COURSE TOWARD NAVAID

15 NM DME FIX   10 NM DME FIX

TYPICAL PROCEDURE AT DME FIX

Holding procedures keep aircraft in a known chunk of airspace while awaiting further clearance from air traffic control. Typical procedures are shown here.

HANDOFF — An action taken to transfer the radar identification of an aircraft from one controller to another if the aircraft will enter the receiving controller's airspace and radio communications with the aircraft will be transferred.

HAVE NUMBERS — Used by pilots to inform ATC that they have received runway, wind, and altimeter information only.

HAZARDOUS INFLIGHT WEATHER ADVISORY SERVICE/HIWAS — A program for broadcasting hazardous weather information (See AWW's, SIGMET's, Convective SIGMET's, CWA's, AIRMET's, and Urgent PIREP's) on a continuous basis over selected VOR's. (Refer to AIM)

HEAVY (AIRCRAFT) — (See Aircraft Classes)

HEIGHT ABOVE AIRPORT/HAA — The height of the Minimum Descent Altitude above the published airport elevation. This is published in conjunction with circling minimums. (See Minimum Descent Altitude)

HEIGHT ABOVE LANDING/HAL — The height above a designated helicopter landing area used for helicopter instrument approach procedures. (Refer to FAR Part 97)

HEIGHT ABOVE TOUCHDOWN/HAT — The height of the Decision Height or Minimum Descent Altitude above the highest runway elevation in the touchdown zone (first 3,000 feet of the runway). HAT is published on instrument approach charts in conjunction with all straight-in minimums. (See Decision Height, Minimum Descent Altitude)

HELICOPTER/COPTER — Rotorcraft that, for its horizontal motion, depends principally on its engine-driven rotors.

HELIPAD — A small, designated area, usually with a prepared surface, on a heliport, airport, landing/takeoff area, apron/ramp, or movement area used for takeoff, landing, or parking of helicopters.

HELIPORT — An area of land, water, or structure used or intended to be used for the landing and takeoff of helicopters and includes its buildings and facilities if any.

HERTZ/HZ — The standard radio equivalent of frequency in cycles per second of an electromagnetic wave. Kilohertz (KHz) is a frequency of one thousand cycles per second. Megahertz (MHz) is a frequency of one million cycles per second.

HIGH FREQUENCY/HF — The frequency band between 3 and 30 MHz. (See High Frequency Communications)

HIGH FREQUENCY COMMUNICATIONS/HF COMMUNICATIONS — High radio frequencies (HF) between 3 and 30 MHz used for air-to-ground voice communication in overseas operations.

HIGH SPEED TAXIWAY/EXIT/TURNOFF — A long radius taxiway designed and provided with lighting or marking to define the path of aircraft, traveling at high speed (up to 60 knots), from the runway center to a point on the center of a taxiway. Also referred to as long radius exit or turn-off taxiway. The high speed taxiway is designed to expedite aircraft turning off the runway after landing, thus reducing runway occupancy time.

HOLD/HOLDING PROCEDURE — A predetermined maneuver which keeps aircraft within a specified airspace while awaiting further clearance from air traffic control. Also used during ground operations to keep aircraft within a specified area or at a specified point while awaiting further clearance from air traffic control. (See Holding Fix) (Refer to AIM)

HOLDING FIX — A specified fix identifiable to a pilot by NAVAID's or visual reference to the ground used as a reference point in establishing and maintaining the position of an aircraft while holding. (See Fix, Hold, Visual Holding) (Refer to AIM)

HOLD FOR RELEASE — Used by ATC to delay an aircraft for traffic management reasons; i.e., weather, traffic volume, etc. Hold for release instructions (including departure delay information) are used to inform a pilot or a controller (either directly or through an authorized relay) that a departure clearance is not valid until a release time or additional instructions have been received.

HOMING — Flight toward a NAVAID, without correcting for wind, by adjusting the aircraft heading to maintain a relative bearing of zero degrees. (See Bearing)

HOVER CHECK — Used to describe when a helicopter/VTOL aircraft requires a stabilized hover to conduct a performance/power check prior to hover taxi, air taxi, or takeoff. Altitude of the hover will vary based on the purpose of the check.

HOVER TAXI — Used to describe a helicopter/VTOL aircraft movement conducted above the surface and in ground effect at airspeeds less than approximately 20 knots. The actual height may vary, and some helicopters may require hover taxi above 25 feet AGL to reduce ground effect turbulence or provide clearance for cargo slingloads. (See Air Taxi, Hover Check) (Refer to AIM)

HOW DO YOU HEAR ME? — A question relating to the quality of the transmission or to determine how well the transmission is being received.

IDENT — A request for a pilot to activate the aircraft transponder identification feature. This will help the controller to confirm an aircraft identity or to identify an aircraft. (Refer to AIM)

IDENT FEATURE — The special feature in the Air Traffic Control Radar Beacon System (ATCRBS) equipment. It is used to immediately distinguish one displayed beacon target from other beacon targets. (See Ident)

IF FEASIBLE, REDUCE SPEED TO (SPEED) — (See Speed Adjustment)

IF NO TRANSMISSION RECEIVED FOR (TIME) — Used by ATC in radar approaches to prefix procedures which should be followed by the pilot in event of lost communications. (See Lost Communications)

IFR AIRCRAFT/IFR FLIGHT — An aircraft conducting flight in accordance with instrument flight rules.

IFR CONDITIONS — Weather conditions below the minimum for flight under visual flight rules. (See Instrument Meteorological Conditions)

IFR DEPARTURE PROCEDURE — (See IFR Takeoff Minimums and Departure Procedures) (Refer to AIM)

IFR MILITARY TRAINING ROUTES (IR) — Routes used by the Department of Defense and associated Reserve and Air Guard units for the purpose of conducting low-altitude navigation and tactical training in both IFR and VFR weather conditions below 10,000 feet MSL at airspeeds in excess of 250 knots IAS.

IFR TAKEOFF MINIMUMS AND DEPARTURE PROCEDURES — FAR, Part 91, prescribes standard takeoff rules for certain civil users. At some airports, obstructions or other factors require the establishment of nonstandard takeoff minimums, departure procedures, or both to assist pilots in avoiding obstacles during climb to the minimum en route altitude. Those airports are listed in NOS/DOD Instrument Approach Charts (IAP's) under a section entitled "IFR Takeoff Minimums and Departure Procedures." The NOS/DOD IAP chart legend illustrates the symbol used to alert the pilot to nonstandard takeoff minimums and departure procedures. When departing IFR from such airports or from any airports where there are no departure procedures, SID's, or ATC facilities available, pilots should advise ATC of any departure limitations. Controllers may query a pilot to determine acceptable departure directions, turns, or headings after takeoff. Pilots should be familiar with the departure procedures and must assure that their aircraft can meet or exceed any specified climb gradients.

ILS CATEGORIES —

    1. **ILS Category I** — An ILS approach procedure which provides for approach to a height above touchdown of not less than 200 feet and with runway visual range of not less than 1,800 feet.

    2. **ILS Category II** — An ILS approach procedure which provides for approach to a height above touchdown of not less than 100 feet and with runway visual range of not less than 1,200 feet.

    3. **ILS Category III.**

        a. **IIIA** — An ILS approach procedure which provides for approach without a decision height minimum and with runway visual range of not less than 700 feet.

        b. **IIIB** — An ILS approach procedure which provides for approach without a decision height minimum and with runway visual range of not less than 150 feet.

        c. **IIIC** — An ILS approach procedure which provides for approach without a decision height minimum and without runway visual range minimum.

IMMEDIATELY — Used by ATC when such action compliance is required to avoid an imminent situation.

INCREASE SPEED TO (SPEED) — (See Speed Adjustment)

INFORMATION REQUEST/INREQ — A request originated by an FSS for information concerning an overdue VFR aircraft.

INITIAL APPROACH FIX/IAF — The fixes depicted on instrument approach procedure charts that identify the beginning of the initial approach segment(s). (See Fix, Segments of an Instrument Approach Procedure)

INITIAL APPROACH SEGMENT — (See Segments of an Instrument Approach Procedure)

INNER MARKER/IM/INNER MARKER BEACON — A marker beacon used with an ILS (CAT II) precision approach located between the middle marker and the end of the ILS runway, transmitting a radiation pattern keyed at six dots per second and indicating to the pilot, both aurally and visually, that he is at the designated decision height (DH), normally 100 feet above the touchdown zone elevation, on the ILS CAT II approach. It also marks progress during a CAT III approach. (See Instrument Landing System) (Refer to AIM)

INSTRUMENT APPROACH PROCEDURE/IAP/ INSTRUMENT APPROACH — A series of predetermined maneuvers for the orderly transfer of an aircraft under instrument flight conditions from the beginning of the initial approach to a landing or to a point from which a landing may be made visually. It is prescribed and approved for a specific airport by competent authority. (See Segments of an Instrument Approach Procedure) (Refer to FAR Part 91, AIM)

    1. U. S. civil standard instrument approach procedures are approved by the FAA as prescribed under FAR Part 97 and are available for public use.

    2. U.S. military standard instrument approach procedures are approved and published by the Department of Defense.

    3. Special instrument approach procedures are approved by the FAA for individual operators but are not published in FAR Part 97 for public use.

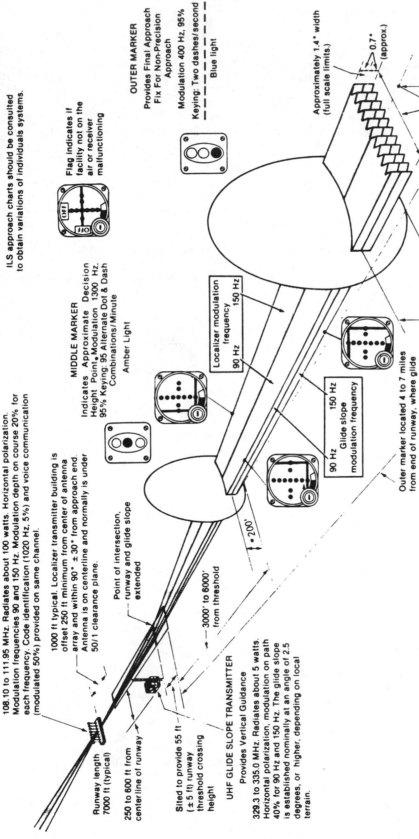

ILS
[FAA INSTRUMENT LANDING SYSTEM]
STANDARD CHARACTERISTICS AND TERMINOLOGY

ILS approach charts should be consulted to obtain variations of individuals systems.

OUTER MARKER
Provides Final Approach Fix For Non-Precision Approach
Modulation 400 Hz, 95%
Keying: Two dashes/second
Blue light

MIDDLE MARKER
Indicates Approximate Decision Height Point. Modulation 1300 Hz, 95% Keying: 95 Alternate Dot & Dash Combinations/Minute
Amber Light

Flag indicates if facility not on the air or receiver malfunctioning

Approximately 1.4° width (full scale limits.)

0.7° (approx.)

3° above horizontal (optimum)

Course width varies; between 3°–6° tailored to provide 700 ft at threshold (full scale limits)

VHF LOCALIZER
Provides Horizontal Guidance.

108.10 to 111.95 MHz. Radiates about 100 watts. Horizontal polarization. Modulation frequencies 90 and 150 Hz. Modulation depth on course 20% for each frequency. Code identification (1020 Hz, 5%) and voice communication (modulated 50%) provided on same channel.

1000 ft typical. Localizer transmitter building is offset 250 ft minimum from center of antenna array and within 90° ± 30° from approach end. Antenna is on centerline and normally is under 50/1 clearance plane.

Localizer modulation frequency
90 Hz   150 Hz

150 Hz
90 Hz   Glide slope modulation frequency

Point of intersection, runway and glide slope extended

3000' to 6000' from threshold

Outer marker located 4 to 7 miles from end of runway, where glide slope intersects the procedure turn (minimum holding) altitude, ± 50 ft vertically.

All marker transmitters approximately 2 watts of 75 MHz modulated about 95%

Figures marked with asterisk are typical. Actual figures vary with deviations in distances to markers, glide angles and localizer widths.

Runway length 7000 ft (typical)

250 to 600 ft from centerline of runway

Sited to provide 55 ft (± 5 ft) runway threshold crossing height

200'

UHF GLIDE SLOPE TRANSMITTER
Provides Vertical Guidance

329.3 to 335.0 MHz. Radiates about 5 watts. Horizontal polarization, modulation on path 40% for 90 Hz and 150 Hz. The glide slope is established nominally at an angle of 2.5 degrees, or higher, depending on local terrain.

NOTE:
Compass locators, rated at 25 watts output 190 to 535 KHz, are installed at many outer and some middle markers. A 400 Hz or a 1020 Hz tone, modulating the carrier about 95%, is keyed with the first two letters of the ILS identification on the outer locator and the last two letters on the middle locator. At some locators, simultaneous voice transmissions from the control tower are provided, with appropriate reduction in identification percentage.

RATE OF DESCENT CHART
(feet per minute)

Speed (Knots)	Angle		
	2 1/2°	2 3/4°	3°
90	400	440	475
110	485	535	585
130	575	630	690
150	665	730	795
160	707	778	849

INSTRUMENT FLIGHT RULES/IFR — Rules governing the procedures for conducting instrument flight. Also a term used by pilots and controllers to indicate type of flight plan. (See Visual Flight Rules, Instrument Meteorological Conditions, Visual Meteorological Conditions) (Refer to AIM)

INSTRUMENT LANDING SYSTEM/ILS — A precision instrument approach system which normally consists of the following electronic components and visual aids:

    1. **Localizer.** (See Localizer)

    2. **Glideslope.** (See Glideslope)

    3. **Outer Marker.** (See Outer Marker)

    4. **Middle Marker.** (See Middle Marker)

    5. **Approach Lights.** (See Airport Lighting)

(Refer to FAR Part 91, AIM)

INSTRUMENT METEOROLOGICAL CONDITIONS/IMC — Meteorological conditions expressed in terms of visibility, distance from cloud, and ceiling less than the minima specified for visual meteorological conditions. (See Visual Meteorological Conditions, Instrument Flight Rules, Visual Flight Rules)

INSTRUMENT RUNWAY — A runway equipped with electronic and visual navigation aids for which a precision or non-precision approach procedure having straight-in landing minimums has been approved.

    a) **Non-precision Approach Runway.** An instrument runway served by visual aids and a nonvisual aid providing at least directional guidance adequate for a straight-in approach.

    b) **Precision Approach Runway, Category I.** An instrument runway served by ILS and visual aids intended for operations down to 60 m (200 feet) decision height and down to an RVR of the order of 800 m.

    c) **Precision Approach Runway, Category II.** An instrument runway served by ILS and visual aids intended for operations down to 30 m (100 feet) decision height and down to an RVR of the order of 400 m.

    d) **Precision Approach Runway, Category III.** An instrument runway served by ILS to and along the surface of the runway and:

    A — Intended for operations down to an RVR of the order of 200 m (no decision height being applicable) using visual aids during the final phase of landing;

    B — Intended for operations down to an RVR of the order of 50 m (no decision height being applicable) using visual aids for taxiing;

    C — Intended for operations without reliance on visual reference for landing or taxiing.

    Note 1. — See Annex 10 Volume I, Part I Chapter 3, for related ILS specifications.

    Note 2. — Visual aids need not necessarily be matched to the scale of non-visual aids provided. The criterion for the selection of visual aids is the conditions in which operations are intended to be conducted.

INTERMEDIATE APPROACH SEGMENT — (See Segments of an Instrument Approach Procedure)

INTERMEDIATE FIX/IF — The fix that identifies the beginning of the intermediate approach segment of an instrument approach procedure. The fix is not normally identified on the instrument approach chart as an intermediate fix (IF). (See Segments of an Instrument Approach Procedure)

INTERNATIONAL AIRPORT — Relating to international flight, it means:

    1. An airport of entry which has been designated by the Secretary of Treasury or Commissioner of Customs as an international airport for customs service.

    2. A landing rights airport at which specific permission to land must be obtained from customs authorities in advance of contemplated use.

    3. Airports designated under the Convention on International Civil Aviation as an airport for use by international commercial air transport and/or international general aviation. (Refer to Airport/Facility Directory and IFIM).

INTERNATIONAL CIVIL AVIATION ORGANIZATION/ INTERNATIONAL FLIGHT INFORMATION MANUAL/ IFIM — A publication designed primarily as a pilot's preflight planning guide for flights into foreign airspace and for flights returning to the U.S. from foreign locations.

INTERROGATOR — The ground-based surveillance radar beacon transmitter-receiver, which normally scans in synchronism with a primary radar, transmitting discrete radio signals which repetitively request all transponders on the mode being used to reply. The replies received are mixed with the primary radar returns and displayed on the same plan position indicator (radar scope). Also, applied to the airborne element of the TACAN/DME system. (See Transponder) (Refer to AIM)

INTERSECTING RUNWAYS — Two or more runways which cross or meet within their lengths. (See Intersection)

INTERSECTION —

    1. A point defined by any combination of courses, radials, or bearings of two or more navigational aids.

    2. Used to describe the point where two runways, a runway and a taxiway, or two taxiways cross or meet.

INTERSECTION DEPARTURE/INTERSECTION TAKE-OFF — A takeoff or proposed takeoff on a runway from an intersection. (See Intersection)
I SAY AGAIN — The message will be repeated.

JAMMING — Electronic or mechanical interference which may disrupt the display of aircraft on radar or the transmission/reception of radio communications/navigation.

JET BLAST — Jet engine exhaust (thrust stream turbulence). (See Wake Turbulence)

JET ROUTE — A route designed to serve aircraft operations from 18,000 feet MSL up to and including flight level 450. The routes are referred to as "J" routes with numbering to identify the designated route; e.g., J105. (See Route) (Refer to FAR Part 71)

COLOR AND TYPE OF SIGNAL	ON THE GROUND	IN FLIGHT
STEADY GREEN	Cleared for takeoff	Cleared to land
FLASHING GREEN	Cleared to taxi	Return for landing (to be followed by steady green at proper time)
STEADY RED	Stop	Give way to other aircraft and continue circling
FLASHING RED	Taxi clear of landing area (runway) in use	Airport unsafe— do not land
FLASHING WHITE	Return to starting point on airport	
ALTERNATING RED & GREEN	General Warning Signal—Exercise Extreme Caution	

Light signals have been used for ground-to-air communication since the earliest days of aviation. These standard meanings should be memorized by every pilot for use in case of radio failure.

JET STREAM — A migrating stream of high-speed winds present at high altitudes.

JETTISONING OF EXTERNAL STORES — Airborne release of external stores; e.g., tiptanks, ordnance. (See Fuel Dumping) (Refer to FAR Part 91)

JOINT USE RESTRICTED AREA — (See Restricted Area)

KNOWN TRAFFIC — With respect to ATC clearances, means aircraft whose altitude, position, and intentions are known to ATC.

LANDING/TAKEOFF AREA — Any locality either on land, water, or structures, including airports/heliports and intermediate landing fields, which is used, or intended to be used, for the landing and takeoff of aircraft whether or not facilities are provided for the shelter, servicing, or for receiving or discharging passengers or cargo.

LANDING DIRECTION INDICATOR — A device which visually indicates the direction in which landings and takeoffs should be made. (See Tetrahedron) (Refer to AIM)

LANDING MINIMUMS/IFR LANDING MINIMUMS — The minimum visibility prescribed for landing a civil aircraft while using an instrument approach procedure. The minimum applies with other limitations set forth in FAR Part 91 with respect to the Minimum Descent Altitude (MDA) or Decision Height (DH) prescribed in the instrument approach procedures as follows:

1. **Straight-in landing minimums** — A statement of MDA and visibility, or DH and visibility, required for a straight-in landing on a specified runway, or

2. **Circling minimums** — A statement of MDA and visibility required for the circle-to-land maneuver.

Descent below the established MDA or DH is not authorized during an approach unless the aircraft is in a position from which a normal approach to the runway of intended landing can be made and adequate visual reference to required visual cues is maintained. (See Straight-in Landing, Circle-to-Land Maneuver, Decision Height, Minimum Descent Altitude, Visibility, Instrument Approach Procedure) (Refer to FAR Part 91)

LANDING ROLL — The distance from the point of touchdown to the point where the aircraft can be brought to a stop or exit the runway.

LANDING SEQUENCE — The order in which aircraft are positioned for landing. (See Approach Sequence)

LAST ASSIGNED ALTITUDE — The last altitude/ flight level assigned by ATC and acknowledged by the pilot. (See Maintain) (Refer to FAR Part 91)

LATERAL SEPARATION — The lateral spacing of aircraft at the same altitude by requiring operation on different routes or in different geographical locations. (See Separation)

LIGHTED AIRPORT — An airport where runway and obstruction lighting is available. (See Airport Lighting) (Refer to AIM)

LIGHT GUN — A handheld directional light signaling device which emits a brilliant narrow beam of white, green, or red light as selected by the tower controller. The color and type of light transmitted can be used to approve or disapprove anticipated pilot actions where radio communication is not available. The light gun is used for controlling traffic operating in the vicinity of the airport and on the airport movement area. (Refer to AIM)

LOCALIZER — The component of an ILS which provides course guidance to the runway. (See Instrument Landing System) (Refer to AIM)

LOCALIZER TYPE DIRECTIONAL AID/LDA — A NAVAID used for nonprecision instrument approaches with utility and accuracy comparable to a localizer but which is not a part of a complete ILS and is not aligned with the runway. (Refer to AIM)

LOCALIZER USABLE DISTANCE — The maximum distance from the localizer transmitter at a specified altitude, as verified by flight inspection, at which reliable course information is continuously received. (Refer to AIM)

LOCAL TRAFFIC — Aircraft operating in the traffic pattern or within sight of the tower, or aircraft known to be departing or arriving from flight in local practice areas, or aircraft executing practice instrument approaches at the airport. (See Traffic Pattern)

LONGITUDINAL SEPARATION — The longitudinal spacing of aircraft at the same altitude by a minimum distance expressed in units of time or miles. (See Separation) (Refer to AIM)

LORAN/LONG RANGE NAVIGATION — An electronic navigational system by which hyperbolic lines of position are determined by measuring the difference in the time of reception of synchronized pulse signals from two fixed transmitters. Loran A operates in the 1750-1950 kHz frequency band. Loran C and D operate in the 100-110 kHz frequency band. (Refer to AIM)

LOST COMMUNICATIONS/TWO-WAY RADIO COMMUNICATIONS FAILURE — Loss of the ability to communicate by radio. Aircraft are sometimes referred to as NORDO (No Radio). Standard pilot procedures are specified in FAR Part 91. Radar controllers issue procedures for pilots to follow in the event of lost communications during a radar approach when weather reports indicate that an aircraft will likely encounter IFR weather conditions during the approach. (Refer to FAR Part 91, AIM)

LOW ALTITUDE AIRWAY STRUCTURE/FEDERAL AIRWAYS — The network of airways serving aircraft operations up to but not including 18,000 feet MSL. (See Airway) (Refer to AIM)

LOW ALTITUDE ALERT, CHECK YOUR ALTITUDE IMMEDIATELY — (See Safety Alert)

LOW ALTITUDE ALERT SYSTEM/LAAS — An automated function of the TPX-42 that alerts the controller when a Mode C transponder-equipped aircraft on an IFR flight plan is below a predetermined minimum safe altitude. If requested by the pilot, LAAS monitoring is also available to VFR Mode C transponder-equipped aircraft.

LOW APPROACH — An approach over an airport or runway following an instrument approach or a VFR approach including the go-around maneuver where the pilot intentionally does not make contact with the runway. (Refer to AIM)

LOW FREQUENCY/LF — The frequency band between 30 and 300 KHz. (Refer to AIM)

MACH NUMBER — The ratio of true airspeed to the speed of sound; e.g., MACH .82, MACH 1.6. (See Airspeed)

MAINTAIN —

    1. Concerning altitude/flight level, the term means to remain at the altitude/flight level specified. The phrase "climb and" or "descend and" normally precedes "maintain" and the altitude assignment; e.g., "descend and maintain 5,000."

    2. Concerning other ATC instructions, the term is used in its literal sense; e.g., maintain VFR.

MAKE SHORT APPROACH — Used by ATC to inform a pilot to alter his traffic pattern so as to make a short final approach. (See Traffic Pattern)

MANDATORY ALTITUDE — An altitude depicted on an instrument Approach Procedure Chart requiring the aircraft to maintain altitude at the depicted value.

MARKER BEACON — An electronic navigation facility transmitting a 75 MHz vertical fan or boneshaped radiation pattern. Marker beacons are identified by their modulation frequency and keying code, and when received by compatible airborne equipment, indicate to the pilot, both aurally and visually, that he is passing over the facility. (See Outer Marker, Middle Marker, Inner Marker) (Refer to AIM)

MAXIMUM AUTHORIZED ALTITUDE/MAA — A published altitude representing the maximum usable altitude or flight level for an airspace structure or route segment. It is the highest altitude on a Federal airway, jet route, area navigation low or high route, or other direct route for which an MEA is designated in FAR Part 95 at which adequate reception of navigation aid signals is assured.

MAYDAY — The international radiotelephony distress signal. When repeated three times, it indicates imminent and grave danger and that immediate assistance is requested. (See Pan-Pan) (Refer to AIM)

METEOROLOGICAL IMPACT STATEMENT/MIS — An unscheduled planning forecast describing conditions expected to begin within 4 to 12 hours which may impact the flow of air traffic in a specific center's (ARTCC) area.

METERING — A method of time-regulating arrival traffic flow into a terminal area so as not to exceed a predetermined terminal acceptance rate.

METERING FIX — A fix along an established route from over which aircraft will be metered prior to entering terminal airspace. Normally, this fix should be established at a distance from the airport which will facilitate a profile descent 10,000 feet above airport elevation (AAE) or above.

MIA — (See Minimum IFR Altitudes)

MICROBURST — A small downburst with outbursts of damaging winds extending 2.5 miles or less. In spite of its small horizontal scale, an intense microburst could induce wind speeds as high as 150 knots (Refer to AIM)

MICROWAVE LANDING SYSTEM/MLS — A precision instrument approach system operating in the microwave spectrum which normally consists of the following components:

    1. **Azimuth Station.**

    2. **Elevation Station.**

    3. **Precision Distance Measuring Equipment.** (See MLS Categories)

Military Training Routes crisscross the United States along defined dimensions, both lateral and vertical. Military aircraft cleared to fly along these routes often exceed 250 knots and fly at low level. The prudent pilot checks with air traffic control before a flight to determine which military routes are active at the time of his flight.

MIDDLE COMPASS LOCATOR — (See Compass Locator)

MIDDLE MARKER/MM — A marker beacon that defines a point along the glide slope of an ILS normally located at or near the point of decision height (ILS Category I). It is keyed to transmit alternate dots and dashes, with the alternate dots and dashes keyed at the rate of 95 dot/dash combinations per minute on a 1300 Hz tone, which is received aurally and visually by compatible airborne equipment. (See Marker Beacon, Instrument Landing System) (Refer to AIM)

MID RVR — (See Visibility)

MILITARY AUTHORITY ASSUMES RESPONSIBILITY FOR SEPARATION — A condition whereby the military services involved assume responsibility for separation between participating military aircraft in the ATC system. It is used only for required IFR operations which are specified in letters of agreement or other appropriate FAA or military documents.

MILITARY OPERATIONS AREA/MOA — (See Special Use Airspace)

MILITARY TRAINING ROUTES/MTR — Airspace of defined vertical and lateral dimensions established for the conduct of military flight training at airspeeds in excess of 250 knots IAS. (See IFR (IR) Military Training Routes and VFR (VR) Military Training Routes)

MINIMUM CROSSING ALTITUDE/MCA — The lowest altitude at certain fixes at which an aircraft must cross when proceeding in the direction of a higher minimum en route IFR altitude (MEA). (See Minimum En Route IFR Altitude)

MINIMUM DESCENT ALTITUDE/MDA — The lowest altitude, expressed in feet above mean sea level, to which descent is authorized on final approach or during circle-to-land maneuvering in execution of a standard instrument approach procedure where no electronic glide slope is provided. (See Nonprecision Approach Procedure)

MINIMUM EN ROUTE IFR ALTITUDE/MEA — The lowest published altitude between radio fixes which assures acceptable navigational signal coverage and meets obstacle clearance requirements between those fixes. The MEA prescribed for a Federal airway or segment thereof, area navigation low or high route, or other direct route applies to the entire width of the airway, segment, or route between the radio fixes defining the airway, segment, or route. (Refer to FAR Part 91 and FAR Part 95; AIM)

MINIMUM FUEL — Indicates that an aircraft's fuel supply has reached a state where, upon reaching the destination, it can accept little or no delay. This is not an emergency situation but merely indicates an emergency situation is possible should any undue delay occur. (Refer to AIM)

MINIMUM HOLDING ALTITUDE/MHA — The lowest altitude prescribed for a holding pattern which assures navigational signal coverage, communications, and meets obstacle clearance requirements.

MINIMUM IFR ALTITUDES/MIA — Minimum altitudes for IFR operations as prescribed in FAR Part 91. These altitudes are published on aeronautical charts and prescribed in FAR Part 95 for airways and routes, and in FAR Part 97 for standard instrument approach procedures. If no applicable minimum altitude is prescribed in FAR Parts 95 or 97, the following minimum IFR altitude applies:

1. In designated mountainous areas, 2,000 feet above the highest obstacle within a horizontal distance of 5 statute miles from the course to be flown; or
2. Other than mountainous areas, 1,000 feet above the highest obstacle within a horizontal distance of 5 statute miles from the course to be flown; or

3. As otherwise authorized by the Administrator or assigned by ATC. (See Minimum En Route IFR Altitude, Minimum Obstruction Clearance Altitude, Minimum Crossing Altitude, Minimum Safe Altitude, Minimum Vectoring Altitude) (Refer to FAR Part 91)

MINIMUM OBSTRUCTION CLEARANCE ALTITUDE/ MOCA — The lowest published altitude in effect between radio fixes on VOR airways, off-airway routes, or route segments which meets obstacle clearance requirements for the entire route segment and which assures acceptable navigational signal coverage only within 25 statute (22 nautical) miles of a VOR. (Refer to FAR Part 91 and FAR Part 95)

MINIMUM RECEPTION ALTITUDE/MRA — The lowest altitude at which an intersection can be determined. (Refer to FAR Part 95)

MINIMUM SAFE ALTITUDE/MSA —

1. The minimum altitude specified in FAR Part 91 for various aircraft operations.

2. Altitudes depicted on approach charts which provide at least 1,000 feet of obstacle clearance for emergency use within a specified distance from the navigation facility upon which a procedure is predicated. These altitudes will be identified as Minimum Sector Altitudes or Emergency Safe Altitudes and are established as follows:

   a. **Minimum Sector Altitudes** — Altitudes depicted on approach charts which provide at least 1,000 feet of obstacle clearance within a 25-mile radius of the navigation facility upon which the procedure is predicated. Sectors depicted on approach charts must be at least 90 degrees in scope. These altitudes are for emergency use only and do not necessarily assure acceptable navigational signal coverage.

   b. **Emergency Safe Altitudes** — Altitudes depicted on approach charts which provide at least 1,000 feet of obstacle clearance in nonmountainous areas and 2,000 feet of obstacle clearance in designated mountainous areas within a 100-mile radius of the navigation facility upon which the procedure is predicated and normally used only in military procedures. These altitudes are identified on published procedures as "Emergency Safe Altitudes."

MINIMUM SAFE ALTITUDE WARNING/MSAW — A function of the ARTS III computer that aids the controller by alerting him when a tracked Mode C- equipped aircraft is below or is predicted by the computer to go below a predetermined minimum safe altitude. (Refer to AIM)

MINIMUMS/MINIMA — Weather condition requirements established for a particular operation or type of operation; e.g., IFR takeoff or landing, alternate airport for IFR flight plans, VFR flight, etc. (See Landing Minimums, IFR Takeoff Minimums, VFR Conditions, IFR Conditions) (Refer to FAR Part 91, AIM)

MINIMUM VECTORING ALTITUDE/MVA — The lowest MSL altitude at which an IFR aircraft will be vectored by a radar controller, except as otherwise authorized for radar approaches, departures, and missed approaches. The altitude meets IFR obstacle clearance criteria. It may be lower than the published MEA along an airway or J-route segment. It may be utilized for radar vectoring only upon the controller's determination that an adequate radar return is being received from the aircraft being controlled. Charts depicting minimum vectoring altitudes are normally available only to the controllers and not to pilots. (Refer to AIM)

MISSED APPROACH —

1. A maneuver conducted by a pilot when an instrument approach cannot be completed to a landing. The route of flight and altitude are shown on instrument approach proce-

dure charts. A pilot executing a missed approach prior to the Missed Approach Point (MAP) must continue along the final approach to the MAP. The pilot may climb immediately to the altitude specified in the missed approach procedure.

2. A term used by the pilot to inform ATC that he is executing the missed approach.

3. At locations where ATC radar service is provided, the pilot should conform to radar vectors when provided by ATC in lieu of the published missed approach procedure. (See Missed Approach Point) (Refer to AIM)

MISSED APPROACH POINT/MAP — A point prescribed in each instrument approach procedure at which a missed approach procedure shall be executed if the required visual reference does not exist. (See Missed Approach, Segments of an Instrument Approach Procedure)

MISSED APPROACH SEGMENT — (See Segments of an Instrument Approach Procedure)

MLS — (See Microwave Landing System)

MLS CATEGORIES —

1. **MLS Category I** — An MLS approach procedure which provides for an approach to a height above touchdown of not less than 200 feet and a runway visual range of not less than 1,800 feet.

2. **MLS Category II** — Undefined until data gathering/analysis completion.

3. **MLS Category III** — Undefined until data gathering/analysis completion

MODE — The letter or number assigned to a specific pulse spacing of radio signals transmitted or received by ground interrogator or airborne transponder components of the Air Traffic Control Radar Beacon System (ATCRBS). Mode A (military Mode 3) and Mode C (altitude reporting) are used in air traffic control. (See Transponder, Interrogator, Radar) (Refer to AIM)

MODE C INTRUDER ALERT — A function of certain air traffic control automated systems designed to alert radar controllers to existing or pending situations between a tracked target (known IFR or VFR aircraft) and an untracked target (unknown IFR or VFR aircraft) that requires immediate attention/action. (See Conflict Alert)

MOVEMENT AREA — The runways, taxiways, and other areas of an airport/heliport which are utilized for taxiing/hover taxiing, air taxiing, takeoff, and landing of aircraft, exclusive of loading ramps and parking areas. At those airports/heliports with a tower, specific approval for entry onto the movement area must be obtained from ATC.

MOVING TARGET INDICATOR/MTI — An electronic device which will permit radar scope presentation only from targets which are in motion. A partial remedy for ground clutter.

MSAW — (See Minimum Safe Altitude Warning)

MULTICOM — A mobile service not open to public correspondence used to provide communications essential to conduct the activities being performed by or directed from private aircraft (See FAR 87.277).

NAS STAGE A — The en route ATC system's radar, computers and computer programs, controller plan view displays (PVDs/Radar Scopes), input/output devices, and the related communications equipment which are integrated to form the heart of the automated IFR air traffic control system. This equipment performs Flight Data Processing (FDP) and Radar Data Processing (RDP). It interfaces with automated terminal systems and is used in the control of en route IFR aircraft. (Refer to AIM)

NATIONAL AIRSPACE SYSTEM/NAS — The common network of U.S. airspace; air navigation facilities, equipment and services, airports or landing areas; aeronautical charts, information and services; rules, regulations and procedures, technical information, and manpower and material. Included are system components shared jointly with the military.

NATIONAL BEACON CODE ALLOCATION PLAN AIRSPACE/NBCAP AIRSPACE — Airspace over United States territory located within the North American continent between Canada and Mexico, including adjacent territorial waters outward to about boundaries of oceanic control areas (CTA)/Flight Information Regions (FIR). (See Flight Information Region)

NATIONAL FLIGHT DATA CENTER/NFDC — A facility in Washington D.C., established by FAA to operate a central aeronautical information service for the collection, validation, and dissemination of aeronautical data in support of the activities of government, industry, and the aviation community. The information is published in the National Flight Data Digest. (See National Flight Data Digest)

NATIONAL FLIGHT DATA DIGEST/NFDD — A daily (except weekends and Federal holidays) publication of flight information appropriate to aeronautical charts, aeronautical publications, Notices to Airmen, or other media serving the purpose of providing operational flight data essential to safe and efficient aircraft operations.

NATIONAL SEARCH AND RESCUE PLAN — An interagency agreement which provides for the effective utilization of all available facilities in all types of search and rescue missions.

NAVAID CLASSES — VOR, VORTAC, and TACAN aids are classed according to their operational use. The three classes of NAVAID's are:

T — Terminal.

L — Low altitude.

H — High altitude.

The normal service range for T, L, and H class aids is found in the AIM. Certain operational requirements make it necessary to use some of these aids at greater service ranges than specified. Extended range is made possible through flight inspection determinations. Some aids also have lesser service range due to location, terrain, frequency protection, etc. Restrictions to service range are listed in Airport/Facility Directory.

NAVIGABLE AIRSPACE — Airspace at and above the minimum flight altitudes prescribed in the FAR's including airspace needed for safe takeoff and landing. (Refer to FAR Part 91)

NAVIGATIONAL AID/NAVAID — Any visual or electronic device airborne or on the surface which provides point-to-point guidance information or position data to aircraft in flight. (See Air Navigation Facility)

NDB — (See Nondirectional Beacon)

NEGATIVE — "No," or "permission not granted," or "that is not correct."

NEGATIVE CONTACT — Used by pilots to inform ATC that:

    1. Previously issued traffic is not in sight. It may be followed by the pilot's request for the controller to provide assistance in avoiding the traffic.

    2. They were unable to contact ATC on a particular frequency.

NIGHT — The time between the end of evening civil twilight and the beginning of morning civil twilight, as published in the American Air Almanac, converted to local time.

NO GYRO APPROACH/VECTOR — A radar approach/vector provided in case of a malfunctioning gyro-compass or directional gyro. Instead of providing the pilot with headings to be flown, the controller observes the radar track and issues control instructions "turn right/left" or "stop turn" as appropriate. (Refer to AIM)

NONAPPROACH CONTROL TOWER — Authorizes aircraft to land or takeoff at the airport controlled by the tower or to transit the airport traffic area. The primary function of a nonapproach control tower is the sequencing of aircraft in the traffic pattern and on the landing area. Nonapproach control towers also separate aircraft operating under instrument flight rules clearances from approach controls and centers. They provide ground control services to aircraft, vehicles, personnel, and equipment on the airport movement area.

NONCOMPOSITE SEPARATION — Separation in accordance with minima other than the composite separation minimum specified for the area concerned.

NONDIRECTIONAL BEACON/RADIO BEACON/ NDB — An L/MF or UHF radio beacon transmitting nondirectional signals whereby the pilot of an aircraft equipped with direction finding equipment can determine his bearing to or from the radio beacon and "home" on or track to or from the station. When the radio beacon is installed in conjunction with the Instrument Landing System marker, it is normally called a Compass Locator. (See Compass Locator, Automatic Direction Finder)

NONPRECISION APPROACH PROCEDURE/NONPRECISION APPROACH — A standard instrument approach procedure in which no electronic glide slope is provided; e.g., VOR, TACAN, NDB, LOC, ASR, LDA, or SDF approaches.

NONRADAR — Precedes other terms and generally means without the use of radar, such as:

    1. **Nonradar Approach** — Used to describe instrument approaches for which course guidance on final approach is not provided by ground-based precision or surveillance radar. Radar vectors to the final approach course may or may not be provided by ATC. Examples of nonradar approaches are VOR, NDB, TACAN, and ILS/MLS approaches. (See Final Approach-IFR, Final Approach Course, Radar Approach, Instrument Approach Procedure)

    2. **Nonradar Approach Control** — An ATC facility providing approach control service without the use of radar. (See Approach Control, Approach Control Service)

    3. **Nonradar Arrival** — An aircraft arriving at an airport without radar service or at an airport served by a radar facility and radar contact has not been established or has been terminated due to a lack of radar service to the airport. (See Radar Arrival, Radar Service)

    4. **Nonradar Route** — A flight path or route over which the pilot is performing his own navigation. The pilot may be receiving radar separation, radar monitoring, or other ATC services while on a nonradar route. (See Radar Route)

    5. **Nonradar Separation** — The spacing of aircraft in accordance with established minima without the use of radar; e.g., vertical, lateral, or longitudinal separation. (See Radar Separation)

NORDO — (See Lost Communications)

NORTH AMERICAN ROUTE — A numerically coded route preplanned over existing airway and route systems to and from specific coastal fixes serving the North Atlantic. North American Routes consist of the following:

    1. **Common Route/Portion** — That segment of a North American Route between the inland navigation facility and the coastal fix.

    2. **Non-Common Route/Portion** — That segment of a North American Route between the inland navigation facility and a designated North American terminal.

    3. **Inland Navigation Facility** — A navigation aid on a North American Route at which the common route and/or the non-common route begins or ends.

    4. **Coastal Fix** — A navigation aid or intersection where an aircraft transitions between the domestic route structure and the oceanic route structure.

NOTICES TO AIRMEN PUBLICATION — A publication designed primarily as a pilot's operational manual containing current NOTAM information considered essential to the safety of flight as well as supplemental data to other aeronautical publications. (See Notice to Airmen/NOTAM)

NOTICE TO AIRMEN/NOTAM — A notice containing information (not known sufficiently in advance to publicize by other means) concerning the establishment, condition, or change in any component (facility, service, or procedure of, or hazard in the National Airspace System) the timely knowledge of which is essential to personnel concerned with flight operations.

    1. **NOTAM(D)** — A NOTAM given (in addition to local dissemination) distant dissemination beyond the area of responsibility of the Flight Service Station. These NOTAM's will be stored and available until canceled.

2. NOTAM(L) — A NOTAM given local dissemination by voice and other means, such as telautograph and telephone, to satisfy local user requirements.

3. FDC NOTAM — A NOTAM regulatory in nature, transmitted by USNOF and given system wide dissemination.

Class I Distribution. Distribution by means of telecommunication.

Class II Distribution. Distribution by means other than telecommunications.

NUMEROUS TARGETS VICINITY (LOCATION) — A traffic advisory issued by ATC to advise pilots that targets on the radar scope are too numerous to issue individually. (See Traffic Advisories)

OBSTACLE — An existing object, object of natural growth, or terrain at a fixed geographical location or which may be expected at a fixed location within a prescribed area with reference to which vertical clearance is or must be provided during flight operation.

OBSTRUCTION — Any object/obstacle exceeding the obstruction standards specified by FAR Part 77, Subpart C.

OBSTRUCTION LIGHT — A light or one of a group of lights, usually red or white, frequently mounted on a surface structure or natural terrain to warn pilots of the presence of an obstruction.

OFF-ROUTE VECTOR — A vector by ATC which takes an aircraft off a previously assigned route. Altitudes assigned by ATC during such vectors provide required obstacle clearance.

OFFSET PARALLEL RUNWAYS — Staggered runways having centerlines which are parallel.

ON COURSE —

1. Used to indicate that an aircraft is established on the route centerline.

2. Used by ATC to advise a pilot making a radar approach that his aircraft is lined up on the final approach course. (See On-Course Indication)

ON-COURSE INDICATION — An indication on an instrument, which provides the pilot a visual means of determining that the aircraft is located on the centerline of a given navigational track, or an indication on a radar scope that an aircraft is on a given track.

OPTION APPROACH — An approach requested and conducted by a pilot which will result in either a touch-and-go, missed approach, low approach, stop-and-go, or full stop landing. (See Cleared for the Option) (Refer to AIM)

ORGANIZED TRACK SYSTEM — A moveable system of oceanic tracks that traverses the North Atlantic between Europe and North America the physical position of which is determined twice daily taking the best advantage of the winds aloft.

OUT — The conversation is ended and no response is expected.

OUTER AREA (associated with ARSA) — Nonregulatory airspace surrounding designated ARSA airports wherein ATC provides radar vectoring and sequencing on a full-time basis for all IFR and participating VFR aircraft. The service provided in the outer area is called ARSA service which includes: IFR/IFR — standard IFR separation; IFR/VFR — traffic advisories and conflict resolution; and VFR/VFR — traffic advisories and, as appropriate, safety alerts. The normal radius will be 20 nautical miles with some variations based on site-specific requirements. The outer area extends outward from the primary ARSA airport and extends from the lower limits of radar/radio coverage up to the ceiling of the approach control's delegated airspace excluding the ARSA and other airspace as appropriate. (See Controlled Airspace — Airport Radar Service Area/ARSA, Conflict Resolution)

OUTER COMPASS LOCATOR — (See Compass Locator)

OUTER FIX — A general term used within ATC to describe fixes in the terminal area, other than the final approach fix. Aircraft are normally cleared to these fixes by an Air Route Traffic Control Center or an Approach Control Facility. Aircraft are normally cleared from these fixes to the final approach fix or final approach course.

OUTER MARKER/OM — A marker beacon at or near the glide slope intercept altitude of an ILS approach. It is keyed to transmit two dashes per second on a 400 Hz tone, which is received aurally and visually by compatible airborne equipment. The OM is normally located four to seven miles from the runway threshold on the extended centerline of the runway. (See Marker Beacon, Instrument Landing System) (Refer to AIM)

OVER — My transmission is ended; I expect a response.

OVERHEAD APPROACH/360 OVERHEAD — A series of predetermined maneuvers prescribed for VFR arrival of military aircraft (often in formation) for entry into the VFR traffic pattern and to proceed to a landing. The pattern usually specifies the following:

1. The radio contact required of the pilot.

2. The speed to be maintained.

3. An initial approach 3 to 5 miles in length.

4. An elliptical pattern consisting of two 180 degree turns.

5. A break point at which the first 180 degree turn is started.

6. The direction of turns.

7. Altitude (at least 500 feet above the conventional pattern).

8. A "Roll-out" on final approach not less than 1/4 mile from the landing threshold and not less than 300 feet above the ground.

PAN-PAN — The international radio-telephony urgency signal. When repeated three times, indicates uncertainty or alert followed by the nature of the urgency. (See MAYDAY) (Refer to AIM)

PARALLEL ILS/MLS APPROACHES — Approaches to parallel runways by IFR aircraft which, when established inbound toward the airport on the adjacent final approach courses, are radar-separated by at least 2 miles. (See Final Approach Course, Simultaneous ILS/MLS Approaches).

PARALLEL OFFSET ROUTE — A parallel track to the left or right of the designated or established airway/route. Normally associated with Area Navigation (RNAV) operations. (See Area Navigation)

PARALLEL RUNWAYS — Two or more runways at the same airport whose centerlines are parallel. In addition to runway number, parallel runways are designated as L (left) and R (right) or, if three parallel runways exist, L (left), C (center), and R (right).

PERMANENT ECHO — Radar signals reflected from fixed objects on the earth's surface; e.g., buildings, towers, terrain. Permanent echoes are distinguished from "ground clutter" by being definable locations rather than large areas. Under certain conditions they may be used to check radar alignment.

PHOTO RECONNAISSANCE (PR) — Military activity that requires locating individual photo targets and navigating to the targets at a preplanned angle and altitude. The activity normally requires a lateral route width of 16NM and altitude range of 1,500 feet to 10,000 feet AGL.

PILOT BRIEFING/PRE-FLIGHT PILOT BRIEFING — A service provided by the FSS to assist pilots in flight planning. Briefing items may include weather information, NOTAMS, military activities, flow control information, and other items as requested. (Refer to AIM)

PILOT IN COMMAND — The pilot responsible for the operation and safety of an aircraft during flight time. (Refer to FAR Part 91)

PILOTS AUTOMATIC TELEPHONE WEATHER ANSWERING SERVICE/PATWAS — A continuous telephone recording containing current and forecast weather information for pilots. (See Flight Service Station) (Refer to AIM)

PILOT'S DISCRETION — When used in conjunction with altitude assignments, means that ATC has offered the pilot the option of starting climb or descent whenever he wishes and conducting the climb or descent at any rate he wishes. He may temporarily level off at any intermediate altitude. However, once he has vacated an altitude, he may not return to that altitude.

PILOT WEATHER REPORT/PIREP — A report of meteorological phenomena encountered by aircraft in flight. (Refer to AIM)

POSITION REPORT/PROGRESS REPORT — A report over a known location as transmitted by an aircraft to ATC. (Refer to AIM)

POSITION SYMBOL — A computer-generated indication shown on a radar display to indicate the mode of tracking.

POSITIVE CONTROL — The separation of all air traffic within designated airspace by air traffic control. (See Positive Control Area)

POSITIVE CONTROL AREA/PCA — (See Controlled Airspace)

PRACTICE INSTRUMENT APPROACH — An instrument approach procedure conducted by a VFR or an IFR aircraft for the purpose of pilot training or proficiency demonstrations.

PRECIPITATION — Any or all forms of water particles (rain, sleet, hail, or snow) that fall from the atmosphere and reach the surface.

PRECISION APPROACH PROCEDURE/PRECISION APPROACH — A standard instrument approach procedure in which an electronic glideslope/glidepath is provided; e.g., ILS/MLS and PAR. (See Instrument Landing System, Microwave Landing System, Precision Approach Radar)

PRECISION APPROACH RADAR/PAR — Radar equipment in some ATC facilities operated by the FAA and/or the military services at joint-use civil/military locations and separate military installations to detect and display azimuth, elevation, and range of aircraft on the final approach course to a runway. This equipment may be used to monitor certain nonradar approaches, but is primarily used to conduct a precision instrument approach (PAR) wherein the controller issues guidance instructions to the pilot based on the aircraft's position in relation to the final approach course (azimuth), the glidepath (elevation), and the distance (range) from the touchdown point on the runway as displayed on the radar scope. (See Glidepath, PAR) (Refer to AIM)

The abbreviation "PAR" is also used to denote preferential arrival routes in ARTCC computers. (See Preferential Routes)

Note. — Precision approach radars are designed to enable pilots of aircraft to be given guidance by radiocommunication during the final stages of the approach to land.

PREFERENTIAL ROUTES — Preferential routes (PDR's, PAR's, and PDAR's) are adapted in ARTCC computers to accomplish inter/intrafacility controller coordination and to assure that flight data is posted at the proper control positions. Locations having a need for these specific inbound and outbound routes normally publish such routes in local facility bulletins, and their use by pilots minimizes flight plan route amendments. When the workload or traffic situation permits, controllers normally provide radar vectors or assign requested routes to minimize circuitous routing. Preferential routes are usually confined to one ARTCC's area and are referred to by the following names or acronyms:

1. **Preferential Departure Route/PDR** — A specific departure route from an airport or terminal area to an en route point where there is no further need for flow control. It may be included in a Standard Instrument Departure (SID) or a Preferred IFR Route.

2. **Preferential Arrival Route/PAR** — A specific arrival route from an appropriate en route point to an airport or terminal area. It may be included in a Standard Terminal Arrival (STAR) or a Preferred IFR Route. The abbreviation "PAR" is used primarily within the ARTCC and should not be confused with the abbreviation for Precision Approach Radar.

3. **Preferential Departure and Arrival Route/PDAR** — A route between two terminals which are within or immediately adjacent to one ARTCC's area. PDAR's are not synonomous with Preferred IFR Routes but may be listed as such as they do accomplish essentially the same purpose. (See Preferred IFR Routes, NAS Stage A)

PREFERRED IFR ROUTES — Routes established between busier airports to increase system efficiency and capacity. They normally extend through one or more ARTCC areas and are designed to achieve balanced traffic flows among high density terminals. IFR clearances are issued on the basis of these routes except when severe weather avoidance procedures or other factors dictate otherwise. Preferred IFR Routes are listed in the Airport/Facility Directory. If a flight is planned to or from an area having such routes but the departure or arrival point is not listed in the Airport/Facility Directory, pilots may use that part of a Preferred IFR Route which is appropriate for the departure or arrival point that is listed. Preferred IFR Routes are correlated with SID's and STAR's and may be defined by airways, jet routes, direct routes between NAVAID's, Waypoints, NAVAID radials/DME, or any combinations thereof. (See Standard Instrument Departure, Standard Terminal Arrival, Preferential Routes, Center's Area) (Refer to Airport/Facility Directory and Notices to Airmen Publication)

PREVAILING VISIBILITY — (See Visibility)

PROCEDURE TURN INBOUND — That point of a procedure turn maneuver where course reversal has been completed and an aircraft is established inbound on the intermediate approach segment or final approach course. A report of "procedure turn inbound" is normally used by ATC as a position report for separation purposes. (See Final Approach Course, Procedure Turn, Segments of an Instrument Approach Procedure)

PROCEDURE TURN/PT — The maneuver prescribed when it is necessary to reverse direction to establish an aircraft on the intermediate approach segment or final approach course. The outbound course, direction of turn, distance within which the turn must be completed, and minimum altitude are specified in the procedure. However, unless otherwise restricted, the point at which the turn may be commenced and the type and rate of turn are left to the discretion of the pilot.

Note 1. — Procedure turns are designated "left" or "right" according to the direction of the initial turn.

Note 2. — Procedure turns may be designated as being made either in level flight or while descending, according to the circumstances of each individual approach procedure.

PROFILE DESCENT — An uninterrupted descent (except where level flight is required for speed adjustment; e.g., 250 knots at 10,000 feet MSL) from cruising altitude/level to interception of a glide slope or to a minimum altitude specified for the initial or intermediate approach segment of a nonprecision instrument approach. The profile descent normally terminates at the approach gate or where the glide slope or other appropriate minimum altitude is intercepted.

PROGRAMMABLE INDICATOR DATA PROCESSOR/ PIDP — The PIDP is a modification to the AN/TPX-42 interrogator system currently installed in fixed RAPCON's. The PIDP detects, tracks, and predicts secondary radar aircraft targets. These are displayed by means of computer-generated symbols and alphanumeric characters depicting flight identification, aircraft altitude, ground speed, and flight plan data. Although primary radar targets are not tracked, they are displayed coincident with the secondary radar targets as well as with the other symbols and alphanumerics. The system has the capability of interfacing with ARTCC's.

PROGRESSIVE TAXI — Precise taxi instructions given to a pilot unfamiliar with the airport or issued in stages as the aircraft proceeds along the taxi route.

PROHIBITED AREA — (See Special Use Airspace).

PROPOSED BOUNDARY CROSSING TIME/PBCT — Each center has a PBCT parameter for each internal airport. Proposed internal flight plans are transmitted to the adjacent center if the flight time along the proposed route from the departure airport to the center boundary is less than or equal to the value of PBCT or if airport adaptation specifies transmission regardless of PBCT.

PUBLISHED ROUTE — A route for which an IFR altitude has been established and published; e.g., Federal Airways, Jet Routes, Area Navigation Routes, Specified Direct Routes.

QUADRANT — A quarter part of a circle, centered on a NAVAID, oriented clockwise from magnetic north as follows: NE quadrant 000-089, SE quadrant 090-179, SW quadrant 180-269, NW quadrant 270-359.

QUICK LOOK — A feature of NAS Stage A and ARTS which provides the controller the capability to display full data blocks of tracked aircraft from other control positions.

QUOTA FLOW CONTROL/QFLOW — A flow control procedure by which the Central Flow Control Function (CFCF) restricts traffic to the ARTC Center area having an impacted airport, thereby avoiding sector/area saturation. (See Air Traffic Control Systems Command Center) (Refer to Airport/Facility Directory)

RADAR/RADIO DETECTION AND RANGING — A device which, by measuring the time interval between transmission and reception of radio pulses and correlating the angular orientation of the radiated antenna beam or beams in azimuth and/or elevation, provides information on range, azimuth, and/or elevation of objects in the path of the transmitted pulses.

1. **Primary Radar** — A radar system in which a minute portion of a radio pulse transmitted from a site is reflected by an object and then received back at that site for processing and display at an air traffic control facility.

2. **Secondary Radar/Radar Beacon/ATCRBS** — A radar system in which the object to be detected is fitted with cooperative equipment in the form of a radio receiver/transmitter (transponder). Radar pulses transmitted from the searching transmitter/receiver (interrogator) site are received in the cooperative equipment and used to trigger a distinctive mission from the transponder. This reply transmission, rather than a reflected signal, is then received back at the transmitter/receiver site for processing and display at an air traffic control facility. (See Transponder, Interrogator) (Refer to AIM)

RADAR ADVISORY — The provision of advice and information based on radar observations. (See Advisory Service)

RADAR APPROACH — An instrument approach procedure which utilizes Precision Approach Radar (PAR) or Airport Surveillance Radar (ASR). (See PAR Approach, Surveillance Approach, Airport Surveillance Radar, Precision Approach Radar, Instrument Approach Procedure) (Refer to AIM)

RADAR APPROACH CONTROL FACILITY — A terminal ATC facility that uses radar and nonradar capabilities to provide approach control services to aircraft arriving, departing, or transiting airspace controlled by the facility (see Approach Control Service). Provides radar ATC services to aircraft operating in the vicinity of one or more civil and/or military airports in a terminal area. The facility may provide services of a ground controlled approach (GCA); i.e., ASR and PAR approaches. A radar approach control facility may be operated by FAA, USAF, US Army, USN, USMC, or jointly by FAA and a military service. Specific facility nomenclatures are used for administrative purposes only and are related to the physical location of the facility and the operating service generally as follows:

Army Radar Approach Control/ARAC (Army).

Radar Air Traffic Control Facility/RATCF (Navy/FAA).

Radar Approach Control/RAPCON (Air Force/FAA).

Terminal Radar Approach Control/TRACON (FAA).

Tower/Airport Traffic Control Tower/ATCT (FAA). (Only those towers delegated approach control authority.)

RADAR ARRIVAL — An aircraft arriving at an airport served by a radar facility and in radar contact with the facility. (See Nonradar Arrival)

RADAR BEACON — (See Radar)

RADAR CONTACT —

1. Used by ATC to inform an aircraft that it is identified on the radar display and radar flight following will be provided until radar identification is terminated. Radar service may also be provided within the limits of necessity and capability. When a pilot is informed of "radar contact," he automatically discontinues reporting over compulsory reporting points. (See Radar Flight Following, Radar Contact Lost, Radar Service, Radar Service Terminated). (Refer to AIM)

2. The term used to inform the controller that the aircraft is identified and approval is granted for the aircraft to enter the receiving controllers airspace.

RADAR CONTACT LOST — Used by ATC to inform a pilot that radar identification of his aircraft has been lost. The loss may be attributed to several things including the aircraft's merging with weather or ground clutter, the aircraft's flying below radar line of sight, the aircraft's entering an area of poor radar return, or a failure of the aircraft transponder or the ground radar equipment. (See Clutter, Radar Contact)

RADAR ENVIRONMENT — An area in which radar service may be provided. (See Radar Contact, Radar Service, Additional Services, Traffic Advisories)

RADAR FLIGHT FOLLOWING — The observation of the progress of radar identified aircraft, whose primary navigation is being provided by the pilot, wherein the controller retains and correlates the aircraft identity with the appropriate target or target symbol displayed on the radar scope. (See Radar Contact, Radar Service) (Refer to AIM)

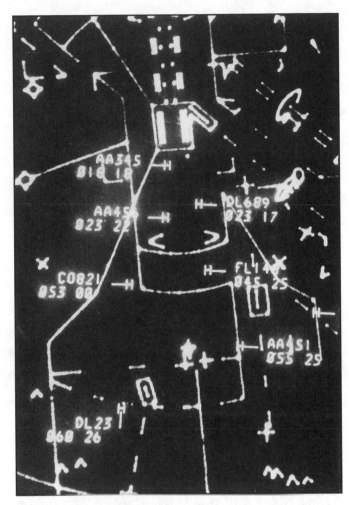

When a controller says "radar contact," he is telling the pilot that his aircraft is identified on the radar display and radar flight following will be provided until terminated. In this photo, aircraft are in radar contact with Dallas-Fort Worth air traffic controllers. Their data blocks are marching southward away from the parallel runways at the busy DFW airport. (FAA photo by S. Michael McKean)

RADAR IDENTIFICATION — The process of ascertaining that an observed radar target is the radar return from a particular aircraft. (See Radar Contact, Radar Service)

RADAR IDENTIFIED AIRCRAFT — An aircraft, the position of which has been correlated with an observed target or symbol on the radar display. (See Radar Contact, Radar Contact Lost)

RADAR MONITORING — (See Radar Service)

RADAR NAVIGATIONAL GUIDANCE — (See Radar Service)

RADAR POINT OUT/POINT OUT — Used between controllers to indicate radar handoff action where the initiating controller plans to retain communications with an aircraft penetrating the other controller's airspace and additional coordination is required.

RADAR REQUIRED — A term displayed on charts and approach plates and included in FDC Notams to alert pilots that segments of either an instrument approach procedure or a route are not navigable because of either the absence or unusability of a NAVAID. The pilot can expect to be provided radar navigational guidance while transiting segments labeled with this term. (See Radar Route and Radar Service)

RADAR ROUTE — A flight path or route over which an aircraft is vectored. Navigational guidance and altitude assignments are provided by ATC. (See Flight Path, Route)

RADAR SEPARATION —(See Radar Service)

RADAR SERVICE — A term which encompasses one or more of the following services based on the use of radar which can be provided by a controller to a pilot of a radar identified aircraft.

    1. Radar Monitoring — The radar flight-following of aircraft, whose primary navigation is being performed by the pilot, to observe and note deviations from its authorized flight path, airway, or route. When being applied specifically to radar monitoring of instrument approaches; i.e., with precision approach radar (PAR) or radar monitoring of simultaneous ILS/MLS approaches, it includes advice and instructions whenever an aircraft nears or exceeds the prescribed PAR safety limit or simultaneous ILS/MLS no transgression zone. (See Additional Services, Traffic Advisories)

    2. Radar Navigational Guidance — Vectoring aircraft to provide course guidance.

    3. Radar Separation — Radar spacing of aircraft in accordance with established minima.

RADAR SERVICE TERMINATED — Used by ATC to inform a pilot that he will no longer be provided any of the services that could be received while in radar contact. Radar service is automatically terminated, and the pilot is not advised in the following cases:

    1. An aircraft cancels its IFR flight plan, except within a TCA, TRSA, ARSA, or where Stage II service is provided.

    2. An aircraft conducting an instrument, visual, or contact approach has landed or has been instructed to change to advisory frequency.

    3. An arriving VFR aircraft, receiving radar service to a tower-controlled airport within a TCA, TRSA, ARSA, or where Stage II service is provided, has landed; or to all other airports, is instructed to change to tower or advisory frequency.

    4. An aircraft completes a radar approach.

RADAR SURVEILLANCE — The radar observation of a given geographical area for the purpose of performing some radar function.

RADAR TRAFFIC ADVISORIES — Advisories issued to alert pilots to known or observed radar traffic which may affect the intended route of flight of their aircraft. (See Traffic Advisories)

RADAR TRAFFIC INFORMATION SERVICE — (See Traffic Advisories)

RADAR WEATHER ECHO INTENSITY LEVELS — Existing radar systems cannot detect turbulence. However, there is a direct correlation between the degree of turbulence and other weather features associated with thunderstorms and the radar weather echo intensity. The National Weather Service has categorized radar weather echo intensity for precipitation into six levels. These levels are sometimes expressed during communications as "VIP LEVEL" 1 through 6 (derived from the component of the radar that produces the information — Video Integrator and Processor). The following list gives the "VIP LEVELS" in relation to the precipitation intensity within a thunderstorm:

    Level 1. WEAK

    Level 2. MODERATE

    Level 3. STRONG

    Level 4. VERY STRONG

    Level 5. INTENSE

    Level 6. EXTREME

RADIAL — A magnetic bearing extending from a VOR/VOR-TAC/TACAN navigation facility.

RADIO —

    1. A device used for communication.

    2. Used to refer to a flight service station; e.g., "Seattle Radio" is used to call Seattle FSS.

RADIO ALTIMETER/RADAR ALTIMETER — Aircraft equipment which makes use of the reflection of radio waves from the ground to determine the height of the aircraft above the surface.

RADIO BEACON — (See Nondirectional Beacon)

RADIO MAGNETIC INDICATOR/RMI — An aircraft navigational instrument coupled with a gyro compass or similar compass that indicates the direction of a selected NAVAID and indicates bearing with respect to the heading of the aircraft.

RAMP — (See Apron)

READ BACK — Repeat my message back to me.

RECEIVING CONTROLLER/FACILITY — A controller/facility receiving control of an aircraft from another controller/facility.

REDUCE SPEED TO (SPEED) — (See Speed Adjustment)

RELEASE TIME — A departure time restriction issued to a pilot by ATC (either directly or through an authorized relay) when necessary to separate a departing aircraft from other traffic.

REMOTE COMMUNICATIONS AIR/GROUND FACILITY/RCAG — An unmanned VHF/UHF transmitter/receiver facility which is used to expand ARTCC air/ground communications coverage and to facilitate direct contact between pilots and controllers. RCAG facilities are sometimes not equipped with emergency frequencies 121.5 MHz and 243.0 MHz. (Refer to AIM)

REMOTE COMMUNICATIONS OUTLET/RCO AND REMOTE TRANSMITTER/RECEIVER/RTR — An unmanned communications facility remotely controlled by air traffic personnel. RCOs serve FSSs. RTRs serve terminal ATC facilities. An RCO or RTR may be UHF or VHF and will extend the communication range of the air traffic facility. There are several classes of RCOs and RTRs. The class is determined by the number of transmitters or receivers. Classes A through G are used primarily for air/ground purposes. RCO and RTR class O facilities are nonprotected outlets subject to undetected and prolonged outages. RCO (Os) and RTR (Os) were established for the express purpose of providing ground-to-ground communications between air traffic control specialists and pilots located at a satellite airport for delivering en route clearances, issuing departure authorizations, and acknowledging instrument flight rules cancellations or departure/landing times. As a secondary function, they may be used for advisory purposes whenever the aircraft is below the coverage of the primary air/ground frequency.

REMOTE TRANSMITTER/RECEIVER/RTR — (See Remote Communications Outlet)

REPORT — Used to instruct pilots to advise ATC of specified information; e.g., "Report passing Hamilton VOR."

REPORTING POINT — A geographical location in relation to which the position of an aircraft is reported. (See Compulsory Reporting Point) (Refer to AIM)

REQUEST FULL ROUTE CLEARANCE/FRC — Used by pilots to request that the entire route of flight be read verbatim in an ATC clearance. Such request should be made to preclude receiving an ATC clearance based on the original filed flight plan when a filed IFR flight plan has been revised by the pilot, company, or operations prior to departure.

RESCUE COORDINATION CENTER/RCC — A search and rescue (SAR) facility equipped and manned to coordinate and control SAR operations in an area designated by the SAR plan. The U.S. Coast Guard and the U.S. Air Force have responsibility for the operation of RCC's.

RESTRICTED AREA — (See Special Use Airspace).

RESUME OWN NAVIGATION — Used by ATC to advise a pilot to resume his own navigational responsibility. It is issued after completion of a radar vector or when radar contact is lost while the aircraft is being radar vectored. (See Radar Contact Lost, Radar Service Terminated)

RNAV — (See Area Navigation)

RNAV APPROACH — An instrument approach procedure which relies on aircraft area navigation equipment for navigational guidance. (See Instrument Approach Procedure, Area Navigation)

ROAD RECONNAISSANCE (RC) — Military activity requiring navigation along roads, railroads, and rivers. Reconnaissance route/route segments are seldom along a straight line and normally require a lateral route width of 10NM to 30NM and an altitude range of 500 feet to 10,000 feet AGL.

ROGER — I have received all of your last transmission. It should not be used to answer a question requiring a yes or a no answer. (See Affirmative, Negative)

ROLLOUT RVR — (See Visibility)

ROUTE — A defined path, consisting of one or more courses in a horizontal plane, which aircraft traverse over the surface of the earth. (See Airway, Jet Route, Published Route, Unpublished Route)

ROUTE SEGMENT — As used in Air Traffic Control, a part of a route that can be defined by two navigational fixes, two NAVAID's, or a fix and a NAVAID. (See Fix, Route)

RUNWAY — A defined rectangular area on a land airport prepared for the landing and takeoff run of aircraft along its length. Runways are normally numbered in relation to their magnetic direction rounded off to the nearest 10 degrees; e.g., Runway 01, Runway 25. (See Parallel Runways)

RUNWAY CENTERLINE LIGHTING — (See Airport Lighting)

RUNWAY CONDITION READING/RCR — Numerical decelerometer readings relayed by air traffic controllers at USAF and certain civil bases for use by the pilot in determining runway braking action. These readings are routinely relayed only to USAF and Air National Guard Aircraft. (See Braking Action)

RUNWAY END IDENTIFIER LIGHTS — (See Airport Lighting)

RUNWAY GRADIENT — The average slope, measured in percent, between two ends or points on a runway. Runway gradient is depicted on Government aerodrome sketches when total runway gradient exceeds 0.3%.

RUNWAY HEADING — The magnetic direction indicated by the runway number. When cleared to "fly/maintain runway heading," pilots are expected to fly the heading indicated by the runway number, not the actual magnetic heading of the runway; e.g., Runway 04, actual magnetic heading 045 degrees, fly heading 040 degrees. Do not apply drift correction.

RUNWAY IN USE/ACTIVE RUNWAY/DUTY RUNWAY — Any runway or runways currently being used for takeoff or landing. When multiple runways are used, they are all considered active runways.

RUNWAY LIGHTS — (See Airport Lighting)

RUNWAY MARKINGS — (See Airport Marking Aids.)

RUNWAY PROFILE DESCENT — An instrument flight rules (IFR) air traffic control arrival procedure to a runway published for pilot use in graphic and/or textual form and may be associated with a STAR. Runway Profile Descents provide routing and may depict crossing altitudes, speed restrictions, and headings to be flown from the en route structure to the point where the pilot will receive clearance for and execute an instrument approach procedure. A Runway Profile Descent may apply to more than one runway if so stated on the chart. (Refer to AIM)

RUNWAY USE PROGRAM — A noise abatement runway selection plan designed to enhance noise abatement efforts with regard to airport communities for arriving and departing aircraft. These plans are developed into runway use programs and apply to all turbojet aircraft 12,500 pounds or heavier; turbojet aircraft less than 12,500 pounds are included only if the airport proprietor determines that the aircraft creates a noise problem. Runway use programs are coordinated with FAA offices, and safety criteria used in these programs are developed by the Office of Flight Operations. Runway use programs are administered by the Air Traffic Service as "Formal" or "Informal" programs.

1. **Formal Runway Use Program** — An approved noise abatement program which is defined and acknowledged in a Letter of Understanding between Flight Operations, Air Traffic Service, the airport proprietor, and the users. Once established, participation in the program is mandatory for aircraft operators and pilots as provided for in FAR 91.87.

2. **Informal Runway Use Program** — An approved noise abatement program which does not require a Letter of Understanding, and participation in the program is voluntary for aircraft operators/pilots.

RUNWAY VISIBILITY VALUE — (See Visibility)

RUNWAY VISUAL RANGE — (See Visibility)

SAFETY ALERT — A safety alert issued by ATC to aircraft under their control if ATC is aware the aircraft is at an altitude which, in the controller's judgment, places the aircraft in unsafe proximity to terrain, obstructions, or other aircraft. The controller may discontinue the issuance of further alerts if the pilot advises he is taking action to correct the situation or has the other aircraft in sight.

1. **Terrain/Obstruction Alert** — A safety alert issued by ATC to aircraft under their control if ATC is aware the aircraft is at an altitude which, in the controller's judgment, places the aircraft in unsafe proximity to terrain/obstructions; e.g., "Low Altitude Alert, check your altitude immediately."

2. **Aircraft Conflict Alert** — A safety alert issued by ATC to aircraft under their control if ATC is aware of an aircraft that is not under their control at an altitude which, in the controller's judgment, places both aircraft in unsafe proximity to each other. With the alert, ATC will offer the pilot an alternate course of action when feasible; e.g., "Traffic Alert, advise you turn right heading zero niner zero or climb to eight thousand immediately."

The issuance of a safety alert is contingent upon the capability of the controller to have an awareness of an unsafe condition. The course of action provided will be predicated on other traffic under ATC control. Once the alert is issued, it is solely the pilot's prerogative to determine what course of action, if any, he will take.

SAIL BACK — A maneuver during high wind conditions (usually with power off) where float plane movement is controlled by water rudders/opening and closing cabin doors.

SAY AGAIN — Used to request a repeat of the last transmission. Usually specifies transmission or portion thereof not understood or received; e.g., "Say again all after ABRAM VOR."

SAY ALTITUDE — Used by ATC to ascertain an aircraft's specific altitude/flight level. When the aircraft is climbing or descending, the pilot should state the indicated altitude rounded to the nearest 100 feet.

SAY HEADING — Used by ATC to request an aircraft heading. The pilot should say the actual heading of the aircraft.

SEA LANE — A designated portion of water outlined by visual surface markers for and intended to be used by aircraft designed to operate on water.

SEARCH AND RESCUE FACILITY — A facility responsible for maintaining and operating a search and rescue (SAR) service to render aid to persons and property in distress. It is any SAR unit, station, NET, or other operational activity which can be usefully employed during an SAR Mission; e.g., a Civil Air Patrol Wing, or a Coast Guard Station. (See Search and Rescue)

SEARCH AND RESCUE/SAR — A service which seeks missing aircraft and assists those found to be in need of assistance. It is a cooperative effort using the facilities and services of available Federal, state and local agencies. The U.S. Coast Guard is responsible for coordination of search and rescue for the Maritime Region, and the U.S. Air Force is responsible for search and rescue for the Inland Region. Information pertinent to search and rescue should be passed through any air traffic facility or be transmitted directly to the Rescue Coordination Center by telephone. (See Flight Service Station, Rescue Coordination Center) (Refer to AIM)

SEE AND AVOID — A visual procedure wherein pilots of aircraft flying in visual meteorological conditions (VMC), regardless of type of flight plan, are charged with the responsibility to observe the presence of other aircraft and to maneuver their aircraft as required to avoid the other aircraft. Right-of-way rules are contained in FAR Part 91. (See Instrument Flight Rules, Visual Flight Rules, Visual Meteorological Conditions, Instrument Meteorological Conditions)

SEGMENTED CIRCLE — A system of visual indicators designed to provide traffic pattern information at airports without operating control towers. (Refer to AIM)

SEGMENTS OF AN INSTRUMENT APPROACH PROCEDURE — An instrument approach procedure may have as many as four separate segments depending on how the approach procedure is structured.

1. **Initial Approach** — The segment between the initial approach fix and the intermediate fix or the point where the aircraft is established on the intermediate course or final approach course.

2. **Intermediate Approach** — The segment between the intermediate fix or point and the final approach fix.

3. **Final Approach** — The segment between the final approach fix or point and the runway, airport, or missed approach point.

4. **Missed Approach** — The segment between the missed approach point or the point of arrival at decision height and the missed approach fix at the prescribed altitude. (Refer to FAR Part 97)

SEPARATION — In air traffic control, the spacing of aircraft to achieve their safe and orderly movement in flight and while landing and taking off. (See Separation Minima)

SEVERE WEATHER AVOIDANCE PLAN/SWAP — An approved plan to minimize the affect of severe weather on traffic flows in impacted terminal and/or ARTCC areas. SWAP is normally implemented to provide the least disruption to the

ATC system when flight through portions of airspace is difficult or impossible due to severe weather.

SEVERE WEATHER FORECAST ALERTS/AWW — Preliminary messages issued in order to alert users that a Severe Weather Watch Bulletin (WW) is being issued. These messages define areas of possible severe thunderstorms or tornado activity. The messages are unscheduled and issued as required by the National Severe Storm Forecast Center at Kansas City, Missouri. (See SIGMET, Convective SIGMET, CWA, and AIRMET)

SHORT RANGE CLEARANCE — A clearance issued to a departing IFR flight which authorizes IFR flight to a specific fix short of the destination while air traffic control facilities are coordinating and obtaining the complete clearance.

SHORT TAKEOFF AND LANDING AIRCRAFT/ STOL AIRCRAFT — An aircraft which, at some weight within its approved operating weight, is capable of operating from a STOL runway in compliance with the applicable STOL characteristics, airworthiness, operations, noise, and pollution standards. (See Vertical Takeoff and Landing Aircraft)

SIDESTEP MANEUVER — A visual maneuver accomplished by a pilot at the completion of an instrument approach to permit a straight-in landing on a parallel runway not more than 1,200 feet to either side of the runway to which the instrument approach was conducted. (Refer to AIM)

SIGMET/WS/SIGNIFICANT METEOROLOGICAL INFORMATION — A weather advisory issued concerning weather significant to the safety of all aircraft. SIGMET advisories cover severe and extreme turbulence, severe icing, and widespread dust or sandstorms that reduce visibility to less than 3 miles. (See AWW, Convective SIGMET, CWA, and AIRMET) (Refer to AIM)

SIMPLIFIED DIRECTIONAL FACILITY/SDF — A NAVAID used for nonprecision instrument approaches. The final approach course is similar to that of an ILS localizer except that the SDF course may be offset from the runway, generally not more than 3 degrees, and the course may be wider than the localizer, resulting in a lower degree of accuracy. (Refer to AIM)

SIMULATED FLAMEOUT/SFO — A practice approach by a jet aircraft (normally military) at idle thrust to a runway. The approach may start at a relatively high altitude over a runway (high key) and may continue on a relatively high and wide downwind leg with a high rate of descent and a continuous turn to final. It terminates in a landing or low approach. The purpose of this approach is to simulate a flameout. (See Flameout)

SIMULTANEOUS ILS/MLS APPROACHES — An approach system permitting simultaneous ILS/MLS approaches to airports having parallel runways separated by at least 4,300 feet between centerlines. Integral parts of a total system are ILS/MLS, radar, communications, ATC procedures, and appropriate airborne equipment. (See Parallel Runways) (Refer to AIM)

SINGLE DIRECTION ROUTES — Preferred IFR Routes which are sometimes depicted on high altitude en route charts and which are normally flown in one direction only. (See Preferred IFR Route) (Refer to Airport/Facility Directory)

SINGLE FREQUENCY APPROACH/SFA — A service provided under a letter of agreement to military single-piloted turbojet aircraft which permits use of a single UHF frequency during approach for landing. Pilots will not normally be required to change frequency from the beginning of the approach to touchdown except that pilots conducting an en route descent are required to change frequency when control is transferred from the air route traffic control center to the terminal facility. The abbreviation "SFA" in the DOD FLIP IFR Supplement under "Communications" indicates this service is available at an aerodrome.

SINGLE-PILOTED AIRCRAFT — A military turbojet aircraft possessing one set of flight controls, tandem cockpits, or two sets of flight controls but operated by one pilot is considered single-piloted by ATC when determining the appropriate air traffic service to be applied. (See Single Frequency Approach)

SLASH — A radar beacon reply displayed as an elongated target.

SLOW TAXI — To taxi a float plane at low power or low RPM.

SPEAK SLOWER — Used in verbal communications as a request to reduce speech rate.

SPECIAL EMERGENCY — A condition of air piracy or other hostile act by a person(s) aboard an aircraft which threatens the safety of the aircraft or its passengers.

SPECIAL INSTRUMENT APPROACH PROCEDURE — (See Instrument Approach Procedure)

SPECIAL USE AIRSPACE — Airspace of defined dimensions identified by an area on the surface of the earth wherein activities must be confined because of their nature and/or wherein limitations may be imposed upon aircraft operations that are not a part of those activities. Types of special use airspace are:

1. **Alert Area** — Airspace which may contain a high volume of pilot training activities or an unusual type of aerial activity, neither of which is hazardous to aircraft. Alert Areas are depicted on aeronautical charts for the information of nonparticipating pilots. All activities within an Alert Area are conducted in accordance with Federal Aviation Regulations, and pilots of participating aircraft as well as pilots transiting the area are equally responsible for collision avoidance.

2. **Controlled Firing Area** — Airspace wherein activities are conducted under conditions so controlled as to eliminate hazards to nonparticipating aircraft and to ensure the safety of persons and property on the ground.

3. **Military Operations Area (MOA)** — An MOA is an airspace assignment of defined vertical and lateral dimensions established outside positive control areas to separate/segregate certain military activities from IFR traffic and to identify for VFR traffic where these activities are conducted. (Refer to AIM).

4. **Prohibited Area** — Designated airspace within which the flight of aircraft is prohibited. (Refer to En Route Charts, AIM).

5. **Restricted Area** — Airspace designated under FAR, Part 73, within which the flight of aircraft, while not wholly prohibit-

ed, is subject to restriction. Most restricted areas are designated joint use and IFR/VFR operations in the area may be authorized by the controlling ATC facility when it is not being utilized by the using agency. Restricted areas are depicted on en route charts. Where joint use is authorized, the name of the ATC controlling facility is also shown. (Refer to FAR Part 73 and AIM)

6. **Warning Area** — Airspace which may contain hazards to nonparticipating aircraft in international airspace.

SPECIAL VFR CONDITIONS — Weather conditions in a control zone which are less than basic VFR and in which some aircraft are permitted flight under Visual Flight Rules. (See Special VFR Operations) (Refer to FAR Part 91)

SPECIAL VFR OPERATIONS — Aircraft operating in accordance with clearances within control zones in weather conditions less than the basic VFR weather minima. Such operations must be requested by the pilot and approved by ATC. (See Special VFR Conditions)

SPEED — (See Airspeed, Groundspeed)

SPEED ADJUSTMENT — An ATC procedure used to request pilots to adjust aircraft speed to a specific value for the purpose of providing desired spacing. Pilots are expected to maintain a speed of plus or minus 10 knots or 0.02 mach number of the specified speed.

Examples of speed adjustments are:

1. "Increase/reduce speed to mach point (number)."

2. "Increase/reduce speed to (speed in knots)" or "Increase/reduce speed (number of knots) knots."

SPEED BRAKES/DIVE BRAKES — Moveable aerodynamic devices on aircraft that reduce airspeed during descent and landing.

SQUAWK (Mode, Code, Function) — Activate specific modes/codes/functions on the aircraft transponder; e.g., "Squawk three/alpha, two one zero five, low." (See Transponder)

STAGE I/II/III SERVICE — (See Terminal Radar Program)

STANDARD INSTRUMENT APPROACH PROCEDURE/ SIAP — (See Instrument Approach Procedure)

STANDARD INSTRUMENT DEPARTURE/SID — A pre-planned instrument flight rule (IFR) air traffic control departure procedure printed for pilot use in graphic and/or textual form. SID's provide transition from the terminal to the appropriate en route structure. (See IFR Takeoff Minima and Departure Procedures) (Refer to AIM)

STANDARD RATE TURN — A turn of three degrees per second.

STANDARD TERMINAL ARRIVAL/STAR — A preplanned instrument flight rule (IFR) air traffic control arrival procedure published for pilot use in graphic and/or textual form. STAR's provide transition from the en route structure to an outer fix or an instrument approach fix/arrival waypoint in the terminal area.

STAND BY — Means the controller or pilot must pause for a few seconds, usually to attend to other duties of a higher priority. Also means to wait as in "stand by for clearance." If a delay is lengthy, the caller should reestablish contact.

STATIONARY RESERVATIONS — Altitude reservations which encompass activities in a fixed area. Stationary reservations may include activities, such as special tests of weapons systems or equipment, certain U.S. Navy carrier, fleet, and anti-submarine operations, rocket, missile and drone operations, and certain aerial refueling or similar operations.

STEPDOWN FIX — A fix permitting additional descent within a segment of an instrument approach procedure by identifying a point at which a controlling obstacle has been safely overflown.

STEP TAXI — To taxi a float plane at full power or high RPM.

STEP TURN — A maneuver used to put a float plane in a planing configuration prior to entering an active sea lane for takeoff. The STEP TURN maneuver should only be used upon pilot request.

STEREO ROUTE — A routinely used route of flight established by users and ARTCC's identified by a coded name; e.g., ALPHA 2. These routes minimize flight plan handling and communications.

STOP ALTITUDE SQUAWK — Used by ATC to inform an aircraft to turn-off the automatic altitude reporting feature of its transponder. It is issued when the verbally reported altitude varies 300 feet or more from the automatic altitude report. (See Altitude Readout, Transponder)

STOP AND GO — A procedure wherein an aircraft will land, make a complete stop on the runway, and then commence a takeoff from that point. (See Low Approach, Option Approach)

STOPOVER FLIGHT PLAN — A flight plan format which permits in a single submission the filing of a sequence of flight plans through interim full-stop destinations to a final destination.

STOP SQUAWK (Mode or Code) — Used by ATC to tell the pilot to turn specified functions of the aircraft transponder off. (See Stop Altitude Squawk, Transponder)

STOP STREAM/BURST/BUZZER — Used by ATC to request a pilot to suspend electronic countermeasure activity. (See Jamming)

STOPWAY — An area beyond the takeoff runway designated by the airport authorities as able to support an airplane during an aborted takeoff. (Refer to FAR Part 1)

STRAIGHT-IN APPROACH — IFR — An instrument approach wherein final approach is begun without first having executed a procedure turn, not necessarily completed with a straight-in landing or made to straight-in landing minimums. (See Straight-in Landing, Landing Minimums, Straight-in Approach-VFR)

STRAIGHT-IN APPROACH — VFR — Entry into the traffic pattern by interception of the extended runway centerline (final approach course) without executing any other portion of the traffic pattern. (See Traffic Pattern)

STRAIGHT-IN LANDING — A landing made on a runway aligned within 30° of the final approach course following completion of an instrument approach. (See Straight-in Approach-IFR)

STRAIGHT-IN LANDING MINIMUMS/STRAIGHT-IN MINIMUMS — (See Landing Minimums)

SUBSTITUTE ROUTE — A route assigned to pilots when any part of an airway or route is unusable because of NAVAID status. These routes consist of:

    1. Substitute routes which are shown on U.S. Government charts.

    2. Routes defined by ATC as specific NAVAID radials or courses.

    3. Routes defined by ATC as direct to or between NAVAID's.

SUNSET AND SUNRISE — The mean solar times of sunset and sunrise as published in the Nautical Almanac, converted to local standard time for the locality concerned. Within Alaska, the end of evening civil twilight and the beginning of morning civil twilight, as defined for each locality.

SUPER HIGH FREQUENCY/SHF — The frequency band between 3 and 30 gigahertz (GHz). The elevation and azimuth stations of the microwave landing system operate from 5031MHz to 5091MHz in this spectrum.

SURVEILLANCE APPROACH — An instrument approach wherein the air traffic controller issues instructions, for pilot compliance, based on aircraft position in relation to the final approach course (azimuth), and the distance (range) from the end of the runway as displayed on the controller's radar scope. The controller will provide recommended altitudes on final approach if requested by the pilot. (See PAR Approach) (Refer to AIM)

SYSTEM STRATEGIC NAVIGATION/SN — Military activity accomplished by navigating along a preplanned route using internal aircraft systems to maintain a desired track. This activity normally requires a lateral route width of 10NM and altitude range of 1,000 feet to 6,000 feet AGL with some route segments that permit terrain following.

TACAN-ONLY AIRCRAFT — An aircraft, normally military, possessing TACAN with DME but no VOR navigational system capability. Clearances must specify TACAN or VORTAC fixes and approaches.

TACTICAL AIR NAVIGATION/TACAN — An ultra-high frequency electronic rho-theta air navigation aid which provides suitably equipped aircraft a continuous indication of bearing and distance to the TACAN station. (See VORTAC) (Refer to AIM)

TARGET — The indication shown on a radar display resulting from a primary radar return or a radar beacon reply. (See Radar, Target Symbol)

    1. Generally, any discrete object which reflects or retransmits energy back to the radar equipment.

    2. Specifically, an object of radar search or surveillance.

TARGET SYMBOL — A computer-generated indication shown on a radar display resulting from a primary radar return or a radar beacon reply.

TAXI — The movement of an airplane under its own power on the surface of an airport (FAR Part 135.100-Note). Also, it describes the surface movement of helicopters equipped with wheels. (See Air Taxi, Hover Taxi) (Refer to AIM)

TAXI INTO POSITION AND HOLD — Used by ATC to inform a pilot to taxi onto the departure runway in takeoff position and hold. It is not authorization for takeoff. It is used when takeoff clearance cannot immediately be issued because of traffic or other reasons. (See Hold, Cleared for Takeoff)

TAXI PATTERNS — Patterns established to illustrate the desired flow of ground traffic for the different runways or airport areas available for use.

TELEPHONE INFORMATION BRIEFING SERVICE (TIBS) — A continuous telephone recording of meteorological and/or aeronautical information. (Refer to AIM)

TERMINAL AREA — A general term used to describe airspace in which approach control service or airport traffic control service is provided.

TERMINAL AREA FACILITY — A facility providing air traffic control service for arriving and departing IFR, VFR, Special VFR, and on occasion en route aircraft. (See Approach Control, Tower)

TERMINAL CONTROL AREA — (See Controlled Airspace)

TERMINAL RADAR PROGRAM — A national program instituted to extend the terminal radar services provided IFR aircraft to VFR aircraft. Pilot participation in the program is urged but is not mandatory. The program is divided into two parts and referred to as Stage II and Stage III. The Stage service provided at a particular location is contained in the Airport/Facility Directory.

    1. Stage I originally comprised two basic radar services (traffic advisories and limited vectoring to VFR aircraft). These services are provided by all commissioned terminal radar facilities, but the term "Stage I" has been deleted from use.

    2. Stage II/Radar Advisory and Sequencing for VFR Aircraft — Provides, in addition to the basic radar services, vectoring and sequencing on a full-time basis to arriving VFR aircraft. The purpose is to adjust the flow of arriving IFR and VFR aircraft into the traffic pattern in a safe and orderly manner and to provide traffic advisories to departing VFR aircraft.

    3. Stage III/Radar Sequencing and Separation Service for VFR Aircraft — Provides, in addition to the basic radar services and Stage II, separation between all participating VFR aircraft. The purpose is to provide separation between all participating VFR aircraft and all IFR aircraft operating within the airspace defined as a Terminal Radar Service Area (TRSA) or Terminal Control Area (TCA). (See Controlled Airspace, Terminal Radar Service Area) (Refer to AIM, Airport/Facility Directory)

TERMINAL RADAR SERVICE AREA/TRSA — Airspace surrounding designated airports wherein ATC provides radar vectoring, sequencing, and separation on a full-time basis for

TIME
Standard to UTC

Eastern	.........................+ 5 hr = UTC
Central	.........................+ 6 hr = UTC
Mountain	.........................+ 7 hr = UTC
Pacific	.........................+ 8 hr = UTC
Yukon	.........................+ 9 hr = UTC
Alaskan	.........................+ 10 hr = UTC
Bering	.........................+ 11 hr = UTC

Add one less hour for Daylight Time.

To convert local times into Universal Coordinated Time (UTC), use the figures on this table. During Daylight Saving Time, add one hour less. Suppose it is 2:00 p.m., Central Standard Time. Adding six hours means the time is 8:00 p.m. UTC, expressed as 2000 hours.

all IFR and participating VFR aircraft. Service provided in a TRSA is called Stage III Service. The AIM contains an explanation of TRSA. TRSA's are depicted on VFR aeronautical charts. Pilot participation is urged but is not mandatory. (See Terminal Radar Program) (Refer to AIM, Airport/Facility Directory)

TERRAIN FOLLOWING/TF — The flight of a military aircraft maintaining a constant AGL altitude above the terrain or the highest obstruction. The altitude of the aircraft will constantly change with the varying terrain and/or obstruction.

TETRAHEDRON — A device normally located on uncontrolled airports and used as a landing direction indicator. The small end of a tetrahedron points in the direction of landing. At controlled airports, the tetrahedron, if installed, should be disregarded because tower instructions supersede the indicator. (See Segmented Circle) (Refer to AIM)

THAT IS CORRECT — The understanding you have is right.

THRESHOLD — The beginning of that portion of the runway usable for landing. (See Airport Lighting, Displaced Threshold)

THRESHOLD CROSSING HEIGHT/TCH — The theoretical height above the runway threshold at which the aircraft's glideslope antenna would be if the aircraft maintains the trajectory established by the mean ILS glideslope or MLS glidepath. (See Glide Slope, Threshold)

THRESHOLD LIGHTS — (See Airport Lighting)

TIME GROUP — Four digits representing the hour and minutes from the 24-hour clock. Time groups without time zone indicators are understood to be UTC (Universal Coordinated Time); e.g., "0205." The term "Zulu" is used when ATC procedures require a reference to UTC. A time zone designator is used to indicate local time; e.g., "0205M." The end and the beginning of the day are shown by "2400" and "0000," respectively.

TORCHING — The burning of fuel at the end of an exhaust pipe or stack of a reciprocating aircraft engine, the result of an excessive richness in the fuel air mixture.

TOUCH-AND-GO/TOUCH-AND-GO LANDING — An operation by an aircraft that lands and departs on a runway without stopping or exiting the runway.

TOUCHDOWN —

1. The point at which an aircraft first makes contact with the landing surface.

2. Concerning a precision radar approach (PAR), it is the point where the glide path intercepts the landing surface.

Note. — Touchdown as defined above is only a datum and is not necessarily the actual point at which the aircraft will touch the runway

TOUCHDOWN RVR — (See Visibility)

TOUCHDOWN ZONE — The first 3,000 feet of the runway beginning at the threshold. The area is used for determination of Touchdown Zone Elevation in the development of straight-in landing minimums for instrument approaches.

TOUCHDOWN ZONE ELEVATION/TDZE — The highest elevation in the first 3,000 feet of the landing surface. TDZE is indicated on the instrument approach procedure chart when straight-in landing minimums are authorized. (See Touchdown Zone)

TOUCHDOWN ZONE LIGHTING — (See Airport Lighting)

TOWER/AIRPORT TRAFFIC CONTROL TOWER/ ATCT — A terminal facility that uses air/ground communications, visual signaling, and other devices to provide ATC services to aircraft operating in the vicinity of an airport or on the movement area. Authorizes aircraft to land or takeoff at the airport controlled by the tower or to transit the airport traffic area regardless of flight plan or weather conditions (IFR or VFR). A tower may also provide approach control services (radar or nonradar). (See Airport Traffic Area, Airport Traffic Control Service, Approach Control/Approach Control Facility, Approach Control Service, Movement Area, Tower En Route Control Service/Tower to Tower) (Refer to AIM)

TOWER EN ROUTE CONTROL SERVICE/TOWER TO TOWER — The control of IFR en route traffic within delegated airspace between two or more adjacent approach control facilities. This service is designed to expedite traffic and reduce control and pilot communication requirements.

TPX-42 — A numeric beacon decoder equipment/system. It is designed to be added to terminal radar systems for beacon decoding. It provides rapid target identification, reinforcement of

Controllers in the airport traffic control tower at Chicago's O'Hare International Airport deal with more landings and takeoffs every day than any other terminal facility in the United States. (FAA)

the primary radar target, and altitude information from Mode C. (See Automated Radar Terminal Systems, Transponder)

TRACK — The actual flight path of an aircraft over the surface of the earth. (See Course, Route, Flight Path)

TRAFFIC —

1. A term used by a controller to transfer radar identification of an aircraft to another controller for the purpose of coordinating separation action. Traffic is normally issued (a) in response to a handoff or point out, (b) in anticipation of a handoff or point out, or (c) in conjunction with a request for control of an aircraft.

2. A term used by ATC to refer to one or more aircraft.

TRAFFIC ADVISORIES — Advisories issued to alert pilots to other known or observed air traffic which may be in such proximity to the position or intended route of flight of their aircraft to warrant their attention. Such advisories may be based on:

1. Visual observation.

2. Observation of radar identified and nonidentified aircraft targets on an ATC radar display, or

3. Verbal reports from pilots or other facilities.

The word "traffic" followed by additional information, if known, is used to provide such advisories; e.g., "Traffic, 2 o'clock, one zero miles, southbound, eight thousand."

Traffic advisory service will be provided to the extent possible depending on higher priority duties of the controller or other limitations; e.g., radar limitations, volume of traffic, frequency congestion, or controller workload. Radar/nonradar traffic advisories do not relieve the pilot of his responsibility to see and avoid other aircraft. Pilots are cautioned that there are many times when the controller is not able to give traffic advisories concerning all traffic in the aircraft's proximity; in other words, when a pilot requests or is receiving traffic advisories, he should not assume that all traffic will be issued. (Refer to AIM, Radar Traffic Information Service)

(Identification), TRAFFIC ALERT. ADVISE YOU TURN LEFT/RIGHT (specific heading if appropriate), AND/OR CLIMB/DESCEND (specific altitude if appropriate) IMMEDIATELY. (See Safety Alert)

TRAFFIC ALERT AND COLLISION AVOIDANCE SYSTEM/TCAS — An airborne collision avoidance system based on radar beacon signals which operates independent of ground-based equipment. TCAS-I generates traffic advisories only. TCAS-II generates traffic advisories, and resolution (collision avoidance) advisories in the vertical plane.

TRAFFIC INFORMATION — (See Traffic Advisories)

TRAFFIC IN SIGHT — Used by pilots to inform a controller that previously issued traffic is in sight. (See Negative Contact, Traffic Advisories)

TRAFFIC NO LONGER A FACTOR — Indicates that the traffic described in a previously issued traffic advisory is no longer a factor.

TRAFFIC PATTERN — The traffic flow that is prescribed for aircraft landing at, taxiing on, or taking off from an airport. The components of a typical traffic pattern are upwind leg, crosswind leg, downwind leg, base leg, and final approach.

    1. **Upwind Leg** — A flight path parallel to the landing runway in the direction of landing.

    2. **Crosswind Leg** — A flight path at right angles to the landing runway off its upwind end.

    3. **Downwind Leg** — A flight path parallel to the landing runway in the direction opposite to landing. The downwind leg normally extends between the crosswind leg and the base leg.

    4. **Base Leg** — A flight path at right angles to the landing runway off its approach end. The base leg normally extends from the downwind leg to the intersection of the extended runway centerline.

    5. **Final Approach** — A flight path in the direction of landing along the extended runway centerline. The final approach normally extends from the base leg to the runway. An aircraft making a straight-in approach VFR is also considered to be on final approach.

(See Straight-In Approach-VFR, Taxi Patterns) (Refer to AIM, FAR Part 91)

TRANSCRIBED WEATHER BROADCAST/TWEB — A continuous recording of meteorological and aeronautical information that is broadcast on L/MF and VOR facilities for pilots. (Refer to AIM)

TRANSFER OF CONTROL — That action whereby the responsibility for the separation of an aircraft is transferred from one controller to another.

TRANSFERRING CONTROLLER/FACILITY — A controller/facility transferring control of an aircraft to another controller/facility.

TRANSITION —

    1. The general term that describes the change from one phase of flight or flight condition to another; e.g., transition from en route flight to the approach or transition from instrument flight to visual flight.

    2. A published procedure (SID Transition) used to connect the basic SID to one of several en route airways/jet routes, or a published procedure (STAR Transition) used to connect one of several en route airways/jet routes to the basic STAR. (Refer to SID/STAR Charts)

TRANSITION AREA — (See Controlled Airspace)

TRANSMISSOMETER — An apparatus used to determine visibility by measuring the transmission of light through the atmosphere. It is the measurement source for determining runway visual range (RVR) and runway visibility value (RVV). (See Visibility)

TRANSMITTING IN THE BLIND/BLIND TRANSMISSION — A transmission from one station to other stations in circumstances where two-way communication cannot be established, but where it is believed that the called stations may be able to receive the transmission.

TRANSPONDER — The airborne radar beacon receiver/transmitter portion of the Air Traffic Control Radar Beacon System (ATCRBS) which automatically receives radio signals from interrogators on the ground, and selectively replies with a specific reply pulse or pulse group only to those interrogations being received on the mode to which it is set to respond. (See Interrogator) (Refer to AIM)

TURBOJET AIRCRAFT — An aircraft having a jet engine in which the energy of the jet operates a turbine which in turn operates the air compressor.

TURBOPROP AIRCRAFT — An aircraft having a jet engine in which the energy of the jet operates a turbine which drives the propeller.

T-VOR/TERMINAL-VERY HIGH FREQUENCY OMNIDIRECTIONAL RANGE STATION — A very high frequency terminal omnirange station located on or near an airport and used as an approach aid. (See Navigational Aid, VOR)

TWO WAY RADIO COMMUNICATIONS FAILURE — (See Lost Communications)

ULTRAHIGH FREQUENCY/UHF — The frequency band between 300 and 3,000 MHz. The bank of radio frequencies used for military air/ground voice communications. In some instances this may go as low as 225 MHz and still be referred to as UHF.

ULTRALIGHT VEHICLE — An aeronautical vehicle operated for sport or recreational purposes which does not require FAA registration, an airworthiness certificate, nor pilot certification. They are primarily single occupant vehicles, although some two-place vehicles are authorized for training purposes. Operation of an ultralight vehicle in certain airspace requires authorization from ATC. (See FAR 103)

UNABLE — Indicates inability to comply with a specific instruction, request, or clearance.

UNCONTROLLED AIRSPACE — Uncontrolled airspace is that portion of the airspace that has not been designated as continental control area, control area, control zone, terminal control area, or transition area and within which ATC has neither the authority nor the responsibility for exercising control over air traffic. (See Controlled Airspace)

UNDER THE HOOD — Indicates that the pilot is using a hood to restrict visibility outside the cockpit while simulating instrument flight. An appropriately rated pilot is required in the other control seat while this operation is being conducted. (Refer to FAR Part 91)

UNICOM — A nongovernment communication facility which may provide airport information at certain airports. Locations and frequencies of UNICOMs are shown on aeronautical charts and publications. (Refer to AIM, Airport/Facility Directory)

The standard air-port traffic pattern as shown in the FAA's handbook for pilots. The segment-ed circle shows whether the pattern is standard left-hand or standard right-hand. A wind cone or tetrahedron reveals wind direc-tion to pilots using the airport.

Application of Traffic Pattern Indicators

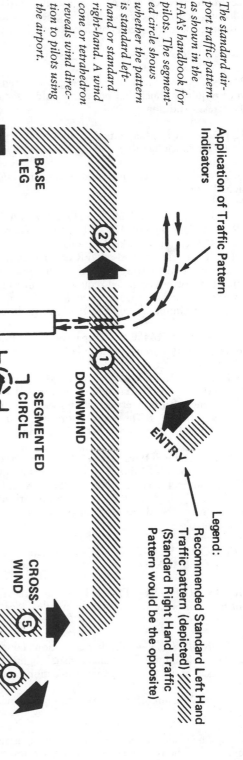

BASE LEG

RUNWAY

DOWNWIND

ENTRY

SEGMENTED CIRCLE

HAZARD OR POPULATED AREA

LANDING DIRECTION INDICATOR

CROSS-WIND

LANDING RUNWAY (OR LANDING STRIP) INDICATORS

WIND CONE

TRAFFIC PATTERN INDICATORS

Legend:
Recommended Standard Left Hand Traffic pattern (depicted)

(Standard Right Hand Traffic Pattern would be the opposite)

① Enter pattern in level flight, abeam the midpoint of the runway, at pattern altitude. (1000' AGL is recommended pattern altitude unless established otherwise.)

② Maintain pattern altitude until abeam approach end of the landing runway, on downwind leg.

③ Complete turn to final at least 1/4 mile from the runway.

④ Continue straight ahead until beyond departure end of runway.

⑤ If remaining in the traffic pattern, commence turn to crosswind leg beyond the departure end of the runway, within 300 feet of pattern altitude.

⑥ If departing the traffic pattern, continue straight out, or exit with a 45° left turn beyond the departure end of the runway, after reaching pattern altitude.

UNPUBLISHED ROUTE — A route for which no minimum altitude is published or charted for pilot use. It may include a direct route between NAVAIDS, a radial, a radar vector, or a final approach course beyond the segments of an instrument approach procedure. (See Published Route, Route)

UPWIND LEG — (See Traffic Pattern)

URGENCY — A condition of being concerned about safety and of requiring timely but not immediate assistance; a potential distress condition.

VECTOR — A heading issued to an aircraft to provide navigational guidance by radar.

VERIFY — Request confirmation of information; e.g., "verify assigned altitude."

VERIFY SPECIFIC DIRECTION OF TAKEOFF (OR TURNS AFTER TAKEOFF) — Used by ATC to ascertain an aircraft's direction of takeoff and/or direction of turn after takeoff. It is normally used for IFR departures from an airport not having a control tower. When direct communication with the pilot is not possible, the request and information may be relayed through an FSS, dispatcher, or by other means. (See IFR Takeoff Minimums and Departure Procedures)

VERTICAL SEPARATION — Separation established by assignment of different altitudes or flight levels. (See Separation)

VERTICAL TAKEOFF AND LANDING AIRCRAFT/VTOL AIRCRAFT — Aircraft capable of vertical climbs and/or descents and of using very short runways or small areas for takeoff and landings. These aircraft include, but are not limited to, helicopters. (See Short Takeoff and Landing Aircraft)

VERY HIGH FREQUENCY/VHF — The frequency band between 30 and 300 MHz. Portions of this band, 108 to 118 MHz, are used for certain NAVAIDS; 118 to 136 MHz are used for civil air/ground voice communications. Other frequencies in this band are used for purposes not related to air traffic control.

VERY LOW FREQUENCY/VLF — The frequency band between 3 and 30 KHz.

VFR AIRCRAFT/VFR FLIGHT — An aircraft conducting flight in accordance with visual flight rules. (See Visual Flight Rules)

VFR CONDITIONS — Weather conditions equal to or better than the minimum for flight under visual flight rules. The term may be used as an ATC clearance/instruction only when:

1. An IFR aircraft requests a climb/descent in VFR conditions.

2. The clearance will result in noise abatement benefits where part of the IFR departure route does not conform to an FAA approved noise abatement route or altitude.

3. A pilot has requested a practice instrument approach and is not on an IFR flight plan.

All pilots receiving this authorization must comply with the VFR visibility and distance from cloud criteria in FAR Part 91. Use of the term does not relieve controllers of their respon-

sibility to separate aircraft in TCAs/TRSAs as required by FAA Handbook 7110.65. When used as an ATC clearance/instruction, the term may be abbreviated "VFR;" e.g., "MAINTAIN VFR," "CLIMB/DESCEND VFR," etc.

VFR-ON-TOP — ATC authorization for an IFR aircraft to operate in VFR conditions at any appropriate VFR altitude (as specified in FAR and as restricted by ATC). A pilot receiving this authorization must comply with the VFR visibility, distance from cloud criteria, and the minimum IFR altitudes specified in FAR Part 91. The use of this term does not relieve controllers of their responsibility to separate aircraft in TCA's/TRSA's as required by FAA Handbook 7110.65.

VFR MILITARY TRAINING ROUTES/VR — Routes used by the Department of Defense and associated Reserve and Air Guard units for the purpose of conducting low-altitude navigation and tactical training under VFR below 10,000 feet MSL at airspeeds in excess of 250 knots IAS.

VFR NOT RECOMMENDED — An advisory provided by a flight service station to a pilot during a preflight or inflight weather briefing that flight under visual flight rules is not recommended. To be given when the current and/or forecast weather conditions are at or below VFR minimums. It does not abrogate the pilot's authority to make his own decision.

VIDEO MAP — An electronically displayed map on the radar display that may depict data such as airports, heliports, runway centerline extensions, hospital emergency landing areas, NAVAID's and fixes, reporting points, airway/route centerlines, boundaries, handoff points, special use tracks, obstructions, prominent geographic features, map alignment indicators, range accuracy marks, minimum vectoring altitudes.

VISIBILITY — The ability, as determined by atmospheric conditions and expressed in units of distance, to see and identify prominent unlighted objects by day and prominent lighted objects by night. Visibility is reported as statute miles, hundreds of feet or meters. (Refer to FAR Part 91, AIM)

1. **Flight Visibility** — The average forward horizontal distance, from the cockpit of an aircraft in flight, at which prominent unlighted objects may be seen and identified by day and prominent lighted objects may be seen and identified by night.

2. **Ground Visibility** — Prevailing horizontal visibility near the earth's surface as reported by the United States National Weather Service or an accredited observer.

3. **Prevailing Visibility** — The greatest horizontal visibility equaled or exceeded throughout at least half the horizon circle which need not necessarily be continuous.

4. **Runway Visibility Value/RVV** — The visibility determined for a particular runway by a transmissometer. A meter provides a continuous indication of the visibility (reported in miles or fractions of miles) for the runway. RVV is used in lieu of prevailing visibility in determining minimums for a particular runway.

5. **Runway Visual Range/RVR** — An instrumentally derived value, based on standard calibrations, that represents the horizontal distance a pilot will see down the runway from the approach end. It is based on the sighting of either high intensity runway lights or on the visual contrast of other tar-

gets whichever yields the greater visual range. RVR, in contrast to prevailing or runway visibility, is based on what a pilot in a moving aircraft should see looking down the runway. RVR is horizontal visual range, not slant visual range. It is based on the measurement of a transmissometer made near the touchdown point of the instrument runway and is reported in hundreds of feet. RVR is used in lieu of RVV and/or prevailing visibility in determining minimums for a particular runway.

> a. **Touchdown RVR** — The RVR visibility readout values obtained from RVR equipment serving the runway touchdown zone.

> b. **Mid-RVR** — The RVR readout values obtained from RVR equipment located midfield of the runway.

> c. **Rollout RVR** — The RVR readout values obtained from RVR equipment located nearest the rollout end of the runway.

VISUAL APPROACH — An approach wherein an aircraft on an IFR flight plan, operating in VFR conditions under the control of an air traffic control facility and having an air traffic control authorization, may proceed to the airport of destination in VFR conditions.

VISUAL APPROACH SLOPE INDICATOR — (See Airport Lighting)

VISUAL DESCENT POINT/VDP — A defined point on the final approach course of a nonprecision straight-in approach procedure from which normal descent from the MDA to the runway touchdown point may be commenced, provided the approach threshold of that runway, or approach lights, or other markings identifiable with the approach end of that runway are clearly visible to the pilot.

VISUAL FLIGHT RULES/VFR — Rules that govern the procedures for conducting flight under visual conditions. The term "VFR" is also used in the United States to indicate weather conditions that are equal to or greater than minimum VFR requirements. In addition, it is used by pilots and controllers to indicate type of flight plan. (See Instrument Flight Rules, Instrument Meteorological Conditions, Visual Meteorological Conditions) (Refer to FAR Part 91 and AIM)

VISUAL HOLDING — The holding of aircraft at selected, prominent geographical fixes which can be easily recognized from the air. (See Hold, Holding Fixes)

VISUAL METEOROLOGICAL CONDITIONS/VMC — Meteorological conditions expressed in terms of visibility, distance from cloud, and ceiling equal to or better than specified minima. (See Instrument Flight Rules, Instrument Meteorological Conditions, Visual Flight Rules)

VISUAL SEPARATION — A means employed by ATC to separate aircraft in terminal areas. There are two ways to effect this separation:

1. The tower controller sees the aircraft involved and issues instructions, as necessary, to ensure that the aircraft avoid each other.

2. A pilot sees the other aircraft involved and upon instructions from the controller provides his own separation by maneuvering his aircraft as necessary to avoid it. This may involve following another aircraft or keeping it in sight until it is no longer a factor. (See See and Avoid) (Refer to FAR Part 91)

VORTAC/VHF OMNIDIRECTIONAL RANGE/TACTICAL AIR NAVIGATION — A navigation aid providing VOR azimuth, TACAN azimuth, and TACAN distance measuring equipment (DME) at one site. (See Distance Measuring Equipment, Navigational Aid, TACAN, VOR) (Refer to AIM)

VORTICES/WING TIP VORTICES — Circular patterns of air created by the movement of an airfoil through the air when generating lift. As an airfoil moves through the atmosphere in sustained flight, an area of low pressure is created above it. The air flowing from the high pressure area to the low pressure area around and about the tips of the airfoil tends to roll up into two rapidly rotating vortices, cylindrical in shape. These vortices are the most predominant parts of aircraft wake turbulence and their rotational force is dependent upon the wing loading, gross weight, and speed of the generating aircraft. The vortices from medium to heavy aircraft can be of extremely high velocity and hazardous to smaller aircraft. (See Aircraft Classes, Wake Turbulence) (Refer to AIM)

VOR/VERY HIGH FREQUENCY OMNIDIRECTIONAL RANGE STATION — A ground-based electronic navigation aid transmitting very high frequency navigation signals, 360 degrees in azimuth, oriented from magnetic north. Used as the basis for navigation in the National Airspace System. The VOR periodically identifies itself by Morse Code and may have an additional voice identification feature. Voice features may be used by ATC or FSS for transmitting instructions/information to pilots. (See Navigational Aid) (Refer to AIM)

VOT/VOR TEST SIGNAL — A ground facility which emits a test signal to check VOR receiver accuracy. Some VOT's are available to the user while airborne, and others are limited to ground use only. (Refer to FAR Part 91, AIM, Airport/Facility Directory)

WAKE TURBULENCE — Phenomena resulting from the passage of an aircraft through the atmosphere. The term includes vortices, thrust stream turbulence, jet blast, jet wash, propeller wash, and rotor wash both on the ground and in the air. (See Aircraft Classes, Jet Blast, Vortices) (Refer to AIM)

WARNING AREA — (See Special Use Airspace)

WAYPOINT — A predetermined geographical position used for route/instrument approach definition, or progress reporting purposes, that is defined relative to a VORTAC station or in terms of latitude/longitude coordinates.

WEATHER ADVISORY/INFLIGHT WEATHER ADVISORY — (See SIGMET, AIRMET)

WEATHER ADVISORY/WS/WST/WA/CWA — In aviation weather forecast practice, an expression of hazardous weather conditions not predicted in the area forecast, as they affect the operation of air traffic and as prepared by the NWS.

WHEN ABLE — When used in conjunction with ATC instructions, gives the pilot the latitude to delay compliance until a condition or event has been reconciled. Unlike "pilot discretion," when instructions are prefaced "when able," the pilot is expected to seek the first opportunity to comply. Once a maneuver has been initiated, the pilot is expected to continue until the specifications of the instructions have been met. "When able," should not be used when expeditious compliance is required.

WILCO — I have received your message, understand it, and will comply with it.

WIND SHEAR — A change in wind speed and/or wind direction in a short distance resulting in a tearing or shearing effect. It can exist in a horizontal or vertical direction and occasionally in both.

WORDS TWICE —

1. **As a request:** "Communication is difficult. Please say every phrase twice."

2. **As information:** "Since communications are difficult, every phrase in this message will be spoken twice."

AVIATION SPECIAL INTEREST GROUPS

AEROSPACE INDUSTRIES ASSOCIATION OF AMERICA, INC.
1250 I Street, NW
Washington DC 20005
(202) 371-8400

AIR LINE PILOTS ASSOCIATION INTERNATIONAL
535 Herndon Parkway
P.O. Box 1169
Herndon, VA 22070
(703) 689-2270

AIR TRAFFIC CONTROL ASSOCIATION
2020 N. 14th Street, Suite 410
Arlington, VA 22201
(703) 522-5717

AIR TRANSPORT ASSOCIATION OF AMERICA
1709 New York Avenue, NW
Washington, DC 20006
(202) 626-4000

AIRCRAFT ELECTRONICS ASSOCIATION
P.O. Box 1981
Independence, MO 64055
(816) 373-6565

AIRCRAFT OWNERS & PILOTS ASSOCIATION
421 Aviation Way
Frederick, MD 21701
(301) 695-2000

AIRPORT OPERATORS COUNCIL INTERNATIONAL, INC.
1220 19th Street, NW
Washington, DC 20036
(202) 293-8500

ALLIED PILOTS ASSOCIATION
P.O. Box 5524
Arlington, TX 76005-5524
(214) 988-3188

AMERICAN ASSOCIATION OF AIRPORT EXECUTIVES
4224 King Street
Alexandria, VA 22314
(703) 824-0500

AMERICAN HELICOPTER SOCIETY
217 N. Washington Street
Alexandria, VA 22314
(703) 684-6777

AMERICAN INSTITUTE OF AERONAUTICS AND ASTRONAUTICS, INC.
370 L'Enfant Promenade, SW
Washington, DC 20024
(202) 646-7400

ASSOCIATION OF FLIGHT ATTENDANTS
1625 Massachusetts Ave, NW
Washington, DC 20036
(202) 328-5400

ASSOCIATION OF PROFESSIONAL FLIGHT ATTENDANTS
1004 West Euless Blvd
Euless, TX 76040
(817) 540-0108

AVIATION DISTRIBUTION AND MANUFACTURERS ASSOCIATION
1900 Arch Street
Philadelphia, PA 19103
(215) 564-3484

DEPARTMENT OF DEFENSE ADVISORY COMMITTEE ON FEDERAL AVIATION
SAFRL, Room 4D865 Pentagon
Washington, DC 20330-3086

EXPERIMENTAL AIRCRAFT ASSOCIATION
Wittman Field
Oshkosh, WI 54903-3086
(414) 426-4800

FLIGHT SAFETY FOUNDATION
5510 Columbia Pike, Suite 303
Arlington, VA 22204
(703) 820-2777

GENERAL AVIATION MANUFACTURERS ASSOCIATION
1400 K Street, NW, Suite 801
Washington, DC 20005
(202) 393-1500

HELICOPTER ASSOCIATION INTERNATIONAL
1619 Duke Street
Alexandria, VA 22314-3439
(703) 683-4646

NATIONAL AERONAUTICS ASSOCIATION
1763 R Street, NW
Washington, DC 20003
(202) 265-8720

NATIONAL AIR CARRIER ASSOCIATION, INC.
1730 M Street, NW
Washington, DC 20036
(202) 833-8200

NATIONAL AIR TRAFFIC CONTROLLERS ASSOCIATION
444 N. Capitol Street, NW
Washington, DC 20001
(202) 347-4572

NATIONAL AIR TRANSPORTATION ASSOCIATION INC.
4226 King Street
Alexandria, VA 22302
(703) 855-9000

NATIONAL ASSOCIATION OF AIR TRAFFIC SPECIALISTS, INC.
4780 Corridor Place
Beltsville, MD 20705
(301) 595-2012

NATIONAL ASSOCIATION OF FLIGHT INSTRUCTORS
P.O. Box 793
Dublin, OH 43017
(614) 889-6148

NATIONAL ASSOCIATION OF STATE AVIATION OFFICIALS
8401 Colesville Road
Silver Spring, MD 20910
(301) 588-1286

NATIONAL BLACK COALITION OF FEDERAL AVIATION EMPLOYEES
P.O. Box 521004
Tulsa, OK 74152
(918) 836-7921

NATIONAL BUSINESS AIRCRAFT ASSOCIATION, INC.
1200 Eighteenth Street, NW
Washington, DC 20036
(202) 783-9000

NATIONAL HISPANIC COALITION OF FEDERAL AVIATION EMPLOYEES
14324 Lemoli Avenue, #3
Hawthorne, CA 90250
(213) 297-1830

**PROFESSIONAL AIRWAYS SYSTEMS
SPECIALISTS**
444 North Capital Street, NW Suite 840
Washington, DC 20001
(202) 347-6065

**PROFESSIONAL AVIATION MAINTENANCE
ASSOCIATION**
500 NW Plaza, Suite 401
St. Ann, MO 63074
(314) 739-2580

PROFESSIONAL WOMEN CONTROLLERS
P.O. Box 44085
Oklahoma City, OK 73144
(213) 297-1379

REGIONAL AIRLINE ASSOCIATION
1101 Connecticut Avenue, NW
Washington, DC 20036
(202) 857-1170

SOCIETY OF AIRWAY PIONEERS
P.O. Box 2809
Friday Harbor, WA 98250
(206) 378-3881

TECHNICAL WOMEN'S ORGANIZATION
920 Westlink
Wichita, KS 67212
(316) 946-4480

ABOUT THE AUTHOR

Walter S. Luffsey was the top Federal official on air traffic control in the late 1980s, as the FAA's Associate Administrator for Air Traffic. He was responsible for overseeing all aspects of air traffic control, including management oversight of more than half the FAA work force.

He began his career in air traffic control as a controller in Norfolk, Virginia. He soon progressed to Supervisory Air Traffic Control Specialist at Atlantic City, N.J. In the ATC portion of his career, he was qualified and worked in all three ATC options: tower, en route, and flight service station. He has comprehensive and direct knowledge in the air traffic control field.

Luffsey was born in Richmond, Virginia, where he majored in mathematics and physics at the University of Richmond. He earned his U.S. Air Force pilot wings in 1956, and is still an active pilot. He holds an Airline Transport Pilot Certificate, having logged several thousand flying hours and flown more than 40 types of aircraft in his career.